# FACE PERCEPTION
## an approach to the study of
# AUTISM

Some other books and chapters
by Tim Langdell, Ph.D.


with Cheri Langdell
from Praeger

*Coping with Vision Loss: Understanding the Psychological,
Social, and Spiritual Effects*


"Being with Alzheimer's" chapter in:
*Dementia-Friendly Worship A Multifaith Handbook
For Chaplains, Clergy, and Faith Communities*
(Jessica Kingsley Publishers)

# FACE PERCEPTION
## an approach to the study of
# AUTISM

By

## TIM LANGDELL, PH.D.

*This book was Dr. Langdell's Psychology Ph.D. thesis submitted to University College London in August 1981, based on his postgraduate Studies from 1975 to 1981*

Oxbridge Publishing Inc.,
Pasadena, CA / Oxford, UK

*"We are forced to speak in images and parables which do not express precisely what we mean. Nor can we avoid occasional contradictions; nevertheless, the images help us to draw nearer to   the real truth."*

Werner Heisenberg.

Oxbridge Publishing Inc.
Oxford/Pasadena
530 South Lake Avenue, 171
Pasadena, CA 91101
www.oxbridgepublishing.com

**Library of Congress Cataloging-in-Publication Data**
Langdell, Tim
      Face Perception: An Approach to the Study of Autism / Tim Langdell
            pages cm
        ISBN: 0-9990928-9-8 (pbk)
        ISBN-13: 978-0-9990928-9-7 (pbk)
        1. Autism    2. Psychology    3. Child Psychology    I. Title

9 8 7 6 5 4 3 2 1

FIRST EDITION

# Contents

PREFACE and AUTISM: A REVIEW.................................................. 1

RESEARCH AND WRITING ON THE TOPIC OF FACIAL
RECOGNITION SINCE 1975-1981..................................................... 13

THE ORIGINAL THESIS................................................................. 25

# PREFACE
## and
## AUTISM: A REVIEW

The body of this book is a facsimile (replica) of my Ph.D. thesis presented to the Medical Research Council department at University College London in August 1981. It fulfilled my requirements for being granted a Ph.D. in Psychology. One reason for my publishing this in book form is that most of the studies in the thesis were never published as academic papers in journals, and thus the important conclusions drawn remain unknown except to those who took the time to seek out the thesis in the stacks at the UCL library. Another reason is so that readers can see that the original work, findings and theories were written in the 1970s, and are not recent additions to a more regular "typeset" book version.

A key finding of my work was that autistic children do not avoid eye contact, but rather they fail to make "normal" eye contact because they pay as much attention to all parts of the face as much as they do to the eyes. There were many other key findings too, regarding autistic children's abilities to recognize upside down faces, and their perception of emotion in faces, and much more. My work was also the first to use computerized measurements of gaze (eye-tracking) with autistic subjects while they were looking at faces and objects. I was also, I believe, the first to propose the amygdala theory of autism, although in hindsight I see I fleshed out this theory more in my conference paper presentations in the 1970s than in the thesis itself. Nonetheless the theory is here.

The one paper I did publish from the thesis was one I was encouraged to publish by my thesis supervisor, Arti Hermelin. She shared my excitement at the results my

1

research was producing, and thus the 1978 paper, *Recognition of Faces: An Approach to the Study of Autism* appeared in Volume 19, Issue 3 of The Journal of Child Psychology and Psychiatry, July 1978, 255-268. Many, I fear, presumed that single paper summarized my entire work on face perception and autism, whereas of course it just reviewed one of the many studies in this thesis. My intention was to publish all of the other studies in this thesis in the months following its submission for my Ph.D. in 1981. Hopefully, while I still work on submitting the individual studies to academic journals, this book will at least make my work, its findings and its theoretical outcomes more widely available to both my fellow academics and to the public.

The thesis covers my research into Childhood Autism during my time as a clinical and experimental psychologist undertaking postgraduate studies at UCL from 1975 to 1981, when I finally produced a version of the thesis I felt was "complete." I took a year off in the late 1970s to take a master's degree in Clinical and Educational Child Psychology from the Elizabeth Newsom at Nottingham University. And I also spent some of the time in Holland at Tilburg University, continuing my research there, as well as spending time in the late 70s at the UCLA *Neuropsychiatric Institute* as a post-doctoral fellow. This was of course before I finished my doctorate: I was very fortunate to gain that honor and to work with both Ivar Lovaas and Bernard Rimland. It was Bernard who arranged my fellowship, getting it approved even though I hadn't yet completed my Ph.D.

In the mid-1970s, I was incredibly lucky to be accepted into the Medical Research Council unit at University College London, run by the inestimably wonderful Neil O'Connor and Beate "Arti" Hermelin. The dynamic duo who were leaders in experimental psychology research into childhood

2

autism. Colleagues there include Uta Frith, and from the MRC I went on to work at the Maudsley Hospital (Institute of Psychiatry) with Lorna Wing and John Rutter. Other colleagues who came to London after I did my initial research included Peter Hobson and Jill Boucher who also went on to do research into ASD. From UCL I took time out to work with Elizabeth Newsom at Nottingham-completing the list of my working with all of the leading researchers in autism in the UK in the 1970s, along with two of the leading U.S. researchers of that time.

Little about this thesis was ordinary, then, since it was interspersed with a variety of detours. Some years into my Ph.D. research I became frustrated that in most institutions because I lacked a clinical certification I was often required to be accompanied by a medical doctor when visiting my autistic patients and research subjects. It became vital that I be able to build trust with them one-on-one, so I took the first detour from UCL to complete the clinical masters at Nottingham, which in turn enabled me to then return to UCL as a certified clinical psychologist within the UK National Health System.

There is novel that I forget the title of where the main character starts writing about a specific topic. As he writes he finds that each thing he considers is connected to something else, and so the work grows. Eventually, it turns into a history of the world. To some extent, writing this Ph.D. thesis felt like that to me since as I explored the landscape of perception and social interaction in autistic children, I found each new area of research connected to some other new area. Hence the thesis grew and grew. I ran long writing it—often a British thesis will take 2-3 years and be around half the length of this work. With the year off in Holland, this took a total of around six years. And even then, I felt it was far from truly "complete," but I was encouraged by my thesis supervisor, the incredible Dr. Arti Hermelin, to draw a line under what I had written so far, and just submit it "as is."

**A Few Words About the Thesis and its Context.**

This thesis was written primarily in the late 1970s and is presented in its original type-written form. Hence, for instance the diagnostic term we used at the time was "Early Childhood Autism." This term was arrived at over years of consideration, replacing the prior term of choice "Infantile Autism," and while we were fully aware of the term "Asperger's," we felt it inappropriate and instead preferred the term "high functioning autistic children/persons." The word "early" was carefully chosen to indicate this is a syndrome that has its onset early in life. That is one reason we didn't opt for a broader term like "autism spectrum" which would leave out the early onset factor we felt was important for differential diagnosis.

One reason we didn't favor the term Asperger's was because it was felt it could be used too loosely to refer to simply mildly eccentric people who did not truly belong in the category of "autistic." Being based in Britain, we have a long history of eccentric characters, and it was felt many well-known personalities would get labeled as Asperger's simply for being a little socially awkward. With wisdom of hindsight, there was merit in identifying those whom others had merely called eccentric as being, as we would now say, "on the spectrum."

Yet it is somewhat ironic that the term Asperger's has gone from not being used as recently as the 1970s and 80s, to becoming a favored description of higher functioning autistic persons, to once again being jettisoned to the scrap heap in 2013 with DSM5 which reduced all of autism to a single

4

category of "autism spectrum disorder." By the way, Asperger himself did not coin the term "Asperger's," his name for the condition was "autistic psychopathy" (see page 1 of the thesis below).

Political correctness was not fully formed in the 1970s when this early work was undertaken. Some terms may thus jar modern sensibilities.

**Still a Good Introduction to Autism**

Despite showing some signs of its age, and despite some progress in the study of autism since the 1970s, the summary of the syndrome in this work still stands as a good introduction. Indeed, despite claims of progress in the understanding of autism, its causes and treatment, this summary shows how little study of the subject has progressed in the past fifty years. Arguably, two of the notable new findings about autism could be said to be its greater prevalence and the idea of autism being a "spectrum." But here in the 1970s we had already defined autism as having a spectrum, although we did not use that specific term.

Indeed, my and my colleagues resistance to the adoption of "Asperger's" at that time arose from a belief that the syndrome was better seen simply as "autism" with a recognition that autistic persons are on a spectrum from "low functioning" to "high functioning." In real terms, then, there has been no progress on the definition and use of the term autism: all that has happened is that in the current era the diagnostic definition went full circle to the norm we established by the mid-1970s.

As to the prevalence, at the time we believed we had determined autism to impact 4.5 children in 10,000. Now, figures like 1 in 54 children having autism are being stated

(National Autism Association website, August 2020). While I don't specifically address it in the thesis, at the time in the late 1070s I found it very difficult to believe that autism was as rare as only around 4.5 in 10,000. I was finding autistic children and adults everywhere I looked (the downside of studying a subject in such depth), and in many cases I observed persons with features of autism that not only had not been diagnosed, but were unlikely to be diagnosed at that time because of where they were in society. Poor children who didn't see doctors, "difficult" children relegated to being hard to educate, but whose teachers or parents had no interest in getting the child diagnosed with a "condition." On the contrary, many did not want their child labelled with a clinical condition or syndrome.

Hence as long ago as the mid-1970s I was certain from my own observations that the prevalence of autism was at least 10 times what was being stated—my estimate being more like 4 in 1,000 rather than 4.5 in 10,000. What then emerged over the ensuing few decades were two major forces impacting the calculation of prevalence: autism being granted a special status that can carry additional financial and medical support, and a dilution of the definition of autism to include persons with autistic-like characteristics. In the past two decades I have met many parents of children diagnosed as autistic who have fought hard for that diagnosis, knowing that with it came additional help—financial, medical and educational—that would not be available to their child if their child was diagnosed with some other term.

The other factor has been the strong push from those supporting autism—a very worthy cause, that I fully support, but one that has attracted a degree of fervor that seeks to elevate autism from its original place in the shadows of childhood disorders (4.5 in 10,000) to a central position of being a common condition, worthy of greater public attention and funding. All of which is fully understandable, given that for many years its prevalence was indeed grossly understated and hence attention to the syndrome, funding of research and treatment, etc., was all below what it should have been.

Indeed, I lost track of the number of people who, during the time I was doing my main research in the 1970s and early 1980s, said to me "Why are you researching such a rare condition, shouldn't you be spending your time on a more common condition like dyslexia?" This would be an appropriate moment to mention what drew me to the study of autism.

Although I do not see the empirical studies yet to support it, my belief is that when autism is more carefully defined (such as to be a truly useful diagnostic category that is not overly broad), the prevalence will likely be found to be what I proposed in the 1970s—namely, around 1 in 250 (the 4 in 1,000 figure I mentioned I was suggesting at that time). That is still a high prevalence, but I do suspect the 1 in 54 is overstated.

I attended university to study astrophysics and computer science. Being a British university, the norm at that time was to select a single topic to study, and then do so intensively for three years. It was also usual to have one or two minors, and so my major of physics was complemented by minors in astronomy and applied mathematics. Indeed, the reason I selected Leicester University was in large part because my space-science hero Professor Ken Pounds was based there, and he was well-known for his studies of black holes in space.

But one year into my time at Leicester I got the "psychology bug," that is, I started to attend psychology classes as a release from the boredom of my physics classes (other than the classes dealing with the then new integrated circuits and those dealing with subatomic particles). As a result, by the end of the first year I had asked the powers that be at Leicester University if I might also be enrolled in the psychology bachelors program as well as physics. At first, they mistakenly thought I was asking to give up physics and switch to psychology and were rather surprised that I was in fact asking to add psychology. Since they had no official joint-major program that would allow me to take these two unrelated subjects, nor did they (at that time) have any kind of combined studies program that would permit it, they stated I would be welcome to add psychology if I would take all three years of it (hence making my tenure at Leicester four years rather than the usual three), and if I could get my home county council of Oxford to finance the additional year.

To this day, I strongly suspect they believed this would be impossible, and were surprised when I got back to them a few weeks later with the approval of the Oxford County authorities. But perhaps I initiated a kind of sea-change at Leicester, since by the time I graduated after four years there, they had now added a combined studies degree that would let students formally study two disparate majors, along with a range of minor topics.

Thus, when it came time for me to select my Ph.D. topic in 1975, I approached the decision with the solid belief that I could bring my knowledge of the scientific method to psychology research. My goal was to find a scientific puzzle to solve, and autistic children represented that perfectly. Here was a condition that spoke to the very core of being human since we are by nature social, and yet here was a syndrome defined by being asocial. I recall telling friends at the time that studying a watch you cannot open that is running slow is not very helpful, but if the watch has specific unusual characteristics, then perhaps one can deduce something about the inner workings without seeing them. Thus, I felt studying autism might reveal something about the human condition in general, and how we as humans perceive the world, the very nature of our social behavior, and so on. I was young, it was typical of my age group to have such lofty ideals.

I still believe there is merit to this: if we can more fully understand autism then we can more fully understand the human condition.

**Key Groundbreaking Findings and Conclusions**
The conclusions I reached were at odds with general theories about autism at that time. Whereas my colleagues spoke of gaze-avoidance as being a key feature of autism (indeed, defined it as a key diagnostic symptom), my studies showed that rather than avoiding another's gaze, autistic children were not making eye contact. Here was a crucial difference: my studies showed that the autistic children were looking at all parts of the face fairly equally, whereas both normal and educationally subnormal children still tended to focus on the eyes and the mouth, ignoring other parts of the face. If the autistic child looked away from the person, my evidence pointed to that being a strategy by the child to cope with perceptual and cognitive overload, rather than gaze avoidance as it is usually understood.

From this I hypothesized that autistic children fail to make constructs which for instance form a connection between the appearance of another's eyes and mouth and emotional states. I focused on the idea of the brain as a hypothesis engine, with autistic children lacking this hypothesis making core ability common to all other children, regardless of intellectual capacity. In turn, I hypothesized that it follows that autistic children easily experience sensory overload, since it is the hypothesis making feature of the brain that enables us to filter perceptual date into what we need to focus on and process, and what we can ignore. I identified the amygdala as key to this theory.

Indeed, the brain usually creates the reality we see, and we do not see the raw data of the perceptual world. The brain makes up a lot of what we see, since to do otherwise would overload us. Rather than take into account every single item of perceptual data, the brain makes assumptions based on synthesis and experience as to what one is likely perceiving, and tends to focus on data that suggests we should alter our perception, rather than trying to cope with the processing of all tens of millions of data points per second we are actually taking in via all our senses.

The data thus suggested to me back in the 1970s that what is unique about autism is that the autistic person is not creating such hypotheses, or at least not as efficiently as cognitively normative persons, hence processing more raw data, and hence experiencing data overload. This in turn explains the lower functioning autistic persons withdrawal, and adoption of stereotypic behavior, to try to deal with the sensory overload. With the higher functioning autistic person, they adopt a more logical sorting of the perceptions, forcing themselves to filter according to logical sorting algorithms, which lead to their stylistic behaviors and in some cases, obsessive behaviors.

But this theory I proposed in the 1970s also explains why we see what are known as islets of ability in otherwise low functioning autistic persons. Hence, the low functioning autistic child who can tell you in milliseconds what day of the week you were born on given just your date of birth, or the one who can tell you exactly how to drive to a location anywhere in a country (because they have memorized the entire street map of that country), or the ones who can draw images with incredible realism despite their apparent brain damage, or the one who can play a complex piano piece having only heard it once.

As so-called normally functioning humans, we throw away or ignore hundreds of thousands of perceptual data points per second in order to function, but the autistic child takes it all in, enabling exceptional abilities that arise because of their lack of "normal" perceptual filtering. Interestingly, more recent studies in the intervening decades are reaching similar conclusions.

### The Birth of Face Perception Studies in Autism

While I published two academic papers drawn from my thesis (the first of which was published in 1978, well before I completed it), the majority of my research has remained solely in the thesis, unavailable to most researchers or those interested in autism. This book hopes to change that—although I still hope to publish the balance of the studies in this thesis as academic papers when, or if, I get time to do so.

But to my delight, my original works does seem to have spawned a large number of further studies of face perception in autism and the amygdala theory, and that these areas of study are still vibrant ongoing ones to this day. I have included an updated bibliography below, listing just some of the hundreds of subsequent studies that have been based either directly or indirectly on my original work in the 1970s.

### The Raw, Unedited Thesis

What follows then is the raw unedited thesis as it was originally presented to University College London in 1981 in fulfillment of the requirements for my Ph.D. That said, there have been a couple of minor edits to make parts of the text more readable, but the wording remains as it was—"warts and all." It is not perfect, I acknowledge that, and it was typed on a typewriter as was more the norm of that time.

In fact, because of my computer science background I had intended this thesis to be one of the first generated by computer software. I recall carrying veritable wheelbarrows full of punch cards to the central University College computer center having typed the entire thesis into a PDP-11 computer terminal at the campus. Each time I tried to get the cards read to produce a printout I could then have bound as a thesis; over and again the cards were rejected for one minor reason or another. Part of why it was late 1981 before I submitted the thesis was because I had to eventually abandon my idea of it being done using the PDP-11. I then had a typist create a manuscript from my hand-written version. The first person I chose, who claimed to be an expert typist, took several months and presented me with a completely unusable stack of paper, so riddled with typing errors I wondered if she in fact knew how to type.

I then had it typed a second time by a better recommended typist, who still made errors, but an acceptable number of them. Hence the state of this final product that follows, including the fact that not every page has a page number, and some of the numbering may be inaccurate. I apologize for any confusion this may cause and renew my intention to eventually reprint the contents as academic papers at some point in the future.

In the meantime, I trust this text is of some interest as an early work in the study of autism.

Dr. Tim Langdell, Ph.D.,
Pasadena, California, August 2020

# RESEARCH AND WRITING ON THE TOPIC OF FACIAL RECOGNITION AND AUTISM SINCE WORK ON THE TOPIC IN 1975-1981

First, I am humbled that my research in the 1970s into face recognition and computerized eye tracking with autistic children gave rise to such a fertile body of research over the ensuing 45 years. I am deeply grateful to all those who took up the work where I left off. Hopefully, by my publishing the entire thesis in this form (pending its publication as separate academic papers), will fill in the gaps in research for some in the field of autism spectrum disorder research, providing information about my findings and conclusions that may prove useful.

Some years ago while on vacation in Hawaii I was approached by a stranger who said he had overheard my name was Langdell, and might I be "the" Langdell who had published on the topic of face perception and autism back in the 1970s? I said I was, whereupon he spoke enthusiastically about how excited I must be that there are now so many groups around the world who followed up on my initial research, and how the topic is now a major one in autism research. I had to candidly confess that I had not stayed current with all the latest research in autism and was unaware that so many studies since the early 1980s had been based on my work.

Back in my hotel room I took a look on Google and was frankly taken aback by the page after page of current and recent research into autism that was either about face perception, or about some other aspect of autism that includes consideration of how autistic persons view faces. Here is just a brief summary of some of the research since I completed my thesis that appears to be either based directly or indirectly on the work I did in that period from 1975-1981. It is apparent to me, though, that in many cases the writers seem only aware of the two papers I published and while they cite my thesis it often appears they have not read it and seem unaware of the other studies I undertook.

First, the two academic papers I published in 1978 and 1981 based on or related to the thesis, then a list of just some of the related studies and books since 1981 (titles in bold for ease or perusal). Each of these newer studies or books either deals primarily with the topic or refers to it within the body of the text. In a number of cases my original work is not properly referenced or omitted from lists of citations one would expect it to be included in. While it may have been more likely that subsequent researchers and writers might have given appropriate cite to my early work had I published the balance of the studies in my thesis at the time, my published papers did exist and all such researchers and writers did have access to my thesis, which was publicly accessible via UCL.

Langdell, Tim (1977) "**Facial Recognition an Approach to the Study of Autism**," *Journal of Child Psychology and Psychiatry*, Vol. 19. Issue 3, July 1978, 255-268

Langdell, Tim & Hammes, J.G.W. (1981), "**Precursors of symbol formation in childhood autism**," *Journal of Autism and Developmental Disorders*, 11, 331-346.

---

And now a selection of papers and books on the same topic since 1981 arising from my or directly related to my original work with a mixture as to whether my earlier work was appropriately acknowledged or not:

Boucher, J., & Lewis, V. (1992). "**Unfamiliar face recognition in relatively able autistic children.**" *Journal of Child Psychology and Psychiatry, 33,* 843–859.

Davies, S., Bishop, D., Manstead, A. S. R., & Tantam, D. (1994). "**Face perception in children with autism and Asperger's syndrome.**" *Journal of Child Psychology and Psychiatry, 35,* 1033–1057.

Hobson, R. P. (1991). "**Methodological issues for experiments on autistic individuals' perception and understanding of emotion.**" *Journal of Child Psychology and Psychiatry, 32,* 1135–1158. (Peter Hobson was a colleague who started work on ASD after I did the main body of my research)

Hobson, R. P., Ouston, J., & Lee, A. (1988). "**What's in a face? The case of autism.**" *British Journal of Psychology, 79,* 441–453.

Klin, A., Sparrow, S. S., de Bildt, A., Cicchetti, D. V., Cohen, D. J., and Volkmar, F. R. (1999). "**A normed study of face recognition in autism and related disorders.**" *J. Autism Dev. Disord.* 29, 499–508.

Schultz, R. T., Gauthier, I., Klin, A., Fulbright, R., Anderson, A., Volkmar, F., Skudlarski, P., Lacadie, C., Cohen, D. J., & Gore, J. C. (2000). "**Abnormal ventral temporal cortical activity among individuals with autism and Asperger Syndrome during face discrimination.**" *Archives of General Psychiatry.*

Tantam, D., Monaghan, L., Nicholson, H., & Stirling, J. (1989). "**Autistic children's ability to interpret faces: A research note.**" *Journal of Child Psychology and Psychiatry, 30,* 623–630.

Volkmar, F. R., Sparrow, S. S., Rende, R. C., & Cohen, D. J. (1989). "**Facial perception in autism.**" *Journal of Child Psychology and Psychiatry, 30,* 591–598.

Posamentier, Mette. (2003), "**Processing Faces and Facial Expressions**," *Neuropsychology Review*, 13, 113-143.

Winoto, Pinata, Yang, Tiffany, Qui, Xiaoyang, & Guan Aonan, (2018), "**Assisting, Not Training, Autistic Children to Recognize and Share Each Other's Emotions via Automatic Face-Tracking in a Collaborative Play Environment**," Conference paper, *International Conference on Universal Access in Human-Computer Interaction*, First online 05 June 2018.

Uljarevic, Mirko & Hamilton, Antonia (2013), "**Recognition of Emotions in Autism: A Formal Meta-Analysis**," *Journal of Autism and Developmental Disorders*, 43, 1517-1526

Baron-Cohen, Simon (1988), "**Social and pragmatic deficits in autism: Cognitive or affective?**" *Journal of Autism and Developmental Disorders*, 18, 379-402

Neely, Leslie, Rispoli, Mandy, Camargo, Siglia, Davis, Heather, & Boles, Margaret (2013), "**The effect of instructional use of an iPad on challenging behavior and academic engagement for two students with autism**," *Research in Autism Spectrum Disorders*, Vol 7, Issue 4, 509-516.

Pierce, Karen, Muller, R.A., Ambrose, J., Allen, G., & Courchesne, E. (2001), "**Face processing occurs outside the fusiform 'face area' in autism: evidence from functional MRI**," *Brain*, Vol 124, Issue 10, October 2001, 2059-2073.

Rutherford, M.D. & McIntosh, Daniel (2007), "**Rules versus Prototype Matching: Strategies of Perception of Emotional Facial Expression in the Autism Spectrum**," *Journal of Autism and Developmental Disorders*, 37, 187-196

Bruyer, Raymond (1986), *The Neuropsychology of Face Perception and Facial Expression*, Psychology Press, New York.

Jemel, Bouthenia, Mottron, Laurent & Dawson, Michelle (2006), "**Impaired Face Processing in Autism: Fact or Artifact?**" *Journal of Autism and Developmental Disorders*, 36, 91-106

Hobson, Peter (1992), "**Social Perception in High-Level Autism**, in *High-Functioning Individuals With Autism* by Eric Schopler & Gary Mesibov (part of the Current Issues in Autism book series of CIAM. 157-184.

Garman, Heather, Spaulding, Christine, Webb, Sara Jane, Mikami, Amori Yee, Morries, James & Lerner, Matthew (2016), "**Wanting It Too Much: An Inverse Relation Between Social Motivation and Facial Emotion Recognition in Autism Spectrum Disorder**," *Child Psychiatry & Human Development*, 47, 890-902.

Fein, Deborah, Barton, Marianne, Eigsti, Inge-Marie, Kelley, Elizabeth, Naigles, Letitia, Schultz, Robert, Stevens, Michael, Helt, Molly, Orinstein, Alyssa, Rosenthal, Michael, Troyb, Eva & Tyson, Katherine (2013) "**Optimal outcome in individuals with a history of autism**," *The Journal of Child Psychology and Psychiatry*, 16 January 2013.

Klin, Ami, Jones, Warren, Schultz, Robert & Volkmar, Fred (2003), "**The enactive mind, or from actions to cognition: lessons from autism**," *Philosophical Transactions of the Royal Society*, 28 February 2003.

Dawson, Geraldine, Carver, Leslie, Meltzoff, Andrew, Panagiotides, Heracles, McPartland, James & Webb, Sara (2003), "**Neural correlates of face and object recognition in young children with autism spectrum disorder, developmental delay, and typical development.**" *Journal of the Society for Research in Child Development*, 28 January 2003.

Brown, Caroline, Gruber, Thomas, Boucher, Jill, Rippon, Gina & Brock, Jon (2005), "**Gamma abnormalities during** perception of illusory figures in autism," *Cortex*, Vol 41, Issue 3, 364-376 (Jill Boucher was another colleague from London University who followed me later with her research into autism).

Chevalier, Pauline, Li, Jamy, Ainger, Eloise, Alcorn, Alyssa, Babovic, Snezana, Charisi, Vicky, Petrovic, Suncica, Shadenberg, Bob, Pellicano, Elizabeth & Evers, Vanessa (2017), **"Dialogue Design for a Robot-Based Face-Mirroring Game to Engage Autistic Children with Emotional Expressions,"** Conference paper, *International Conference on Social Robotics*, printed in *Social Robotics* 546-555 (part of the Lecture Notes in Computer Science book series, LNCS, Vol 10652).

Feuerriegel, Daniel, Churches, Owen, Hofmann, Jessica & keage, Hannah (2015), **"The N170 and face perception in psychiatric and neurological disorders: A systematic review,"** *Clinical Neurology*, Vol 126, Issue 6, 1141-1158

Harms, Madeline, Martin, Alex & Wallace, Gregory (2010), **"Facial Emotion Recognition in Autism Spectrum Disorders: A Review of Behavioral and Neuroimaging Studies,"** *Neuopsychology Review*, 20, 290-322.

Webb, Sara Jane, Faja, Susan & Dawson, Geraldine (2011), **"Face Processing in Autism,"** in the book *Oxford Handbook of Face Perception*, Published July 2011.

Mottron, Laurent (2011), **"The power of autism,"** *Nature*, 479, 33-35 (refers to Dawson's work on face perception and autism but may not reference my earlier work that Dawson followed up on).

Sinzig, Judith, Morsch, Dagmar & Lehmkuhl, Gerd (2008), **"Do hyperactivity, impulsivity and inattention have an impact on the ability of facial affect recognition in children with autism and ADHD?"** *European Child & Adolescent Psychiatry*, 17, 63-72.

Kirchner, Jennifer, Hatri, Alexander, Heekeren, Hauke & Dziobek, Isabel (2011) **"Autistic Symptomology, Face Processing Abilities, and Eye Fixation Patterns,"** *Journal of Autism and Developmental Disorders*, 41, 158-167.

Celani, Giorgio, Battacchi, Marco Walter & Arcidiacono, Letizia (1999) **"The Understanding of the Emotional Meaning of Facial Expressions in People with Autism,"** *Journal of Autism and Developmental Disorders*,29, 57-66.

Weeks, Jane & Hobson, Peter (1987), **"The Salience of Facial Expression for Autistic Children,"** *The Journal of Child Psychology and Psychiatry*, January 1987.

Hobson, Peter (1999), **"Beyond Cognition: A theory of autism,"** Chapter in book *Perspectives on the Nature of Autism*, Routledge, London.

Happe. Francesca (2006), **"The Weak Coherence Account: Detail-focused Cognitive Style in Autism Spectrum Disorders,"** *Journal of Autism and Developmental Disorders*, 36, 5-25.

Newell, Lisa, Best, Catherine, Gastgeb, Holly, Rump, Keiran & Strauss, Mark (2001), **"The development of categorization and facial knowledge: Implications for the study of autism,"** in the book *Infant perception and cognition: Recent advances, emerging theories, and future directions*, Oxford University Press. 223-259.

Tardif, Carole, Laine, France, Rodriguez, Melissa & Gepner, Bruno (2007), **"Slowing Down Presentation of Facial Movements and Vocal Sounds Enhances Facial Expression Recognition and Induces Facial-Vocal Imitation in Children with Autism,"** *Journal of Autism and Developmental Disorders*, 37, 1469-1484.

Fletcher-Watson, Sue (2014), **"A Targeted Review of Computer-Assisted Learning for People with Autism**

Spectrum Disorder: towards a Consistent Methodology," *J. Autism Dev. Disord.*, 1:87-100

Jamal, Wasifa, Das, Saptarshi, Maharatna, Koushik, Pan, Indranil & Kuyucu, Doga (2015), "**Brain connectivity analysis from EEG signals using stable phase-synchonized states during face perception tasks,**" *Physica A: Statistical Mechanics and Its Applications*, Vol 434, 15 Sep 2015, 273-295.

Jamal, Wasifa, Das, Saptarshi, Oprescu, Ioana-Anastasia, Maharatna, Koushik, Apicella, Fabio & Sicca, Federico (2014), "**Classification of autism spectrum disorder using supervised learning of brain connectivity measures extracted from synchrostates,**" *Journal of Neural Engineering*, Vol 11, No 4.

Kandalaft, Michelle, Didehbani, Nyaz, Krawczyk, Daniel, Allen, Tandra & Chapman, Sandra (2013), "**Virtual Reality Social Cognition Training for Young Adults with High-Functioning Autism,**" *Journal of Autism and Developmental Disorders*, 43, 34-44.

Roby, Deborah, Brown, Philippa, Jones, Nicola & Hanley, Mary (2012), "**Brief Report: Faces Cause Less Distraction in Autism,**" *Journal of Autism and Developmental Disorders*, 42, 634-639.

Merin, Noah, Young, Gregory, Ozonoff, Sally & Rogers, Sally (2007), "**Visual Fixation Patterns during Reciprocal Social Interaction Distinguish a Subgroup of 6-Month-Old Infants At-Risk for Autism from Comparison Infants,**" *J of Autism & Dev Disord.*, 37, 108-121.

Tracy, Jessica, Robins, Richard, Schriber, Roberta & Solomon, Marjorie (2011), "**Is Emotion Recognition Impaired in Individuals with Autism Spectrum Disorders?**" *Journal of Autism & Dev. Disord.*, 41, 102-109

Ramdoss, Sathiyaprakash, Machalicek, Wendy, Rispoli, Mandy, Mulloy, Austin, Lang, Russell & O'Reilly, Mark (2011), "**Computer-based interventions to improve social and emotional skills in individuals with autism spectrum disorders: A systematic review**," *Developmental Neurorehabilitation*, Vol 15, Issue 2, 119-135.

Trapp, Sabrina, Schweinberger, Stefan, Hayward, William & Kovacs, Gyula (2018), "**Integrating predictive frameworks and cognitive models of face perception**," *Psychonomic Bulletin & Review*, 25, 2016-2023.

Yirmiya, Nurit, Kasari, Connie, Sigman, Marian & Mundy, Peter (1989), "**Facial Expressions of Affect in Autistic, Mentally Retarded and Normal Children**," *The Journal of Child Psychology and Psychiatry*, Sep 1989.

Golan, Ofer, Sinai-Gavrilov, Yana & Baron-Cohen, Simon (2015), "**The Cambridge Mindreading Face-Voice Battery for Children (CAM-C): complex emotion recognition in children with and without autism spectrum conditions**," *Molecular Autism*, 6, Article No 22.

Baron-Cohen, S., Ring, H.A., Bullmore, E.T., Wheelwright, S., Ashwin, C. & Williams, S.C.R. (2000), "**The amygdala theory of autism**," *Neuroscience & Biobehavioral Reviews*, Vol 24, Issue 3, 335-364. (I believe I was the first to propose the amygdala theory of autism in 1975-77; I have not had time yet to check if this paper mentions that or not).

Landowska, Agnieszka & Robins, Ben (2020), "**Robot Eye Perspective in Perceiving Facial Expressions in Interaction with Children with Autism**," Conference paper, WAINA 2020, *Web, Artificial Intelligence and Network Applications*, 1287-1297.

Sneju, Atsushi, Tojo, Yoshikuni, Dairoku, Hitoshi & Hasegawa, Toshikazu (2004), "**Reflexive orienting in response to eye gaze and an arrow in children with and**

**without autism**," *The Journal of Ch Psychol & Psychiat,* 24 Feb 2004.

Coffman, M.C., Anderson, L.C., Naples, A.J. & McPartland, J.C. (2015), "**Sex Differences in Social Perception in Children with ASD**," *Journal of Autism and Dev Disord.*, 45, 589-599

Wagner, Jennifer, Hirsch, Suzanna, Vogel-Farley, Vanessa, Redcay, Elizabeth & Nelson, Charles (2013), "**Eye-Tracking, Autonomic, and Electrophysiological Correlates of Emotional Face Processing in Adolescents with Autism Spectrum Disorder**," *Journal of Autism and Dev Disord.*, 43, 188-199.

Sepeta, Leigh, Tsuchiya, Naotsugu, Davies, Mari, Sigman, Marian, Bookheimer, Susan & Dapretto, Mirella (2012), "**Abnormal social reward processing in autism as indexed by pupillary responses to happy faces**," *Journal of Neurodevelopmental Disorders*, 4, Article No 17.

Jambaque, I., Mottron, L., Ponsot, G. & Chrion, C. (1998), "**Autism and visual agnosia in a child with right occipital lobectomy**," *Journal of Neurology, Neurosurgery & Psychiatry*, 65, 555-560.

Herrington, John, Taylor, James, Grupe, Daniel, Curby, Kim & Schultz, Robert (2011), "**Bidirectional communication between amygdala and fusiform gyrus during facial recognition**," *NeuroImage*, 4, 15, 2348-2355.

Woynaroski, Tiffany, Kwakye, Leslie, Foss-Feig, Jennifer, Stevenson, Ryan, Stone, Wendy & Wallance, Mark (2013), "**Multisensory Speech Perceptions in Children with Autism Spectrum Disorders**," *Journal of Autism and Dev. Disord.*, 43, 2891-2902.

Baron-Cohen, Simon (1991), "The Development of a Theory of Mind in Autism: Deviance or Delay?" *Psychiatric Clinics*, 14, 1, 33-51.

Oberman, Lindsay & Ramachandran, Vilayanur (2007), "The simulating social mind: The role of the mirror neuron system and the simulation in the social and communicative deficits of autism spectrum disorders," *Psychological Bulletin*, 133(2) 310-327.

Strathearn, Lane (2009), "The elusive etiology of autism: nature *and* nurture?" *Behav. Neurosci.*, 20 July 2009.

Dawson, G., Webb, S. J., Wijsman, E., Schellenberg, G., Estes, A., Munson, J., and Faja, S. (2005a). "Neurocognitive and electrophysiological evidence of altered face processing in parents of children with autism: implications for a model of abnormal development of social brain circuitry in autism." *Dev. Psychopathol.*, 17, 679–697.

Dawson, G., Webb, S. J., and McPartland, J. (2005b). "Understanding the nature of face processing impairment in autism: insights from behavioral and electro-physiological studies." *Dev. Neuropsychol.*, 27, 403–424.

Evers, Kris, Steyaert, Jean, Noens, Ilse & Wagemans, Johan (2015), "Reduced Recognition of Dynamic Facial Emotional Expressions and Emotion-Specific Response Bias in Children with an Autism Spectrum Disorder," *Journal of Autism and Dev. Disord.*, 45, 1774-1784.

Jones, Catherine, Pickles, Andrew, Falcaro, Milena, Marsden, Anita, Happe, Francesca, Scott, Sophie, Sauter, Disa, Tregay, Jenifer, Phillips, Rebecca, Baird, Gillian, Simonoff, Emily & Charman, Tony (2010), "A multimodal approach to emotion recognition ability in autism spectrum disorders," *J. Ch. Psych. & Psychia.*, 18 Oct 2010.

Lozier, Leah, Vanmete, John & Marsh, Abigail (2014), "**Impairments in facial affect recognition associated with autism spectrum disorders: A meta-analysis,**" *Dev. And Psychopath.*, 2014, 1-13.

THE ORIGINAL THESIS
AS IT WAS SUBMITTED
TO UNIVERSITY COLLEGE
LONDON IN 1981

FACE PERCEPTION: AN APPROACH TO THE

STUDY OF AUTISM

by

Tim Langdell

Thesis submitted for the Degree of Doctor of Philosophy
at the University of London.        August, 1981.

"We are forced to speak in images
and parables which do not express
precisely what we mean.  Nor can
we avoid occasional contradictions;
nevertheless, the images help us to
draw nearer to the real truth."


Werner Heisenberg.

ABSTRACT

The autistic child's ability to identify others' faces and their expressions was investigated in comparison with the ability of non-autistic children. A study of the children's ability to identify peers' from isolated facial areas revealed that the autistic children were abnormally good at this task. Reasons for these findings were investigated in a series of experiments which revealed that the autistic children were also abnormally good at recognising inverted faces and inverted text. The conclusion was drawn that the autistic children's performance was due to their possessing a perceptual integration deficit which prevents them seeing stimuli like faces and words as meaningful wholes. This was investigated further by tests of their ability to discern facial expression and the results of these studies supported the above conclusion. Tests of the children's ability to lip read revealed that the autistic children also had problems with between modality perceptual integration. Studies of their ability to produce facial expressions showed them to be poor at both spontaneous and elicited expressions. Further, whilst they were as good as controls at copying facial expression, they were less able to make use of visual feedback to improve their attempts. This was seen as further evidence for a perceptual integration deficit. Finally, a computerised study of autistic children's eye movements whilst viewing live facial expressions and other stimuli supported much of the previous findings, adding the finding that they had abnormally brief visual fixation times and that they engaged in very few feature-to-feature gaze shifts. The results were discussed and found to favour a theory in which the autistic child's problems with social and communicative competence are linked to his problems with perceptual integration. The possession versus the use of abilities was discussed, as was possible sites of neurological damage, and the possibility that autistic children lack some vital usually 'innate' abilities and propensities.

ACKNOWLEDGEMENTS

I am extremely grateful for the very generous help given to me by my supervisor Beate Hermelin, and I gratefully acknowledge,too, the many fruitful hours of discussion she and I had on the ideas and experiments in this thesis. My thanks are also due to my colleagues in the MRC Developmental Psychology Unit in London, and especially to its director Neil O'Connor, and also to my colleagues in the Psychology Department of University College London who helped fire my thoughts. I also wish to acknowledge the help given to me by the technicians at University College and at Tilberg University in Holland, and that of Drs.Jacques Hammes in Tilberg too. For financial assistance I am indebted to the grant given to me by the Medical Research Council. My thanks to the children who took part in the studies, and to their teachers and head teachers, especially: Mrs. Brown, Head of the Helen Allison School for Autistic Children at Gravesend; Mr. Pickering, Head of the Dedisham School for Autistic Children near Horsham; Mr. Stenlake of the Claybourne School for ESN(M) children near Weybridge; Mr. Harris, Head of the Holy Trinity Middle School in West End; and finally to the heads and staff of the eight further schools for autistic children which I had the opportunity to visit in England, Holland, Germany and California. I am grateful to Mrs. Jean Willoughby for her excellent typing. Finally, I extend my thanks to my wife Cheri whose support and understanding have made this thesis possible.

# CONTENTS

| | Page |
|---|---|
| WHYS AND WHEREFORES: A FOREWORD | i |
| CHAPTER 1 - AUTISM: A SYNOPSIS | 1 |
| 1.1 An Introduction | 1 |
|     1.1.1 Theories of aetiology | 7 |
| 1.2 Experimental Studies | 13 |
|     1.2.1 Memory | 13 |
|     1.2.2 Perception | 22 |
|     1.2.3 Cognition | 28 |
|     1.2.4 Arousal | 40 |
|     1.2.5 Language and sociability | 42 |
| 1.3 Terminology, Diagnosis and the Selection of Subjects | 48 |
|     1.3.1 Terminology | 48 |
|     1.3.2 Diagnosis | 51 |
|     1.3.3 Selection of Subjects | 55 |
| CHAPTER 2 - FACE PERCEPTION AND MUTUAL GAZE | 70 |
| 2.1 The Onogeny of Face Perception | 70 |
|     2.1.1 The first year of life | 73 |
|     2.1.2 Childhood and adolescence | 92 |
| 2.2 The Role of Gaze and Mutual Gaze in Normal Development | 99 |
| 2.3 Person Perception and Gaze Contact in Autistic Children | 102 |
| CHAPTER 3 - RECOGNITION OF FACES AND RELATED ISSUES | 110 |
| 3.1 Recognition of Peers' Faces | 110 |
| 3.2 Sorting Schematic Houses | 150 |
| 3.3 Lip Reading Studies | 159 |
|     3.3.1 Recognition of peers' faces by hard-of-hearing subjects | 160 |
|     3.3.2 Lip reading by autistic children | 171 |
|     3.3.3 The contribution of lip reading to speech perception | 175 |

3.4   Further Studies of the Inverted Mode                                194

    3.4.1    Recognition of inverted halves of faces        194

    3.4.2    Recognition of inverted words                  208

    3.4.3    General discussion of the inverted mode
             studies                                        212

3.5   Summary and Conclusions to the Studies so Far                        216


CHAPTER 4 - IDENTIFICATION AND PRODUCTION OF FACIAL EXPRESSIONS:
           THE NORMAL CHILD                                             220

4.1   Introduction                                                        220

4.2   Emotional Expression in the Normal Infant and Young
      Child                                                             221

4.3   The Recognition of Emotion                                          230

4.4   Lack of Opportunity to Learn Expressions                            234

4.5   Acting Expressions                                                  239

4.6   Presence of Opportunity                                             241


CHAPTER 5 - IDENTIFICATION AND PRODUCTION OF FACIAL EXPRESSIONS:
           THE AUTISTIC CHILD                                           242

5.1   The Identification of Expressions                                   242

    5.1.1    The abilities of the autistic children        242

    5.1.2    Identification of expression in upright and
             inverted faces                                 247

    5.1.3    Identification of expression in  faces
             containing two conflicting expressions.        258

    5.1.4    Discussion of studies of identification
             of expressions.                                267

5.2   Production of Facial Expressions                                    270

    5.2.1    The autistic children's abilities             270

    5.2.2    Elicited expressions                          273

    5.2.3    Copying facial expressions                    281

5.3   Discussion                                                          288

CHAPTER 6 - EYE MOVEMENTS WHEN PERCEIVING FACES.                    295

  6.1  Introduction                                                      295

  6.2  Computer Based Study of Autistic Children's Eye
      Movements.                                                         299

  6.3  Summary and General Conclusions                                    349


CHAPTER 7 - PRESENT FINDINGS, THEORETICAL IMPLICATIONS AND
           SUGGESTIONS FOR FURTHER RESEARCH                          359

  7.1  Introduction                                                      359

  7.2  A Summary of the Present Findings                                 360

  7.3  Theoretical Implications                                          373

      7.3.1    Is face perception innate?                             373

      7.3.2    Is face perception unique?                             374

      7.3.3    Facial expression and its relation to
               identity.                                          379

      7.3.4    Hemispheric processing and face perception             380

      7.3.5    Hemispheric processing and the identification
               of facial expression                               387

      7.3.6    Neurological aetiologies of autism suggested
               by other authors                                   394

      7.3.7    Some theoretical considerations                        406

               a) Perceptual integration deficits in autism        407

               b) Possible connections between an integration
                  deficit and language and thought                 412

               c) Speculations as to the nature of brain
                  dysfunction in autism                            423

               d) The possession of abilities versus the
                  use of them                                      427

               e) Do autistic children lack any normally
                  'innate' behaviours?                             429

  7.4  Suggestions for Further Research                                  431

APPENDIX 1                                                            438a

REFERENCES                                                            439

# LIST OF TABLES

Table

1.1 The Subjects Used in this Thesis

1.2 Summary of Pathological Data: Autistic Children

3.1 The Subjects

3.2 Mean Per Cent Errors for Each Group in Each Condition

3.3 Analysis of Variance on the Mean Per Cent Errors

3.4 Subjects in House Sorting Study

3.5 Number of Children in Each Group who Sorted by Each of the Characteristics.

3.6 Hard-of-Hearing Subjects' Details

3.7 Average Per Cent Errors by Each Group in Each Condition

3.8 Subjects in Study of Contribution of Lip Reading to Speech Perception.

3.9 Mean Per Cent Correct by Each Group when Lip Reading Words, and the Mean Level of Noise Required by Each Group so that the Auditory-Only Scores were Equivalent to the Visual-Only Ones.

3.10 Subjects in the Study of Ability to Recognise Inverted Halves of Faces.

3.11 Mean Per Cent Correct for Each Group when Recognising Inverted Upper and Lower Halves of Faces.

5.1 Subjects in the Study of Identification of Facial Expression.

5.2 Mean Per Cent Correct for Each Group Sorting Upright and Inverted Full and Half Expressional Faces.

5.3 Mean Per Cent Correct by each Group, Scored by the Mouth's Expression, for the Parted and Complete Composite Expressional Faces.

5.4 Details of the Subjects in the Study of Elicited Expressions.

5.5 Mean Scores Given by Raters to Each Group's Attempts to Pull Happy and Sad Faces.

5.6 Details of the Subjects in the Study of Copies Expressions.

5.7 Mean Scores Given by the Raters on a Seven Point
Scale when the Children were Trying to Copy a
Model's Expression once without Feedback, and
again with Feedback.

6.1 Details of the Three Subjects Tested in the
Computerised Study of Eye Movements while
Looking at Faces.

6.2 Average Fixation Times when Looking on the Stimuli;
and when Looking at Them, the Average Fixation
Times in the Upper and Lower Halves.

6.3 Details of the Average Number of Fixations on, and
the Average Time Spent Looking at, the Passive Face
and the One with its Eyes Closed.

6.4 Average Number of the Two Types of Gaze Shift
Exhibited by the Children.

LIST OF FIGURES

Figure

2.1  Stimuli which elicit smiles in babies.

2.2  Fixation 'preferences' with increasing age.

3.1  Scanning pattern when viewing faces.

3.2  Example of problematic stimuli in Goldstein and
     Mackenberg's study of 1966.

3.3  Examples of faces to be recognised.

3.4  Mean percentage errors by young children when
     viewing parts of faces.

3.5  Mean percentage error by the older children when
     viewing parts of faces.

3.6  Mean percentage error by the younger and older
     autistics when viewing parts of faces.

3.7  Example of 'focussing hypothesis'.

3.8  Schematic houses to be sorted by the children.

3.9  Pictures used in lip-reading experiment.

3.10 Percentage correct by the groups in the lip reading
     study, with a relative scoring method.

3.11 Percentage correct by each group in the lip reading
     study, with an absolute scoring method.

3.12 Words read in reading experiment.

5.1  Contextual clues given for expressional faces test
     in Odom et al's study.

5.2  Examples of actors making happy and sad faces.

5.3  Examples of children's attempts to pull happy and sad faces.

5.4  Examples of the children's attempts to copy facial
     expressions.

6.1  Eye movements when looking at faces.

6.2  Schematic of components of eye movement apparatus.

6.3  Example of apparatus set up for use.

6.4  Arrangement of apparatus in present study.

6.5  Example of calibrations grid used.

6.6       Schematic houses viewed by children

6.7       Examples of recordings of eye movements.

6.8       Average time spent looking at each house/face.

6.9       Average number of fixations on each house/face.

6.10 )
6.11 )   Three children's results when viewing faces
6.12 )   with open and closed eyes.

6.13 )
6.14 )   Three children's results when viewing talking
6.15 )   and smiling faces.

6.16 )
6.17 )   Three children's results when viewing sad and
6.18 )   averted faces

6.19      Three children's results when viewing schematic
houses.

7.1       Examples of the difficulty one experiences in
viewing inverted stimuli.

7.2       Examples of the difficulty in determining inverted
facial expressions.

7.3       Example of degraded stimulus for perceptual
integration task.

WHYS AND WHEREFORES: A FOREWORD

Autism is a syndrome characterised by an impaired ability to form

social relationships and an impaired use of language for communicative

purposes.  Not surprisingly, the anecdotal and clinical literature is

dominated by descriptions of the autistic child's problems in these

areas.  However, scientific investigations have tended to be based

upon hypotheses about the nature of autism and have thus often only

investigated one aspect of the condition.  The assumption has often

been that one aspect is central to the syndrome and all the other

symptoms are secondary:  social competence and language have predictably

been the most common suggestions for central aspects, and there has

ensued a conflict over which underlies the other.  Empirical studies

of autistic children have investigated various aspects of their

perception, cognition, memory and language competence.  In brief, such

studies have found that a central cognitive deficit may underlie the

autistic children's problems in perception, thinking and transference

to long-term memory.  A central cognitive deficit may also account for

the trouble some autistic children have with syntax and semantics.

However, the intersection of most of the autistic child's problems,

which might be described as the cognitive implications of person

perception, has rarely been studied.  It was thus the primary aim

of this thesis to examine autistic children's perception of social

stimuli and discuss the cognitive implications of any findings.  But

this immediately raised the question "What is a social stimulus?"

Social stimuli include speech, bodily gestures, facial expression and the representation of faces. Various aspects relating to human beings such as items of clothing, immobile limbs etc, cannot be classed as social stimuli. Rather it is those aspects which are directly related to interpersonal relations which can be referred to as 'social'. Thus the face epitomises social stimuli and perception of it stands at the intersection of the autistic child's problems.

There is some controversy in the literature on face perception as to whether faces form a unique class of visual stimuli. However there can be little doubt of the primary role that the face plays in human social relations. At least three levels of information can be gathered from other's faces: the relatively invariant facial aspects may be used for identification, both mobile and static elements may be utilized to determine how another feels, and lip movements may provide linguistic information. It is not surprising, then, to find that the face plays an important part in the socialisation of the child (Schaffer, 1971). The normal infant is found to smile more at faces than at other stimuli (Wolff, 1963), and from the first few weeks of life the infant can discriminate a pattern of two dots which resemble eyes (Ahrens, 1954). It seems equally significant that the infant should initially have his focus of vision fixed at some 8 inches away - approximately the distance he is from the mother's face during breast feeding (Schaffer, ibid).

As the normal child develops he progresses from a basic tendency to respond to eye-like patterns, to the discrimination of an increasing number of facial features, and eventually to being able to distinguish his mother's face from that of strangers. Gradually he learns the meaning of others' facial expressions, and becomes increasingly able to read more and more subtle emotions and feelings into these expressions (Ekman, 1973). Although from around 7 months evidence suggests that infants perceive faces as gestalts (Ahrens, 1954; Phillips, 1977), the eye area retains primary importance in identification of faces, and the determination of most facial expressions.

Nothing is known, by contrast, about the development of face perception in autistic children. Some insight into the deviance of the autistic's condition may be gained from the following passage (my emphasis):

> As the name 'autism' implies, one of the key features consists of an autistic-type abnormality in interpersonal relationships. This may be shown in early childhood by a relative lack of eye-to-eye gaze, limited emotional attachments to parents, little variation in facial expression, and an appearance of aloofness and distance together with an apparent lack of interest in people.
>
> (Rutter and Bartak, 1971).

From birth the autistic child may have failed to form an anticipatory posture prior to being picked up, or when picked up he may have failed to adjust his position to the shape of his mother (Wing, 1976b). In addition many autistic babies are reported to lack the basic propensity to communicate to others. They may be very 'good' babies who never learn that crying can be used to request or demand something, or they may be very difficult babies who cry unconsolably. Many mothers of such babies also report that they could never have a 'conversation without words' with their child - although they knew the experience from a former normal child they had cared for (Newson, 1980).

In what way does the autistic child's initial lack of responsiveness to social stimuli    like  human  faces   affect the manner in which he perceives faces at a later age?  What parts of the face does he use to identify others by, or utilise to formulate impressions of how they feel (if indeed he does formulate them)?

These questions are the primary concern of this thesis.  In particular it will address itself to such questions as whether or not the autistic child does tend to actively avoid mutual gaze (as some workers have suggested), or whether their abnormal social behaviour can best be understood in terms of an underlying cognitive deficit.

The first chapter will deal with an overview of the present state of knowledge of the syndrome, and includes coverage of some of the many theories about it.  The chapter will also survey the results from psychological experiments with autistics and will end with a discussion of the problems of diagnosis and the selection of subjects for the present studies.

The second chapter will consist of an overview of the literature on face perception by normal children from birth to adolescence.  This chapter includes a discussion of the role of mutual gaze in normal children and contrasts normal gaze activity with autistic children's problems with interpersonal relations.  A third chapter is devoted to an experimental study of autistic children's ability to recognise peoples' faces, and the issues that arise from this study. In the fourth chapter a survey of the literature on normal children's abilities to identify and produce facial expressions will be given, whilst the fifth chapter will report several experimental studies of such abilities in autistics. The sixth chapter deals with a computerised study of the eye movements of children who are looking at faces. Finally, the seventh chapter will attempt to bring the results and conclusions of the thesis together, suggest implications for the study and theory of autism, and give ideas for further research.

CHAPTER 1

AUTISM: A SYNOPSIS

1.1. An introduction

Cases of mental disturbance in childhood which might be termed
'psychotic' date back to at least the eighteenth century (Haslan, 1799),
and Bender (1969) relates the details of many of these. Notable among
them was the case of "the wild boy of Averyon" (Itard, 1801), who may
well have been an autistic child. However, Maudsley (1867) was the
first psychiatrist to attempt an overview of psychoses in childhood,
and it was considerably later that such conditions became more generally
recognised. In 1906 De Sanctis coined the term 'dementia precocissima'
to describe psychoses in prepubital children. Later Heller (1930)
described a disintegrative psychosis in which relatively normal
development up to about 3 years of age is followed by a severe
regression to a speechless state with the onset of stereotypies and
restless behaviour. Potter (1933) proposed a set of criteria for
childhood examples of schizophrenia, and in 1943 Kanner published the
first clear delineation of a syndrome he called 'infantile autism'.
In the same year Frye (published 1968) was working with what appears
to be the same type of children as Kanner described. The following
year saw Asperger's (1944) clinical description of a similar condition
which he independently called 'autistic psychopathy'. Bender    then
(1947) wrote   about a broad and ill-defined group of children
labelled as 'childhood schizophrenics'. Several concepts of psychosis
appeared over the ensuing years, such as Mahler and Gosliner's (1955)
'symbiotic psychosis', and Rank's (1955) 'atypical child'. Since that

time many papers on the topic of childhood psychosis have been written and a host of classification schemes have been forthcoming (Laufer and Gair, 1969; Rutter et al., 1969; Churchill et al., 1971; Rutter, 1971; Ornitz, 1973; Miller, 1974; Wing, 1976).

From the late 1950's onwards there was a tendency to group all childhood psychoses together under the general title of 'childhood schizophrenia' (see Creak, 1961). However, there has been a substantial amount of evidence in the literature attesting to the fact that adult schizophrenia is quite unlike the syndromes seen in early childhood in many ways. For instance, there are clear genetic factors in schizophrenia, autistic children rarely have halucinations which are a characteristic of schizophrenia, and whereas autistic children's parents tend to be middle class there is no class bias in schizophrenia (see Rutter, 1974). Broadly speaking, it is now accepted that childhood psychoses fall into three main groups. First are those children whose onset of symptoms is in the first 30 months of life and who are characterised by a lack of signs of brain damage, and who possess the characteristics of 'autism'. Next are the children whose onset is after about seven years of age and who resemble adult schizophrenics in many of their symptoms. Finally, the group in between, which is less well defined. These children may fall into Heller's 'disintegrative psychosis' category, and they frequently show signs of brain damage and evidence of a specific causatory factor, such as a traumatic event.

The most characteristic 'psychosis' of childhood, though, is autism (Rutter, 1976). As mentioned above it was first delineated by Kanner in 1943, who wrote a paper entitled "Autistic Disturbances of Affective Contact". He began his paper by saying:

> Since 1938, there have come to our attention
> a number of children whose condition differs
> so markedly and uniquely from anything reported
> so far, that each case merits ... a detailed
> consideration of its fascinating perculiarities.

He went on to describe in detail the cases of 11 children who he felt constituted an otherwise undelineated syndrome. The main characteristics of these children included a profound lack of affective contact with people, an anxiously obsessive desire for the preservation of sameness, a fascination for objects which are handled with skill in fine movements, mutism or a kind of language which does not seem intended to communicate, and finally the retention of an intelligent physiognomy and evidence of good cognitive potential.

There are several reasons why the application of Kanner's description for diagnostic purposes is problematic. The issue of which diagnostic criteria one should use will be dealt with later in this section. However, it should be noted here that Kanner's last point mentioned above is particularly misleading. While it is true that many autistic children have islets of relatively good ability amongst an otherwise low level of functioning, it is spurious to take this good ability as indicative of their 'real' cognitive potential. Similarly, there is a host of evidence suggesting that autistic children are poor at expressing their feelings through gesture. It is thus also misleading to refer to their physiognomies as 'intelligent'. Nonetheless, it is notable that autistic children tend not to look subnormal even though about 75% of them are reported to be so (Rutter, 1975).

The following 4 points may be kept in mind as giving the best description of autism to date:

1.    An impairment development of language and all modes of communication, which has certain well defined characteristics and is out of keeping with the child's general intellectual level.

2.    Impaired social development which is characterised by a number of special features such as a failure to develop empathy. This impairment of social relations is out of keeping with the child's general intellectual level.

3.    Evidence of rigidity and inflexibility of thought processes reflected in an insistence upon sameness, stereotypies, abnormal preoccupations, and a resistance to change.

4.    An onset of symptoms before 30 months of age.

(After, Rutter, 1978; Newson, 1980).

As mentioned above the problems of diagnosis will be returned to later in this chapter.

Two major presenting characteristics of autism are thus impairments in social development and in communicating with others. It has also been noted that the first three above aspects are not isolated factors which are unrelated to each other (Newson, 1977). Newson (ibid) has pointed out that what makes the autistic child stand out is the interrelationship of his difficulties. His language and attempts at communication are characterised by the rigidity of thought processes noted in the third point above. The act of communication itself is social in nature, and the development of language occurs in the social environment of early mother/infant interaction (see, Bruner, 1975a,b; Lock, 1978).

As will be noted in a later section, theories of autism have frequently been criticised for positing a single generalised factor (such as poor mothering, chronic high arousal, or excessive 'shyness) to explain the complex pattern of behaviours which autistics' present. Additionally, it will be noted that relatively few experimental studies have been done on the fundamental characteristics of language disorder and social abnormalities. Whilst many excellent studies have investigated the possibility of a central cognitive deficit being at the core of autism, there is still room for a study of the relationships between social perception, cognition and communication. It is noteworthy, for instance, that some children (for instance some Down's children) exhibit poor cognitive performance,yet are affectionate and warm in their interactions with others. Such children may be poor at speech, or even mute, but show a clear understanding of what 'communicating with others' is all about. They will often also show good ability at the use of gesture to make their needs, requests and comments known to others.

There is thus a strong body of evidence which suggests that a child may be socially aware and communicatively competent (albeit less so than a normal child with greater intelligence), yet be essentially functioning at an idiot level. But in the case of the autistic child the reverse may be true; an autistic child may be performing at normal or near normal in certain areas of cognitive ability yet be very impaired in his social relationships. One must be careful, then, not to make any simple assumptions about the links between the autistic child's cognitive abilities and his social incompetence. Nonetheless, there is reason to believe that the particular cognitive deficit in autism might well also underlie their poor ability in social situations (Hermelin and O'Connor, 1970; Frith and Hermelin, 1971).

The aim of this thesis is thus to study the autistic child's abilities in areas of social perception which include elements of cognitive processing and communication. It was felt that the human face is unique insofar as it may be regarded as a social stimulus (that is, one with social meaning to the normal person). Because the face serves several different functions (it can tell you who a person is, what they are feeling, and offers other information such as lip movement components of speech) it thus has few rivals for richness of information about others in social situations. This is important, not the least because the face is one of the earliest stimuli that the child perceives, and he does so in the pre-linguistic stage of development in which autism begins.

Consequently, if one was to find any abnormalities in the manner in which autistic children view faces, then such a discrepancy might reflect upon the nature of the dysfunction in their thought processes. Moreover, analysing how autistic children view faces could allow one to find additional information on the way they look at people and thus determine whether there is evidence for their avoiding gaze contact, or if there is evidence for their failing to use the information available in the eye area. Later sections will deal with this topic more fully.

Thus a study of the autistic child's manner of perceiving faces may offer insight into his perceptual, social, communicative, and cognitive abilities. To date, though, there have been no studies of autistic children's abilities to recognise faces or determine facial expressions, or indeed any other aspect of face perception.

The next section will be devoted to a short overview of the theories about the aetiology of autism. Following that will be a section concerned with previous experimental studies of autistic children. To close this chapter there will be a section on the

selection of subjects for the studies in this thesis. This last
section will include a discussion of the problems of diagnosis, and
will also give an outline of the case histories of each of the autistic
children studied herein.

### 1.1.1  Theories of Aetiology

Many causes for autism have been proposed and these fall into two
basic categories:  those which note that autism can occur in the absence
of any obvious neurological damage and hence take a psychogenic viewpoint,
and those which note that the autistic child may be born with a
physiological or metabolic dysfunction but that this need not show
itself in any readily apparent signs.  In addition, some workers have
proposed theories about the psychological problems in autism, which are
thought to be there regardless of the original cause (Wing, 1976).

Several workers have proposed that autism is due to poor child-
rearing in one way or another (Bettelheim, 1967;  Despert, 1951;
Goldfarb, 1961;  Kanner, 1943, 1949;  Rank, 1959;  Zaslow, 1967).  It
has been suggested that the parents of autistic children are cold and
remote, intellectual people (Kanner, 1943), or that the father alone
may have such a personality (Eisenberg, 1957).  Others have noted that
the early environment may be very lacking in stimulation for the child,
and have likened autism to the effects upon war captives of solitary
confinement (Bettleheim, ibid).  Yet others have put forth behaviouristic
theories and claim that mothers of autistic children give inadequate
or inappropriate reinforcement of early behaviour (Ferster, 1961;
Phillips, 1957).

There has been no firm support for any of these theories in the experimental literature. Creak and Ini (1961) found no abnormalities in the personalities of autistic children's parents. Rutter et al (1971) have more recently confirmed this finding of normal personalities in autistic's parents. Wing (1976) noted that about half of the parents of autistic children may have at some time had neurotic or depressive disorders, but this was also true of parents of aphasics, and is thus probably a result of the strains of caring for handicapped children. The only finding which emerged consistently from the studies of parents was that those of autistic children tended to be unusually frequently of the higher social classes (Rutter et al., ibid). DeMyer et al (1972) have noted in this regard that higher social class and intelligence are not usually factors which are associated with poor child-rearing practices. Additionally, Wing (1980) has provided evidence to suggest that there may not be a social class bias in the parents of autistic children. She has noted that in her sample of children drawn from the Camberwell region of London, parental class membership showed no class bias when referral factors had been accounted for. She also noted that there was a higher class bias in the people joining the National Society for Autistic Children nearer its inception, but that this had now tailed off as autism had become more widely known.

Faulty conditioning of autistic children in early childhood and infancy also seems unlikely. On the one hand it is doubtful that conditioning theories can even account for the development of normal babies, and on the other hand it is hard to imagine how caretakers the world over could have conditioned such similar abnormalities of behaviour into their children (Wing, 1976). In conclusion, there is very little support for any of the psychogenic theories of the aetiology of autism.

Genetic abnormalities have been suggested (for example, Kanner, 1949), but there is only a slightly raised prevalence of autism in autistic children's siblings. Rutter (1968) found a 2% rate in sib instead of the 4.5 per 10,000 age specific rate found in the population in general. Folstein and Rutter (1977) did a study of 21 same sex twins where at least one of each set had autism. Of the 25 cases of autism 19 were boys, which gave a girl/boy ratio of 1/3.1, similar to that found in the general population. They found a 36% pairwise concordance for autism in the 11 pairs of monozygotic twins, compared to a 0% concordance in the 10 dyzgotic pairs. Further, in 12 of the 17 pairs discordant for autism there was a tendency for the presence of autism in one twin to be associated with biological damage. Thus this study might provide some support for the idea of dividing autistic children into two groups: those who have few signs of brain damage and may have a genetically determined abnormality and those whose symptoms are due to a form of brain injury. However, this study awaits replication, and it remains possible that the problems of early diagnosis of autism may have led to spurious results in this twin study.

There seems little doubt that brain damage of some form can lead to a disorder which is indistinguishable from autism (Wing, 1976). Indeed, noting the absence of support for psychogenic theories of aetiology, it is almost certain that brain dysfunction or tissue damage is in some way the causatory factor. Evidence pertaining to perinatal injury is conflicting (see Wing, 1976). Chess (1971) found a correlation between the presence of maternal rubella and autistic behaviour in the child. Workers have documented that a history of infantile spasms may precede the onset of autistic behaviour (Kolvin et al, 1971; Taft and Cohen, 1971; Wing, 1975). Wing (1975) also found that conditions such as menengitis, tuberose sclerosis and phenylketonuria may be associated with patterns of behaviour which more-or-less resemble those found in autism. Rutter (1970) reported that by adolescence about a third of autistic children had at some point had epileptic fits. Lotter (1966, 1967) also found that about a third of the autistic children in his epidemiological study had some recorded evidence suggestive of neurological abnormality.

Several theories have been proposed as to where in the brain the lesion might be which causes autism. However, there appear to be three main areas which are favoured as possibilities: the recticular formation, subcortical areas such as the limbic system and temporal lobe, and the left hemisphere. Theories based upon the suggestion that abnormalities of arousal underly autistic behaviour have favoured the reticular formation as the site of a lesion (Rimland, 1964; Hutt et al, 1964, 1965; Hutt and Hutt, 1970; DesLauriers and Carlson, 1969). Rimland suggested that the function of the reticular formation is to sort out incoming information and to imbue it with meaning. This would imply that the basic deficit in autism would be one of coding, which is in good agreement with empirical research (see the next section on experimental studies of autism). However, Rimland's view of the functioning of the reticular formation is one which few neurophysiologists hold. Hutt Hutt and colleagues have proposed that the autistic child is chronically over-aroused. However, their theory has been criticised by Hermelin and O'Connor (1971), who have also presented evidence which suggests that autistic children's arousal is no different from matched controls. DesLauriers and Carlson's theory posits a deficit in the interaction of the limbic system and the reticular formation (both of which affect arousal). The deficit

as they suggest it amounts to the autistic child being hypothesised to
be in a state of (functional) sensory deprivation.  However, their view
of the function of these 2 systems has yet to be borne out in the
physiological literature, and it is uncertain whether one could account
for the wide variety of symptoms of all autistic children by an arousal
theory alone.

Work in the field of possible biochemical abnormalities in autism
is probably best summed up by quoting Wing (1976):

> The work in the field of biochemistry is at present
> hard to interpret because of the poverty of clinical
> data concerning the children studied, lack of
> repetition of experiments by other workers and the
> difficulty of knowing how to relate biochemical
> abnormalities to the details of the clinical syndrome.
>
> (p.87)

Turning now to theories which do not necessarily base themselves
on any particular suggestion of brain dysfunction, it is notable that
the earliest theory of autism (that of Kanner) said that autistic
children are born with a lack of ability to relate affectively to others.
Undoubtably autistic children do have problems relating to others
(cf. the four points above which describe the syndrome).  However, a
concept of a general deficiency of affect is too global.  DeMyer et al.
(1970) pointed out that autistic children are often cooperative so long
as tasks are within their ability.  Hermelin and O'Connor (1971)
discussed the fact that their studies had shown autistic children to
approach and orient towards adults as frequently as matched subnormal
children.  They concluded that it would be more fruitful to look at
the social and interpersonal behaviour of autistic children in terms
of an absence of basic skills which underlie normal social and linguistic
behaviour.

Hermelin and O'Connor (1971) were led to the conclusion that a central cognitive deficit might underlie autism. This theory was later elaborated in collaboration with Frith to include the inability of autistic children to extract meaning and features (such as rules) from their perceptual input. Because their ideas came from a series of experimental studies, it will be dealt with again in the following section on experiments with autistics.

Some investigators have suggested that autistic children have abnormalities of perception and attention (Koegal and Schreibmann, 1974; Lovaas and Koegal, 1973; Orintz and Ritvo, 1968). Lovaas and his colleagues have proposed that autistic children have problems attending to more than one aspect of their input. Thus this leads to an 'overselectivity' in their responses. However, later work by Lovaas (Koegal and Lovaas, 1978) and Litrownik et al, (1978) has shown that this is more due to general subnormality than to autism in particular. Ornitz and Ritvo have posited that the autistic child has faulty modulation of sensory input, which is related to an underlying vestibular dysfunction. In essence, this means that the autistic child lacks stable percepts. However, this suggestion is not supported by the findings of others who provide evidence for stable perception by autistics (DeMyer, 1971).

Finally, some workers have suggested that the autistic child's problems with imitation may lie at the root of the syndrome (DeMyer, 1971; Curico and Piserchia, 1978; for instance). DeMyer links this inability with an underlying inability to integrate visual information with motor acts. This, it is argued, could lead to a lack of communicative competence due to the fact that a lot of early social behaviour is imitative in form. However, it may be the case that a poor ability to imitate is one manifestation of a deeper problem, which also affects cross-modal integration. This point will be returned to later in this thesis.

## 1.2. Experimental Studies

### 1.2.1. Memory

Anecdotal and clinical evidence would tend to suggest that autistic children generally have good memory abilities (Wing, 1976a, for example). They are noted to have excellent rote memory, and the reported 'islets of intelligence' (Creak et al, 1961) are often memory-based (an ability to recall whole pages of telephone directories, to reproduce a piece of music on the piano having only seen it played once, and so forth). However, their abilities to recall items of information are often best when the topic of the items coincides with their obsessive interest. For instance, one might meet an autistic child who had an average (or even poor) memory for most things but who might be obsessed with knowing people's date of birth and be able to tell you what yours is years after you first told him. The clinical impression is also that autistic children's memory is 'echo-box' like (see Hermelin and O'Connor, 1970), that is, what goes in tends to come out in the same form, unchanged by processing. Indeed Rimland (1964) has suggested that an inability to process information with respect to stored knowledge is fundamental to the syndrome. He referred to a 'closed-loop' phenomenon whereby the autistic child tends to parrot what is said to him, even going so far as to repeat what he's heard in the same type of voice. Short-term memory, too, would appear to be good insofar as many autistic children are reported to exhibit echolalia.

Do the experimental studies confirm the above clinical impressions? In general, the answer would seem to be yes, but with some qualifications. Several workers have reported that the children's short-term memory (STM) is as good as that of normal and subnormal children matched for mental age (Tubbs, 1966; O'Connor and Hermelin, 1967a and b ; Hermelin and O'Connor, 1970; O'Connor, 1971; Hermelin and O'Connor, 1975; Prior and Chen, 1976). However, there have been studies which suggest that autistic children have an STM deficit (O'Connor and Hermelin, 1965; Hermelin and O'Connor, 1970; Boucher, 1978). It is therefore worth looking at these studies to search for the source of the discrepancies.

Tubbs (1966) administered the Illinois Test of Psycholinguistic Abilities (ITPA) to a group of autistic children. Two of the sub-tests of the ITPA measure the child's immediate recall of orally and visually presented words. On these subtests the autistic children were as able as normal children, who were matched on their ability at the Peabody Picture Vocabulary Test. This finding was confirmed by Hermelin and O'Connor (1975) who also noted, though, that the autistic children were not as able as matched controls in the backward recall of digits. Hermelin and O'Connor's (1967a) study in which autistic children had to recall random words and sentences also supported the claim that their short-term memory (STM) is good. In fact, the overall ability of the autistic children was found to be better than that of subnormal children matched on the Peabody Vocabulary Test. However, the subnormal children recalled words that were presented in sentences better than they did words which were equally frequent in their lexicon and were presented in random order. This was not the case for the autistic children who recalled the sentences as well as they did the random strings of words. This may well be related to the finding that autistic children excel in tests of STM only when immediate recall is required of stimuli which are not inherently meaningful (like sentences) and not to be recalled in any other way than that in which they were presented.

Further support for this idea was found by Hermelin and O'Connor (1967b)  when  they tested the autistic child's ability to recall meaningfully and randomly arranged words and pictures. However, whilst the autistic children once again failed to benefit from the meaningful ordering of the words, both groups gained equally from the sequential ordering of the visual material. There was thus some evidence that in autistic children echolalia and the random ordering of input were more characteristic of auditory than visual material. Moreover, Hermelin and O'Connor's study found that the autistic children showed a strong tendency to recall what they had heard or seen recently better than what was presented before. Whilst this was also true for the subnormal children the effect was much more marked in the autistic children. The autistic children thus performed as if they had an 'echo-box' memory (Waugh and Norman, 1965;  Craik, 1966).

This concept of an echo-box memory in autistic children was taken up by Boucher (1978). She emphasised that whilst semantic coding normally predominates in memorising earlier portions of lists for immediate recall, acoustic/phonetic coding plays an important role in the recency effect (Glanzer and Cunitz, 1966;  Brown and McNeill, 1966; Baddeley, 1976). Comparing the ability of autistic children with normal children of similar age and digit span revealed that the autistic children were inferior in their recall of orally presented words, randomly ordered. However, as Boucher pointed out, this result is of limited significance since the normal children had better language ability, thus this does not provide evidence against the contention that autistic children's STM is as good as mental age (MA) matched controls. It does, however, give support for the idea that the autistic child does not possess supernormal abilities to use acoustic cues when remembering verbal stimuli. Boucher further reports that by use of Baddeley's (ibid) formula to calculate the capacity of the STM system, autistic and normal children have the same echoic memory capacity (about 2.4 items on average). However, allowing for the variance in the two groups it does seem from Boucher's tables that the STM capacity of the normal children is greater than that of the autistic children, albeit fractionally (about 2.9 and 2.3 items capacity, respectively). Because she matched the normal and autistic groups on digit span, Boucher's study shows that autistic children's STM for digits is better than that for words.

A final source of doubt about the STM ability of autistic children comes from O'Connor and Hermelin's (1965) study in which they investigated various visual analogues to verbal operations. In this study they asked verbal and non-verbal autistic, aphasic, normal and deaf children to perform a variety of visually presented tasks. One of these was the immediate recall by forced choice of the size of a previously seen square. Whilst the speaking autistics were as able to do this as the normal children, the non-speaking autistics were significantly poorer than all their controls. O'Connor and Hermelin draw on the work of Conrad (1964) to explain this. Conrad links good

ability to recall items with the ability to verbally encode stimuli
before storage. Thus, poor STM might exist in the relatively less able
non-verbal autistic child - for visually presented material at least.

From the above studies, it is clear that the relationship between
memory and meaning is of particular interest in the study of autism.
Remembering well may often depend upon one's ability to discern pattern
in the items one is presented and to be able to cluster the items in a
meaningful manner to aid recall. This topic has been explored in a
series of studies by Hermelin and O'Connor (1970) and Frith (1968).
Because this aspect is relevant to our knowledge of the processing
abilities of autistic children, it will be dealt with in full later
in a section on 'cognition'.

There have been comparatively few studies of long-term memory
(LTM) in autistic children. However, Boucher and Warrington (1976)
claim to have shown impairments in autistic children's LTM, which
in some ways resemble that the amnesic patients. In the first
experiment they describe, autistic and subnormal children matched
for non-verbal ability were tested for their ability to recall 10
visual stimuli after a retention interval of 1 minute. They found the
autistic children to be worse than the controls. However, they rightly
pointed out that this might have been due to the subnormal children's
higher verbal ability. It should be noted that the task involved the
children having to verbally recall the drawings that they were shown.
A further experiment was devised which was intended to take this factor
of verbal ability into account. However, Boucher and Warrington claimed
to match some subnormal children to their sample of autistic children
on both language MA and non-verbal reasoning. This matching procedure

is rather puzzling because most autistic children can be expected to possess a higher non-verbal reasoning ability than language level. In contrast, subnormal children do not as a rule show such a biased profile of ability. It seems difficult to understand how they were able to match the groups for both measures. There is thus some doubt as to how well the groups were matched - did they both have about the same language ability? There was also quite a difference in what Boucher and Warrington required the groups to do in this task. This time each child was presented with 40 test items and was asked to name each one. In the recall session, which occurred after a filled interval of 30 seconds, he had to choose one of 40 pairs of items to indicate which he had seen before. Once again the autistic children were inferior in their ability to recall which items they had seen before. However, this test was in fact a recognition paradigm, and the presence of the pictures seen before did not 'cue' the autistic children's memories and allow them to perform as well as the controls. This is of relevance because in three of their studies Boucher and Warrington claim that cued recall in autistic children is unimpaired and significantly better than their free recall. In one experiment they cued the children acoustically, using the initial sound of the test word coupled with the neutral vowel ( ). In a second experiment they gave semantic clues to each word which were short descriptions of the objects the words referred to ('something to sit on', for example). In both experiments the words that the child had to recall were less frequent in their lexicon than at least one other word which had the same initial sound (in the first case) or which might be given the same description (in the second case). However, one must ask whether 'high frequency' words are indeed equally frequent in the lexicons of both autistic and subnormal children. Boucher and Warrington used the Mein (1961) word list , which was prepared from an analysis of words used in conversation by severely subnormal patients. Wing (1976) and others have pointed out, though, that the speech of autistic children is often very idiosycratic. Thus their vocabularies might contain words that are uncommon for the average non-autistic subnormal child and fail to contain some words which are common for most subnormals. It might also be expected that the autistic children's vocabularies vary more from one child to the next than comparable subnormal children. This is a problem which all studies of the language of autistic children face, and it can only be overcome by an extensive examination of the language used by the particular children under study.

Boucher and Warrington claim to show that cued recall (both acoustic and semantic) is as good in autistic children as in subnormal controls. In fact, their data implied that the autistic children were more able than the subnormals to use the semantic cues, however, the experiment attempting to show this was poorly designed. It was impossible for them to directly compare the two groups' abilities in semantically cued recall. The children were read a list of words, and after a filled interval of 30 seconds they were required to recall (freely) as many as they could. Once they had done this the children were given semantic cues to aid their recall of the remaining words. Thus the number of remaining words that could be recalled after semantic cuing varied from group-to-group and from child-to-child. Their conclusion that the subnormal children did not use semantic cues as well as the autistics is based upon logical, not statistical, inference. That is, the autistic children had poorer recall when they were uncued, yet their overall recall ability did not differ from that of the subnormals. However, whilst one might feel able to draw the logical conclusion that the autistic children must have 'made up' the difference in recall

scores by being better at the cued recall, this might be erroneous.

The subnormal children might still possess as good cue recall as the

autistic children, but the words that they would have recalled by

semantic cuing had mainly already been remembered without such aid.

It is a pity that Boucher and Warrington did not give both groups a

separate test of cued and uncued recall on matched items.  In sum

then, it is difficult to agree with Boucher and Warrington's conclusion

fromthis study that their results favour an 'impaired retrieval'

hypothesis rather than one of a central cognitive deficit in autism.

They argue that the latter would predict relatively poor ability to

utilise semantic cues for recall, whereas the former predicts the

opposite finding.  It is certainly surprising given that the series of

of experiments reported by Hermelin and O'Connor (1970) suggest that

it is the semantic aspect of stimuli that gives autistic children the

most problems.

Boucher and Warrington also report a study of the ability of

autistic and normal children to recall written words after a filled

retention interval.  In this experiment they did do two separate

studies of the children's ability to recall the items freely and with

cues.  The cues were the first 3 letters of each of the test words, and

were also the first 3 letters of a more frequent word in their lexicon.

However, they used the Mein word list again, and thus the aforementioned

matching problems applied here too.  In this study they not only found

that the groups were equal in their ability on the cued recall but

also on the free recall.  Thus they once again found evidence to support

the idea that cued recall was better in autistics than subnormals

(although no subnormal group was actually tested), and that this ability to utilise cues was not modality bound.  But the finding that the autistic children were as good at the free recall was not in line with their amnesia/autism parallel.  The finding that the autistic children's long term memory under free recall of visual items might be better than that for verbal items  may parallel the findings of O'Connor and Hermelin (1967a).  In this study O'Connor and Hermelin found that the meaningful ordering of visual stimuli had an equal effect upon the immediate recall ability of normal and autistic children.  Meaningful ordering of verbal items on the other hand helped the autistic children far less than it did the normal controls.  There is thus a body of evidence to suggest that the basic deficit in autism affects the auditory/temporal mode more than the visual/spatial.  This point will be returned to in the section on 'cognition'.

In summary, the autistic child would seem to have an intact STM, and there is some possibility that his LTM is less good than that of matched subnormals.  It seems likely that these findings are linked to the proposition that autistic children fail to process their perceptions meaningfully, which is a primary factor in recall from LTM storage. These findings need not conflict with the clinical reports of exceptional memory feats in autistic children.  It may be that recalling specific stimuli to order is most affected.  When the autistic child is remembering items obsessively (and thus on his own terms, and not in the structured situations noted above), he may perform exceptionally well.  He will also tend to perform much better when the items can be recalled as they were perceived, unprocessed (such as dates, car numbers, etc.).  Finally, there is some evidence that the autistic child's memory problems are greater in the auditory/ temporal realm than in the visual/spatial.

1.2.2.  Perception

Abnormal responses to sensory stimuli are one of the central features of autistic behaviour. They have been noted to be hyper-reactive and hypo-reactive to stimuli, and both forms of response may be present in the same child. A lack of response to sensory stimulation has led some mothers to think that their child is blind or deaf; however, it is often the case that the same mother will also have reason to disbelieve this for the child may ignore loud sounds but seem aware that a sweet is being unwrapped in an adjoining room. Similarly, a child might often present as blind, but will be noted to have a fixation which includes collecting small pieces of cotton that drop onto the carpet (see Wing, 1976a). In fact some investigators have gone so far as to regard autism as the result of multiple sensory handicap. Wing (1967) carried out a comparative study of autistic, blind, deaf, aphasic, Down's syndrome, and normal children. Abnormal responses to visual and auditory stimuli was far more marked in the autistic than in the Down's syndrome or normal groups. This group difference was also noted for the autistics' preference for proximal senses. Overall, the group which the autistic children resembled most was the partially deaf-blind group. Keeler (1958) and Blank (1959) are amongst the many who have noted similarities between blind and autistic children (see Hermelin and O'Connor, 1970; Fraiberg, 1977). Blind children have mannerisms, for instance, which closely resemble those produced by autistic children. The lack of social responsiveness in blind infants (reported by Urwin, 1978) is strongly reminiscent of reports of autistic infants' behaviour (Wing, 1976a for instance). This may well be linked with Walters and Parke's (1965) conclusion that social responsiveness in infancy is related to the role which the distal receptors (vision and hearing) play in normal development.

An abnormal hierarchical structuring of the senses has been proposed for autistic children (Goldfarb, 1961; Schopler, 1965, 1966). Such workers state that autistic children tend to use proximal as much or more than distal senses for exploring their world. Wing (1966) and Rimland (1964) have both noted that autistic children tend to lick, bang, scratch, smell, touch and shake objects. And when they shake, bang or scratch them they seem to be doing so for the vibrations produced rather than for the sounds. But a simple view of preference for proximal senses is not in line with observations of the autistic child having hypo-responsiveness to pain, cold and heat.

Investigating EEG responses to sound and light in autistic, normal and Down's syndrome children, Hermelin and O'Connor (1968) found no group differences in orienting responses to light, but there was a clear indication that continuous noise was more arousing for the autistic children than for the other groups. They also found that the autistic children showed a relative lack of sustained arousal to intermittent visual stimulation. This finding is in line with the results of behavioural measures which showed that autistic children have briefer visual inspection times than do normal or subnormal controls (O'Connor and Hermelin, 1967a). No such group differences were found for the continuous representation of visual stimuli. Hermelin and O'Connor (1970) concluded that the results do not indicate avoidance of visual stimuli due to high arousal levels, but rather a faster decrease in an orientation response.

In another study by Hermelin and O'Connor (1964) they examined autistic subnormal and normal children's responses to light, sound and touch when 2 stimuli were presented at once. The children were rewarded regardless of which of the stimuli (one to their left and the other to their right) they chose to respond to. Hermelin and O'Connor found that all groups responded to light in preference to either touch or sound. However, when the bimodal presentation was of touch and sound alone, subnormal children tended to respond to the sound whereas the autistic children tended to do the opposite. It was also concluded that the autistic child's main problem was not the establishment of a new response (all children could learn to respond to sound rather than light), but the extinction of a dominant response.

Elsewhere O'Connor and Hermelin (1965b) showed that autistic children of fairly low ability tended to respond equally to noise and to words when the two stimuli were in competition. However, this was also true for Down's syndrome children of similar verbal M.A., thus the effect may be entirely due to verbal ability. However, what did differentiate the autistic children was their tendency to respond more according to the position of the stimuli than to the stimuli's intensity. Hermelin and O'Connor (1965a) have also shown that discriminations are easier for autistic children when they can be made on the basis of - and with additional information from - motor movements. In this study the children had to find a reward under one of two boxes, with three possible cues being given as to which box concealed the sweet; in one case it was the box in the higher position, in another the box was larger, and in the third case the box had an arrow pointing in a certain direction drawn upon it. The autistic children only learnt the task of finding the reward when the response included motor movements (high versus low boxes). Although it may be noted that the autistic children who did worst on these tasks were those with lower levels of ability. Support for these findings was also found in Hermelin and O'Connor's later study (1967a).

Thus the above studies do not support a simple theory of abnormal hierarchical organisation of the senses in autism. There is evidence that they prefer to explore objects with proximal senses rather than distal ones, but they respond more to light than sound or touch when the senses are put in competition. They seem to have an abnormal preference for touch over sound, although the factor of M.A. might be important here, it being true only for lower ability children. Certainly there is evidence for autistic children finding discrimination easier when there are motor cues available. Given this, though, what factors characterise autistics ability in visual discrimination?

In their study of visual discrimination, O'Connor and Hermelin (1967a) were concerned with the question of whether autistics were able to perceive differences between various visual stimuli. To do this they employed the paradigm devised by Fantz (1965) in which one measures the child's fixation times whilst looking at two displays. By mounting the displays inside a box with a dark interior, it was possible to give the child a choice of looking at one or two stimuli or at nothing at all. Thus if a child looked significantly more at one of the stimuli than the other, it could be concluded that he could discriminate between them. Because this paradigm relies upon the existence of visual 'preference', it should be noted that an equal fixation time on each stimulus does not necessarily mean that the subject could not perceive any difference between them. Using this method O'Connor and Hermelin were able to investigate identity, size, colour, brightness, pattern, complexity and meaningfulness. The main finding was that the autistic children had generally lower fixation times on all the stimuli. Because the number of their fixations was similar to that of normal and subnormal matched controls,

this meant that they spent more time than the other groups in 'non-
directed gazing' (at the black interior of the box).

There were no group differences in preference for looking at the
stimuli. This meant, for instance, that all groups tended to look
more frequently at the photograph of a face than at a jumbled version
of the same photograph. There was thus no indication that the autistic
children tended to avoid looking at faces - this is a point that will
be returned to later in a survey of the work on social perception in
autism.

It might be suggested from the above studies that autistic
children see and hear but do not look and listen. The evidence
reported so far, and that to be reported in later sections, supports
the view that the autistic child has a central cognitive deficit,
which can lead him to resemble other children whose perceptual
apparatus is not intact (such as blind and deaf children). What the
nature of this deficit is will be pursued in the section on 'cognition'.
However, such a view is not without its opponents.

Ornitz (1969, 1970, 1974) and Ritvo (1976) have proposed that
the autistic child has faulty modulation of sensory input and an
underlying central vestibular dysfunction. This is hypothesised to
lead to 'perceptual inconstancy' and an unsmooth balance of internal
neural excitation and inhibition. All this amounts to saying that
the autistic child lacks stable percepts - which is contrary to the
evidence provided above by the studies of Hermelin and O'Connor.
DeMyer (1971) discussed the hypothesis of perceptual inconstancy
and found little support for it. The autistic children that she

has studied have always shown good test/retest reliability. DeMyer also found that autistic children could copy actions performed when there was a constant visual reference (a doll for example), and thus showed no evidence for unstable percepts. Alpern (1967) has noted that autistic children are stable in their responses to IQ tests (which is supported by Rutter, 1974). Also a neurological study (Small et al, 1971a,b) found that latencies and amplitudes of visual cerebral evoked potentials were quite constant in autistic children. In fact, Small found some evidence for the autistic children's potentials being even more stable than those of normal comparison subjects. DeMyer concludes her discussion (ibid) by saying that Ornitz and Ritvo's theory finds little support in the literature, but a theory which proposes that autistic children fail to attach semantic cue value to sensory input is well supported.

Finally, further evidence for the essentially normal perceptual abilities of autistic children of higher ability comes from Wurst (1976). He found that whilst they demonstrated many problems on tests involving social contact, they showed no problems on perceptual tests. Evidence for a lack of perceptual problems also comes from studies of less able autistic children, too. For instance, Nadia, described by Selfe (1977) had a remarkable ability to draw objects when she was only 5 or 6 years old. Nadia is a very low level child, and when she drew the pictures she was almost entirely mute. Now she has some language ability, and it is possible that the emergence of symbolic function has lessened her ability to draw so remarkably. Nonetheless, it seems clear that Nadia's problems were not in seeing but in the interpretation of what she saw. Thus she represents one retarded autistic child in whom perceptual discrimination, memory, and motor skills are higher in some areas than might be expected from her general development. It seems that there are a fair number of autistic children with good drawing ability, too (Selfe, inter alia). Indeed, autistic children of all levels of ability often have obsessions which reflect the presence of intact perceptual abilities.

### 1.2.3   Cognition

The most extensive studies of autistic children's cognitive abilities have been undertaken by Hermelin, O'Connor and Frith (see: Hermelin and O'Connor, 1970; Hermelin and Frith, 1971; and Hermelin, 1978). In the previous section it was noted that autistic children seem to have intact perceptual systems. That is, whilst they may occasionally behave as if they are blind or deaf, they can nonetheless see and hear quite normally. It appears that the autistic child's main problem is making sense of what he sees and hears - that is, in processing the incoming information. Evidence for an intact STM in these children also supports this idea. Several experiments have been carried out to determine where the autistic child's greatest areas of cognitive disfunction lie.

From very early on in life - some say from birth - the child is able to integrate the information coming through his senses (Bower, 1979). It also seems that the storage of information coming in through the senses is not modality specific. Some, for instance, have proposed that cross modal transfer is language mediated (Blank and Bridger, 1964). Others have suggested that an area of the brain is concerned with modality independent storage of information (eg. Geschwind, 1965).

In contrast Atteneave and Benson (1969) concluded that spatial information is primarily represented in visual terms regardless of which modality the relevant data entered through. On the other hand, it seems likely that temporal information is processed primarily in auditory terms, and hence verbal coding may play a strong role in this processing (Hermelin, 1972).

To begin with, can autistic children make normal use of visual cues to aid performance on motor task? Frith and Hermelin (1969) studied the role of visual and motor cues for autistic, subnormal and normal children. In each group there were two subgroups distinguished on the basis of perceptual age (PA, determined with the Frostig scales), chronological age (CA), and mental age (MA). They asked the children to construct jig-saw puzzles which were a series of cards that had to be put into a specific order. In one puzzle the order could only be determined by the shape of the edges of the cards. In another the cards had flat edges and the only clue as to the correct ordering was a line running through the cards - one thus had to match the lines up at the joining points, rather like making a road. In a third type of puzzle there was both the pictorial and edge shape information available to help the child. In the first type, then, the shape/tactile cues were maximised whereas in the second the visual cues were maximised. All the groups except the autistic children with low ability found the second type of puzzle to be harder than the first. The low PA autistic children demonstrated a trend to find the second easier than the first. Thus these autistic children alone showed that they could perform well when they had to deal with trial and error motor-based strategies but performed poorly when visual information was available which might have improved their performance. The possibility of poor visual/motor integration led Hermelin and Frith to examine the same groups' abilities to follow a maze-like track with a metal stylus. The children were required to do this once without being able to see what they were doing, and again with visual feed-back. When the children were able to look the autistic children were as fast as normal children. However, when they were denied visual feedback, particularly when the track to be traced was complex in form, the normal children were significantly faster than the autistic children. Hermelin and Frith concluded that autistic children fail to compensate for a deficit in processing and integrating visual information by alternative strategies. The strategies which autistic children can use efficiently are those based upon immediate feedback from kinesthetic or motor cues.

Hermelin (1972) reported studies of the autistic child's ability to code information. She asked each child to place his hands such that the middle and forefingers of one hand were spread open and immediately behind the equivalent fingers of the other hand. The child's 4 fingers were touched in turn and for each one a word was said. The child had to repeat the word that went with each finger. When the child had learnt the correspondance the experimenter changed the hands around so that the fingers of the left hand now occupied the places of the right hand and vice versa. Having done this the child had 2 choices. He could either decide that the labels went with the place or with the specific finger regardless of its position. It was found that both sighted normal and autistic subjects responded with the finger that was labelled, whereas blind children tended to report

the location. It is thus a pity that blindfolded autistic children
could not have been used, for it would have been interesting to see
if they resembled the blind children. In a second experiment also
reported by Hermelin (1972) autistic, normal and congenitally deaf
children were presented with a display of numbers to be recalled.
The numbers appeared in windows which were side-by-side. It was
thus possible to make the temporal order in which the numbers were
presented differ from the spatial order (thus, the order might have
been 397 left-to-right, but 973 first-to-last). Both autistic and
deaf children reported the numbers in spatial terms whereas the normal
children reported them according to the temporal order.

The above results concur findings from earlier studies by Hermelin and
O'Connor (1964) in which they found that autistic children have normal
orientation to visual stimuli, and show no preference for proximal
receptors. However, in both the above studies autistic children used
the information about discrete location in space, and were less liable
to locate events according to their temporal position. The main
result is thus that like deaf children autistic children may not readily
translate and rehearse events in space and time in a verbal form.

Temporal processing deficits have been shown in other studies by
Hermelin, O'Connor and Frith. Hermelin and Frith (1971) report the
most important of these studies (see also, Hermelin and O'Connor 1970;
Frith, 1968; Frith 1970a,b). Normal, subnormal and autistic children
were required to repeat words spoken to them. One experiment tested
the ability of the children to repeat words that formed an orderly
sequence (a sentence) with their memory for words which were randomly
arranged. It is well known that people can remember sentences better
than random word strings (Miller and Selfridge, 1953). This phenomenon

can be explained by assuming that people make use of their knowledge about and familiarity with language and its inherent redundancies. Because of our knowledge about syntax we can guess what a sentence might be given only the key words, and thus considerably relieve the load on our memory. Both normal and subnormal children were able to recall the sentences better than the random words, and were thus able to make use of the redundancy. However, whilst the autistic children (of about MA 4 years) also found sentences easier to recall than random words, the effect was far less marked than with the other 2 groups. The autistic children were as able (or better on occasion) to recall the random words as were the normal children, but they were much worse at the sentences. There was also a strong tendency for the autistic children to recall mainly the last thing that they heard. It is possible that some of the autistic children were simply echoing what they had just heard.

A second experiment attempted to see if the autistic children could overcome their tendency to recall the last thing that they heard. In this study the child was presented with word strings which were half made up of random words and half of meaningful strings (sentences). Thus the child might be asked to recall "wall long cake send where is the ship", or "read them your book way spoon here like". Because half the time the sentence began the string and the other half it followed the random words, it was possible to tell whether a child was merely repeating the last thing that he heard, or taking note of the redundancy present in the sentence half of the word string. Normal children were found to recall sentences better than the random words regardless of where they came in the word string. In contrast the autistic children tended to recall what was most recently said to them regardless of whether this was the meaningful half or not. This supports the clinical observation that some autistic children echo what is said to them, with little understanding for meaning. Even the relatively able autistic child may use words without fully understanding the meaning and implications of them.

Hermelin and O'Connor (1967b) also attempted to show whether or not the association processes    shown by 'clustering' are impaired in autistic children. Subnormal and autistic children were matched for digit span and tested on their immediate recall of supra-span lists of words which contained words drawn from two meaningful sets of objects. For instance, they might have been presented with "blue three red five six white green eight". As can be seen, the ability to cluster these 8 words into 2 meaningful sets of 4 would greatly aid recall (ie. blue, red, white, green/three five, six, eight). Thus if any subject was to recall more items than he normally was able to from a list of random words, he would have to appreciate the value of clustering. The subnormal children showed this clustering in their recall whereas this was found to a much lesser extent in the autistic children. Thus Hermelin and O'Connor confirmed their hypothesis that autistic children do not actively reorganise material according to its meaning.

Frith hypothesised (Frith, 1968) that autistic children are impaired in their ability to detect lawful patterns in their perceptual input; thus the above problems with realising that clustering meaningful items would aid recall might only be one example of a more fundamental deficit. The children were consequently presented with

series of words which were simply variations upon either repetition
(eg. one-one-one) or alternation (eg. one-two-one-two). More complex
patterns could thus be created by mixing repetitions and alternations
together (eg. one-one-two-one). Subnormal, normal and autistic
children were once again matched for their immediate memory ability
and were required to recall lists of supra-span length. The results
showed that the control groups could remember highly redundant strings
of words (eg. mouse-mouse-mouse-bag-bag-bag) far better than the
autistics. However, as might be expected from the matching procedure,
both groups did equally well when recalling more random strings. Once
again the autistic children failed to make use of the structure in
the stimuli. It may be noted that these findings are similar to those
reported above for recall of random words together with sentences.
However, whereas the structure of the earlier tests items was syntactic,
that of the later one was not. Thus, the deficit displayed by the
autistic children in extracting rules is not restricted to grammar.

Frith also noted the type of errors made by the groups. Just as
the known rules about syntax might enable one to reconstruct a sentence
from keys words, so it might be possible to reconstruct the 'binary'
strings presented in Frith's study by noting the dominant rule of the
sequence (repetition or alternation). For instance, brown-blue-brown-
brown consists of mainly alternations. Thus the application of this
rule to aid recall might produce: brown-blue-brown-blue.. The results
revealed that subnormal and normal children's recalled sequences
tended to reflect correctly the main rule present in the input sequence.
If the input sequence tended to contain repetitions then the control
groups recalls tended to contain even more repetitions. The autistic
children performed quite differently. They tended to almost always apply
the repetition rule, whether or not it was dominant in the input.

Thus Frith was drawn to the conclusion that whereas the control groups could correctly determine and use the rule present in the word strings, the autistic children tended to rigidly apply one rule regardless of the input. She noted that feature extraction and the imposition of rules might be relatively independent of each other. They may be likened, in fact, to Piaget's "accommodation" and "assimilation" (See Piaget and Inhelder, 1969).[*] Frith suggests that the stereotyped rigid and ritualistic behaviours in autistic children might be regarded as an exaggerated form of pattern imposition. On the other hand, the often inappropriate and unpredictable behaviour of such children might be the result of the autistic's impaired ability to extract features from his environment.

Frith (ibid) also undertook a study which aimed to investigate the pattern imposition tendencies of the autistic children. A pack of cards was used, each card being either black or red. The child was required to guess which colour card would be turned up next. Only subnormal, normal and autistic children who appeared to understand the game were included. Nearly every child tended to repeat or alternate his responses. - very rarely did children use mixtures of the two. All the children tended to impose their own simple patterns in this unstructured situation. Similar results were found when children had to spontaneously construct rows of coloured counters.

These experiments led Hermelin and Frith (1971) to conclude that the deficit possessed by autistic children may extend beyond their language problems, and it may account for a wider range of cognitive dysfunctions. This basic deficit would appear from these studies to be an inability to extract features from organised input, coupled

---

* Footnote: However, for Piaget "accommodation" and "Assimilation" are not independent, but are rather more like two sides of the same coin.

with a tendency to impose rigid patterns. Frith concluded that in certain circumstances this imposition of pattern might be appropriate, but in relatively complex and flexible situations (such as social interaction, symbolic play, etc.) such a tendency would be a gross handicap. However, it is possible that the pattern imposition tendency of autistic children may itself be a secondary manifestation of a more fundamental deficit. This possibility will be considered later in this thesis.

Whilst the autistic child's good short-term recall of items implies that he possesses the ability to form internal images, Hermelin and O'Connor decided to test this ability more directly (see Hermelin, 1978). Hermelin (1978) noted that in Piagetian terms the ability to form images is a necessary precursor to symbol formation in the child. The first experiment she reported involved blindfolded normal, congenitally blind, and blindfolded autistic children. Each child had to feel two shapes and say whether the shapes could fit together to form a complete square. The shapes were fixed to a board a small distance apart, and thus one could not directly test their ability to fit together. The shapes were presented in two different ways: in one case the shapes were in the correct rotation to fit together if it was possible; in the second case the smaller shape was rotated around 180 degrees so that the child might have to "rotate it in his mind" to determine if it would fit. No differences were found between the groups on either mode of presentation. However, Hermelin pointed out that the task could have been solved by tactile exploration alone and may have required a minimum of visual imagery. O'Connor and Hermelin (1975) also required blind, blindfolded normal and blindfolded autistic children to say whether a plastic 'hand' given to them to feel was a left one or a right one. The hands were identical in shape, one being a mirror image of the other. Thus, orientation features were the only distinguishing cues in this task. Blindfolded normal children were both faster and more often correct than were the blind or blindfolded autistic children. Hermelin (ibid) thus concluded that like the blind, autistic children may lack a spatial reference frame with visual dimensions to help them in making a decision.

In the same study, Hermelin and O'Connor (1975) also asked blind and blindfolded subjects to reproduce different aspects of a limb movement. The question which concerned them was whether kinesthetic data were sufficient for the derivation and storage of movement components in the absence of kinesthetic invariants. The experiment involved each child moving a lever up a rod for a distance which was determined both by the starting point and by the presence of a 'stopper'. After the practice trials the stopper was removed and the child was required to reproduce the same end position from a different starting position. Thus, if in the practice trials the child had been asked to move the lever from the base up to a height of 15cm, then in the test he may have been required to lift the lever once again to the 15cm position but this time to start already 5cm up the rod (thus the distance to be produced in the latter case would be 5cm shorter than in the former). In a second condition the child had to reproduce the same distance from a different starting position (thus he might have had to lift the lever from 5cm to 20cm rather than from the base to 15cm). They found no group differences on the first task -ie. when the same location had to be reproduced. Thus the position of the arm could be recalled by all 3 groups (blind, blindfolded normal and blindfolded autistic) on the basis of kinesthic information. However, in the second task the children needed to involve a degree of visual imagery, for there are no receptors in one's muscles or joints which signal distance of limb travel.[*] Large group differences were found, the blindfolded normal children being more correct than the blind or autistic children. Hermelin and O'Connor thus concluded that autistic children seem to be unable to evoke the necessary visual images to supplement information derived from movement.

Hermelin (ibid) ended her discussion of the above results by saying that it is unwise to treat the autistic child's problems as if they lay entirely in the realm of language. She pointed out that it is not language which enables us to think, but rather the ability to think and form symbols which allows us to develop language. It is thus of relevance to the studies that Piaget considers the construction of internal images to be essential precursors to symbolic acts in the child. She concluded by saying, "....(our experiments) seem to indicate to us that autistic children do not tend to integrate current experience with schemas and representations stored from previous sensory impressions". (p. 153; Hermelin 1978). However, she also notes that autism may well be present from birth, and thus from a period before the normal child can handle symbols and images, and that the behavioural pathology in autism must be due to "other psychological mechanisms and processes" than the ability to handle symbols and images. This is a topic that will be returned to later in this thesis.

---

*Footnote: Recent work throws doubt upon this statement (Greer, *inter alia*).

DeMyer's (1971) claim that autistic children have problems in transferring information from the visual to the motoric systems thus gains some support from Hermelin and O'Connor's work. DeMyer's work in turn offers support for Hermelin and O'Connor's findings. DeMyer tested normal, subnormal and autistic children for their ability to imitate bodily movements. Some of the movements involved an object, such as a doll, and some left no visual trace at all, such as raising a hand. She found that autistic children could copy actions with a doll fairly well, but were significantly poorer at the other body movement imitations than the other two groups. Her explanation centres on the fact that when an action is done with a doll there is a visual referent available, whereas body movements leave no visual traces. The child thus has no cues in the latter case as to which of the possible body movements in his repertoire is required. However, it may be possible to see these findings as support for Boucher and Warrington's (1976) contention that autistic children have normal cued recall abilities but poor free recall competence.

In conclusion, it would seem most likely that the essential deficit in autism can be described as 'cognitive' in nature. Autistic children have problems in extracting meaning from their perceptions. Their good immediate recall supports the idea that they can retain information, but the idiosyncrasy of their LTM implies that they tend not to encode sensory data meaningfully. Relatively low ability autistic children tend to have poor pattern detection abilities and also tend to impose their own patterns upon their perceptions regardless of the appropriateness of the imposition. Autistic children appear to be able to form internal images, but they seem poor at integrating these images with prior perceptions. They are also poor at using information from the visual modality to aid their performance on motor tasks. In several respects, then, they resemble blind children. They resemble the deaf, too, insofar as they tend to code visual stimuli spatially rather than temporally, regardless of the nature of the stimuli. Finally, it is worthy of note that autism may be present from birth and thus begin at a stage in development which is precursory to the normal child's ability to handle symbols and images.

1.2.4   Arousal

Arousal is of relevance to several parts of this thesis, however, it will be covered briefly here due to the fact that relatively little is known of this complex variable. One may measure 'arousal' by several methods. One can, for instance, record a subjects heart-rate, or his EEG or observe his behaviour. However, it is possible that one level of arousal may be indicated by one of these measures and a quite different level be suggested by another measure - at the same time, in the same subject. Some workers have proposed that autistic children have arousal problems (Hutt et al, 1964; Rimland, 1964; Schopler, 1965; DesLauriers and Carlson, 1969). Although most of these workers have implicated a defect in the reticular formation of autistic children, it is notable that they do not all posit the same deficit. Hutt et al suggests that the autistic child is over-aroused and cite EEG evidence to support their claim. They claim that autistic children's resting EEG records have a predominance of low-voltage, fast, desynchronised waves and that the decrease of stereotypic behaviours in such children accompanies a greater synchronisation of the waves. However, Hermelin and O'Connor (1968) found no abnormalities in the resting EEGs of autistic children. Hermelin and O'Connor (1971) also note that

Hutt et al's claim that chronic high arousal is linked to the autistic child's avoidance of 'social stimuli' was not supported by their studies. Autistic children were not found to avoid 'social' stimuli when their behaviour in a room containing objects and a person was noted, nor when they were required to look at faces with their eyes closed or faces with their eyes open (see O'Connor and Hermelin, 1967a).

Rimland (1964) suggested that autistic children are under-aroused and suggested that a lot of their behaviour could be seen as self-stimulatory. However, his theory is based upon a view of the functioning of the reticular formation which few physiologists hold and there is no supporting experimental evidence. DesLauriers and Carlson (1969) suggest that autistic children have problems of both under- and over-arousal. Though they hypothesis remains a possibility, no empirical evidence has been forthcoming to support it. It is also unclear as yet whether their view of the reticular formation and the relationship of it with the limbic system is upheld by physiological research.

Wing (1976) in reviewing the ideas about arousal and autism concludes by saying that whilst autistic children almost certainly have abnormalities of arousal, these are likely to be secondary to other abnormalities. "In any case it is difficult to explain the specific patterns of impairments and skills found in autism on the basis of anything as generalised as over- or under-arousal". (Wing, ibid; p.86).

## 1. 2.5   Language and Sociability

Language and sociability will be dealt with in one section. This
is partly because a major point to be made in this thesis is that the
two aspects are closely related in the normal child, and partly because
few experimental studies have been done of these areas. This latter
point is perhaps rather surprising given that problemswith communication
and social interaction are fundamental to autism. However, the reason
is perhaps that such aspects of the child are easier to investigate by
ethological, observational means rather than laboratory based
experimental approaches. Language has nonetheless been studied - as
the above sections have shown - and whilst language may not have
always been the central variable being measured, it has often been a
part of various experimental designs (children have frequently been
required to voice their responses). One must also not overlook the
fact that most experiments take place in a social setting.

Abnormal responses to people are a fundamental aspect of clinicians'
reports of the behaviour of autistic children. It is thus important
to know whether the autistic child does indeed behave differently
towards people than do other children of similar mental capacities.
If this is the case, then one must further enquire if their abnormal
response to people is peculiar to the social situation or whether it
is just one manifestation of a more general deficit in the autistic
child.

A more specific aspect of the general topic of social interaction
and autism is the claim that autistic children avoid eye contact.
This will be discussed in more detail in a later section, however it
will be noted here that it seems that autistic children have unusual

gaze behaviour which is more connected to their inability to use gaze correctly than for avoidance of others' eyes. It also appears that an autistic child may seem to avoid another's gaze when in fact he has an abnormally low fixation time on all objects, not just others' eyes (Hermelin and O'Connor, 1970). There is evidence of this kind, too, relating to the proximity which autistic children keep to people compared to that of control subjects.

Hermelin and O'Connor (1963a) noted the amount of approach to, and orientation towards, various stimuli in autistic and control children. The various stimuli were placed in an otherwise empty room and the children were observed one at a time through a one-way mirror. Part of this study included a measure of the children's proximity and response to an adult. The adult spent 9 minutes in the room. For the first 3 minutes she sat still and silent. In the next 3 minutes she attempted to make physical contact with the child (cuddling, tickling, and engaging him in play). In the final 3 minutes the adult asked the child some questions and gave some simple verbal commands. The results showed no difference between the groups in the number of approaches and responses they made, as long as these were non-verbal. However, speaking or responding to speech divided the groups. Many of the autistic children failed to respond to speech, seeming not to understand or to be unattentive. However, they also found that when there were objects, pictures and a person in the room, all children oriented more often and for longer periods to the person than to the objects.

Another study (O'Connor and Hermelin, 1963) confirmed that autistic children are like subnormal controls in their preferential orientation to people. In this study they were once again observed whilst in a room. The physical distance of the children from a variety of objects placed at one end of the room was compared. The objects included both 'social' and non-social stimuli: a box, a rocking platform, a blanket, a life-size model of a woman, a person and a voice being played through a loudspeaker. It was found that subnormal children spent more time in the vicinity of the box, blanket and rocking platform than the autistic group, but there were no differences on the other (social) stimulus conditions.

Two further studies by O'Connor and Hermelin (1967) pertain to the gaze avoidance controversy, which will be dealt with in full later. They measured the children's fixation times whilst looking at various stimuli in a box. This type of experiment was described in the above section on 'perception' and essentially involves the use of Fantz's stimulus preference method devised for use with infants. The child has two stimuli to look at in an otherwise dark interior of a box, and his visual fixations are noted. Two of the stimuli Hermelin and O'Connor used were a photograph of a face, and a jumbled version of the same photograph. Like subnormal and normal children, the autistic children looked more frequently and for longer at the unscrambled face than at the scrambled one. However, their gaze behaviour was characterised by extremely brief fixations whereas that of the other groups was not. Hermelin and O'Connor also modified the apparatus so that a person could look into the opposite end of the box from that which the child looked through. Thus the child could see a live face illuminated at the far end. Hermelin and O'Connor measured the children's eye movements when the face had its eyes open compared to when they were closed. Both autistic and control children looked as frequently at both displays. However, once again the autistic children had abnormally brief fixation times.

In conclusion to their section on responsiveness to people, Hermelin and O'Connor remark, "Our results gave no support to the view that the behaviour of autistic children towards people or images of people is specifically impaired in comparison with their behaviour towards other objects." (1970, p.120). Nonetheless, abnormal social response is one of the most clear symptoms which presents itself to the clinician. It is also undoubtedly true that people as a class of objects differ from most objects in crucial ways, and thus present specific problems for any child who has a 'cognitive dysfunction'. This point will be returned to later.

It should be noted, though, that some workers have put a more primary emphasis on the social problems of the autistic child (Kanner 1943, 1949, 1954; Hutt and Ounsted, 1966; Richer, 1976). Hutt and Ounsted claimed to find that autistic children specifically avoided looking at social stimuli and related their findings to the theory (Hutt et al., 1965) that the autistic child is chronically over-aroused. However, they have been criticised (Hermelin and O'Connor, 1971, p.17) for drawing conclusions which go beyond the experimental evidence they obtained. They also had very few subjects in their experiment. Their study has also not yet been replicated, although results presented in this thesis are of relevance.

Richer and Coss (in Coss 1972) also did a study which claimed to show that autistic children specifically avoid looking at people's eyes. This experiment and criticisms of it will be given later; suffice to say at this juncture that the results they obtained are highly questionable. Finally, approaches to the study of autistic children such as that of Richer (1976) and Tinbergen and Tinbergen (1972) have been strongly criticised(Ricks and Wing, 1976, for example).

To summarize, then, there is a body of experimental evidence (albeit small and unreplicated) which suggests that the social handicap of the autistic child might be secondary to a more basic handicap. Whilst autistic children and subnormal children alike seem to respond more to people than to objects, the autistic child appears to have a less differentiated response to people. It is perhaps primarily the autistic child's failure to find meaning in his perceptions which leads him to be less sociable than other children.

Experimental studies of autistic children's language have been scarce. There has, however, been a lot of space in the literature devoted to the description of the syndrome which has been given to the topic of the language. In several papers, Rutter (1968, 1972, 1974, 1978) has emphasised his belief that language problems are at the heart of autism. Over the years Rutter has summarised the trends in thought about language and autism. Briefly, this has covered a period when Rutter referred to autistic children as having a "language delay" (and spoken language was mainly referred to), through a period when the deviance of their language was emphasised, and most recently to the emphasis on the language deficit being global insofar as it affects all modes of communication. Distinctive characteristics of their speech have been noted. For instance, they tend to begin their speech development with echolalia which is unlike that of normal children in that autistic children repeat what they hear as it is heard, unmodified by the level of their grammatical competence. In contrast, normal children's echolalia is modified by the level of their grammatical competence. Related to the echolalia is the tendency for autistic children to go through a much longer period than normal in which they reverse pronouns.* They also frequently display abnormal

---

* Footnote: Or, more accurately, fail to use them correctly--the implication that they reverse pronouns is misleading.

prosody (rhythm, pitch and contour of the speech), tending to speak all
utterences in a monotone or with a particular idiosyncratic phrasing.
As with the normal child in the early stages of language development,
they show such features as naming difficulties, neologisms,
abbreviations and telegrammatic speech.

Hermelin and O'Connor's (1971) above mentioned studies of recall
of meaningful and randomly organised word strings tend to suggest that
the less able autistic child has problems with both the syntactical
and semantic aspects of speech. However, this was not so for the
more able autistic children, whose abilities in these areas of language
may approach or equal those of subnormal children with similar M.A.s.
Frith (1969), in collaboration with Hermelin and O'Connor, has also
tested the effect of word stress upon recall by autistic and subnormal
children. It was found that both groups tended to recall the stressed
words better than the unstressed ones.

Baltaxe and Simmons (1975, 1977a,b) and Baltaxe (1977, 1979,
1980) have undertaken a series of studies of the language of autistic
children. The major results of their work have been the delineation
of pragmatic factors of speech as the core symptoms. This has also
been noted by others (Langdell, 1977, 1980; Frith, 1980). Such factors
refer primarily to the use to which language is put. This is bound up
with an awareness of the social aspects of speech, the context in which
utterences occur, the shared understandings between speaker and listener,
and the use of prosody. Baltaxe has focused on the latter factor of
prosody as a primary aspect, but to do so may obscure more relevant

'interpersonal' aspects of autistics' language. The pragmatic aspects of autistic children's language is important and will be dealt with fully later in this thesis.

In conclusion, few studies of autistic children's language have been undertaken. It would appear that the lower ability autistic child has problems with all aspects of speech (indeed many of the least able autistic children are mute), whereas the more able autistic child may more realistically be described as having problems with the use to which language is put. It is noted, though, that the latter aspect of linguistic pragmatics is a new area in the study of autism, and as yet little is known about it beyond the level of description. Pragmatics and the relationship between verbal and non-verbal factors will be a focus of this thesis.

## 1.3 Terminology, Diagnosis and the Selection of Subjects

The aim of this section is to survey the issue of the terminology of the syndrome and to discuss the problems of diagnosing autistic children. After this the selection procedure of the subjects used in the thesis will be given as well as a brief summary of the case history of each autistic child.

### 1.3.1 Terminology

Since Kanner (1943) first called the syndrome "infantile autism" workers have used various other labels, such as Creak et al's(1961) "childhood schizophrenia" and Goldfarb's "childhood psychosis". All three labels are open to criticism for several reasons. In the first place Kanner's use of the term "infantile" might imply that the syndrome is particularly related to infancy. However, Rutter (1974) has noted that symptoms which are indistinguishable from those which Kanner described may be found in children who develop normally up to 2 or 3 years of age. The term "schizophrenia" is also very misleading in that it implies a connection with adult schizophrenia, which does not appear to be true. For instance, adult schizophrenics are reported to have hallucinations whereas autistic children do not, and schizophrenics are more likely to come from unskilled or semi-skilled parents whereas autistic children are more likely to have middle class parents (although this last point has recently been questioned by Wing,(1980)). For a more complete discussion of the differences between autism and schizophrenia the reader is referred to Wing (1976), or Rutter (1974).

The term "psychosis" is also potentially misleading for similar reasons. Wing (1976) states that "childhood psychosis" includes autism, but it may also be used to describe many other conditions of childhood whose symptoms differ greatly from those of autism. "Psychosis" may also cause confusion because of the implication of 'thought disorder' which it carries (the Oxford English Dictionary defines psychosis in terms of a severe mental derangement involving the whole personality). Whilst the autistic child may display a rigidity of thought patterns it is perhaps less than accurate to refer to his thought as 'deranged'. Certainly autism is not a personality disorder in the usual sense of the term.

What term should one use then? Wing (1976) suggests "early childhood autism". Her reasons for the choice of this is that it allows for the fact that autism is not always evident from birth but also has the virtue of implying that the "autism" (i.e. the withdrawal) may be present only in the early years. Wing further suggests that the term might be changed when more is known about the underlying neurological impairment present in autistic children. However, it has yet to be shown that a single such impairment exists.

There are though two viable alternatives to the above term. First, one might return to calling the syndrome by its delineator (hence "Kanner's Syndrome") as it was once referred to. Although this might lead to argument, too, as others have laid claim to referring to similar children at about the same time as Kanner, or even sooner. Second, one might suggest that the term "autism" alone be adopted. The reason usually given as to why one does not do this is that the term on its own has unfortunate connotations. It was first used by Bleuler (1919) to refer to schizophrenic patients who have withdrawn into an inner world of fantasy. This is not the case for the autistic child, who is characterised by his lack of fantasy and inner language (Ricks and Wing, 1976). However, it may be noted that throughout the literature even those writers who agree on the merits of one term or another, may still use the shorthand term of "autism" or "autistic". The reasons are perhaps obvious, and the present author has been guilty of doing this throughout this thesis. Words have a habit of coming to mean what their use implies that they mean. Thus by use a word like "awful" has come to mean the opposite of its etymological derivation. Already it might be suggested that many workers in the field of childhood mental disorders are not likely to confuse childhood autism with Bleuler's original term - and it could be argued that in many cases they are unaware of its other, original use. Thus whilst the present author is in agreement with Wing's reasons for choosing "early childhood autism" as the best available widespread term to date, it is nonetheless noted that common usage will probably cause the singular term "autism" to be widely and unconfusingly applied. The area of terminology is thus rather confused, and undoubtedly made too much of.

## 1.3.2 Diagnosis

As mentioned in the first section of this chapter, Kanner first singled out 5 points which characterise the autistic child:

1. A profound lack of contact with other people
2. An anxiously obsessive desire for the preservation of sameness.
3. A fascination for objects which are handled with skill in fine motor movements.
4. Mutism or a type of language which does not seem intended to communicate.
5. The retention of an intelligent physiognomy and evidence of good cognitive potential as shown by such abilities as an excellent rote memory or their skill on performance tests.

It was also mentioned above that there are many problems with application of the above five points as diagnostic criteria. First, it is misleading to imply that any islets of ability in the autistic child are evidence for essentially good cognitive potential. Most autistic children remain in the subnormal range of functioning. There is also evidence that particular cognitive deficits (see Hermelin and O'Connor, 1971) may allow a child to have a few seemingly good abilities and yet still handicap him tremendously. Whilst it is undoubtably true also that subnormal autistic children do not <u>look</u> subnormal (unlike many other subnormal children) it is again misleading to refer to their appearance as "intelligent". Such a set of descriptions might lead one to think that the child is essentially normal but temporarily withdrawn for psychosocial reasons only.

Wing also notes (1976, p.17) that people who have tried to apply Kanner's criteria have been loath to include any child who shows any signs of awareness of others. This thus excludes virtually every eligible child. The main problems seem to have arisen from the fact that clinicians have tended to refer to his five points and not considered what he meant by them in the light of the eleven case histories he presented in great detail (1943).

Several other diagnostic schemes have been criticised on the grounds or being potentially misleading. Creak et al's "9 points" have been faulted for containing too much ambiguity of meaning. In addition, many workers have taken 4 out of the 9 points listed by Creak et al. as their criterion for autism. Whilst it is agreed that not all 9 points outlined by them are essential, by taking only 4 one might wrongly classify a child with no real social or language problems as autistic. A similar criticism can be made about Rendle-Short's 14 diagnostic points (see Rendle-Short, 1971; Clancy et al, 1969). He suggested that only 7 of the 14 points need be present for the diagnosis of autism. However, once again this would allow one to give the label to a child who showed none of the accepted basic characteristics of autism. In fact, one of the 14 points was counter indicative of autism, for it was claimed that the autistic child uses gesture instead of language. This is quite contrary to the clinical observations which have revealed that autistic children have particular problems with the production and use of gesture (see Bartak et al., 1975).

Rutter and his colleagues have been concerned to discover which characteristics are specific to autism (Rutter, 1966, 1974; Rutter and Lockyer, 1967). Rutter (1974) reported that only two behavioural characteristics were common to all autistic children: a profound and general failure to develop social relationships, and language problems which include lack of comprehension, echolalia, and pronominal reversal. Ritualistic and stereotyped behaviours were reported in the majority of autistic children but were also frequent in other types of children, too. It should be noted here that autistic children's echolalia and their tendency to reverse pronouns are both aspects of their general inability to understand what language is used for.

More recently Rutter (1978) has updated his criteria in response to the observations and empirical research of the past decade. It has been noted for some time that it is important to emphasise that the language problems of the autistic child do not constitute a delay, but are rather abnormalities (Newson, 1977). It is also imperative to note that the autistic child is impaired in all modes of communication, not just the verbal aspects (see Tubbs, 1966, for example). Thus the best diagnostic points at this time would appear to be:

1. An impairment of language and all modes of communication, which has certain well-defined characteristics and is out of keeping with the child's general intellectual level.
2. Impaired social development which is characterised by a number of special features such as a failure to develop empathy. This impairment of social relations is out of keeping with the child's general intellectual level.
3. Evidence of rigidity and inflexibility of thought processes reflected in an insistance upon sameness, stereotypies, abnormal preoccupations, and a resistance to change.
4. An onset of symptoms before 30 months of age.

(Drawing on Rutter, 1978, and Newson, 1980).

It is clear that a glossary is needed to be able to apply these diagnostic pointers, especially the first two. Although several workers have written in some detail about the specific characteristics of autism

(Rutter, 1978 for instance), this does not detract from the fact that the factors which lead to diagnosis are complex and may make the correct labelling of a child difficult.

Wing (1976) indicates the complexity of diagnosis when she refers to the fact that a lengthy interview with parents is almost obligatory. The problem is that an accurate diagnosis is dependent upon full details of the child's history. There is every indication that no list of pointers can replace first-hand knowledge of a large number of children with autistic features. Newson (1977) has also emphasised that the problem with toting up any list of points is that it misses what she terms the whole nature of autism. That is, to tot up points allows the clinician to miss the fact that in autism every kind of impairment links up with every other kind of impairment. The impairments flow into each other, and it is the interaction between the different parts of the syndrome which is most characteristic of autism. As Creak et al.(1961) pointed out, every characteristic in autism can be found in the normal child at some stage in his development.

The diagnosis of autism is thus rather complicated by various factors. Indeed there are some workers who feel that autism may not be a separate syndrome but may be part of a spectrum of language or social disorders in childhood (Wing, inter alia, for instance). The fundamental problem is that autistics, like schizophrenics, do not all share some easily definable characteristic (as do Down's children or those with PKU). Autistic children rather tend to form a family, where not all members look alike but all resemble some other members. Together with this is a common aspect of all autistic children which may be likened to the "look" of a family.

1.3.3.  Selection of Subjects

The first step in the choice of autistic children to be used in
the present studies was to visit as many schools for autistic children
as was practical.  Seven schools were visited, five of these on a fairly
regular basis, and two of them weekly during the first year of research.
More recently schools in Holland, Germany and the United States have
been visited to consolidate the subjective impressions of autism against
various cultural and linguistic backgrounds.  As the result of the
visits to English schools a pool of 20 autistic children were chosen
from just 2 schools (both of which belong to the National Society for
Autistic Children).  Thus these children were chosen not only with the
academic concept of "syndrome typicality" in mind, but also with the
experience gained from seeing some 250 children who had received the
label of "autistic".  This coupled with the reports of experienced
psychiatrists and psychologists (where available) was seen to be the
safest method of choosing a subject pool of autistic children for
experimental purposes.

Each child was screened, though, to make sure that he complied
with the then most used system of classification (Rutter, 1971).
This was essentially a list of 4 points which closely resemble those
mentioned near the end of the last section.  That is, a delay in language
development, an impairment in the formation of relationships, ritualistic
and compulsive behaviour, and an onset before 30 months.

The subject pool was initially chosen for the first study to be
reported in this thesis.  This involved children having to identify
faces, and it was necessary that the subjects have some verbal ability.
This consequently narrowed the sample to relatively able children who

TABLE 1.1    The Subjects

| | "Younger" groups | | | | "Older" groups | | | |
|---|---|---|---|---|---|---|---|---|
| | Autistic | Matched Normal (M.A.) | Matched Normal (C.A.) | Matched subnormal (M.A.&C.A.) | Autistic | Matched Normal (M.A.) | Matched Normal (C.A.) | Matched Subnormal (M.A.&C.A.) |
| Mean chronological age (yr) | 9.80 | 5.62 | 9.64 | 9.75 | 14.10 | 8.10 | 13.57 | 13.70 |
| Standard deviation (yr) | 1.00 | 0.23 | 1.51 | 0.98 | 1.10 | 0.66 | 0.40 | 1.27 |
| Mean full I.Q.* | 60.30 | | | 61.30 | 63.00 | | | 60.20 |
| Standard deviation | 15.62 | | | 5.36 | 14.22 | | | 7.71 |
| Mean performance I.Q.* | 73.50 | | | 62.40 | 78.00 | | | 63.10 |
| Standard deviation | 15.25 | | | 8.06 | 18.30 | | | 7.87 |

* All I.Q. measures are from a complete administration of the WISC.  The I.Q.s of the normal children were not taken, but all children were chosen as "average performers" by their teachers.

were at least 8-years-old. The details of the children are given
in table 1.1. As can be seen (p. 67) the ratio of males to females was high,
and thus in accord with the ratio found in the general population
(Rutter, 1974). Again, because of the requirements of the first
experiment, the children were split into two groups according to
their chronological ages. Comparison groups were also chosen at two
age levels. If one is trying to show abnormal performance or response
in an autistic child, then one must also test a normal child of similar
mental age. But if the autistic child is found to perform/respond
differently to the normal child, it might still be because of the
subnormal nature of his cognitive abilities. Thus the child must also
be compared to a subnormal child of similar mental and chronological
age who is not autistic. Finally, should the autistic child perform
well on a task, one wishes to know how good his performance is compared
to that of a normal child of similar chronological age. Thus three
comparison groups were chosen, each at two levels of age, to match the
autistic groups. Two groups were of normal children who were matched
to the mental ages of the 2 groups of autistic children (on WISC scores).
Another two groups were of normal children matched to the chronological
ages of the children in the two autistic groups. Finally, there were
two groups of subnormal children who were matched with the autistic
children for both mental (WISC scores) and chronological ages. Only
if the autistic children's performances differ from all the other groups
can one conclude that the results are due to their 'autism'. The
subnormal children were all free of autistic symptoms, and the normal
children matched to the C.A. of the autistics were chosen as being
'average' performers according to teachers' reports.

As will be seen, in most of the studies after the first one, it was decided that the subnormal children were the most pertinent comparison group. Because of their general abilities, the subnormal children will hereafter be referred to as 'ESN' children.

There follows a brief summary of the information gathered on the autistic children. It will be noted that in most cases the files on the children were fairly uninformative, particularly with reference to the child's development prior to school entry. The children's parents were not available for the collection of any further information. However, any sparsity of critical information (such as age of onset of symptoms) was compensated for by consultation with the heads of the schools.

Child 1 : Paul B.  D.O.B. 5/6/63.

Paul is the second born of a family of five. His two siblings are female (one a year older, the other about two and a half years younger). The pregnancy was normal but birth was delayed. The first suspicion of abnormality was at around 15 months when Paul was noted to head-bang. He was a difficult child to manage at home, had no speech at 18 months, took no notice of others, had no bowel/bladder control and seemed not to be able to understand the simplest of commands. Diagnosis of autism was made at 24 months. There is no known history of mental illness in Paul's family. The change in Paul's condition has been very dramatic. At about 4 to 5 years old he was still in nappies day and night. He could not dress himself, and had virtually no speech. He would take people's hands if he wanted something and would happily spend his day fitting puzzle-type games and objects together. By the

time he was first seen by the present author (at 12 years old) he had
fluent speech and was certainly not socially withdrawn. As is typical
of the more able autistic child (Wing, 1976) Paul's main problems are
now in the realm of the 'do's' and 'do nots' of social interaction,
and not in the presence or absence of it. He still retains his greater
ability in spatial/non-verabl taks but he is only slightly delayed in
his linguistic abilities.

Child 2 : Gary. D.O.B. 29/3/65.

Gary is an only child. His Mother claims that she knew there
was something wrong with him from his very first cry. Both parents are
qualified mental nurses. He began to walk at about 12 months, talk at
3 years, and had bladder control at 4 years. There is no noted
abnormality in the pregnancy, his birth or his early life. There are
no neurological signs. Autism was first suspected in the last quarter
of the first year. He did not play, was very resistant to any change,
banged his head when frustrated, flapped hands and arms, looked out
of the corner of his eye at things, and his sentences were stereotypic/
echolalic in nature. As with Paul, Gary's symptoms of withdrawal from
social contact have given way now to problems with social interaction.
He can still be aloof, but may paradoxically indulge in attention-
seeking routines. Once again the WISC showed him to be more able to
do non-verbal tasks than verbal ones. In common with many fairly able
autistic children, communication with Gary is quite possible so long
as it takes place on his terms.

Child 3:  Clive D.O.B. - 15/4/65.

Clive is the third born of his family and quite a lot younger than his two brothers.  Because the brothers were born in 1953 and 1958 one may assume that his mother was of mature years when she had Clive.  However, the pregnancy and birth are recorded as normal and nothing out of the ordinary is noted in his earliest development.  In fact, it seems that his mother did not notice anything wrong with him even at 3 years.  At this age he went to a nursery and immediately a nurse there suspected that Clive might be autistic.  Thus one must assume that the statement of Clive's normal development up to 3 years must be looked upon with suspicion.  Clive walked at 14 months, but continence by 2½ years, had some words at 1 year and spoke at 18 months.  However, his mother said that his speech was never "conversational" and that he has always "tapped things".  He is also aloof, even now to some extent.  His mother has taken a very long time to concede that there might be anything wrong with Clive but admits that his present disinterest in others has always been there - certainly prior to 30 months.  Today Clive is not withdrawn, but he is "distant" in his manner.  He will hardly ever initiate a conversation, and when he does his topics are likely to be sterotypic or bizarre.

Child 4:  Christopher, D.O.B. - 19/9/65

Christopher is a firstborn.  There were no pregnancy problems, but the second stage of labour was prolonged, with signs of foetal distress.  There is no history of mental illness in his family.  The first signs of abnormality came within the first 30 months of life.  He was described as a hyperactive child, who was aloof and slow to develop language.  Little else is known about his early development, but there would seem to be no overt signs of brain damage. He is now still fairly aloof, and his linguistic abilities are certainly out of keeping with his intellectual level. His language is particularly poor when it comes to using it to communicate.

Child 5: Michael, D.O.B. - 19/1/62.

Michael is the second child of a family of four. Both parents are university graduates. The head of the school remembered that he was born prematurely, but there was no note of pregnancy or birth problems in his file. Abnormality was first suspected at 18 months because the words he had acquired by then were not being extended or put to conversational use. The label of autism, though, was not given to Michael until some 4 years of age. He had always been noted as a distant child, but he is now somewhat more sociable. He will readily engage in social conversation now, but does so mainly on stereotypic topics. He will greet one by name, but shows few totally normal social behaviours.

Child 6: Martin K. D.O.B. - 24/11/66

Martin is an only child. He first walked unaided at 16 months, was not fully continent until 5 years, possessed some words by 2-years-old and some phrases by 3 years. His parents have taken a long time to accept that there is anything abnormal about Martin. Thus reliable data about his early development is not available. He seems to have had no major illnesses. There are no hard signs of neurological problems. There is nothing noted regarding pregnancy or birth problems. However, Martin seems always to have been abnormal in his social behaviour. In early life he was a "solitary person" and his words and phrases were almost totally echolalic. In early childhood, he was diagnosed as having a personality disorder, but the information fits more exactly the diagnosis of autism which he has more recently been given. Today Martin is more sociable, but his speech is full of obsessive phrases and is delivered in a fairly high-pitched and monotonous manner. He is still a solitary child, and has many obsessions - most of which are verbal.

Child 7:  Robert, D.O.B. - 26/2/62

The file on Robert is very brief and essentially tells one that he is of below average ability. However, the head is certain that his birth and the pregnancy were normal and that his earliest development did not lead to suspicions of abnormality. However, before 30 months of age, his aloofness and non-communicative use of language provided indications of autism. Certainly, when first seen Robert presented as a fairly typical autistic child of above average ability. He had a distant manner, and his attempts at social interaction were invariably abnormal. Whilst his speech is good, it is notable that he scores well below his age level on the verbal tasks of the WISC. His being particularly poor on the comprehension of language gave support to the description of him as autistic.

Child 8:  Rebecca, D.O.B. - 4/6/67

Very little pertaining to Rebecca's early life is included in her file. At first her development was presumably seen as normal for she was sent to a normal village school. However, she was always out of place there. She failed to keep up with the others of her age and was frequently "picked on" by other children. Because of her "underachievemen she was sent to an ESN school where she was later diagnosed as autistic.

At first sight one might doubt Rebecca's diagnosis. However, she now presents as a bright autistic child. One also notes that it may be very hard to diagnosis "mild" autism early in life. The more intelligent autistic child may only appear as a difficult child when seen in the context of a normal school. Further questioning of the parents by the head of the autistics' school revealed that Rebecca was always a loner at school. She made no friends and played very little, if at all. The head also commented on Rebecca's tendency to wiggle her fingers in front of her eyes occasionally, and was told that Rebecca had done that since infancy - it was not seen as abnormal by the parents and thus was not mentioned. Thus there would seem little doubt that Rebecca is a fairly able autistic child whose symptoms of social aloofness and abnormalities of language stem from within the first 30 months of life. Her social behaviour is still out of keeping with her intellectual level, and her language is also abnormal in the ways described by Rutter (1978).

Child 9: David B. D.O.B. - 13/12/62

The notes on David are poor. He is the fifth child of the family. He was seen to be abnormal early in his development. A doctor who was a friend of the family suggested early on that David might be autistic. His symptoms began very early (before 30 months) and certainly included many typical autistic features (such as aloofness, slow speech development, and lack of communicative speech when it did develop).

Child 10: Cathy, D.O.B. - 29/4/63

The notes on Cathy are also scant. She is the second of two children in the family, and her sister is reported to have language problems. As far as is known she has had no illnesses which may have given rise to her condition. There are no hard signs of brain damage. Pregnancy and birth were reputedly normal. Her gross language problems and social abnormalities have been evident since before 30 months of age. Today she presents as a distant child who is "more with it" than one first imagines. That is, she seems to be intellectually very slow and has little clear speech, but her comprehension of speech as revealed by her following commands is higher than her verbal performance would imply.

Child 11: Mark, D.O.B. - 31/12/61

Mark is an only child. His mother fell downstairs in the 6th month of pregnancy, but no immediate consequences were apparent. The birth was normal and as a baby he seemed to develop fairly normally. He loved to be cuddled and would laugh when tickled, but he seemed too placid and lacked normal reactions to outside stimuli. His father suspected something to be wrong when Mark was 2 years old because he was not developing speech. His mother was young at his birth (16) and he may have been an unwanted child as divorce followed relatively soon after his birth. However, there is nothing to connect Mark's condition with this early upheaval. Today Mark presents as an extraordinary child. Although autistic in his distance from others (especially peers) and his naievity when it comes to socialising, he has an exceptional musical ability. He has been shown to have perfect pitch, an excellent sense of key, and his memory for music is outstanding.

Child 12: Paul Mc. D.O.B. - 1/5/66

The notes on Paul are incomplete. However, it is known that his mother was unconcious during the first stage of labour for four hours. This has no effect on the baby as far as could be told at that time.

There are no signs of brain damage. Paul is an only child. His autism was suspected at about 19 months because of his extreme placidity. He was late to develop language, and he spoke mainly echolalically for some time. Today Paul presents as a fairly typical autistic child as per Rutter's (1978) classification. He is a fairly bright child, although a formal test delivers a mildly subnormal score.

Child 13: Stewart, D.O.B. - 8/10/65

Stewart's file was almost bereft of information. He has one older sibling (F, 18/5/62). As far as is known his birth went without problems, as did the pregnancy. He showed typical autistic features in his early childhood.

Child 14: Stephen Q, D.O.B. - 2/3/68

He is an only child. Autism was first suspected at 18 months (language was not developing, and he presented as an aloof child). He attended his first school for autistic children at the age of 4 yrs 11 months.

Child 15: Chrissy, D.O.B. - 16/1/67

He has one female sibling who is two years older. His notes tell that he was first suspected as autistic at about 18 months. Little information about his early life is available, and there is no evidence of prenatal, perinatal or postnatal problems. No evidence exists for neurological dysfunction or damage.

Child 16: John, D.O.B. - 7/12/62

He is a first born child, with one sibling (M, 3 years younger). At 9 months John was suspected of being deaf because of his lack of response to auditory stimuli. However, hearing tests found nothing to support the suspicions. It was later realised that his aloofness and slow language development were in fact aspects of his autism. There is no evidence for neurological abnormality. Since very young he has assembled puzzles at 90 degrees from normal, and has been able to do them when no picture is present. At 7 yrs 9 mths, he was tested to have a performance IQ of 124. Although his ability here is now much more in the normal range, he is nonetheless very able at non-verbal tasks.

Child 17: Steven, D.O.B. - 1/5/61

Steven is an only child. Some abnormality was indicated as early as 18 months, but the diagnosis of autism itself was not made until he was 4 years. His onset of symptoms is said to have been concurrent with the break up of his parent's marriage. However, it seems unlikely that Steven's problems were in any sense "caused" by the separation. He was walking at 15 months, but did not start to talk until 4 years of age. The birth and pregnancy are reported to have been without complication. Steven is now a slow child for his age and undoubtably presents as an autistic.

Child 18: David, C. D.O.B. - 21/7/60.

David had a normal birth, and the pregnancy was not complicated. He was adopted at 7 weeks of age. Thus although he is reported to have one sibling who is 3 years his senior, this child would seem to be his half-brother. It is very likely that he is therefore a first born. His condition was first noticed at 24 months when he was slow to acquire communicative language and presented as a distant child.

TABLE 1.2    Summary of Pathological Data: Autistic Children

(n = 20)

| | |
|---|---|
| Early Onset | 20 |
| Males | 18 |
| First Born | 13 |
| Premature | 1 |
| Pregnancy Complications | 1 |
| Birth Complications | 3 |
| Low Intelligence in One or Both Parents | 0 |
| Mental Illness or Subnormality in sibs | 1 |
| Seizures | 0 |
| "Soft" Neurological Signs | 0 |
| No speech | 0 |

Child 19:  Martyn, D.O.B. - 1/7/62

Martyn was a firstborn thus although his mother claims to have felt there was something wrong from the time of labour, one cannot be sure this was so. There is certainly no medical evidence to support prenatal problems. His head was stuck in and forceps were used. It is not known whether this has any causative connection with his present condition. However, there are no signs of neurological impairment. Abnormality was first suspected by the parents at 6 months, but they did not feel sure until 2 years. Martyn was diagnosed as autistic at 4½ years of age.

Child 20:  Neil, D.O.B. - 13/4/59

Little information on Neil's early development was available. However, it seems certain that his development in infancy was fairly normal. But speech was late to emerge and developed in a non-communicative manner. He has always been a loner, and even now presents as someone in a world of his own at times. Suspicion of autism occurred early in his life and the onset of symptoms was within the first 30 months. Today Neil is a very bright autistic child. He possesses a remarkable ability to add up long strings of numbers in his head and is able to mentally multiply 6 finger numbers. It is also claimed that he can readily state on which day of the week a person was born on given only their birth date.

1.3.4    Themes in the pathological data

In table 1.2 it can be seen that there is a high preponderance of first-borns amongst the sample of autistic children (13 out of 20). To date it is unclear whether there is any relationship between birth order and autism. Several authors have noted a tendency for autistic children to be first born (Rimland, 1964; Kanner, 1954; Creak and Ini, 1960; Pitfield and Oppenheim, 1964; Rutter, 1967). However, Wing (1967) states that whereas the firstborn of two sibs has a higher risk than in other sibship sizes, there is no significant association between birth rank and abnormalities when it is classified into first-born, intermediate and last-born. Nonetheless, Hermelin and O'Connor (1970) found that of their sample of 27 autistic children, 20 were first-born. Should there indeed be a preponderance of first-borns amongst the autistic population, then this would tend to implicate birth injury as a possible cause of the syndrome.

Complications in pregnancy and birth are sometimes reported to be quite high in autism (Knoblock and Pasamack, 1962; Gardner, 1976). Although they do not discuss the topic, it may be noted that Hermelin and O'Connor (1970) found a fairly high incidence of pregnancy and birth complications in their "small" sample. The sample of this thesis, in contrast, have very few incidents of such problems. This may be in part due to the general level of ability of the children in the present studies compared to that of the children studied by the above cited workers. Certainly the children studied by Hermelin and O'Connor and by Gardner were mostly of relatively low intelligence. It may well be the case that pregnancy and birth complications are more frequently associated with the autistic child of lower ability.

Chapter 2

FACE PERCEPTION AND MUTUAL GAZE

2:1  The Ontogeny of Face Perception

> Instead of searching for drives to 'explain' social development
> it is more profitable to conceive of sociability as originating
> in the infant's perceptual encounters with other people.

> (Schaffer, 1971, p.57).

One of the first and most consistent of the perceptual encounters
to which Schaffer refers is the human face.  It is thus hardly surprising
that the perception of people's faces figures prominently in discussions
of the unfolding of the child's sociability.  An abundance of studies on
the topic reflects an immense interest in the ontogeny of face perception
(Ellis, 1975), but sadly leaves us with a somewhat confused picture of
the subject (Gibson, 1969).  Perhaps a substantial part of this confusion
is due to the fact that our knowledge about the infant's perception of
faces is drawn from a wide variety of studies dealing with a wide range
of topics, and not necessarily with the ontogeny of face perception per
se.  For example, studies of smiling have aimed to establish which aspects
of the infant's perceptual environment lead to a smiling response (Ambrose,
1961;  Wolff, 1963;  Spitz, 1946):  not surprisingly the human face, or
parts of it, has been found to be a prominent releaser of smiles in the
newborn.  Other workers have been more interested in the general perceptual
abilities of the child (Gibson, 1969;  Thomas, 1965), or in the formation
of specific perceptual schemata (Kagan et al, 1966), or in the perception
of object orientation (Watson, 1966) - with the result that they have
provided useful information about the development of face perception in a
somewhat serendipitous manner.  Nevertheless, many studies have addressed
themselves directly to the topic and have generally fallen into two basic

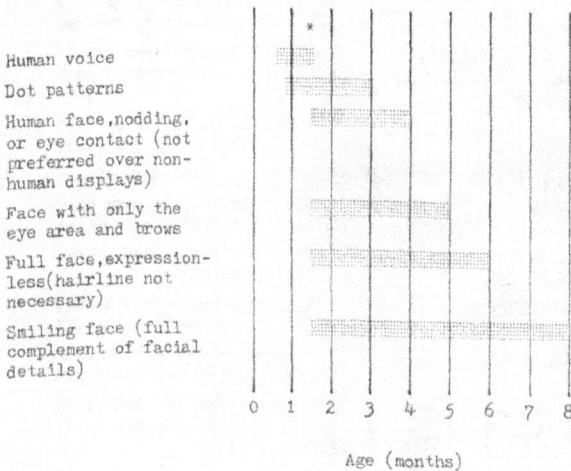

Human voice

Dot patterns

Human face,nodding,
or eye contact (not
preferred over non-
human displays)

Face with only the
eye area and brows

Full face,expression-
less(hairline not
necessary)

Smiling face (full
complement of facial
details)

0 1 2 3 4 5 6 7 8

Age (months)

Figure 2.1 The stimuli which elicit smiles from normal babies -
note that with increasing age they become more
specific to human faces (details from Ahrens,1954,
and Bower, 1977)

[*Note that the full 'social' smile emerges at 6 weeks]

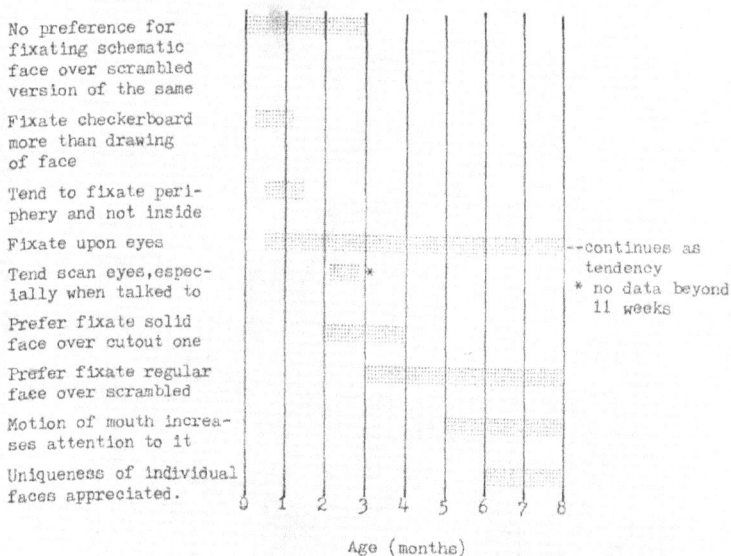

No preference for
fixating schematic
face over scrambled
version of the same

Fixate checkerboard
more than drawing
of face

Tend to fixate peri-
phery and not inside

Fixate upon eyes

Tend scan eyes,espec-
ially when talked to

Prefer fixate solid
face over cutout one

Prefer fixate regular
face over scrambled

Motion of mouth increa-
ses attention to it

Uniqueness of individual
faces appreciated.

--continues as
  tendency
* no data beyond
  11 weeks

Age (months)

Figure 2.2  Fixation 'preferences' with increasing age.
(details from Gibson,1969; Ahrens,1954;
Haith et al.,1977)

types: those interested in the possible innateness of face perception
(see Schaffer, 1971) and those concerned with the delineation of the
stages in the development of social perception (e.g. Ahrens, 1954;
Fantz, 1965).

With the foregoing in mind, a summary will be presented of the
present state of our knowledge about the ontogeny of face perception.
As will be seen, this is at times somewhat contradictory, and far from
complete. Figures 2.1 and 2.2 show which stimuli elicit smiles, and
which are preferentially fixated in the first 8 months of life. Reference
to these figures may prove helpful to the understanding of the following
sections.

2.1.1:    THE FIRST YEAR OF LIFE

          (a)  Birth to four weeks of age

          A question of major pertinence to this section is: "Is face
perception an innate property of the human infant?" If by this we mean
that the infant is born with the ability to recognize the basic pattern
of a face qua face from birth, then the answer is simply "No". However,
it does seem quite possible that certain biases exist within the newborn's
perceptual organization that do favour the human face as an attractor
of infant attention par excellence.

          A number of studies have come to the conclusion that the newborn
exhibits no 'preferential' fixation of real faces over other complex
stimuli, including stimuli whose elements are those of a face but are
in scrambled form (Hershenson et al, 1967; Herschenson, 1966; Fantz,
1965, 1966; Thomas, 1965; Koopman & Ames, 1968). Early reports that
the human face might be a unique stimulus for the newborn were confused
by the uncontrolled variable of complexity (e.g. Fantz, 1963). However,

they gave clear indications that a schematic face is 'preferred' to:
coloured discs (Fantz, 1963, 1965); bull's eyes (Fantz, 1963); dice
(Stechler, 1964); newsprint (Fantz, 1963, 1965); red squares (Fantz,
1967); or a lighted orange bulb (Fantz, 1967). Indeed, Fantz himself
found (1965) that for infants in the first week of life, visual preferences,
as measured by lengths of fixation, were solely dependent upon the
complexity of the stimuli presented; there is in fact a body of evidence
to support the view that infants prefer a certain level of complexity
(Hershenson, 1964; Brennan, 1965). Typically, these studies have
succeeded in showing that newborns tend to fixate a checkerboard with
a particular number of squares in 'preference' to those with either less
or more squares. Thus it would seem quite possible that 'visual preference
studies' have done little more than to demonstrate this finding - that
complicated patterns (such as newsprint) and simplistic ones (such as
red squares and dice) lie either side of an optimum level of complexity
that is more closely approximated by a schematic face. The helpfulness
of these findings is thus rather unclear, and even less so when one
considers that real (live) faces possess a quite different level of
complexity than the drawings that have been used in most of the studies.
It may also be noted that the word 'preference' is being used in a very
loose sense and refers to the activity on the part of the infant of
looking at one visual stimulus longer than at another. Obviously,
there could be many reasons why the newborn might do this, and hence
the unqualified usage of this term is to be criticized.

It has been reported that infants in the first month or so of life
have a tendency to only scan the perimeters of objects presented to
them (see Maurer & Maurer, 1976; Haaf, 1974; Kessen et al, 1972);
Nelson & Kessen, 1966, 1973). The face would seem to be no exception

to this, as Haith et al (1977) have found; their study of the
scanning behaviour of infants from birth to 11 weeks showed that in
the first few weeks of life the child will hardly look at a face
presented to it at all. When its gaze does fall on the face it is
almost exclusively restricted to the periphery (hair, outline, and
chin). As the weeks pass, the infant will, with increasing regularity,
allow his gaze to wander into the interior of an object (Maurer &
Salapatek, 1976). Again, this was borne out by Haith et al.'s study
(ibid); a glance at their data reveals that whenever the infant of
less than 3 weeks looked inside the perimeter of the face then his
gaze almost inevitably rested upon the eyes in preference to other
features.

Other writers have stressed the importance of such basic stimulus
factors as brightness, contrast and mobility as those which have a
major part to play in the determination of the infant's gaze behaviour
(Gibson, 1969; Salzen, 1964). In fact, these factors may hold such
a monopoly upon the infant's fixations (Kessen et al., 1970) that the
finding that the eyes receive a disproportionate amount of attention
may simply be due to their possessing these qualities.

In a sense, so far so good. There seems to be nothing innate
whatsoever about face perception as such, but rather that the human face
possesses those properties which the newborn child 'prefers' to fixate.
Given this and the fact that the face is one of the most frequently
viewed stimuli in the infant's environment, one cannot be suprised to
find that 'faces' as a class of visual stimuli often appear to be unique
(Ellis, 1975). However, we are still left with the puzzle - if puzzle
it be - that when the infant starts to look inside things it is necessarily

the eyes that come to have no intramodal rival in attracting his
attention. Why, for instance, should the eyes dominate his looking
behaviour when other aspects of the face also possess the properties
of contrast and movement (in particular the talking mouth)? Indeed,
Haith et al (1977) designed their experiment in such a way as to throw
light upon this subject. They found that the additional variable of
talking did not have any statistically significant effect upon the
3-week-old's scanning. This may have been due to a baseline effect of
those subjects showing so few face fixations anyway. Nonetheless,
even the 5- and 7-week-old infants did not increase the number of mouth
fixations when the face was talking. On the contrary, there was a
clear trend for the addition of this variable to increase the five- and
seven-week-old's percentage of fixations to the eyes. This point will
be returned to in the next section.

Is there any evidence that perception of faces or parts of them
is an innate ability? Several workers have suggested that the eyes
may form an elementary gestalt (see Ahrens, 1954; Spitz, 1951; Argyle
& Cook, 1976). However, although one would expect that any discussion
of innateness would naturally fall into this first section, in fact most
of the work which tries to support such an ethological stand-point has
taken as its response measure the social smile, which does not manifest
itself until some 6 weeks of age. Such studies have claimed to show
that the eyes enjoy a unique position as releasers of smiling in the
young infant (Ahrens, 1954; Ambrose, 1961);* and it has been argued
that the two-eye configuration may act as an innate releasing mechanism

---

\* However, Bower (1974) has rightly pointed out that babies deprived
of visual contact with others' faces also produce full smiles. Thus
the question of the uniqueness of the eye-pattern is in question.
The topic will be dealt with more fully in the second half of this
thesis, devoted to the development and recognition of expression.

in a similar way that 'eye spots' appear to do within the animal

kingdom (Spitz, 1965; Coss, 1972). Support for this is drawn from

studies that have found that two eyes are necessary to provoke smiling

(see Gibson, 1969, for a summary) and, more pertinently, that more than

two dots may prove to be a more effective releaser of smiles than just

the two dot 'eye pattern' alone (Ahrens, 1954; Coss, 1972). Thus,

one may see this as a supra-optimal stimulus functioning more effectively

than nature herself (Tinbergen, 1951). As Schaffer (1971) concludes,

this may be taken as evidence for a natural endowment of evolutionary

advantage:

> And the human infant, too, is structured in such a fashion
> that certain biologically important stimulus-response sequences
> - such as smiling to eye-like patterns - are part of his innate
> endowment, bringing him into contact with other human beings
> and thereby increasing his chances of care, protection and
> survival.
>
> (Schaffer, 1971, p.69)

Argyle and Cook (ibid) claim that such an innate tendency might not

show itself in the first few weeks of life due to the "immaturity" of

the newborn's perceptual system. Is this a valid point? Certainly the

newborn's visual system is immature when set alongside that of an adult,

but is nonetheless surprisingly well developed from the first few days

(Kessen et al., 1970). The infant has good acuity in the first weeks

(certainly fine enough to perceive eyes) and it has been shown that

babies exhibit "following behaviour" to mobile objects within the first

few hours of life (Kessen et al., ibid). It is thus not immediately

clear precisely which aspects of the newborn's "immaturity" Argyle and

Cook might be referring to. Perhaps one of the most restricting

limitations of the early visual system in humans is that the child has

a fixed focus of approximately 20 cm (roughly 8 inches) (Haynes et al.,

1964). This rigidity of accommodation may well be advantageous to the

young child in his early perception of depth, etc. (see Maurer &
Maurer, 1976). It also means that the infant's clear vision is
limited to a distance which corresponds closely   to that of the
caretaker's face from the child during feeding. This restriction
would seem to be one that would favour the discrimination of the
eyes, not hinder it.

The picture so far is thus rather a confused one, in which the
infant would seem to be geared to favour the eyes by virtue of the
facts that: (a) he tends to fixate objects of high contrast and mobility,
and (b) that his focussing is at first fixed at a distance that favours
eye perception under primarily social situations. And yet he is found
to scan the periphery of the face, virtually ignoring the eyes until
the fourth week.Thus, if we are to consider some kind of an innate
mechanism, then it must be in some way delayed until the start of the
second month.

However,another explanation for why the eyes are so favoured by
the young infant can be drawn the ideas presented by Bower (1974)
and Newson (1974). Bower discusses what he refers to as 'the strange
case of the smile'. He is drawn to the conclusion that babies may
smile because they perceive contingency between two or more of their
perceptions. Thus the infant's tendency to smile at upright faces
more than upside-down ones (Watson, 1966) might be due to the fact
that the face is seen in an upright orientation when contingency
games such as peek-a-boo are being played. Whilst this may not be
so (see the later chapter on facial expressions), it nonetheless
introduces the possibility that babies' smiling is at least partly
due to their detection of contingency. Newson (ibid) notes that

infant attention is best gained by object's which are mobile, self-deforming, brightly coloured, and noise-emitting. These features, he notes, are quintessentially those of the human face. He also notes that human beings have another feature which means that they can monopolize an infant's attention; the adult is able to react selectively depending upon the immediately preceding activities of the baby himself. Thus a mother has the unique feature of 'contingent reactivity' which makes her an object of compelling interest to her baby.

But in early infancy one is not talking of the whole mother being an attractive visual stimulus to her baby. As noted above, it is her head, and particularly the eyes, which attract the baby's attention. By extending Bower and Newson's suggestions it might be possible to explain this in terms of 'contingent reactivity'. That is, the caretaker's eyes are moving, the eye-lids blinking and screwing up, etc. in time with the baby's own behaviour. Thus the eyes in particular present a visual stimulus whose movement is contingent upon that of the baby. Furthermore, the adult possesses the ability to predict what the baby will do, and thus the eyes may be moving not only in response to what the baby just did, but also in response to what he is doing in the present moment. In terms, then, of 'contingent reactivity' the eyes may have no rival in the perceptual world of the infant (save possibly the human voice).

Whether or not the above idea is sufficient to explain the fact that babies are so attracted to people's eyes will be returned to later in this thesis. For the moment it should be noted that if babies

are born with an innate attraction for eyes (the 'dot detector' idea)
then it is very unusual that they do not look inside faces until about
the fourth week.  Also, if the eye configuration is learnt, then one
must question why the young infant does not seem to use the earliest
opportunities available to him to look at the eyes.  This is particularly
pertinent in the light of the finding that babies have their gaze
fixation set at such an appropriate distance at this early age and yet
do not at this time fixate the eyes.  Finally, there is some support for
the contention that the eyes are particularly attractive to infants
partly because of innate tendencies to look at bright, mobile self-
deforming objects, and partly because the caretaker's eye movements
are contingent upon the behaviour of the infant.  This necessarily
implies that infants are born with a tendency to search out and attend
to contingency between perceptual events and inner states.  The full
ramifications of this will be discussed at the end of this thesis.

    (b)  <u>Six-to-Sixteen-Weeks</u>

       At about six weeks of age, the infant begins to smile in a
social context for the first time.  It is at this time that Wolff
(1963) and Greenman (1963) report that mothers first experience real
eye contact with their baby.  The infant is seen to scan the face
until the eyes are found, and their discovery elicits a great deal
of excitement and smiling.  Ahrens (1954) too found that one of the
earliest and most efficient releasers of the smile response was simply
a pair of dots drawn in the fashion of eyes upon a white oval disc.
Spitz and Wolff (1946) also found data harmonious with this in that
by the end of the second month all that is needed to elicit smiles
is a face<u>like</u> stimulus which must have two correctly placed "eyes",
and some movement.  In finding this they were effectively replicating

Kaila's (1932) findings that in order for a baby to smile at a face
it must be presented en face, with movement, and preferably itself
possessing a smile. Both eyes were found to be necessary in that no
smiles ensued if the face was seen in profile or with one eye covered
up by a hand (see also Spitz & Wolff, ibid). However, Kaila stated
that although a smiling face was smiled at more than a non-smiling one,
this could not be due to imitation: when imitation begins, it starts
with facial movements that are much more simple than those involved in
smiling. In addition, the infant will still smile at a face that has
the mouth covered. Presumably Kaila's findings might be attributable
to the fact that a smiling face possesses more movement than an
unsmiling one.

The predominance of the eyes is also borne out by studies of
visual fixation. As noted above, Haith et al (1977) showed that
infants between five and eleven weeks of age spent the majority of
the time looking at their Mother's eyes. Moreover, it would appear
that if their mother starts to speak,        rather than increasing his
fixations to her mouth region  the infant fixates her eyes with greater
intensity and tightness of scanning. Because they also found that
the mother's movement had the effect of increasing the child's response,
it may well be that the increase in looking at her eyes in their study
was brought about simply by the additional movement inherent in a
talking face. In fact, this constitutes the major flaw of Haith et al's
work: their "talk" condition was the same as their "movement" condition,
in which the mother swayed from side to side, with the sole addition
that she talked to the child as she moved. In consequence, we are not
given any direct uncontaminated comparison between the still face and
one that talks. The variable of movement itself has been shown in many

studies to increase the infant's reponse and thus increase his tendency to look at the eyes. It may therefore follow that movement enhances the attractiveness of the eyes and thus provides excessively strong competition for the mouth when it moves. A comparison between a 'still' face and a 'talking' one might possibly reveal a greater number of fixations of the mouth.

Bearing in mind the above-mentioned ideas about contingency detection by infants, it might be that Haith et al.'s results can be explained in these terms. That is, without being spoken to the infant may be attracted to the eyes because they move in time with his behaviour. When the mother starts to talk as well her lip movements too will usually be contingent upon the baby's inner state as reflected by his movements. Her speech will therefore be correlated with her eye movements; thus contingency will exist not only between the baby's inner state and the movement of the mother's eyes but also between the sound he perceives and the eye movements. This might cause the baby to attend with renewed vigor to the eyes, as Haith et al. found.

Caron et al. (1973) also provide support for the view that the eyes are of major importance up to about four months of age. By presenting schematic faces repetitively to infants, they were able to test which of a number of 'distortions' of the schematic faces caused a release from proactive inhibition. In this manner they found that the eyes were by far the most salient feature at four months, and that they had to be symmetrically placed in the upper half of the face-like stimuli.

It seems that the discrimination of the eyes in the upper half of the face is the real developmental step that occurs in this period.

Watson (1966) found that the infant of some three months of age will smile more at an upright face than at an inverted one. In fact, Watson's study is rather more interesting than other writers have implied. His work does not really show what he claims as such - that the infant of less than six months can respond to changes in orientation - but rather shows the unpredicted finding that differential response to human faces in different orientations only occurs for infants of about 14 weeks of age. This effect was very dramatic, was restricted to the change of orientation from upright ($0^o$) to inverted ($180^o$), and did not occur at all to the half turn ($90^o$).

The results of Caron et al (ibid.) have bearing on this in that they found that at four months an infant will respond to inversions of facial outlines but remains insensitive to inversions of the inner face itself. By five months, the child will have become primarily sensitive to changes in the orientation of the inner face and unresponsive to changes in the outline. This can be viewed in terms of the emergence of the importance of the outline with respect to the eye position as a factor, as mentioned above. At four months the infant probably has no schema for the face itself (the eyes/nose/mouth gestalt), and in consequence the positioning of the eyes in relation to the hair will be of prime importance. By five months, however, it would appear that the face itself is perceived as a unity. Thus the infant starts to view the features of the face with respect to each other, and not with respect to an outline. Hence it seems quite natural that the infant's sensitivity should change its focus.

However, that the infant should become insensitive to the orientation of the outline does not ring true. Perhaps this was an artifact due to the simplistic nature of the schematic stimuli used in their experiment (the "inverted outline" leaving the face upright does in fact look like an acceptable representation of a bearded man). One would expect that the importance of the inner facial configuration should be established with respect to the position of the hair, ears, and so forth. The emergence of a relationship between facial features and the facial outline is evidenced in Watson's work (ibid.): the unique sensitivity of the infant at about 14-weeks-old may well be due to his making the 'hypothesis' that the eyes must be in the top of the head, but his failing to hypothesise as to the position of the face with regard to its outline. When this 'hypothesis' emerges, at five months or so, then an inverted head which still satisfies this rule is not seen as incongruous, and this is precisely what Watson's results imply.

Whilst up to about six weeks a pair of dots suffices to elicit a smiling response, regardless of the contour, by about three months it is found that the more realistic the representation of the eyes, the greater the response (Ahrens, 1954). With increasing age isolated features begin to lose their effectiveness in eliciting smiles, and Ahrens reports an increasing integration of the features which is reflected in the more organized scanning of the face by the infant (see Figure 2.1).The emergence of the importance of realism at two months plus is supported by such studies as that of Fantz (1965) where he found that a contoured model of a head was preferred to a flat cutout. He also found evidence to corroborate Caron et al.'s findings regarding the establishment of the eyes/outline relationship by four months of age: Fantz discovered that at three months or so the child will only fixate an eye-spot pattern if it is symmetrically positioned within a facelike outline.

Ahrens found that by four months of age whereas both a schematic and realistic portrayal of a face would produce smiling, a real face was better. Polak et al. (1964) also found that by three months the infant will smile sooner, longer, and more strongly to a real face than a life-size colour photograph of a real face. Prior to this time the photograph had been equally effective. It is hard to agree, however, with their main conclusion that this is evidence for the emergence of depth perception at this age. As Gibson (1969) points out, there is no evidence to suggest that the infant's perception of depth is like that in a 2-D photograph prior to this stage in his development.

Bearing the above in mind, it is hardly surprising that workers should have found that about two to three months of age the infant will tend to look at a 'regular' face (be it schematic or photographic) more than a 'scrambled' version (Fantz, 1965; Kagan et al. 1966; Lewis, 1965).

By way of conclusion to this section, one may say that "the eyes have it" when it comes to attracting the two- to four-month-old's attention or eliciting his smiles. In addition, it seems clear that as he becomes older he requires the stimulus presented to him to be increasingly realistic before he will smile.

(c)  Five months to one year

As noted above, the main characteristic of the fifth month is the emergence of the importance of the mouth as a feature (Caron et al. 1973). By this stage Ahrens (ibid) notes that for the first time the mouth must be present before smiles will ensue. A widely drawn mouth has greatest salience, and mouth widening as such rather than smiling is important (see also Spitz and Wolff, 1946). The face itself as a perceptual gestalt of eyes/nose/mouth seems to be appreciated and, as was mentioned in the last section, an inverted head is no longer seen as incongruous (Watson, 1966). Once again, there is strong evidence that the more lifelike the stimulus, then the more the infant will look at it or smile at it (Ahrens, ibid; Lewis, 1969;  Kagen, 1971).

Gibson summarizes the achievements of the fifth month by saying that the child has differentiated the plastic, solid surfaces of faces, has discriminated not only the eyes but also the mouth as necessary features, and has determined that faces tend to have an oval outline. However, there is as yet no appreciation of individual faces, nor of emotions. Although Caron et al. (ibid.) suggests that the mouth has become as salient as the eyes by this age, this is questionable. They fail to note the child's increasing requirement of realism as a prime factor, with the consequence that their five-month-old subject actually tended to be less disturbed by the eye 'distortions' than did the four-month-olds. This may well be due to the excessive simplicity of their schematic stimuli. Indeed, even in adulthood the eyes still remain the most discriminable part of faces (Ellis, 1975). In addition, even though the face as a unit emerges at about five months, it would seem that changes to the upper half may be still more readily perceived than those to the lower half (Meili, 1957;  Benjamin, 1963).

At about the sixth month of life, the child begins to be able to tell what the sex of the face is (Gibson, 1969). Some variation is noted, though, in this finding: whilst Cornell (1974) has found evidence for sex discrimination as early as five and a half months, Fagan (1976) feels that this is not achieved until about seven months.

Fagan's (ibid.) other findings for seven-month-olds are also of interest: they were able to appreciate that a face still belonged to the same person even when quite different views of it were presented. The infant even seems to have grasped the idea of a 'pose' in that he can respond to a face as 'familiar' when it follows a different but similarly posed face.

The emergence of the child's first negative reactions to human faces also occurs at about five-to six-months of age (Ahrens, 1954). An angry face will produce avoidance by the infant, as will artificial stylized eyes. However, negative responses have not been noted by some to become firmly established until about eight months (Gibson, 1969). At about this age there is a greater refinement in the infant's differentiation of faces and the first real evidence for negative responses to strangers is found. This latter topic has perhaps been insufficiently investigated (Schaffer, 1971; Gibson, ibid.), and there are those workers who have failed to find unequivocal evidence for it prior to some twelve months of age (e.g. Morgan & Riccuiti, 1965). Concomitant, though, with the emergence of negative responses is the finding that smiling does not occur unless in response to a facial display to which smiling is a socially acceptable response (Gibson, ibid.). Thus, there is a sense in which the eighth month brings with it an important step in the development of the child as a primarily

social being. It is now that the appreciation of basic emotions
displayed by faces comes into existence: indeed, the development of
such appreciation of emotions goes on for the rest of the child's life
(see Charlesworth & Kreutzer, 1973; Ekman et al., 1972).

The study of children from six to twelve months would appear to
have received far less attention than that of the first six months.
However, it would seem to be the case that the infant grows into early
childhood by developing his appreciation of individual features and
of individual person's faces, by preferring more and more realistic
portrayals, and by becoming more and more interested in violations of
the basic face 'schema' (Gibson, 1969; Kagan et al., 1966; Lewis,
1969).

As a final note to this section, it must be mentioned that the
above findings have been found using normal, home-reared infants as
subjects. Evidence exists to show that other rearing practices and
different early environments (such as institutions) may well retard
both the emergence of social smiling and its related appreciation of
faces and also the strength of such responses when they do emerge
(Schaffer, 1971, summarizes this point).

(d) Summary and conclusions to the first year

Our present knowledge of the ontogeny of face perception
within the first year of life is a patchwork of fact and speculation
that is somewhat difficult to pull together into a unified whole.
Precisely what propensities the infant is born with is unclear, let
alone whether or not it is possible to infer some sort of innate
mechanism which directs his attention specifically towards others'
faces.

There is a distinct feeling that some important pieces of the puzzle have yet to be turned up: we find the newborn 'prefers' stimuli that have the qualities that eyes possess, and that he has a fixed focal distance which corresponds to the distance away of the caretaker's eyes during feeding, and yet for the first three to four weeks he fails to make eye contact. Has this preliminary period served as a time in which the child has learnt the social value of the eyes? It would appear that this obvious 'learning theory' answer fails to fit the data, since during this first month the infant does not seem to be utilizing his opportunity to learn about the eyes.

A discrepency exists in the literature and was purposely avoided in the first section: the infant is found to prefer certain levels of complexity from the first days of life and yet several workers have found that he tends not to look inside shapes at this stage. If this is true, then it is rather difficult to understand how Fantz (1965) and others have obtained preference differences for varieties of facelike stimuli that differ from each other only in level of complexity and not in outline shape. To 'explain' this one may be drawn to propose that the newborn is not necessarily using his foveal vision to scan things, but rather using his peripheral or 'perifoveal' vision. Whilst there is no evidence for such a thesis (Kessen et al., 1970), and it would be rather hard to produce any, nonetheless it may be noted that Lewis et al. (1978) have shown that newborns can see both fovally and peripherally and that the periphery is often associated with 'movement detectors'. Therefore, although one is now in the realms of pure speculation, it is possible that the infant's attention is initiated by certain factors such as brightness and contrast (see Gibson, 1969) but is maintained by other factors such as movement - which are at first scanned peripherally and not foveally. The advantage of this conjecture is that it offers a concrete 'explanation' for the data to date which no other theory seems able to do.

The question of innateness is one that must be approached with caution. In what sense could face perception, or the propensity to fixate eyes (to be more precise) be innate? It would seem extremely naive to expect an inborn mechanism to exist that causes the infant to look specifically at another person from the first hours of life. Rather, it is most likely, as Schaffer (1971 quoted above) infers, that the context in which contact with other human beings can occur and social perception be initiated, should be created by the infant's innate endowment.

Hershenson (1967) notes that a variety of studies report a qualitative difference in 'looking' of younger and older infants: the younger infant seems to be "captivated by stimuli" (Ames & Silfen, 1965), to show "obligatory attention" (Stechler & Latz, 1966); the older infant in contrast appears to be "capturing stimuli with his visual behaviour" (Ames & Silfen, ibid.). Thus, whilst the newborn may be responding in an obligatory manner to the visual world he is born into in accord with his innate propensities, the older infant may be in the process of forming schemata. Whereas at first attention may well be initiated by one basic factor (such as brightness or contrast) and maintained by another (such as movement), it may be the case that the older infant orients towards stimuli that possess such qualities, but that the length of his fixation is determined more by the "closeness-of-fit" to his emergent schemata (Kagen et al., 1966). In fact, Lewis (1969) goes so far as to suggest that fixation and smiling are the responses to two quite different things: that length of fixation is indeed determined by schema-development, but that smiling is determined solely by releasing mechanisms and/or social learning. However, such a view seems to offer no explanation for the findings noted above - that those elements which are necessary to produce smiling are also those which tend to be fixated. The two processes appear to be linked, not differentiated.

The contention that infants seek contingency in their perceptions (both between two or more present perceptions and between past and present ones) may offer the strongest alternative to the above ideas. To be accurate, though, it is not totally different from the previous ideas because it is a synthesis of Lewis and Wilson's (1972) and Bower's (1974) views. There is also some evidence that certain types of contingency may engage the infant's attention but other types may sustain it. Infants are known to give a lot of attention to mobiles that they can move, and which therefore move contingent upon their behaviour. Such mobiles receive most attention, however, if there is a delay between the baby's action and the mobile's movement, and if the movements are different from moment to moment. The infant thus tends to orient towards something which is both contingent and novel. But his interest in a stimulus may be sustained by its ability to continue to satisfy his curiosity. Thus it may be that contingency of a stimulus to the baby's ongoing behaviour causes him to orient towards it, but contingency to past experience (his schemata) effects the sustenance of his interest. More research will be necessary before this contention can be fully assessed.

## 2.1.2   CHILDHOOD AND ADOLESCENCE

It is noted throughout the literature that most cognitive abilities show improvement with age increase - particularly in the period from birth to early adulthood. However, the results pertaining to facial recognition do not appear to be so clearly defined. For instance, Cross et al (1971) were not able to find a significant improvement in correct recognition scores for adolescent faces by subjects in age groups: seven years, twelve years, seventeen years (mean chronological ages), and adults. However, they did find that the younger subjects made more false identifications than the other age groups. Thus they combined the recognition scores with the false identifications to form a 'statistical decision theory discrimination parameter' (d'), which then showed a clear developmental trend (7 years - d' = 0.61; 12 years - d' = 0.93; 17 years - d' = 0.99 and adults - d' = 1.95). One should note, though, that this is hardly a surprising result, as young children are well known for doing their very best to help/comply with experimenters in just such tasks as these. The younger child, unlike the older one, when asked a question for which he has not learnt an answer is very likely to 'make one up' (Piaget, 1929). Thus, one must question whether Cross et al. are really telling us anything about the facial recognition ability of younger children. Moreover, as their study was of American children, one should note that such children are brought up, in general, to always try their hardest to answer any question put to them, whereas British children tend to be taught to be silent unless they know the answer (for a further discussion of this, see Hudson, 1966).

A replication of Cross et al.'s work by Ellis et al (1973), using
12-year-old and 17-year-old subjects, found the latter were significantly
superior to facial recognition of young adult faces on the basis of both
correct identification and d' scores (thus, contrary to implications
drawn from Hudson's work, Cross's results do seem applicable to some
British children). In criticism, it may be suggested that the adolescent
subjects would be more familiar with the stimulus material. The factor
of age of face in photographic stimulus with respect to age of subject
was taken into account in Goldstein and Chance's 1964 study; they
concluded that the age of stimulus did not give advantage to any one
group of subjects. However, one should note that their conclusion
was based on two experiments, only one of which gave no relation between
age of stimulus face and recognition ability for subjects of differing
ages. The other experiment reported in the 1964 paper does, in fact,
find the younger children's faces easier to recognize in general, and
especially for the younger children. As this was contrary to their
expectation (viz that the older children's faces would show greater
differences, and that ability to recognize faces increases with age
due to cognitive maturation) they went on to do the second (aforementioned)
experiment. After obtaining different results with different stimulus
pictures, they concluded that the paradox could be resolved by noting
that there are very great differences between faces of the same age and
went on to suggest these differences may be as great as those between
ages! To some extent this is bound to be true for faces of children a
few years apart in age, however, with an age difference of several years
to a decade or more, there are surely very great inter-age differences
(especially from infancy up to early adulthood, the age span in question
in Goldstein and Chance's paper).

Working with disoriented (inverted) photographs of faces, Brooks and Goldstein (1963) found a clear developmental trend for children between three and fourteen years of age - the older children being less affected by the change in stimulus orientation. However, Goldstein did a similar experiment in 1965, which found that adults were more affected by disorientation of stimuli than were children. To resolve "the 'apparent paradox' thus provided by the 1963 and 1965 papers" (Goldstein, 1975) Goldstein did a further replication (1975) using subjects from five to twenty years of age. This time he obtained a general decline in performance with age (although a slight rise in mean % correct scores between the five/six years group to the nine/ten years group was noted, no intervening age group being tested). However, for some strange reason Goldstein argues that, because his experimental methods were very similar in the 1963 and 1975 studies, he is within his rights to combine the scores of the two papers. He thus obtained a curvilinear variation with age (the three/four years old being as poor at recognition as the twenty-year-olds, and the twelve/thirteen year olds providing the peak in ability). He then goes on to suggest that cognitive maturation can explain the increase in ability from three to thirteen years, and that the subsequent reduction in level of performance can be attributed to "rigidity of the perceptual mechanisms as a function of over-learning of a mono-orientated configuration". Many criticisms of this paper come to mind; not the least of which is that of his combining the results of two independent studies. The studies obtained quite different scores for the age groups from five years to thirteen/fourteen years (especially the latter), and yet he still felt the two studies could be integrated for analysis simply on the basis of a similarity in methods. He himself suggests that there may have been quite substantial differences in his subject populations. In addition there was a major difference in the two methods employed; in the 1963 study the subjects saw the stimulus

faces upright prior to identification in the inverted mode. In the
1975 study the pictures were firstly viewed inverted and then upright
later. Possibly, viewing the faces upright initially may have allowed
easier recognition by the older children of the inverted faces (as is
borne out by their results). The drop in ability to recognize the
inverted stimuli by the older subjects in his latest study (1975)
may be due to his method of subject selection and his rationale behind
it. Up to thirteen/fourteen years he used school children (predictably)
and the faces used as stimuli were those of classmates of the subjects.
However, for the seventeen/twenty year age group he used 'sororities'
and 'fraternities' in college as a direct parallel to classes in school.
Sororities and fraternities are not comparable, though, in all but a
vague sense. First, there is likely to be many more 'peers' in one's
sorority or fraternity than in one's class at high school. Second,
there is a larger possibility that college students may recognize a
sorority/fraternity member's face less well because unlike classmates,
sorority and fraternity members do not meet regularly as a group on
a daily basis.

Finally, Goldstein and Mackenberg (1966) found a clear developmental
trend in children from three years to eleven years in recognition of
faces from isolated facial features. The older children were more
able to give a correct identification on the basis of a smaller area
of the face being shown (e.g. just the nose, just the eyes, etc.).
As Goldstein and Mackenberg point out, one might argue that the older
children may simply have known each other longer than the younger
children, especially in stable school populations. However, they
feel this interpretation is weak because the kindergarten children
had been together for at least seven months prior to testing.

Additionally, Chance, Goldstein and Schicht (1966) found that when they replicated this experiment, taking length of association into account, the ability to identify a face on the basis of viewing a part did increase with age, but would not a function of increased acquaintance. The other major finding of this latter paper was that the younger children, of their sample of six-year-old to twelve-year-old children, tended to identify a face of a 'friend' more often than a face of a child who was not a friend. In fact, the increase in ability for the older children only seems to apply to recognition of non-friends in Chance et al.'s 1967 study.

Table 2.1: % correct responses in Chance et al.'s 1967 paper:-

| GROUP | FRIENDS AS STIMULI | NON-FRIENDS AS STIMULI | OVERALL SCORE |
|---|---|---|---|
| Kinder' | 57 | 41 | 44 |
| 1st Grade | 73 | 56 | 56 |
| 2nd Grade | 67 | 58 | 58 |
| 6th Grade | 66 | 64 | 66 |

Two possible interpretations of these results come to mind[1]. On the one hand, one might tentatively suggest that the 'increased ability' of the older child is not purely cognitive but rather is largely due to his increased socialization. That is, the younger child may be more egocentric in every sense, and thus only take close notice of the appearance of his friends and his relatives to the exclusion of others. With age he comes to more readily take the other's position into account (viz,the emergence of sympathy and empathy), and with increased

---

[1] One cannot ignore, though, a third interpretation: as the friends formed a much smaller sample size, if a developmental effect was present it may have required many more subjects to obtain a statistically significant trend.

Besides, who has the most friends?

socialization, he may notice more closely the appearance of all others he meets, both acquaintances and friends. On the other hand, one can still propose an explanation in terms of 'cognitive maturity', as the young child may simply need longer and more continuous visual contact with another in order to recognize his face (this he would presumably obtain with close relatives and friends). However, Cross et al. found that length of acquaintance was not a factor in recognition and that the disparity between the younger children's ability to recognize friends and non-friends was large, it seems to imply that a social rather than just a cognitive explanation may apply here.

Goldstein and Mackenberg (ibid.) also found that all of the children they studied found the upper facial features easier to recognise than the lower ones. This better recognition of the upper halves was related to the presence of the eyes: when they were visible the children could identify the faces easier than when they were not. Thus the importance of the eye area in early childhood persists throughout childhood into adolescence (and apparently into adulthood too, see Argyle and Cook, 1976). This topic will be returned to in the following section on the function of gaze contact in normal people.

## Summary and conclusions

The results of the studies relating to age as a factor in the recognition of faces are very mixed. There is certainly a need for many of the experiments to be replicated. It seems that there are no age trends in children's abilities to recognise faces, when one looks at percentage correct scores. But if false identifications are noted, then younger children are found to make more of these than older children. However, not all studies have found this. Another study, for example, found that older children do recognise faces better, both in terms of percentage correct scores and false identification scores. A third study obtained different results again. In this study the children had to recognise upside-down faces, and it was found that the older children were worse at this than the younger ones. All these studies were criticised, though, and none have results which can be unquestionably taken as fact. It was also suggested that faces themselves may be more or less difficult to recognise depending on the person's age. Two studies by the same investigator revealed conflicting results. In one study there was no difference between the ease of recognising young faces and old; in the other the younger faces were found to be easier to recognise than the older ones.

A less flawed paper on the ability of children to recognise peers from isolated areas of photographs of their faces showed that older children could identify correctly from relatively smaller areas than could younger children. Thus the ability to recognise a whole from a small part seems to improve with age.

Finally, the eyes, which became important to the child in the sixth week of life, seem to retain their position of prime salience into late adolescence. The tendency to fixate others' eyes is true regardless of the age of child and seems to radically affect the manner in which children recognise faces.

## 2.2: The role of gaze and mutual gaze in normal children

Of the five senses sight alone possesses a range of possibilities in which the input may be enhanced or attenuated. For example, the eyelids may be opened or closed; gaze may be averted to bring a stimulus into peripheral vision, or it may be fixated directly; the pupils may be constricted or dilated; the skin surrounding the eyes may be screwed up so as to peer through a mere slit or stretched out to allow maximum light to enter. All this adds up to a system which is far more flexible than that of audition, which may only be significantly affected by an action like putting one's hands over one's ears.

The visual system matures very quickly too. The newborn baby soon gains almost adult visual capabilities (Rheingold, 1961; Kessen et al., 1970; Klaus et al., 1971). Vision is not only mature from early in life, but visual fixation and following are the only neonatal reflexes that do not drop off with time (Greenman, 1963; Robson, 1967). It is hardly surprising, then, that vision should play a critical role in the development of social relations (Walters and Parke, 1965; Schaffer, 1971, 1977).

Infants' gaze at about 10 days is fairly passive and often out of the corner of their eyes; they will follow movements of the mother's face, but only so long as she is facing her child. At about four weeks, eye contact occurs between mother and child for the first time. Wolff

(1963) reports how an infant of this age will scan an adult's face until the eyes are found. Mothers begin to spend much more time interacting with their babies at about the fourth week. They report (Wolff, ibid.) that they feel the baby can see them for the first time. Robson (ibid.) notes that many mothers may not be conscious that eye contact has been established, but they may rather report that interaction with the baby is suddenly much easier.

Once gaze contact is established, there is evidence that the gaze of mother and child takes on a 'conversation-like' quality (Jaffe et al, 1973; Peery and Stern, 1974). Pawlby (1977) has also noted that baby and mother will take turns in their looking behaviour. It seems that the behaviour may be innate, for it is similarly and precisely timed in both mother and infant (Jaffe et al, ibid.; Trevarthan, 1974a, b). Thus in a sense mother and infant share something from very early on in their relationship. A phasing of their behaviours exists such that very few clashes occur (Newson, 1974) and such phasing can take place because the patterns of behaviour (including gaze) are common to mother and child, making the child predictable to interact with. The mother can thus gain a real sense of 'contact' with her child from very early on. And the contact is two-way, for Schaffer and Emerson (1964) found that interruption of visual contact produced more protests in six-month-olds than did interruption of physical contact.

Richards (1971) studied mothers' interaction with two-month-olds. He noted that when the infants sat on the mothers' laps there were repeated cycles in which the mother would smile and move her head rhythmically to-and-fro from the baby's face. The infant responded with rapt attention, a widening of his eyes, and a stilling of body movements. He would become more and more excited and gradually begin to move and vocalise, at which point he would turn from the mother and the cycle would begin again.

The making and breaking of mutual gaze seems to be one of the earliest interactions between mother and infant. Bruner and his colleagues (see Ratner and Bruner, 1977) describe the patterns of rule-governed behaviour which develop between mother and child. Games such as peek-a-boo are common and basically consist of the breaking and re-making mutual gaze contact.

It is worth emphasising that gaze contact is just that - contact. That is, it allows the other to know that you are attending to him and aside from vocalising it is the only effective way of establishing contact between people at a distance. Above it was noted that mothers may suddenly feel contact with their children for the first time when mutual gaze is established. Certainly where such contact is not possible (in blind children, for example) children may suffer great problems in the development of sociability and language.

Language development may have a great deal to do with early inter-changes such as those noted above. Collis and Schaffer (1975) showed that babies follow their caretaker's line of regard, and the caretaker follows theirs. Being able to look at the same thing is a first step towards shared understandings. If the child looks at something, then the mother will frequently try to determine what the child is looking at and comment upon it or 'mark' the experience. Bruner (1975a,b) has gone so far as to claim that language develops to regulate such shared understandings, and thus they are essential to the ontogenesis of speech.

Consequently, gaze serves to tell someone what you are attending to, and this role will continue into adult life as an important aspect of communicating with others (Bates, 1976; Urwin, 1978; Trevarthan and Hubley, 1978). There are many unconscious activities which adults carry out with mutual gaze or by the direction of their gaze. For instance, when another is speaking and one wishes to indicate that one has something to say, then one will attempt to establish eye contact. However, if the other person wishes to continue to talk, then he will avoid mutual gaze. Mutual gaze also gives cues as to whose turn it is to speak, and it can be used to convey paralinguistic aspects of communications such as boredom, assertion, aggression, disagreement, etc.

Although this section has been kept brief, several pertinent conclusions may be drawn about gaze and mutual gaze. In early life mutual gaze helps to establish contact between mother and child. It also serves to enable adult and infant to establish joint reference that underlies shared understandings. The establishment of joint reference has been suggested to be essential for the development of language (see Bruner 1975a,b) and is undoubtably involved in the normal development of social relations (Schaffer, 1977). Later, gaze serves its earlier role of establishing joint reference but it is also used to regulate conversations and give paralinguistic cues to the meaning of utterances and responses.

## 2.3: Person Perception and Gaze Contact in Autism

When one considers that the presence of gaze avoidance has been an often mentioned (see Wolff & Chess, 1964), and by implication fundamental, aspect of the syndrome of early childhood autism, then it is perhaps rather surprising that there have been so few studies of the topic (see Rutter, 1974). This is partially due to its being a difficult area of study within an experimental context, which means that the behavioural observation methods of ethological workers (e.g. Hutt, et al., 1965) are more readily applicable.

Kanner himself emphasized gaze avoidance as a common aspect of the autistic child's "disturbance of affective contact" (1943). Even in the most recent papers on the subject, this aspect of autism is almost inevitably mentioned even if it is no longer given the importance it once had (Rutter, 1978).

Perhaps one of the most often quoted studies of gaze avoidance in childhood autism is that of Hutt and Ounsted (1965). In this they put forward the idea that gaze avoidance in such children is a reaction to over-arousal. They make an analogy with findings from work with animals in which avoidance of mutual eye gaze is frequently associated with timidity and the avoidance of threatening situations. The autistic child is seen to be in an already high state of arousal, and eye contact is avoided in order to prevent the level of arousal from rising any higher. The evidence they were able to offer to support this claim was very meagre and consisted of a discussion of a limited amount of video recording taken of autistic children during 'interaction' with adults and other children and of the results to a fairly simple experiment. The video recordings, they claimed, showed typical situations in which the autistic child is found to monitor others with his peripheral vision and avert his gaze at the critical moment when someone is about to look at him or in any way demand his attention. The essentially 'anecdotal' nature of this part of their paper makes it difficult for one to accept the findings unquestioningly. The experiment that they reported entailed autistic children being put into a room in which there were four different schematic representations of faces, both animal and human. Their major finding was that the autistic children spent more time looking at the fixtures in the room than did subnormal controls. When the autistic children did look at the drawings they tended to avoid the more obviously social ones looking least at a smiling 'human' face. However, Hutt and Ounsted draw conclusions which are far beyond the findings that they present. A major failing was that they failed to control for such factors as realism and complexity of the stimuli. Given that differential behaviour was found for both types of children, it is difficult to say which factor (or factors) affected the results.

Richer and Coss (1972) also did an experiment designed to investigate gaze aversion in autistic children. An experimenter sat in a room into which the child entered. The adult adopted one of several poses which were aimed to present the autistic child with varying levels of 'threat' (in terms of the presence and absence of eyes especially). The adult sat in the middle of the room and either talked in a normal manner to the child or talked with his mouth or mouth and one eye or his entire face covered by his hands. They claimed to find that the children showed less "aversion" to the covered face than to the partly covered one and less to the partly covered face than to the talking person with his face uncovered. However, when one considers the conditions, it is notable that they differ in degree from what a child might expect an adult to be doing. In consequence, their results may simply show that the autistic children were more interested in what an adult might be doing with his hands over his face whilst talking, than in a normal talking adult - as would be the case surely for any normal child. At least this factor should have been accounted for and discussed.

Such experiments really tell us very little about what they claim
to be studying: there are far too many other factors involved to know
which of the variables is instrumental in producing the results.
Experiments undertaken within a laboratory type of setting may well be
described as less natural, but at least they allow one to be rather
more specific about the variables one is looking at. In this regard,
Hermelin and O'Connor (1967) undertook a study of the gaze behaviour
of autistic children. In one of their experiments they required that
the child look into one end of a 'black box' in which he could only
see an illuminated face at the other side. There were two conditions:
the face either had its eyes open or closed. If the autistic child
avoids eye contact then one would expect them to look longer at a face
with its eyes closed than at one with its eyes open. This was not found
to be the case, and they looked at each condition equally long. Similarly,
they found that the autistic children looked longer at a photograph
of an adult male than they did at a scrambled version of the same face.
However, they did find that the autistic children looked significantly
less long at all the stimuli that they presented to them than did matched
subnormal controls. This led them to hypothesize that the gaze avoidance
noted in the literature as a strong clinical impression may simply be a
result of their exceptionally brief fixation times on all stimuli, not
just human faces. It is also worth noting that if they specifically
asked any of their autistic children to look at them then no gaze
avoidance was noted.

A more recent study by Churchill and Bryson (1972) also failed to
find support for the contention that autistic children actively avoid
looking at people. Theirs was an observational study and involved a
subject being in a room in which there was an adult seated in a cubicled

area. The floor of the room was mapped out according to whether or not the child could see and be seen by the adult. The adult adopted one of two dispositions: either he remained quiet and inattentive to the child, or, still without talking, he paid a lot of (visual) attention to what the child was doing. If the autistic child is hypothesized to avoid looking at people and to be more aversive to attentive adults than non-attentive ones, then clear behavioural differences should have been observed between the autistic children and matched normal control subjects. However, their findings did not bear this out at all; all the children spent most of their time in a position within the room where they could see and be seen by the adult. In addition, all the children tended to look more frequently at the attentive adult than at one who was being less attentive. In fact, the most prominent inter-group differences were in such areas as type of toy play activity and level of communication attempted with the adult: the autistic children were found to play with their toys in a very ritualistic manner and failed to use them in a communicative way; equally, their speech, when it occurred, was of a non-communicative nature. This contrasted strongly with the 'chatter' of the normal children, who were clearly puzzled as to why the adult was so unresponsive, etc. ·

Perhaps one of the more interesting aspects of their study was the reported impressions of the observers who felt that there was a qualitative difference in the looking of the two types of children. The normal children seemed to be attentive in their looking and accompanied it with cessation of unrelated motor activity, turning the entire torso toward the adult, etc; the autistic children did not do so. This links up with Rutter's (1978) description of the gaze behaviour of autistic children.  He points out that it is not so much the amount of gaze contact which differentiates autistic children from normal children, but rather the way in which the eye contact is used. The normal child will use eye contact in a highly discriminating fashion, looking at people when he wants something from them.  The autistic child on the other hand does not engage in such use of mutual gaze.  More important, he does not exhibit the patterns of gaze behaviour that one associates with shy or very anxious children whose eye avoidance is often specific to social interaction of a highly arousing nature.

Whilst an impression of gaze aversion is nonetheless found in the literature of the syndrome, this is almost entirely attributed to children of less than about five years old.  Wing points out that the older autistic child is far less likely to be withdrawn (Wing, 1976), and many adolescent autistics engage in over-extended gaze contact.  Such information is very difficult to marry with the concept that autistic children are avoiding eye-to-eye contact in order to keep their level of arousal as low as possible.  Nor can we see this latter theory as being applicable to the younger autistic child, if not to the older one:  many young autistic children too are reported to "look through" people in a non-aversive manner (Norman, 1955;  Wolff & Chess, 1964).

Differences have been outlined between relatively intelligent autistic children and those of low IQ (Bartak & Rutter, 1976;  Wing, 1978).  However, precisely what effect cognitive level has upon such aspects of gaze contact is slightly unclear.  Whilst Wing found that the difficulty of obtaining eye contact in her sample was positively correlated with cognitive level (especially as measured by language comprehension), Bartak and Rutter found no significant difference

between autistic subjects under IQ 70 and those with an IQ over 70,
either on level of eye contact at the time of study or on presence of
gaze avoidance in the child's history (they had all shown it at some
time). However, they would appear to agree on the general statement that
the autistic child with lower intelligence is much more likely to have
general social deficits and to show much more socially deviant behaviour.
The more intelligent subjects were reported to have a lesser likelihood
of having shown impaired physical responsiveness in infancy, especially
in social situations.

It is now possible to distil some major factors from this section:
the clinical impression, although poorly supported as yet by experimental
evidence, is one of abnormal gaze behaviour in the autistic child, but
this may not involve "avoidance" as such. This may be particularly so
for the more intelligent autistic child, in whom it might be argued
that the syndrome is less confounded with concommitant subnormality
(Bartak & Rutter, ibid.). Certainly, beyond about five years of age
it would seem impossible to attribute a simple theory such as avoidance
of arousing stimuli to the behaviour of the autistic child. The picture
is more one of a failure to use gaze in a normal fashion - an indifference
to gaze contact and not an aversion to it.

Bearing this in mind, perhaps it would be useful to consider the ways
in which normal gaze behaviour influences the manner in which normal
children view other people, and then to go on to investigate the presence
or absence of such factors in the perceptual abilities of autistic children.
To this end the first section of the following chapter is devoted to
such a consideration, and to a comparative investigation of the autistic

child's ability to recognize faces from isolated features. The remaining sections of the next chapter discuss the various findings that this initial investigation revealed.

Chapter 3

RECOGNITION OF FACES AND RELATED ISSUES

3.1:  Recognition of peers' faces from isolated features

In the last chapter it was noted that the normal child between about 4 and 10 years of age tends to find it rather easier to identify faces from the upper regions than from the lower areas. This was particularly so when recognition of different parts of a face involved the presence or absence of the eyes - when the eyes were present the children found it much easier to identify the person in the photograph. From this and other studies (see Ellis, 1975, for a summary), the conclusion may be drawn that it is most probably the normal child's proclivity for gaze contact and his use of information in the eyes to discern how others are feeling that leads to the particular salience which the eye area possesses.

This being the case, it would seem reasonable to assume that the converse may also be so: that visual avoidance of the eye area may lead to a lesser knowledge of that part of the face, and consequently lead a gaze-avoiding child to possess an abnormal pattern of knowledge of facial features. Thus an experimental paradigm which sets out to test autistic children's knowledge of the various parts of a face may well prove fruitful in providing an indication as to which parts of the face they know best, and presumably look most frequently at. However, in the last chapter it was noted that whilst some workers have claimed that the autistic child avoids eye contact, others have proposed that the autistic child is simply indifferent, giving no more attention to a person's eyes than to other stimuli which he experiences. As Beate Hermelin once put it "If you were a table, you too would complain that the autistic child was not looking at you". How may an experiment which aims to test a child's ability to identify known faces from isolated features provide data to indicate which of the foregoing statements about the autistic child's gaze behaviour is the more likely?

On the one hand there is the idea that the autistic child may actively avoid looking into people's eyes. If this is true then it might well be the case that his knowledge of the eye area, and that alone, would be poor in comparison to that of other non-autistic children. On the other hand an indifference to looking into the eyes of others might be expected to lead to quite different results. The child's knowledge of the various parts of a face may well then be decided by basic attractive properties, which in consequence would lead to a much more homogeneous knowledge of the face - more so, in fact, than that of the normal child who is biased towards gaze contact. More to the point, one would especially not expect such a child to possess a relatively poor knowledge of the eye area.

However, these are not the only predictions that one can make: the literature on face perception contains many studies which attest to the fact that our habitual manner of perceiving faces causes them to be abnormally difficult to recognize when viewed upside-down (Ellis, 1975). Precisely what it is which causes this is not yet known (Ellis, ibid.); but it would, at least, not seem to be simply a question of faces being unlike other 'objects' in so far as they are usually only seen in one orientation. Other so-called "mono-

Figure 3.1.  Normal eye movements when viewing a face
(Yarbus, 1967).

oriented" stimuli have been consitently found to be relatively easier
to recognize when inverted (Yin, 1969). Nor would it appear to be a
matter of complexity, for other equally complex stimuli have also been
reported to be easier to identify when upside-down (Ellis, ibid).
However, there would seem to be a consensus of opinion amongst the workers
in this field that it is primarily the social aspects of face perception
that give rise to this finding. Moreover, it seems likely that in order
to gain social information from a face one needs to be able to integrate
the various features into a whole or 'gestalt'. Thus, normal subjects
great problems with identifying inverted faces may be related to the
difficulty in telling the expression of an inverted face (Yin, 1970),
and hence to the problem of integrating the various facial features
when they are viewed in an unusual orientation. Others have stressed
such aspects as the manner in which one scans faces in order to gather
social information (e.g. Rock, 1974; Noton & Stark, 1971; see
figure 3.1). Such workers claim that these scanning strategies become
inadequate when one is attempting to identify an upside-down face.
However, it may equally be because certain scanning patterns are
appropriate to viewing a known gestalt configuration, whereas others
are more appropriate when viewing a complex stimulus which would
normally be seen as a whole but which is presented in an unfamiliar
orientation.

It is of interest to note here that if a child were able to
identify inverted faces with greater ease than is normal, then it may
either be because he is indifferent to the expression on other's faces
or because he is unable to discern such expression. In addition it may
mean that such a child is unable, or poorly able, to integrate his
perceptions into meaningful gestalten.

It was also noted in the last chapter that the factor of age
has an effect upon the child's ability to recognize photographs of

faces (Ellis, _ibid._ ; Goldstein & Mackenberg, _ibid._). In addition workers have reported a clear developmental trend in the autistic child's responsiveness to people; the older autistic child tends to be more responsive and to show less behaviour that gives the clinical impression of gaze aversion. Consequently, one might expect such aspects to manifest themselves in the autistic child's pattern of ability to recognize faces. There is, for instance, the finding that older normal children can recognize peers' faces from a small portion than can younger subjects (Goldstein & Mackenberg, _ibid._). Do autistic children also show this developmental trend from a basic knowledge of the whole to a knowledge of constituent parts? And is the increase in sociability in the autistic child with age reflected in a trend towards a more normal pattern of recognition ability?

To investigate all the above, an experiment was carried out which, in essence, utilized the same procedure which Goldstein and Mackenberg had used with normal American children. In this experiment, each child was presented with a photograph of a classmate's face which was partially covered so as to allow only one feature or a selected few of them, to be visible. However, this previous study's methodology was not followed precisely: using a large number of subjects, Goldstein and Mackenberg showed each child only one example of each part of the face under test. Thus each child saw only _one_ face with the eyes alone being visible, only _one_ where the face from the nose downwards was visible, and so forth. But this procedure led them to produce a few nonsensical results, which in turn throw doubt on their general findings. For instance, the method gave rise to their 5th grade subjects seeming to do better with only the immediate eye area (45% correct) than with the condition which allowed them to see an entire band of the face from ear-to-ear (15% correct; see Figure 3.2).

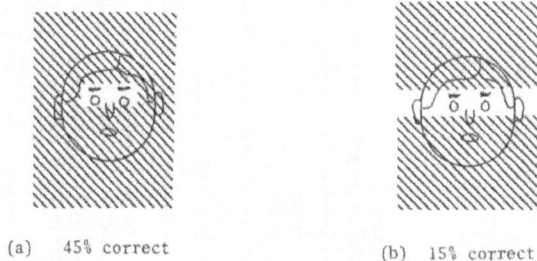

(a)    45% correct                    (b)  15% correct

Figure 3.2:  Two of the conditions used by Goldstein and Mackenberg
             (1966) with the respective percentage correct obtained
             by 5th grade subjects underlayed.

In order to avoid such puzzling results, the following experiment

required that all the subjects would see all the photographs under all

the possible masking conditions.

To investigate possible age effects, two groups of autistic children

were selected and will be nominally referred to as the 'older' and

'younger' autistic children.  However, it should be made clear that

there was an unavoidable lower limit set upon the age level of the sample

as a whole.  Each child was required to have sufficient language ability

to be able to comprehend, and respond to, the requirements of the various

tasks.  No autistic child below about eight years of age was found to be

able to do this.

TABLE 3.1    The Subjects

| | "Younger" groups | | | | "Older" groups | | | |
|---|---|---|---|---|---|---|---|---|
| | Autistic | Normal (M.A.) | Normal (C.A.) | Subnormal | Autistic | Normal (M.A.) | Normal (C.A.) | Subnormal |
| Mean chronological age (yr) | 9.80 | 5.62 | 9.64 | 9.75 | 14.10 | 8.10 | 13.57 | 13.70 |
| Standard deviation (yr) | 1.04 | 0.23 | 1.51 | 0.98 | 1.10 | 0.66 | 0.40 | 1.27 |
| Mean full I.Q.* | 60.30 | | | 61.30 | 63.00 | | | 60.20 |
| Standard deviation | 15.62 | | | 5.36 | 14.22 | | | 7.71 |
| Mean performance I.Q.* | 73.50 | | | 62.40 | 78.00 | | | 63.10 |
| Standard deviation | 15.25 | | | 8.06 | 18.30 | | | 7.87 |

\*   All I.Q. measures are from a complete administration of the WISC.  The I.Q.'s of the normal children were not taken, but all children were chosen as "average performers" by their teachers.

## The Children Tested

In total, eighty children took part in this study. Of these twenty were autistic children who were attending one of two special schools and had been diagnosed by experienced psychiatrists. These children are the 'pool' of autistic children for this thesis and they have been described in detail in the first chapter. The autistic sample was divided equally into an "older" and a "younger" group according to their chronological age. Table 3.1 gives details of all the subjects used in this study.

Two groups of ten normal children acted as controls according to the chronological ages of the autistic children. A further two groups of ten normal children were chosen to control for the mental ages of the autistic sample. In addition, two groups of ten subnormal children were selected to match both the chronological and mental ages of the two autistic groups. All the subnormal children attended a school for the educationally subnormal, and were free of autistic symptoms.

In choosing the children for this investigation, care was taken not to include any child who had unduly obvious distinguishing features (such as scars, glasses, etc.) or who had any known defect of vision.

## The Materials Used

The stimuli for each group were black and white photographs of the faces of the members of that group, each measuring 14cm by 10cm. All signs of clothing were excluded, together with any distinguishing features in the background that might have aided or confused recognition. An attempt was made to have all the children in a natural pose, which in almost all cases was fairly expressionless with mouth closed. The

Figure 3.3. Two of the faces to be recognised; the lower one has the Low$_3$ mask in place.

same lighting conditions, photographic equipment, and processing procedures were used for each photograph to ensure a good match of tone, definition and contrast. It was decided that black and white photographs should be used, as recognition of them is reported to be in no way inferior to that of colour photographs (Laughery, et al., 1971), and colour photographs were thought to involve insurmountable difficulties in the matching of skin tones, and so forth. Each photograph was large enough for isolated features to be readily distinguishable without loss of clarity and detail. Samples of the photographs are shown in Figure 3.3. In order to present isolated features and areas of the faces, cardboard masks were prepared that could be placed over the photograph during presentation to allow only specific facial areas to be viewed. A stop-watch was used to record the response times of each subject.

The Testing Procedure

Each child was taken individually to a quiet room to be tested. All ten photographs of the members of his group (i.e. of the nine peers and of himself) with all masking conditions were shown to each subject. There were seven "masks" in all and one condition in which the face was shown upside-down. A consistent order of presentation was used, to ensure that no child gained any advantage to be had from differences in presentation order, and that as little learning as possible could occur of the particular photographs that might have aided recognition.

The eight conditions were as follows, and they were presented to the child in the order in which they will be described. First, all the pictures were shown upside-down, as it has been found that prior experience of a face in a different mode can greatly affect its recognition when inverted (Goldstein, 1975):

1. The 'inverted' condition (Inv.*)

When all of the faces had been seen in such a manner then the child was shown just the noses of all the faces:

2. The 'nose-only' condition (Nose)

Then the child saw just the eyes of each face:

3. The 'eyes-only' condition (Eyes)

After this the child saw just the mouth and chin of each face:

4. 'Mouth and chin' condition ($Low_1$)

---

* Abbreviations are included for the conditions in order to facilitate the drawing up of the tables and graphs.

When he had made his guess the card was moved a little to reveal the nose area of the face as well:

5. 'Nose, mouth and chin' condition ($Low_2$)

Following his next guess, or reaffirmation of the first one, the eyes were revealed by a further move of the card:

6. 'Eyes, nose and mouth' condition ($Low_3$)

The 'lower half' of the face of the next photograph was then shown in a similar way, and so on until all ten photographs had been seen in all of these last three conditions.

The 'upper half' of each face was revealed next in two stages;[*] firstly the child was allowed to see only the hairline and forehead:

---

* Footnote: The photos were randomized before proceding with the next step.

7. The 'forehead only' condition (Up$_1$)

Then, following the child's guess, the card was moved down to reveal the eyes as well:

8. 'Forehead and eyes' condition (Up$_2$)

This procedure was repeated for each of the ten photographs in turn. It was impressed upon the child each time the card was moved that he did not have to change his mind - it did not necessarily mean that his guess had been incorrect. No feedback whatsoever was given as to the subject's number of errors.

Finally, the child was shown all the faces in the normal upright uncovered manner, to ensure that he knew the identity of each face. If the child failed to recognize any face in this final condition then his previous errors on that face were discounted.

TABLE 3.2     Table of the mean per cent errors for each group in each condition

Groups*

| Masks+ | Older autistic | Younger autistic | Older normal (C.A.) | Older normal (M.A.) | Older subnormal | Younger normal (C.A.) | Younger normal (M.A.) | Younger subnormal |
|--------|---------------|------------------|---------------------|---------------------|-----------------|-----------------------|-----------------------|-------------------|
| Up 1   | 15.61 | 60.69 | 24.40 | 38.40 | 47.70 | 37.41 | 34.98 | 36.90 |
| Up 2   | 8.28  | 29.42 | 7.20  | 21.00 | 15.20 | 15.52 | 23.32 | 10.60 |
| Low 1  | 26.52 | 35.19 | 68.90 | 77.70 | 64.00 | 71.04 | 85.00 | 74.00 |
| Low 2  | 11.06 | 21.97 | 43.70 | 71.90 | 46.90 | 56.59 | 78.04 | 64.30 |
| Low 3  | 4.31  | 7.64  | 20.30 | 35.50 | 14.60 | 25.96 | 35.82 | 21.30 |
| Nose   | 74.60 | 77.63 | 80.89 | 90.60 | 92.30 | 81.45 | 90.00 | 93.50 |
| Eyes   | 64.32 | 89.34 | 60.60 | 80.29 | 86.40 | 66.79 | 86.12 | 83.60 |
| Invert | 28.33 | 48.18 | 52.40 | 55.70 | 70.30 | 53.08 | 56.10 | 79.70 |

\*   For full details of the groups see "Subjects" section and Table 3.1
+   For full details of the various masking conditions used see text.

123

Each child was told that he was to see "some pictures of the
other children in your class/school" and that the task was "a sort of
game" in which he was told "let's see if you can tell me whose
picture I'm going to show you". Additionally, each subject was told
that he should have no hesitation in saying if he didn't know, as
the experimenter quite understood that some might be a little difficult.
Nonetheless, the child was encouraged to "have a guess" whenever
possible. Subjects were kept fully informed as to how much of the
face they could expect to see at any one time to avoid the possibility
of their delaying a response until more was revealed.

After the child had seen a condition (or series of conditions when
the "halves" of the face were revealed) with all of the ten photographs,
the pictures were thoroughly randomized before proceeding with the
next stage of the presentation.

Although no time limit was set for the presentation of each
stimulus, a record was kept of the response times of each child, who
was told to guess as soon as he felt fairly certain whose face was
being presented.

## The Results of the Study

### a) The basic analysis

An analysis of variance was performed on the percentage error
scores of the various groups (the means are shown in Table 3.2) to
compare the performance by the different types of children (autistic,
normal and subnormal) in the different conditions, across the two
age groups. Significant main effects of age, conditions, and type of
child were obtained, together with significant interactions of
conditions x type and of conditions x type x age. Because the sources

TABLE 3.3     Analysis of variance on the mean per cent errors

(i) Comparing types of child across two age levels

| Source | df | SS | MS | F | P |
|---|---|---|---|---|---|
| Age | 1 | 6722.00 | 6722.00 | 5.41 | 0.023 |
| Type | 3 | 43687.19 | 14562.39 | 11.71 | 0.001 |
| Conditions | 7 | 338205.56 | 48315.08 | 216.13 | 0.001 |
| C x T | 21 | 49415.63 | 2353.13 | 10.53 | 0.001 |
| C x T x A | 21 | 10707.88 | 509.90 | 2.28 | 0.001 |

(ii) Older autistics and their controls

| Source | df | SS | MS | F | P |
|---|---|---|---|---|---|
| Type | 3 | 40949.19 | 13649.73 | 12.21 | 0.001 |
| Conditions | 7 | 178881.50 | 25554.50 | 126.13 | 0.001 |
| T x C | 21 | 22349.00 | 1064.24 | 5.25 | 0.001 |

(iii) Younger autistics and their controls

| Source | df | SS | MS | F | P |
|---|---|---|---|---|---|
| Type | 3 | 8444.06 | 2814.69 | 3.01 | 0.032 |
| Conditions | 7 | 121162.81 | 20193.80 | 78.15 | 0.001 |
| T x C | 21 | 43819.00 | 2434.39 | 9.42 | 0.001 |

of the conditions x type interaction are of particular interest to us in this study, and noting that the 'age' factor was significant, two further analyses of variance were computed: one to compare the older autistic group with their controls; and a second to compare the performance of the younger autistic children with that of their controls. Significant effects of type and conditions were obtained in both cases, along with a significant interaction of type x condition in each case. The results of these analyses are given in Table 3.3.

b) An overview of the findings

The main results of the study can be summarized as follows (note that the terms 'upper half' and 'lower half' are used in the way they were in the description of the presentation).

(i) On nearly all the masking conditions, there were no significant differences between the mean percentage errors of the normal and subnormal groups. The trend for all these children was concordant with the results of previous experiments (e.g. Goldstein & Mackenberg, ibid.), and indicated that they found the features of the upper half of the face generally easier to recognize than those of the lower half.

(ii) In contrast to their normal and subnormal controls, the younger autistic children were significantly better at identifying the lower half of the face than the upper half.

(iii) The older autistic children's mean percentage of errors were not significantly different from those of the younger autistic children when recognizing the lower half of the face. Unlike the younger autistic children, however, they did not differ significantly

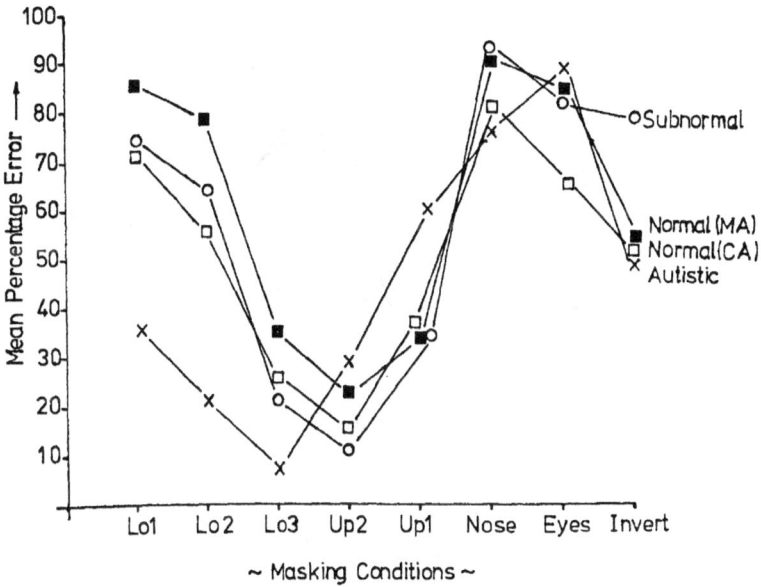

Figure 3.4. Mean percentage errors by the young children.

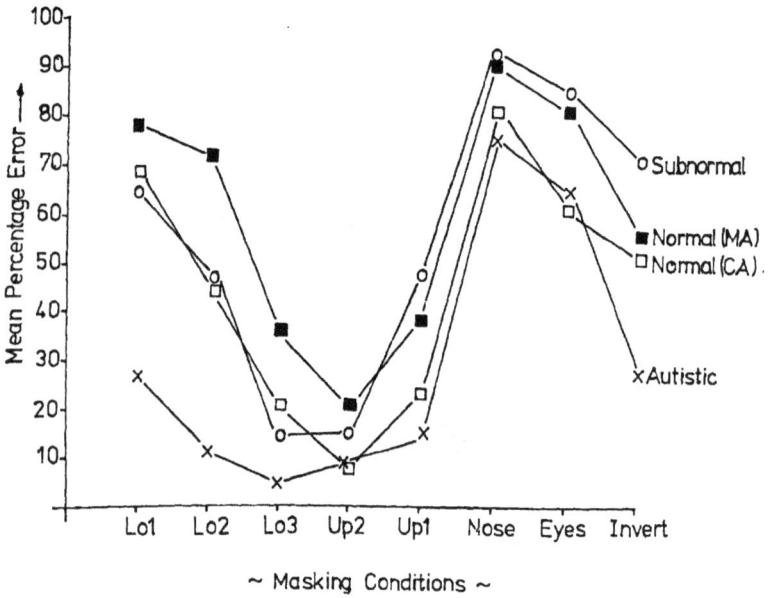

Figure 3.5. Mean percentage errors by the older children.

from their normal control group matched for chronological age
on their ability to recognize the uppermost area of the face
(the 'forehead only'). In fact, their pooled mean percentage
error for the upper two areas of the face (the 'forehead only'
and the 'forehead and eyes') did not differ from that of the
lower 'half' (the three conditions which gradually revealed
the lower features from 'mouth only' up to 'eyes, nose and
mouth').

(iv) The remaining major finding was that while the younger
autistic children did not differ from their controls in their
ability to recognize upside-down faces, the older autistic
children were much better at this than any other group (including
their younger counterparts).

c) Further analysis: some basic comparisons

Selected comparisons were made, using Scheffé's procedure (Winer,
1971) to investigate the sources of the two significant interaction
terms of the first analysis of variance above.

The analysis of variance revealed that the pattern of performance
over the various conditions differed according to the type of child.
The first interaction indicated that the autistic children as a whole
had quite different error rates on the upper and the lower halves of
the face than did the other types of children (the difference between
$Low_1$, $Low_2$, $Low_3$ and $Up_1$, $Up_2$ differed between the types of child,
$F_{77,2} = 89.87$ (p $<$ 0.01). The differences between the groups' error
rates are shown in figures 3.4 and 3.5. As can be seen, the major
source of this was due to the autistic children being so good at the
'Low' mask conditions, i.e., the lower areas of the face.

The other significant interaction was a second order one of conditions-by-type of child-by-age. This essentially indicated that there were age level differences, along with the between group variations, for the two halves of the face. The Scheffé comparison showed that whilst the older normal and subnormal children resembled their younger counterparts in their pattern of ability, the older autistic children were significantly better than the younger ones on the two upper areas ('forehead only' and 'eyes and forehead'; $F_{77,2}$ = 22.65, p < 0.05). Figure 3.6 shows the differences between the autistic groups.

By a combination of Schaffé's procedure with the Duncan's Range statistic (Winer, 1971; McGuigan, 1968), the sources of the groups-by-conditions interaction were further investigated separately at each age level. First, the results of these comparisons for the younger children will be described.

d) <u>The results of the younger subjects</u>

A comparison of the upper most and lower most parts of the face ($Up_1$ and $Low_1$), where the eyes were not present, for the four groups of younger children revealed that the groups' performances were different ($F_{36,3}$ = 67.50, p < 0.01). i.e.:

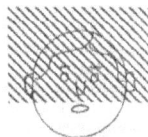

|  | $Up_1$ | $Low_1$ |
|---|---|---|
| Normal (M.A.) | 34.98% | 85.00% |
| Normal (C.A.) | 37.41% | 71.04% |
| Subnormal | 36.90% | 74.00% |
| Autistic | 60.69% | 35.19% |

(average errors)

The difference was clearly due to the subnormal and normal children finding the uppermost area easier, but the autistic children finding the lowermost area easier (df = 62, $p < 0.05$ in each case; Duncan's Range). The normal and subnormal children thus performed almost indistinguishably on these two conditions, and the contrast with the younger autistic children's performance could hardly have been more marked.

It is also of interest to look at the difference which the contribution of the presence of the eyes made to the identification of the lower 'half' of the face. i.e.:

| | $Low_2$ | versus | $Low_3$ |
|---|---|---|---|
| Normal (C.A.) | 56.59% | | 25.69% |
| Normal (M.A.) | 78.04% | | 35.82% |
| Subnormal | 64.30% | | 21.30% |
| Autistic | 21.97% | | 7.64% |

(average errors)

It is immediately obvious that the autistic children did better in both conditions than all the control children ($p < 0.05$ in all cases). It is also obvious that the presence of the eyes made the faces easier to recognize for all four groups. However, the interaction was just significant at the $p = 0.05$ level ($F_{36,3} = 9.11$). Within group comparisons showed that this was because whilst the normal and subnormal groups' errors were significantly reduced when the eyes were present (df = 62, $p < 0.01$ in each case), the difference for the autistic children just failed at the $p = 0.05$ level. But it should be noted

that the autistic children had very few errors without the eyes being
present, and thus the effect of the presence of the eyes may have been
obscured by a ceiling effect. Thus the lack of significant reduction
of errors by the autistic children when the eyes were allowed to be seen,
should not be taken as evidence that they knew them less well than the
control subjects. Indeed, the younger autistic children were quite as
able to identify the faces in the 'eyes-only' and 'forehead and eyes'
($Up_2$) conditions as the other children matched for mental age, i.e.:

|  | eyes-only | $Up_2$ |
|---|---|---|
| Normal (M.A.) | 86.12% | 23.32% |
| Subnormal | 83.60% | 10.90% |
| Autistic | 89.34% | 24.42% |

(average errors)

The comparison designed to look at the contribution which the
eyes made to the recognition of the upper area of the face also showed
that the autistic children knew the eye area well, i.e.:

|  | $Up_1$ | $Up_2$ |
|---|---|---|
| Normal (C.A.) | 37.41% | 15.52% |
| Normal (M.A.) | 34.98% | 23.32% |
| Subnormal | 36.90% | 10.60% |
| Autistic | 60.69% | 29.42% |

(average errors)

All four groups found identification much easier when the eyes were present, though the effect was much greater for the autistic children, primarily because they were so poor on the 'forehead only' condition (all within group comparisons were significant at $p < 0.01$ on the Duncan's Range). The autistic children were significantly worse on the 'forehead only' condition than all the control children ($p < 0.01$ in all cases).

It is noteworthy that the younger autistic children still found the lower part of the face from the eyes downwards ($Low_3$) easier to identify than the part from the eyes upwards ($Up_2$). i.e.:

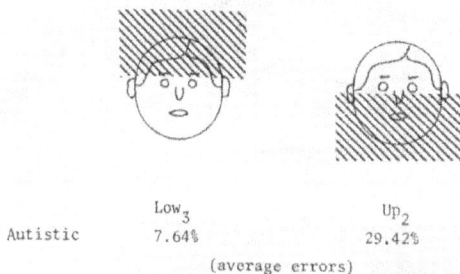

|  | $Low_3$ | $Up_2$ |
|---|---|---|
| Autistic | 7.64% | 29.42% |

(average errors)

This was not the case for any of the other younger groups, who tended to find the reverse was true (see figure 3.4), although the difference did not quite reach significance for these groups.

Finally, no significant differences were found between the groups on either the 'nose-only' or the 'inverted' conditions.

134

e)  The results of the older subjects

    As was mentioned in the initial summary of the results, the
older control subjects performed almost identically to their younger
counterparts.  Once again, the presence of the eyes significantly
reduced the number of errors they made in recognising upper and lower
halves of the face. i.e.:

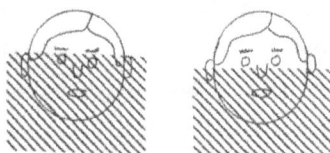

|  | $Up_1$ | $Up_2$ |
|---|---|---|
| Normal (C.A.) | 24.40% | 7.20% |
| Normal (M.A.) | 38.40% | 21.00% |
| Subnormal | 47.70% | 15.20% |
| Autistic | 15.61% | 8.28% |

(average errors)

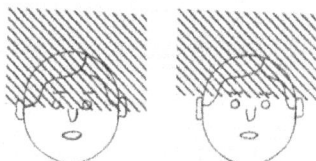

|  | $Low_2$ | $Low_3$ |
|---|---|---|
| Normal (C.A.) | 43.70% | 20.30% |
| Normal (M.A.) | 71.90% | 35.50% |
| Subnormal | 46.90% | 14.60% |
| Autistic | 11.06% | 4.31% |

(average errors)

As can be seen, nearly all the control groups had fewer errors
when they could see the eyes, in both cases (the normal children in
the first above instance were the exceptions; the other children had
significantly different errors at $p < 0.01$). Unlike the younger autistic
children, the older ones did not produce fewer errors when the eyes
were made visible in either case. However, as with the younger
autistics' ability on the lower two areas, this may have been due to
a ceiling effect, because they were already making very few errors on
the lower areas where the eyes were absent. A ceiling effect might also
have prevented the normal children doing any better on the 'forehead and
eyes' than on the 'forehead only'. Lastly, it is noted that the older
autistic children made fewer erros than all the other groups on all
the conditions except the 'forehead and eyes' one ($Up_2$), where they
were no better than their normal controls matched for chronological
age ($p < 0.05$ in all the other instances).

The comparison of the older subjects' abilities to recognize the
'forehead only' and the 'mouth only' conditions revealed a similar
pattern to that described above for the younger children, i.e.:

| | $Up_1$ | $Low_1$ |
|---|---|---|
| Normal (C.A.) | 24.40% | 68.90% |
| Normal (M.A.) | 38.40% | 77.70% |
| Subnormal | 47.70% | 64.00% |
| Autistic | 15.61% | 26.52% |

(average errors)

As before, the normal and subnormal children found the uppermost part easier to identify than the lowermost one ($p < 0.05$ in all cases). However, unlike the younger autistic children, the older ones found the two conditions almost equally easy (the difference was not significant). The autistic children were very much better on the 'mouth only' condition than their controls ($p < 0.01$ in all cases).

What is particularly interesting about the older autistic groups' results is the homogeneity of their knowledge across the parts of the face (the 'nose only' and 'eyes only' excepted). In fact, the only comparison which reached significance was between the 'mouth only' and 'eyes, nose and mouth' conditions ($Low_1$ and $Low_3$; $p < 0.05$), where the information available was quite different, i.e.:

$Low_1$                          $Low_3$

Autistic        26.52%                          4.31%

(average errors)

This uniform knowledge of the face also extended to the inverted mode, for errors here were only found to differ significantly from the 'eyes, nose and mouth' condition, in which recognition was nearly perfect ($p < 0.01$, Duncan's Range).

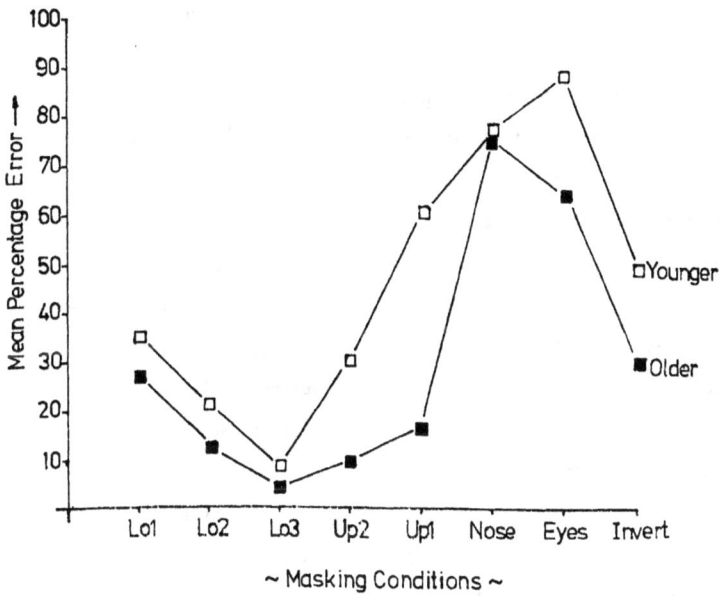

Figure 3.6.  Comparison of younger and older autistic children's results.

The mention of the inverted mode leads to the final major result of this section, namely that the older autistic children found it far easier to recognize upside-down faces than did any of the other groups (and this includes the younger autistics too).

The 'nose only' condition produced no group differences whatsoever.

f) Age differences in performance

In the above section many of the similarities and dissimilarities between the older and younger children were highlighted. It was noted that the increase in age had very little effect upon the scores of the normal and subnormal groups. In fact, reference to the previous graphic representation (Figures 3.4 and 3.5) reveals only a general trend for an increase in recognition ability of about 5% to 10%. However, the autistic children differed substantially with age on the upper portions of the face: the older children were substantially better on the 'forehead only' (p $<$ 0.01, Duncan's Range) and somewhat better on the 'forehead and eyes' condition. The older autistic children were also significantly better on the 'eyes only' condition than were the younger autistics (p $<$ 0.01). There was also a trend for the normal groups to show better ability with age on the 'eyes only' condition, and thus the difference may be attributable to no more than an increase in skills with age. Nonetheless, it is of interest that whilst the younger autistic children performed only at their mental age level on this condition, the older autistic children were well up to a normal chronological age ability.

g) IQ differences in performance

The WISC scores for the autistic children were used to test the possibility of a correlation between IQ and performance on the tasks. A Pearson-Bravais product moment coefficient (see McGuigan, 1968) was computed for both groups' mean percentage error scores versus both full and performance IQ. No significant correlation was found.

h) Some additional points

The mean response times attained by each group were not significantly different. Thus it can be concluded that there was no tendency to give any group any advantage that might be had from viewing the stimuli for a longer period.

Finally, in all the conditions where the autistic childrn's results differed significantly from those of their normal control subjects, the subnormal children were found not to differ in their ability from at least one of the normal control groups. In consequence, it can be inferred with some confidence that the deviant results of the autistic children which have been described above are not likely to be simply due to their 'subnormality' but rather to their 'autism'.

i) Summary of the main findings

In such a complex analysis it is worth briefly summarizing the most outstanding points again before discussing the results as a whole.

i) The autistic children's pattern of ability was clearly different in many respects from that of the control groups - most of the differences being in the direction of the autistic children performing better than the normal or subnormal children.

ii) It was notable that whereas all the control groups found the
upper parts of the face easier to recognize than the lower parts,
the younger autistic children found the reverse to be true. The
older autistic children differed again in that they seemed to find
all areas of the face almost equally easy to identify.

iii) Neither autistic group showed any evidence of knowing the eye
area poorly in comparison to their controls.

(iv) The largest 'age' effects for the autistic children occurred
in their abilities to recognize the uppermost facial regions, and
to identify the inverted faces. The older autistics were much
better than the younger ones in both cases.

## Discussion of the findings

Three main questions have arisen from this study. First, why are
young autistic children better able to recognize photographs of their
peers when shown the lower rather than the upper facial features?
Second, why, in contrast to normal and subnormal children, should older
autistic children possess a more homogeneous knowledge of the entire
face, such that they can use the upper as well as the lower features
effectively for recognition? Third, why are the older autistic children
better able than any others in this study to recognize upside-down faces?

In searching for explanatory hypotheses for these results, it
should be borne in mind that they may not reflect a single aspect but rather
a compound of aspects of autism. Thus, the results can be viewed both
in the light of the autistic child's perceptual abilities, and also
his failure, or deviant attempts, to discern the social signals conveyed

by the face. However, as was noted above these aspects may well be interrelated; indeed they may represent two sides of the same coin.

First, in terms of social factors of face perceptions, it is noted that the results of the experiment do not seem to support the gaze avoidance theory proposed by Hutt et al. (e.g. Hutt and Ounsted, 1966). It will be remembered that in the introductory section of this study, it was suggested that the reason for the eye area's usual salience in face perception might be the fact that one tends to engage in mutual gaze contact and use eye contact for communicative purposes (Argyle and Cook, 1976). By reverse argument, a child who avoids gaze contact might be expected to have an abnormally poor knowledge of the eye area. Clearly this was not so for either of the groups of autistic children.

There are two remaining ways in which the results may be interpreted: either the autistic child has something akin to the normal and subnormal child's tendency to view upper halves of faces and has an additional reason for looking at, and hence knowing well, the lower facial features; or the autistic child lacks the normal tendency to focus upon the eye area, and instead has an abnormally even knowledge of all the facial features due to an absence of social awareness causing him to fixate any one area in particular.

The younger autistic children found the uppermost facial regions harder to identify than did their matched controls, whereas these autistic children found the lowermost areas easier to recognise than did the controls. Whatever the reason for the younger autistic children's good knowledge of lower areas, they do not share all the characteristics of the normal and subnormal children's socially biased knowledge of the upper regions. What might lead to a better-than-average knowledge of lower facial features? In view of the younger autistic child's poor social competence it is hardly surprising to find evidence which suggests that he may have failed to learn either that the eye area is an important source of information about another's inner state, or that a social convention exists concerning mutual gaze contact. Thus a lack of knowledge, to some degree, of upper facial features can be understood without reference to gaze avoidance, but why should a bias towards the mouth stem from this? A possible relevant observation reported by Dodd (1977) is that normal subjects, when presented with a spoken communication against a noisy background, tend to rely upon visual cues (i.e. lip reading) regarding the content of the communication. Thus it might be inferred that the younger autistic child attends to the mouth area because he is trying to compensate for an inability to extract the full meaning from the auditory component of speech. This inability, in turn, might arise from a cognitive deficit affecting the processing of all auditory stimuli (see Hermelin and O'Connor, 1970).

This hypothesis leads to the postulation that the autistic child should either possess better-than-normal lip-reading powers, or at least a greater-than-normal reliance upon the cues given by the lips in spoken communications. Yet a contrasting hypothesis may account for the results equally well. If the child is aware that the lip movements are related to what he hears but is unable to integrate the two sources of information, his attention may well be drawn toward the mouth of the speaker as a source of conflict. In spite of this focussing of attention, his lip reading powers may nevertheless be somewhat poorer than normal.

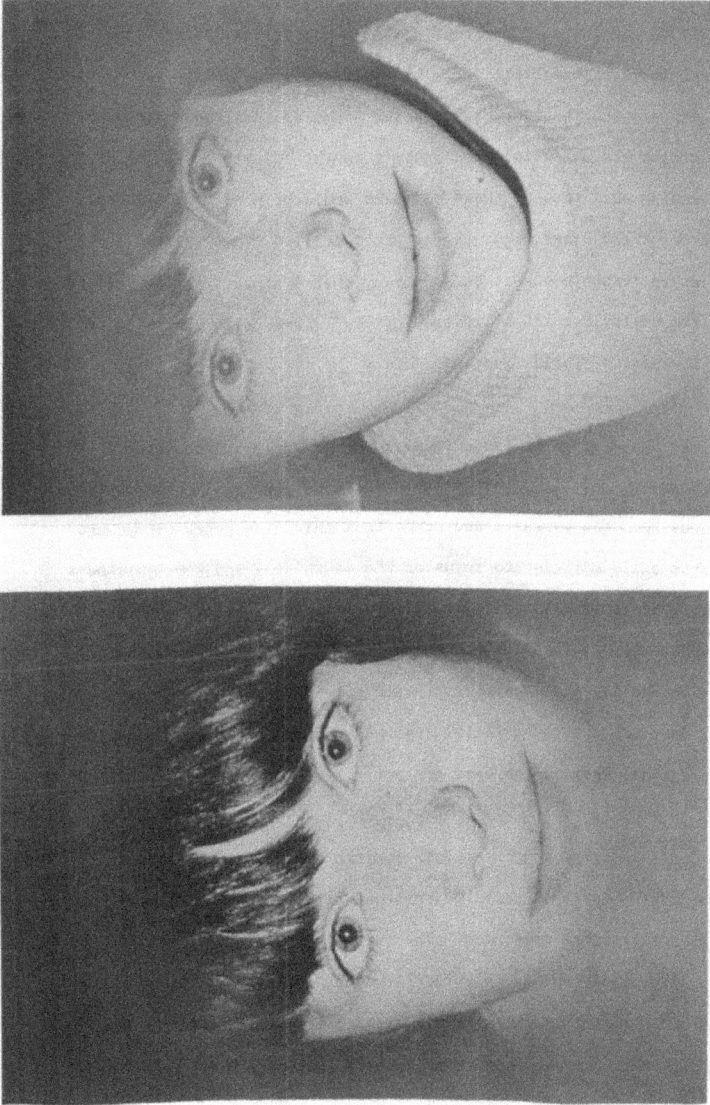

Figure 3.7. Illustration of the focusing hypothesis showing the differing areas attended to when fixating (i) the eyes and (ii) the mouth.

On the other hand, the autistic child may be envisaged as being able to utilize information from visual and auditory modalities and be able to combine such information to compensate maximally for a central linguistic deficit. On the other hand, the child may be unable to integrate the two sources yet being aware of their connexion may concentrate his attention on another's mouth. Clearly, a study of the lip-reading abilities of these children would help to decide whether either of these views might in fact be justified. Naturally, conclusive evidence cannot be sought by such a study - it may well be that the autistic child's lip-reading powers are quite unrelated to his knowledge of facial features.

The above argument leads to what one may call a 'focussing hypothesis'. That is, whereas the normal and subnormal children tend to focus upon the eye area and hence know this area best, the younger autistic child may tend to focus on the mouth area and know this best. The hypothesis is illustrated in figure 3.7, and gives some idea of how a tendency to focus on the eye area may mean that the mouth is not attended to, and in contrast a tendency to focus on the mouth area means that the uppermost facial regions tend to be out of the sphere of attention, whereas the eyes are not.

Could such hypotheses account for the older autistic children's performance? These children possessed a better-than-normal knowledge of lower facial features, too. The autistic syndrome has been regarded , in a sense, as a language disorder (Rutter, 1978), for the autistic child's problems with language stay with him for life even though his 'social' behaviour may improve remarkably (Rutter, 1974). Thus, if it is argued that the linguistic deficit in the younger autistic child leads to a better knowledge of the mouth area then one can expect the older autistic child to also possess this knowledge. But as was noted above, the growing autistic child may also become more socially competent (though rarely, if ever, normal in this respect). Thus he may be expected to acquire at least the rudiments of social communication - including the use of the eye area as a source of information, even if his ability to read complex meaning into this area is deficient. To exemplify this, one older and more able autistic boy said, "I know people talk with their eyes but I don't know what they are saying". Sufficient knowledge that the eye area conveys meaning relevant to interpersonal communication, but an inability to decipher this meaning, could lead to the over-extended gaze contact noted by Wing (1976b) and hence to a knowledge of the upper half of the fact which can equal that of normal subjects. In short, the reasons for both of the autistic group's good knowledge of the mouth area might be the same, and the difference between their abilities on the upper regions might be explicable in terms of the growth of social awareness.

The major alternative to the above interpretation of the results is to view them in terms of the autistic child's lack of social competence leading him to view the face as a pattern devoid of socially meaningful information. His knowledge of the various facial features might thus be determined by the inherent attraction and discriminability of the features. Implicit in this, though, is the assumption that the autistic child is viewing the face as a collection of separate parts rather than as a unified meaningful whole or 'gestalt'. Given that the eye and mouth areas might be considered to be the most easily discriminable regions one might expect the child's ability to identify faces to be best when both of these areas are present, less good when only one area is visible, and worst when neither are present. This, in fact, accurately describes the younger autistic children's results (see figure 3.4). Once again the difference between the two autistic groups may be viewed as due to maturation, but this time maturation of the ability to discriminate parts of wholes rather than maturation of social competence. Evidence that older children are better than younger ones at discerning isolated features was one of the findings reported by Goldstein and Mackenberg (1966) and is well supported by the literature on gestalt perception in children (Ghent, 1956).

This hypothesis thus emphasises the social factors in the normal child's perception of faces in contrast to the possibility that autistic children view faces as collections of disparate features rather than as meaningful, expressionful wholes. If this is true then the social factors which make inverted faces so hard to recognise (Yin, 1970) ought to be absent in the autistic; in addition the autistic child ought to be poor at recognising facial expression because this requires the integration of facial features, and indeed poor at perceptual tasks in general which require perceptual integration. The present experiment allows one to look at one of these points, namely the identification of inverted faces.

The older autistic children's mean percentage error for recognising inverted faces was much lower than that of all the other groups, whereas that of the younger autistic children was not significantly different from that of their controls. Nonetheless, there was a slight trend towards the younger autistic children being particularly good on the inverted faces. These results do not offer clear support for either of the above theories. The older autistic children's exceptional ability to recognise upside down faces does seem to agree with the contention that they view faces as collections of parts rather than as 'gestalten'. Thus whereas the normal and subnormal children had to try to rotate mentally not only the facial features but also the relationships between them, the older autistic children merely had to identify a feature which they recognised as unique to a peer's face. It is possible that the younger autistic children also view faces as collections of parts but are poor at identifying inverted faces simply because they are not as good at identifying single inverted features as their older counterparts are.

These results with inverted faces may also be interpreted in terms of the above mentioned 'focussing hypothesis'. One may argue that both normal and younger autistic children possess a centre of attention (the eyes for the former and the mouth for the latter) the position of which changes when a face is inverted. If, as has been suggested, (Noton and Stark, 1971) people tend to have specific scanning strategies when viewing faces, then these strategies may be organised about a subject's 'focal centre'.[*] Inversion of the face thus disrupts the child's scanning strategy. This disruption may account for the relatively poor performance of both the normal and younger autistic children. The older autistic children, by contrast, seem to have no particular focal centre and thus their scanning strategy might be more flexible. If this is so then their strategy might be less affected by inversion of the stimulus. The difficulty with this interpretation

---

* Footnote: See Figure 3.1 for an example of a normal person's scanning

though, is that no matter how flexible the older autistic child's scanning strategy is hypothesised to be, one would expect it to still be organised around the upright arrangement of the facial features. In addition, it does seem unlikely that the autistic child possesses such a sophisticated perceptual ability in this realm given his well reported problems with perceptual tasks (Hermelin and O'Connor, 1970).

However, there may be a simpler reason why the older autistic child is so good at recognising inverted faces: it may simply be due to the fact that he possesses a more detailed knowledge of the mouth and that this feature is easier to rotate mentally. His superior performance over the younger autistic child may in turn be due to the development of his cognitive/perceptual skills to put such knowledge to use. This idea can simply be tested by presenting the child with inverted halves of faces to recognise. It would thus be expected that the older autistic child's ability to recognise inverted lower halves would be superior to his ability to recognise inverted upper halves. This point will be followed up in a section devoted to the 'inverted mode' further on in this chapter.

### Summary and Concluding Remarks

This study has brought to light a number of interesting findings which now need to be investigated further. Those hypotheses proposed in the above discussion which lend themselves to experimental study will be dealt with in the remaining sections of this chapter in the order in which they are summarised below.

i) It was suggested that autistic children might have a tendency to scan the lower halves of all objects presented to them.

(ii) Two possible hypotheses were proposed to account for the autistic child's tendency to know the lower halves of faces which allow clear (if opposing) predictions about the lip-reading abilities of such children.

(iii) Having noted that the older autistic children possessed a better-than-average ability to identify inverted faces, three possible explanations presented themselves:  it may be a result of the scanning patterns employed by the children;  it may be due to their possessing a detailed knowledge of a part of the fact which is easy to recognise upside down;  finally and related to this last idea, they may regard faces as collections of disparate features rather than as 'gestalten' and hence have an advantage over non-autistic children who habitually view faces as integrated meaningful wholes and who are thus presented with difficulties when viewing faces presented in an unfamiliar orientation.  The first of these possibilities will be dealt with to some degree in Chapter Six, and the last possibility will be returned to in Chapter Five when autistic children's knowledge of facial expression is investigated.

## 3.2 Sorting schematic houses

In the last section it was seen that both groups of autistic children were far more able to recognize faces from features of the lower facial areas than were normal or subnormal children. Is it possible that this could be the result of the autistic children possessing a tendency to scan the lower halves of all things? Whilst there is nothing in the literature on autism to suggest this, it is nonetheless a potentially parsimonious explanation of the autistic children's results, and as such must be investigated.

Possibly the most direct method of investigation would be to study the eye movements of autistic children whilst they are looking at various objects. However, there are many methodological problems inherent in such studies, not the least of which is the fundamental requirement that subjects must remain fairly motionless. The results of a study of this nature will in fact be reported later in this thesis, but are not presented at this point due to the rather inconclusive findings they revealed.

Another approach to the problem is to give the children a simple task in which a set of cards must be sorted into two piles. By designing the stimuli in such a manner that there can be no 'wrong' way of sorting them, it is possible to leave it to the child concerned to choose the criterion on which they are sorted. Thus if a child has a proclivity to attend to the lower half of things he may be expected to choose one or more feature of the lower-half of the stimuli to sort by.

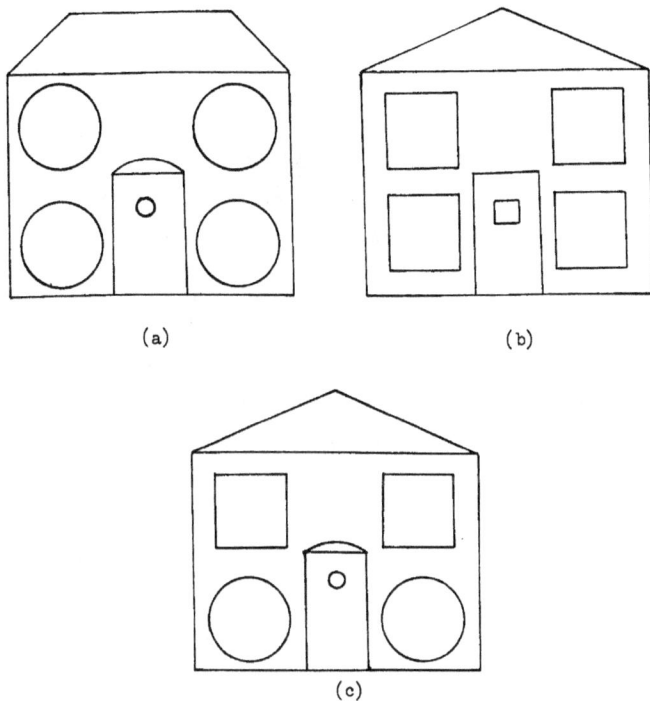

(a)          (b)

(c)

Figure 3.8  The two 'basic houses ('a' and 'b') to be sorted by
and an example of a variation.

## Materials

A set of drawings of schematic houses was prepared. In the first instance two 'basic' house designs were chosen, and they are shown in Figure 3.8 as 'type A' and 'type B'. As can be seen, the details of 'type A' are fairly square and angular in style, whereas those of 'type B' are rather more rounded. The houses on the set of cards to be sorted into two piles were each variations upon these basic houses and contained elements from each of them. Thus (as can be seen in Figure 3.8) one variation, for instance showed the roof and two upper windows of 'type B ' together with the door and two lower windows of 'type A'. The child could thus elect to sort according to any of four main features, i.e. type of roof, shape of upper windows, shape of lower windows, or door. This would allow the examiner to test whether the lower placed features, i.e. doors and lower windows, would be predominantly selected as crucial to the autistic children. Care was taken to draw the houses in complementary pairs (as in Figure 3.8).* That is, if one variation was modelled upon 'type A' with a few elements from 'type B', then a complementary drawing based upon 'type B' with the same elements changed to those of 'type A' was also included. A 'square' house having two rounded windows would always be complemented by a 'round' house with two square windows. In this way it was ensured that any consistent strategy of sorting would give rise to an equal number of houses being placed in each pile.

All the houses (Basic and variations) were drawn in black ink upon white card 10 cm x 8 cm in size. Figure 3.8 shows full scale examples of the drawings. In total, twenty variations were prepared modelled upon the two basic houses.

---

* This was omitted in error. A fourth house with upper features from type A and lower ones from type B should also have been shown

TABLE 3.4          Subjects in house sorting study

| Group | N | Mean C.A. (s.d.) | Mean full IQ (s.d.) |
|-------|---|------------------|---------------------|
| Autistic | 9 | 11.66 yrs (2.21) | 62.89 (15.24) |
| ESN | 9 | 11.82 yrs (2.10) | 60.91 (8.12) |

For reasons that will be made clear in the procedure section, additional sets of variations were prepared, each based upon two new basic houses. For example, twenty variations were drawn modelled upon two roofless basic houses and another set based upon two doorless basic houses.

## Subjects

In all, eighteen children took part in this experiment. Nine of these were autistic children, who were randomly chosen from the twenty who took part in the previous study. No age factor was included, because the good ability of the autistic children to recognize lower facial features was found across both age levels. The remaining nine subjects were those subnormal children from the last study who were matched with these nine autistic children according to mental and chronological age. Details of the subjects are given in Table 3.4.

## The Testing Procedure

All children were tested individually in a quiet room. The experimenter placed the two drawings of the basic houses (type A and type B) on a table in front of the child. The child was then given the set of twenty variations upon these two basic houses and was told that they were drawings of houses which looked like the two already displayed. The child was then instructed to "put those houses which look like this one (pointing to type A) here (pointing to a place adjacent to type A) and those which look like this one (pointing to type B) here (pointing to as adjacent spot)". No indication was given to the child as to how he was to sort. To avoid the confusion which might have arisen from too many houses being visible at one time, the houses already sorted and those yet to be sorted were kept face downwards (leaving only the two basic houses continuously visible).

When the child had completed his sorting of the cards the
experimenter examined the two piles to ascertain the most likely feature
(or possibly features) by which the child had sorted. This was invariably
quite easy to do as, for example, all the houses with 'type A' roofs
would be in the pile by 'type A', and similarly for 'type B'. Following
this, the feature used by the child as his sorting criterion was omitted
from the drawings of the next two 'basic' houses. Thus, in the above
example, the old cards would be removed from sight and two new basic
houses displayed; these were identical to types A and B but without
roofs.

As was mentioned in the materials section, variations upon these
new basic houses were also drawn, and these were now given to the
child. Once again, identical instructions were given which directed
the child to sort according to similarity.

The rationale behind the removal of the crucial sorting feature was
that the subsequent results would give an idea as to the hierarchy of
importance of the features for the two groups of children. Thus, for
example, if the autistic children tend to look at the lower halves of
things, then we would expect them to sort according to a lower feature
regardless of the stimuli. If they were indeed found to sort by a
lower feature in the first run then this might arguably be due to
an imbalance in the design of the houses. Buf if, when the lower
feature in question is removed the autistic child goes on to sort
according to another lower feature, then perceptual bias in these
children may be inferred (although, of course, such an interpretation
is dependent upon the performance of the ESN subjects).

TABLE 3.5    Number of children in each group who sorted by each
of the characteristics

| Type of Child | Basic houses | | When no roof | | When no upper windows |
| | By roof | By upper windows | By door | By upper windows | By roof |
|---|---|---|---|---|---|
| Autistic | 8 | 1 | 8 | 0 | 1 |
| Subnormal | 9 | 0 | 8 | 1 | 0 |

(N = 9)

Results

The results are shown in Table 3.5 . They were very clear-cut and
did not support the hypothesis that autistic children tended to look
at the lower half of objects. Both groups of children chose to sort
by the roofs in the first run, with the sole exception of one autistic
child who sorted according to the shape of the upper windows. Of
those children who sorted by the roofs, all except one went on to
sort the 'roofless' houses by their door type. The exception was an
ESN child who went on to sort by the upper windows. Finally, the
autistic child who sorted by upper windows in the first run was found
to sort by the roofs when no upper windows were present. No support
can be gathered from these results to infer that the autistic child
is in any way abnormal in his scanning of objects.


Discussion

Clearly, the autistic children performed almost identically to
the ESN subjects in their sorting of schematic houses. Both groups
chose to sort according to an upper feature - the roof - even though
it may be noted that the number of upper and lower elements were the
same (although this is not to imply that the drawings were in some
sense 'perfectly balanced' in their upper and lower features).

With this upper feature absent, both types of children tended
to switch to sorting by a lower feature (the door), as one might
expect from looking at the somewhat door-dominated appearance of the
roofless houses.

It could, of course, be argued that these particular stimuli
were not closely comparable to the faces used in the previous study.
However, in schematic form there is a fair similarity between faces

and the type of house picture used in this study. In fact, it might be argued that real faces contain more salient information in their upper halves than do such schematic houses. Thus, if a bias towards lower halves of faces was found for the autistic children, then an even larger bias might have been expected for them with the houses.

Caution must be exercised in drawing a causal connection between sorting strategies and scanning behaviour (after all, we may tend to visually fixate people's eyes and yet still choose to sort a selection of faces according to such criteria as sex, age, presence or absence of facial hair, etc.). However, taking our knowledge of autism as a whole, this study would seem to give further evidence that no such simple phenomenon can explain the results obtained in the face-identification study. It would seem, therefore, somewhat unlikely that autistic children's good knowledge of lower facial features is the result of their possessing a proclivity to scan the lower area of all things.

## Summary and Conclusion

The hypothesis that the autistic child's abnormally good knowledge of lower facial features is due to their looking at the lower halves of all objects was tested. They were given a task in which they had to sort a selection of schematic houses into two piles. The manner in which they sorted these indicated that they did not tend to scan the lower half of the houses. Their strategy for sorting was found to be almost identical to that of ESN children who were matched for age and general IQ. Thus the contention that autistic children tend to look at the lower half of things was rejected.

## 3.3 Lip-Reading

In the face perception experiment, it was found that the autistic children were remarkably good at recognizing the lower halves of faces. Two possibilities were proposed to explain this, and it was noted that these implied opposite expectations about the lip-reading ability of autistic children. On the one hand it was suggested that an inability to fully extract information from the auditory component of speech might lead the autistic child to have an abnormally great reliance upon the visual cues given by the mouth. Thus a tendency to lip-read more frequently than a normal child could lead to a better-than-normal knowledge of the lower facial features. In consequence, it would be expected that the autistic child's lip-reading ability would be somewhat better than that of mental age matched controls, and their reliance upon such cues to be somewhat greater.

On the other hand, the autistic children may possess a fairly normal, or even poor, ability to lip-read and yet be unable to integrate the two types of information from the speech-sounds and the visual movement of the lips. Such a lack of ability to bring the two types of information together into a coherent unity, might lead to increased attention to these sources of confusion. If the child's attention were to be drawn to the mouth, he may get to know the lower facial area well. However he would not be expected to possess a particularly good lip-reading ability, nor would one expect to find indications of an abnormally enhanced attention to the visual aspects of speech in contrast to the auditory components.

To investigate these possibilities, two routes may be taken: a direct one and an indirect one. The indirect route involves a study of the face perception abilities of hard-of-hearing subjects who are known to lip-read. If the supposition that such activity leads to an enhanced knowledge of the mouth area should turn out to be untrue, this would invalidate the first of the above hypotheses. The more direct way is to investigate the autistic child's lip-reading ability in comparison to that of subnormal children matched for mental and chronological age. In particular, it would be interesting to discover whether the contribution of lip-reading to speech perception is similar in both autistic and subnormal children.

First, a study of face perception in deaf and hard-of-hearing subjects will be reported, followed by an investigation of the lip-reading abilities of autistic children.

### 3.3.1 Recognition of peer's faces by hard-of-hearing subjects

Hermelin (1978) has made the point that there are two basic and contrasting approaches to the experimental study of autism. The more usual of these is to match autistic with other children of like cognitive ability who do not show any autistic symptoms. Any group differences thus obtained, assuming that the criteria for matching were valid, may be ascribed to the autistic children's "autism" rather than to general cognitive deficits. However, the alternative approach can often lead to equally enlightening findings. In this, autistic children and children with another well-defined impairment but different cognitive ability (the deaf or blind for example) are presented with an experimental task, and the results are scrutinized for communalities in spite of IQ differences between the two groups. Hermelin and O'Connor were able to show that autistic childen at times performed as if they were deaf, and at other times as if they were blind.

TABLE 3.6       Hard-of-hearing subjects' details

| N | Mean Full IQ | Mean chronological Age |
|---|---|---|
| 5 | 70.80 (sd = 4.76) | 27.60 (sd = 8.56) |

In the study of face perception in autistic children, it has been shown that there are differences between their performance and that of matched controls, which may be ascribed to their autism. However, the second approach may now be useful in deciding which of the several hypotheses raised to explain the results might be true. One of these was that the autistic child may have a proclivity to lip-read. Consequently, it may be useful to investigate the face perception abilities of subjects who are known to lip-read in everyday life. To this end a number of the tasks given to the children in the previous face perception experiment were also given to a small sample of hard-of-hearing subjects.

## The subjects who took part

The object of this study was not to match a set of subjects to the autistic sample on the basis of such factors as mental or chronological age. Instead, five hard-of-hearing adults were used who were all inpatients of one hospital. Details of these are given in Table 3.6. Although no attempt at matching was made, the subjects each had to meet two criteria: first they should be proficient at lip-reading and known to be using this ability in their daily life; second, they were chosen to be of below average intelligence such that their mental level was not greatly at variance with that of the autistic children used in the previous face perception study. None of these subjects had any specific deficit other than hearing loss and, in particular, none showed any autistic symptoms.

## Materials

As with the previous face identification experiment, black and white photographs were prepared with the same attention to details as was outlined in the 'materials' section of the previous study;

the pictures were of the same size with natural poses, no

distinguishing features, etc. The same cardboard masks were utilized

once again to present isolated areas of the faces. The faces used in

this study were those of members of staff at the hospital unit where

the subjects lived. It was decided not to use photographs of the

subjects themselves as this would limit the number of faces they had

to choose from. The staff members were well known to all the subjects;

and there were ten such photographs in all.

## The experimental procedure

This study was essentially a rerun of the previous experiment but

using the hard-of-hearing subjects, and fewer masking conditions. It

was decided that the subjects' performance on the upper and lower

upright halves was of prime importance; thus only two conditions

showing upper features, and two showing lower features, were used:

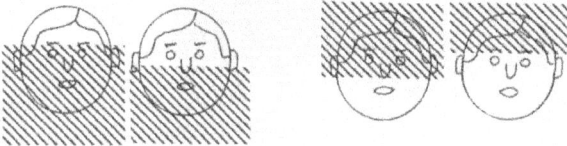

Once again, the subject was asked to guess whose face was being

shown to him. He was told that they were photographs of people in the

hospital. First, each subject saw just the 'mouth and chin' of one

of the faces:

When he had made his guess, the mask was removed to reveal the area up to and including the eyes:

Having either reaffirmed the face's identify or given his new guess, the next of the ten faces was presented in an identical manner. When all twenty faces had been seen in these two conditions, the photographs were thoroughly randomized before showing just the forehead of one of them:

The subject made his guess as to whose face it was, and then the mask was lowered to just below the eyes - at which point the subject was asked if he still thought it was the same person or whether he thought it was someone else:

When a response was given, the next face was presented under the same two conditions. This was repeated until the subject had seen all ten photographs under all conditions.

Finally, the subject was shown all the faces in a normal uncovered upright mode and asked to identify the people. If he made a mistake on a face in this run through, his previous errors on that face were discounted for the purpose of analysis.

TABLE 3.7    Average percent errors by each group on each
condition (see section 3.1)

| Group | Condition | | | |
|---|---|---|---|---|
| | Mouth and Chin (Low$_1$) | Eyes downwards (Low$_3$) | Forehead (Up$_1$) | Eyes upwards (Up$_2$) |
| Deaf | 48.02 | 24.46 | 48.44 | 27.80 |
| Older autistic | 26.52 | 4.31 | 15.61 | 8.28 |
| Younger autistic | 35.19 | 7.64 | 60.69 | 29.42 |
| Older normal (C.A.) | 68.90 | 20.30 | 24.40 | 7.20 |
| Older normal (M.A.) | 77.70 | 35.50 | 38.40 | 21.00 |

Results

The percentage of correct scores for the four conditions, along with those of the normal subnormal and autistic children from the previous experiment, are given in Table 3.7. Due to the small number of subjects who took part in this experiment, no attempt was made to compare these results statistically. Indeed, the basic aim of this study was not to undertake such a strict inter-group comparison of each condition, but rather to determine whether or not it was readily apparent that differences existed between the groups in their pattern of performance. This having been said, however, the performance of the normal and subnormal children on these four conditions was very homogeneous, both between groups and over the entire age range. Thus on the basis of such factors as chronological and mental age, there are few grounds for expecting the hard-of-hearing subjects' average percentage correct scores to be particularly different from those of the previous study's control children.

Clearly, though, this is not totally the case for the hard-of-hearing subjects performed rather better than did those other subjects on the condition in which only the mouth and chin were present. Thus the common-sense prediction that lip-reading may lead to an enhanced knowledge of the mouth area would seem to have gained some support. It is worthy of note that this is the only condition in which the hard-of-hearing subjects' performance was substantially different from that of the normal or subnormal children. [*]

On the other hand, the results obtained from the autistic children are quite different from those of all the other subjects on all the conditions, except that in which the face is visible from

---

[*] Footnote: The hard-of-hearing subjects did not differ from the normal subjects matched-for-M.A. on "Up2."

the eyes upwards ($Up_2$). Both groups of autistic children are still substantially better than all the others on the lower facial features ($Low_1$ and $Low_3$). The hard-of-hearing subjects are certainly better than the 'control' groups on the 'mouth and chin only' condition, but their performance here does not seem as exceptional as that of the autistic children.

Of course, too much emphasis should not be placed upon these scores for there are many uncontrolled factors involved. However, on the whole, it may be seen that the normal and subnormal children tend to be better on the upper features than the lower and they are certainly better when the eyes are available compared to when they are not. In contrast, the hard-of-hearing subjects seem to possess a more 'balanced' knowledge of the face - 'balanced' in as much as their knowledge of the uppermost and lowermost areas is almost the same:

$Up_1$

48.44%

$Low_1$

48.02%

The same is true of the areas from the eyes downwards and the eyes upwards:

$Low_3$

24.46%

$Up_2$

27.80%

The younger autistic children thus had a better knowledge of the lower facial features than the upper ones. The subnormal and normal children by contrast had a better knowledge of the upper features than the lower ones. Both the hard-of-hearing subjects and the older autistic children had a more homogeneous knowledge of the face. However, the two autistic groups both showed a much better knowledge of the lower areas than the hard-of-hearing subjects.

## What conclusions can be drawn?

The fact that the hard-of-hearing subjects found it easier to recognize the faces from just the mouth and chin area than the normal and subnormal children tends to support the thesis that habitual lip-reading enhances the knowledge of this area. Equally, the pattern of scores bears this out in as far as it shows that relative to their own scores on the other conditions, the hard-of-hearing subjects' knowledge of the mouth area is better. However, their percentage correct scores on this condition are not as impressive as those of the autistic children, and thus it would seem that a lip-reading propensity cannot be the full explanation for the autistic children's performance. Certainly, as far as the recognition of faces from the eyes downwards is concerned, the autistic children are still far and away the best performers. Thus it could still be argued that autistic children's attention to the mouth area of a face does not imply that they attempt to lip-read. Their excellence at recognizing the lower portions may merely reflect a greater capability to identify spatial patterns than that of the hard-of-hearing subjects. The next logical step would seem to be to examine the autistic children's lip-reading abilities.

TABLE 3.8    Subjects in study of contribution of lip-reading to
speech perception

| Group | N | Mean C.A. (sd) | Mean full IQ (sd) |
|-------|---|----------------|-------------------|
| Autistic | 6 | 14.42 yrs (1.52) | 65.33 (14.09) |
| ESN | 6 | 14.20 yrs (1.12) | 62.67 (9.12) |

3.3.2.  Lip-Reading by Autistic Children

It will be recalled that there was no statistically significant difference between the two groups of autistic children's abilities to recognize the faces from the mouth and chin only. Thus in an investigation of the lip-reading abilities of these children, the factor of age is not of particular concern. With this in mind, it was decided to select a sample of six autistic children from those who took part in the original face perception experiment and to give these children a simple test of their ability to lip-read. Details of the children selected are given in Table 3.8. In order to have some 'norm' against which to compare the results of the autistic children, a group of six control subjects were also tested. Bearing in mind that the subnormal and normal children's performances on the 'mouth only' condition were almost identical, a selection of subnormal children were chosen as a comparison group. These ESN children were six of those who took part in the original experiment and were chosen to match the autistic children for general IQ and chronological age. The details of these children may also be found in Table 3.8.

Procedure and method

In this experiment the child was required to lip-read the names of some of his peers. To have presented the names by silently 'mouthing' them could have led to too many errors of apparent articulation, placement of vowels etc. Thus in order to avoid such complications the children were fitted with noise-reducing headphones. With these in place the child was quite unable to hear a whispered word at about a metre away from the speaker.

Each child was tested separately in a quiet room free from distraction. He was told that he was going to have some headphones on, which would not allow him to hear what was being said to him. The experimenter made it clear to the child that he would see him say the names of some of his classmates/schoolmates. At this point five photographs of the faces of peers of the subject were placed in a row on a table in front of him. The child was asked to point to the face of the person whose name he thought the experimenter had said. The noise-reducing headphones were then put in position and the experimenter whispered the name of each of the represented peers in random order, naming each twice in all. No feedback was given to the child as to whether his guesses were right or wrong.

## Results

The autistic and subnormal groups were equally good at this task: the ESN children obtained a mean percentage correct score of 79.17% (s.d. = 20.60), and the autistic children an average of 73.33% (s.d. = 22.51). There was no significant difference between these means ( $t = 0.47$; $d.f. = 10$).

## Discussion

No attempt was made to match the stimuli used in this study, with the consequence that one group may have had an objectively easier task than the other (the peers' names for the two groups were of course not identical). Thus, the results really only reveal that the autistic children could lip-read, although this in itself is perhaps an interesting and salient finding.

Having established that autistic children can lip-read and that
they may be able to do so as well as matched ESN controls, it seemed
worthwhile to investigate their lip-reading abilities further.  In
order to do this the lip-reading task utilized by Dodd (1977) was
employed in an adapted form.  The reason for choosing this procedure
was that it not only provides a more thorough test of lip-reading
ability by use of matched stimuli, but it also allows the quantification
of the extent to which lip-reading contributes towards speech perception
in the child.  Dodd found that in normal speech-perception by children,
the contributions of what was seen and what was heard were statistically
equal.  However, if the two sensory sources were made to compete by
giving the child disparate auditory and visual information, vision was
found to dominate over hearing in the determination of what the child
reported that he perceived.

For several reasons, Dodd's experiment could not be repeated in
its original form with the children used in the present experiments.
Perhaps the greatest difficulty was the time which it would have taken
to establish the lip-reading ability of autistic children and match
this with an 'auditory-only' presentation (Dodd's subjects took up to
100 trials to reach her criteria).  Consequently it was decided to
assume the results that Dodd found for normal children with respect to
there being an equal contribution of sight and hearing to speech
perception under normal circumstances and to see if the autistic
children also showed the reported dominance of vision when the two
modalities were put in opposition.

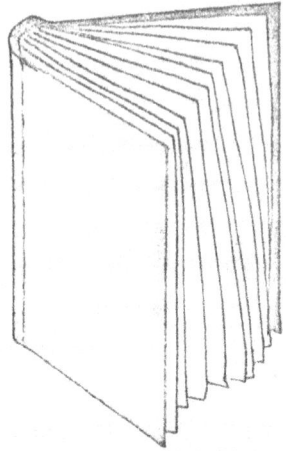

Figure 3.9. Four pictures to choose from in the lip-reading study ("house" was seen, "book" was heard and "boy" was the related distractor).

### 3.3.3 The Contribution of Lip-Reading to Speech Perception

Materials

Given that it is meaningful to describe autistic children as having a language deficit (Rutter, 1974, 1978), it was decided to keep the language content of this necessarily highly 'language loaded' study to a minimum. To ensure this, the children were not required to make a verbal response to the experimenter's questions but were requested to point to pictures of objects instead.

The first step was to give the child a test of his lip-reading abilities using a standardized list of words. It was felt that one of the most important factors determining the choice of these words was that they be equally familiar to each of the children. The choice of words was also restrained by the decision that they should be monosyllabic and lend themselves easily to visual representation. When dealing primarily with subnormal children rather than abnormal ones, it might have been possible to use Mein's Word List (Mein & O'Connor, 1960, Mein, 1961). This would have allowed a selection of words of high frequency for subnormal children. However, such studies have not been undertaken on the vocabularies of autistic children. Autistic children, being known for their verbal idiosyncrasies, may have vocabularies which differ considerably from that of their subnormal peers with similar overall mental ability. To circumvent this difficulty, the classroom materials in both the autistic and subnormal schools were inspected and material was found in the form of packs of cards which were in general use as aids to language learning. These cards each showed a simple picture depicting common objects with monosyllabic names (Appendix I gives a full list of those used). Examples of the pictures may be found in Figure 3.9 Each child's teacher was asked to confirm that the child knew the names of all the chosen schematized objects.

In addition to these materials, some electronic equipment was also used in the auditory presentation of the words: this included a tape recorder, microphone and headphones. The names of the objects depicted on the above-mentioned cards were read onto a tape to provide a standard source of auditory information. A constant volume amplifier was also employed in order to maintain constant loudness of the presentation of these words. A white noise generator coupled with an attenuator (graduated in decibels) was used to vary the difficulty of perceiving the words presented from the tape. Finally, noise-reducing headphones were once again used in the test of lip-reading.

## The procedure

Step one: The child was first shown all the pictures which he would see in the course of the experiment and was asked to name each of them. If the child's spontaneous label for an item differed from that which had been used in the list of words (such as calling a 'ship' a 'yacht') then he was corrected and told: "No, we'll call this a ship". This procedure ensured that the children knew the names of the stimuli and that they were all equally well informed as to the specific names given to the pictures within this study's context.

Five of the pictures were then set out in a row in front of the child, and as in the last experiment, he was told that he would wear headphones which would not allow him to hear what the experimenter was saying. Again, it was made clear to the child that he would see the names of the objects mouthed and should point to which of them he thought had been named. The noise-reducing headphones were then placed over his ears, and the name of one of the objects was whispered. The

child was quite unable to pick up any auditory cues. This process
was repeated twenty times, and each time the child had five randomly
chosen pictures to choose from. The percentage correct thus obtained
by the child was noted down to be used in the next step.

Step two: For this stage of the experiment, the child was fitted
with ordinary headphones into which white noise could be fed at a
controllable level. These headphones were also connected to a tape
recorder on which had been recorded the names of all the pictures used
during the first step. The intention of this stage of the proceedings
was to ascertain what level of noise would need to be mixed with the
constant-volume presentation of the words in order for the child to
get the same average percentage correct as he had obtained with vision
alone in step one. The criterion for ascertaining the level of noise
was that the child should obtain the same number of items correct out
of the twenty presented at a particular noise level as he had done in
the lip-reading task alone.

To do this, a "method of limits" was employed in which the
experimenter first estimated the level of noise which would produce the
required percentage correct score. The child then had ten of the
pictures placed before him and heard each of their names against the
white noise background in a random order. His task was to point to the
picture of the object which he had heard named - no spoken response was
required. There was also no feedback given as to how well he was
performing.

Inevitably, the estimated noise level would prove to be too high
or too low, thus another estimate was made on the other side of the

required level; for example, if the child had achieved a percentage correct score of eighty in the visual-only (lip-reading) condition, and if the first estimate of the necessary noise level returned an approximate average of 60%, then the noise level which would return a performance of between 90% and 100% was estimated. It was then a relatively simple matter to deduce by mathematical means the noise level which would be required to meet the criterion. If Xmin is the first percentage correct score, Xmax is the one which is higher than the criterion, and Xcri is that of the criterion; and if Ymin is the attenuation in decibels of the noise corresponding to Xmin, and Ymax is that corresponding to Xmax, then Ycri, which is the level that we seek, is:

$$\frac{Xcri - Xmin}{Xmax - Xmin} \text{ x } (Ymax - Ymin) + Ymin = \underline{Ycri}$$

Thus, in the example above, if a 25 dB attenuation was associated with 60% correct, and a 35 dB attenuation of noise produced 90% correct, and the goal was to find that level which is needed to return 80%, then the formula could be used to deduce that a 2/3 increase in percentage correct corresponds to a 2/3 decrease in noise, which is approximately 32 dB.

The noise level was then set at the calculated value and twenty trials were given to establish its accuracy. In each of the trials the subject had a different set of five pictures from which he had to pick the one which he had heard named. In practice, the level of noise deduced in this manner was found to be within 1 dB or 2 dB of the required value.

By using this method, the matching of the child's ability on the visual-only and on the auditory-only conditions could be engineered in a minimum of time. This was important for several reasons. For instance, the autistic children were found to become distressed if they were required to listen to the white noise for too long; in addition, this method meant that each child took very nearly the same number of trials to reach the criterion, with the consequence that they all had almost precisely the same exposure to the experimental materials and situation.

With the percentage correct scores on the visual and auditory only conditions being set as equal it was now possible to create a 'dubbed' condition in which the child heard one word and saw another one mouthed. To do this the level of white noise was kept constant for each child and a pre-recorded list of words was played. However, this was done in such a way that the child could not be certain whether he was hearing the words directly from the tape or via a microphone which the experimenter was holding. Due to the employment of a constant volume amplifier there was no detectable difference between words spoken by the experimenter which had been recorded on the tape and those presented live via the microphone.

It should be noted that many of the instructions had been given to the child whilst the headphones were in place, by the use of the microphone. Thus each child had become accustomed both to listening to a tape recording and to the experimenter speaking via the amplification system. The instructions now given were to look at the experimenter and point to the picture of the object that he said. By phrasing the instruction in the form: "What did I say?" the implication of whether 'seen' or 'heard' was meant was avoided.

The sound of a brief 'knock' was recorded onto the tape two seconds prior to each of the words. This sound was recorded at such a low level that the child was unaware of its presence. However it allowed the experimenter to synchronize the seen and heard words. The process was practiced many times prior to running the experiment with the children in order that the synchrony could be as near perfect as possible.

Once again the pictures of objects were used. In each trial the child would have four of these placed on the table in front of him One of the pictures was of the word he was to hear and one of the word he was to see the experimenter mouth. A third was what may be termed a 'related distractor' because it was of a word which had either its beginning or its end in common with either the heard or the seen word. The final picture was of an object whose name bore no resemblance at all to either the seen or the heard word. Thus for one trial the four cards may have been:

| HEARD | SEEN | RELATED | UNRELATED |
|-------|------|---------|-----------|
| Tree | House | Train | Boy |

The 'unrelated distractor' was included to control for guessing.

A series of five trials like this were run at the level of noise determined previously for that child in the auditory-only condition.

It was mentioned in the introduction to this section that Dodd (1977) has found that when the two inputs are set in competition as above (by creating an equal percentage correct in each modality separately), then subjects tend to report more of the seen words than those heard. The

above five trials averaged across the subjects in each group thus allows
the determination of whether such a visual dominance exists for the
autistic and subnormal children.

If this is so, then it would be of interest to know to what degree
the children rely upon the visual rather than the auditory information.
To investigate this, the noise level was reduced in four steps of two
decibels each, with five trials being run at each of these steps (with
the exception of the final step where only four trials were run due to
a shortage of appropriate materials).

As was mentioned above, autistic children may have an abnormal
tendency to rely upon visual input rather than auditory. Thus, even
if the noise level is decreased, the autistic children might still
report what they saw rather than what they heard. In contrast, the
subnormal children might exhibit a more normal reliance upon auditory
cues as the noise is reduced. It is possible that visual dominance may
only be present when the two modalities are in direct competition. If
the child's reliance upon one modality is greater than the other, then
it would be expected that words presented in that dominant modality
would always be more readily reported. Thus, by setting the noise level
such that auditory and visual presentations alone result in equal scores,
modality dominance becomes apparent when the two stimulus sources are
in direct conflict. Additionally, as the noise is reduced, one could
expect the subnormals to quickly switch to reporting what they heard.

There is also the possibility that the autistic child's attention
is drawn to the mouth because he sees it as a source of confusion over

TABLE 3.9    Mean percentage correct by each group when lip-reading
             words, and the mean level of noise required by each
             group so that the auditory-only scores were equivalent
             to the visual-only ones.  (Note that the higher the dB
             value, the lower the noise level)

| Group | Visual only (lip reading) | Level of noise to obtain same score on auditory-only (dB) |
|---|---|---|
| Autistic | 82.5% (sd = 10.84) | 28.3 (sd = 0.98) |
| ESN | 83.3% (sd = 22.51) | · 33.5 (sd = 5.01) |

what he hears.  If, as suggested earlier, this is the reason for the
autistic child's knowledge of the mouth region, then he should not tend
to report the visually presented words more than the heard ones when
the two modalities are in conflict.  In addition, the effect of reducing
the noise should only be that the autistic child reports the heard
words with increasing accuracy.

Hence, two opposing sets of propositions may be derived from the
hypotheses outlined at the beginning of this section.

Results

First, it can be said that the autistic children were as able as
the ESN subjects at the basic test of lip-reading (the visual-only task;
t = 0.08 ; df = 10) - but not more so.  However, a suprising result
emerged from the auditory-only task, in which an attempt was made to
match the percentage correct with that on the previous lip-reading task.
Surprisingly, the autistic children were found to require a higher
average level of white noise to match an equal level of percentage
correct as the ESN children (t =2.24;df = 10 p< 0.01).  That is, the
autistic children's ability to report the words which they heard was
significantly less affected by the masking white noise than was the
ability of the subnormal children (see Table 3.9).

i)   The Subnormal children and the 'balanced'condition:

Contrary to expectation, the ESN children did not perform in the
manner which Dodd (1977) reported for normal children on the 'dubbed'
condition.  When the level of noise was set such that each child had an
equal ability to identify the words when they could only hear them or
see them, then with the two modalities in conflict the ESN children

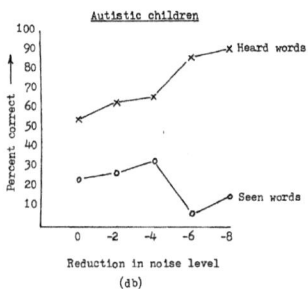

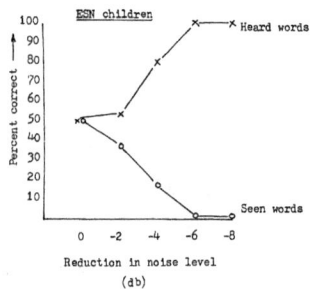

Figure 3.10  Average percent correct reported of seen and heard words by each of the groups - using a 'relative' scoring method.

reported the heard and seen words with equal frequency (t = 0.41 ; df =10, p ⟩ 0.1). Interestingly, this reflected a 50% efficiency in each modality (thus, with an 80% correct average with each modality alone, the percentage correct in each modality fell to about 40% each in the dubbed condition). As the noise level was reduced in two decibel steps, the first step had no apparent effect at all, but the next step brought a sudden and substantial swing towards dominance of the auditory input over the visual one (see Figure 3.11) (t=3.86; df=10, p⟨0.01).

Further reduction of the noise increased this tendency to report what was heard and not what was seen. By the final reduction of noise the ESN children were reporting what they heard with almost total accuracy, totally ignoring (or at least not reporting) the visual input (t=25.4; df=10, p⟨0.001).

(ii) The autistic children and the 'balanced' condition:

The picture presented by the results of the autistic children was rather different. In the first place they did not exhibit an equipartition of response at the initial stage in which the two modalities were in direct conflict. Instead, they showed a significantly greater tendency to report what they heard rather than what they saw (t = 1.85; df = 10, p⟨0.05 - see Figure 3.10). As was the case with the subnormal children, their tendency to report the heard items increased as the noise level was lowered. However, the decrease in noise level had a somewhat weaker effect upon the autistic children's responses. In fact, using an 'absolute' method of scoring (where responses given to the related distractor were scored as incorrect) there was no significant difference in the autistic children's average percentage correct responses to the heard words with various levels of noise (the minimum was 63.3%, the maximum was 83.3%. t = 1.51 - see

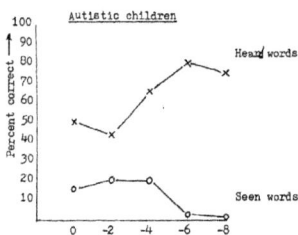
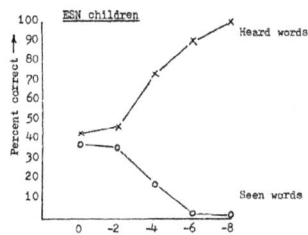

Figure 3.11  Average percent correct reported of seen and heard words by each of the groups - using an 'absolute' scoring method.

Figure 3.11). Even when the responses to the related-distractors were counted as correct (as in the previously mentioned Figure 3.11), only the minimum and maximum average percentage correct scores differed (minimum = 70%, maximum = 91.7%, t = 2.16, p < 0.05). In a similar manner, their percentage correct responses to the seen words also underwent less change as the noise was decreased (the maximum and minimum average percentage correct scores did not differ by either scoring method). It is possible, however, that the low average percentage correct score at the first stage (prior to noise reduction) was such that a significant lowering of performance in this modality could hardly occur. Nonetheless, we may note that neither did their ability to report the seen words fall to zero by the last step of noise reduction, nor did their ability to report the heard words rise to the almost errorless performance of the ESN subjects.

## Discussion

First in this study, the autistic children were as able as the subnormal subjects at lip-reading. In itself, this may be seen as one point against the suggestion that autistic children make greater use of lip-read cues than others. This idea is further contradicted when it is considered that the autistic children were also not found to possess an abnormally great reliance upon lip-read cues in the 'dubbed' condition. In fact, the opposite appeared to be the case, and the autistic subjects had a greater tendency to report what they heard than what they saw. However, the effect of reducing the noise level was far less dramatic for the autistics than for the subnormals. If it is suggested that the tendency to report the heard words before the noise was reduced was due to them selectively attending to the auditory input, then the problem immediately arises of explaining why the noise reduction had little effect. One would have expected that if the child possessed a tendency to attend to the auditory modality rather than the visual, any changes which made perception of the heard words easier would have been expected to facilitate the reporting of these words.

Clearly, there are too many uncontrolled variables in this study to allow any firm conclusions. However, some suggestions may be offered which might provide a basis for some further research. In attempting to account for the above findings, it would be well to consider the other unexpected result that came out of this study: the autistic children tended, on average, to put up with more noise to achieve an average percentage correct score in the auditory-only condition than ESN children. This may be connected with Hermelin & O'Connor's (1968) finding that autistic children are more aroused by continuous white noise than are matched subnormal controls. If it is proposed that a higher level of arousal might heighten attentiveness, then for the autistic children in the present study, it may be suggested that the increase in noise level served two ant_agonistic functions: (1) to mask the signal and thus make it less easy to discriminate; (2) to increase attention to the auditory modality and thus enhance perception of the items which were heard.

This explanation is tentative and obviously not the only one which might be put forward; however, looking at the autistic children's percentage correct scores on the heard words it can be seen that as the noise was reduced their performance hardly changed at all. In the light of the above it may be suggested that as the noise level became lower, the

autistic children simultaneously became less attentive to the auditory
stimuli and yet more able to perceive them; thus, the relatively gradual
increase in the average percentage correct scores may be seen as the
result of these two antoagonistic factors. Nonetheless, we should not
consider the auditory component in isolation, either within the context
of this study or in 'real life' situations. Consequently, the question
remains why the presence of the noise did not also enhance the autistic
children's ability to report the words they saw too. That is, what
reason could there be for an auditory predominance when the two modalities
are set in direct conflict?

It might be conjectured, for instance, that the autistic children
were not tending to integrate the disparate pieces of information into
a unified perception. Clearly, some competition for response selection
was present or else they would have reported the seen-words and heard-
words equally frequently. But with some failure to integrate the inputs
of various modalities, one may speculate that arousing stimulation to
one modality (here, white noise to the auditory) increases sensitivity
specifically to items presented to that modality.* The suggestion that
the autistic children may have had a lesser propensity to integrate the
inputs was bolstered by the finding that two of the autistic children
responded to some of the trials by reporting correctly that they had
seen one word and heard another - which was never reported by any of
the subnormal children. In fact, being aware of the possibility that
the ESN children could equally well have been able to report both heard
and seen words but failed to do so because they felt a single response
was required, additional trials were run at a later date, and it was
specifically pointed out that what was heard and what was seen were
different. The subnormal children were requested to report both of the

---

* Footnote: or that a failure to integrate what was seen with what was heard reduced
the masking effect of the noise.

words and were found to be unable to do so. Instead they pointed
to just one of the choice of four pictures as they had done in the
experimental proceedings.

Evidence exists that human infants integrate what they see and
hear from birth (Wertheimer, 1961), and that by at least ten weeks
of age an infant is capable of detecting when lip-movements are out
of synchrony with the speech he is hearing (Dodd, inter alia), and
this is even the case when a non-native language is being presented
to the baby. In the light of such findings, it could be the case
that an apparent deficit in inter-modal integration in autistic
children has important implications for their ontogeny and can be
seen as an aspect which parallels that of an incompetence in cross-
modal transfer. Evidence for this has been reported in recent
literature (Hermelin, 1978). Such a proposition that autistic
children have problems with the integration of experiences is not
new, and references to it may be found scattered throughout the
writings on childhood autism (e.g. Rimland, 1964; Anthony, 1958).

The results pertaining to noise level and the perception of
aurally presented information needs to be more thoroughly investigated.
One way in which this might be approached would be to replicate the
"auditory only" part of the above experiment but with overall magnitude
of the input being the only variable. Thus having set a low level of
information input, which is overlaid with a similarly low level of noise

to produce an average correct reporting of the stimuli of, say 50 to 60%, the overall volume of the combined input could then be increased in equal decibel steps. For the ESN subjects it would be expected that the overall increase in volume would have little or no effect on their ability to report the words. However, for the autistic children it might be hypothesized that as the overall noise level was increased, so would their average percentage correct scores.

Concerning the sensory integration aspect, the autistic and subnormal children could be presented with a noise over-laid auditory input which was out of synchrony with the lip-movements of the presenter of the items. The performance in this condition would then be compared with that on an "auditory only" condition which utilized the same level of white noise. For the normal, and presumably the ESN children, the conflicting information provided by the out-of-synchrony visual input would cause a lower average percentage correct score than when such a conflicting input is absent (Dodd, 1977). On the other hand, if the autistic subjects were tending not to integrate the two inputs, then it would be expected that their performance on the two conditions would be almost identical. Although this experiment is not included in this thesis, the proposition that autistic children have problems with the integration of sensory data will be returned to later.

In conclusion, this study has mainly brought to light several interesting findings that are outside the scope of the present thesis[*] to follow up. Nonetheless, there would seem to be no support for the contention that the autistic children possess an abnormal tendency to

Footnote: A pilot study of this was run, though, and the results supported the idea that autistic persons have a perceptual integration deficit.

rely upon the visual modality when perceiving speech. In fact, when the two modalities were in conflict the autistic children tended to report what they heard rather than what they saw.

The most parsimonious explanation for the results would seem to be in terms of the children's abilities to integrate their perceptions. Whilst the subnormal children seemed to show evidence of such integration, the autistic children tended not to.

## Summary of the lip-reading studies

It was suggested that autistic children might possess a better-than-average knowledge of the mouth area of faces because they have a tendency to lip-read. Thus it was decided to approach the study of this possibility by examining the face perception ability of subjects known to lip-read in every-day life. Hard-of-hearing subjects were indeed found to know the lower facial regions generally better than did normal and other subnormal subjects. However, their ability to recognize the mouth area of peers' faces was not outstandingly good and was thus felt not to be truly comparable with that of the autistic children in the previous study.

The basic contention was also investigated by studying the lip-reading ability of autistic children in comparison to that of matched ESN children. It was noted that a tendency to look at the mouth area might occur for either of two quite different reasons: it may well be the case that autistic children lip-read, but it may also be that they are poor at integrating the seen and heard aspects of speech perception. The latter deficit might lead to confusion in the autistic child and thus to an enhanced attention to the sources of this confusion. It was thus decided that the first of these two possibilities would imply better-than-average lip-reading powers by autistic subjects and a greater-than-normal reliance upon such visual speech cues. The second possibility, in contrast, would not imply that autistic children would be any better than ESN children at lip-reading, indeed they may be worse. It was also not expected that an inability to integrate the two types of information would lead to an abnormal reliance upon the visual modality.

These possibilities were investigated using a method developed by Dodd (1977) in which the child heard one word and saw another being mouthed. This allowed testing for abnormal modality reliance. The results did not lend themselves to clear interpretation. However, it would seem unlikely that a dependency upon visual speech cues could explain the autistic children's knowledge of lower facial features. Instead, it appeared that a poor ability to integrate the two sources of information about spoken messages was implicated.

3.4  Further Studies of the Inverted Mode

3.4.1   Recognition of inverted halves of faces

In the initial study of face perception (section 3.1), it was found that the older autistic children were exceptionally good at recognising inverted faces. In contrast, the younger autistic children were no better at this than the normal and ESN children tested for comparison. It was therefore concluded that the findings could not be explained purely by reference to the social aspects of face perception. For instance, Yin (1970) has suggested that it is ones ability to discern the expression of an inverted face which makes it particularly difficult to recognise. The less sociable child would thus be expected to have least difficulty recognising inverted faces. However, the younger and less sociable autistic children (see Wing, 1976b) did worse than the older ones at recognising the inverted faces.

It was suggested that a child's scanning strategy might be partially determined by the existence of a 'focal centre', that is, a point or area of the face around which scanning is primarily centred[*]. It was further argued that normal and ESN children might have such a 'focal centre' as the eyes, and the evidence which emerged from the study suggested that the younger autistic children might have the mouth as a centre of scanning. The inversion of the face changes the position of the focal centre with respect to the other facial features, thus for the above three groups inversion of the stimulus might disrupt their scanning strategies.

---

[*]   There is evidence supporting the idea that normal adults have 'focal centres' around which their scanning of a face revolves (Walker-Smith et al., 1977).

In contrast, the older autistic children's fairly homogeneous knowledge of faces might indicate that they possess no such 'focal centre', and thus have no well-defined scanning strategy which could be disrupted by inversion of the stimulus. This suggestion might best be investigated by studying the children's eye movements while looking at inverted faces compared to their eye movements when viewing upright ones. A pilot study of their scanning when viewing upright faces will be presented near the end of this thesis; but it was not possible to carry out the full eye movement study with the older autistic children used in section 3.1.

However, a simpler explanation might also account for the older autistic children's results. It may be that they possess a better than normal knowledge of the mouths of faces and that the mouth area is much easier to recognise upside down than areas that other children know best. This suggestion has common sense validity insofar as the eye area has more elements comprising it than the mouth area. In other words, to recognise the eyes upside down one would have to be able to 'mentally rotate' more elements than when recognising inverted mouths. The fact that older autistic children were better able to recognise inverted faces than younger ones might be due to a maturational factor (it is known that older normal children are more able to identify faces from small areas than younger normal children; Goldstein and Mackenberg, 1966).

If the above is true, then one can predict that older autistic children would find inverted lower halves of faces to be considerably easier to recognise than inverted upper halves. To test this, older autistic children were required to identify inverted halves of peers' faces from black and white photographs. Their performance on this task was compared with that of a group of ESN children matched for age and general ability.

TABLE 3.10    Subjects in the study of ability to recognise
              inverted halves of faces

| Group | N | Mean C.A. (sd) | Mean Full IQ (sd) |
|-------|---|----------------|-------------------|
| Autistic | 10 | 14.17 yrs (1.42 yrs) | 66.70 (13.24) |
| ESN | 10 | 13.92 yrs (1.31 yrs) | 62.80 (8.41) |

## Subjects

The selection of subjects for this study was hampered by two factors. First, of the original ten 'older' autistic children, five were no longer available for testing. Second, because there had been a gap of some 18 months between this experiment and the one presented in section 3.1, the children involved were naturally older. Consequently any differences between the performance of the children in this study and the earlier one might be due to the nature of the task, or to the different photographs, or to the maturation of the subjects over the 18-month period. In an attempt to reduce these problems a new 'older' group of autistic children were chosen on a one-to-one basis to match the age and intelligence of the earlier group. Similar problems of course arose with the choice of ESN children to act as a comparison group. These problems were ameliorated in the same way by choosing a new 'older' ESN group which was matched one-to-one with the former group for age and intelligence. Table 3.10 gives details of the subjects.

## The materials used

As for the experiment in section 3.1, the stimuli for each group were black and white photographs of the faces of the members of that group, each measuring 14 cm by 10cm. A fresh set of photographs was made, of course, because not all members were present in the previous experiment, and this also avoided any advantage being given to a child who could remember the previous photographs. Precautions were once again taken to ensure that no clothing was visible in the pictures, and that they were all of evently good quality. Cardboard masks were again made so that the part of the face the child was not to see could be covered up.

TABLE 3.11    Mean percent correct for each group when recognising
              inverted upper and lower halves of faces

| Group | Inverted lower half | Inverted upper half |
|-------|---------------------|---------------------|
| Autistic | 70.00% | 72.00% |
| ESN | 47.40% | 51.24% |

## Methodology and Procedure

Each child was taken individually to a quiet room to be tested. The child was told that he would see 'upside-down pictures of the faces of children you know in the school'. The inverted pictures of upper and lower parts of the faces were presented one at a time in random order, and the child was asked to say whom he thought the photograph depicted. The upper inverted halves were equivalent to an inversion of the 'Up$_2$' condition from the last experiment. The lower inverted halves were equivalent to the invert of the 'Low$_2$' condition. Although the order of presentation was essentially random, certain contraints were imposed in that the two halves of the same face were not shown consecutively. This method was used in preference to one in which one half of all faces was presented before the child saw the other half, in order to reduce learning effects. Finally, each child was shown the whole of all the faces upright and uncovered, and if he was unable to identify any face in this run then his previous errors on that face were discounted.

## Results

The results are tabularised in table 3.11.

### 1.  The ESN children

As can be seen from the table, the ESN children were approximately as good at recognising each of the inverted halves (the difference was not significant in a related t-test; $t = 0.60$, $p > 0.1$, $df = 8$). Surprisingly, this group performed a little better on these inverted halves than the previous 'older' ESN group did on the full inverted face. However, the difference only reached significance for the comparison between the inverted whole face and the inverted upper half (a related t-test revealed $t = 2.39$, $df = 8$, $p < 0.05$). It is not clear why this should be so.

Comparing the present 'older' ESN group with the previous one on inverted and upright halves revealed significant differences. There was no difference between the previous ESN group's ability to recognise upright lower halves and the present ESN group's ability to recognise inverted lower halves (related t = 0.46, df = 8). However the performance on the inverted upper halves was significantly worse than on the upright upper halves (related t = 2.89, df = 8, p $<$ 0.025). Thus inversion of the faces had little effect on the ESN children's ability to recognise lower halves, but it significantly impaired their ability to recognise upper halves. This finding thus supports the initial proposal that recognition of upper half is more affected by inversion of the stimulus than is recognition of the lower half. It may well be then that the mouth area is easier to rotate mentally than is the eye area.

### The autistic children

The autistic children displayed equal ability to recognise faces from upper and lower inverted halves (related t = 0.31, df = 8, p $>$ 0.1). The autistic children in this study were as good at recognising inverted halves as the group in the previous study had been at recognizing whole inverted faces: full invert versus inverted $Up_2$ gave a related t = 0.27, full invert versus inverted $Low_2$ gave t = 0.05, and neither were significant at p = 0.1. Comparing their abilities at the inverted and upright halves revealed significant differences. They were better on upright lower halves than inverted ones (related t = 3.72, df = 8, p $<$ 0.01), and better on the upright upper halves than the inverted ones (related t = 3.96, df = 8, p $<$ 0.01).

Between group differences

The autistic children were considerably better at recognising faces from inverted lower halves than the ESN children (t = 2.14, df = 17, p < 0.025). The comparison of the groups' abilities to identify inverted upper halves showed a non-significant, but nonetheless clear, trend for the autistic children to be once again better (t = 1.62, df = 17, p < 0.08).

Summary of results

1. The ESN children got about half of the faces correct when viewing either upper, or lower inverted halves. The ability of the autistic children was about equal when requiring to tell identify from either inverted half and was generally better than that of the ESN children

Percentage correct scores

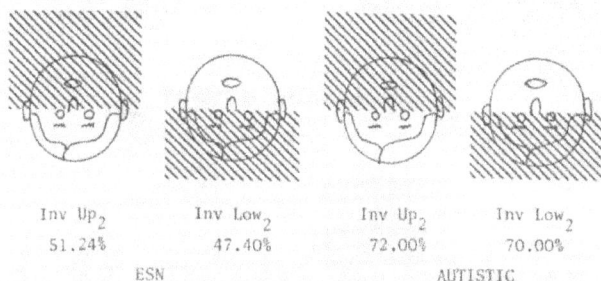

| Inv Up$_2$ | Inv Low$_2$ | Inv Up$_2$ | Inv Low$_2$ |
| 51.24% | 47.40% | 72.00% | 70.00% |
| ESN | | AUTISTIC | |

2. Comparison of the ESN children's ability to recognise inverted halves of faces in this study, with their recognition of upright faces in the previous study, showed that their ability to recognise upper halves was more affected by inversion than was their recognition of lower halves. This supports the contention that the lower half of the faces contains more easily mentally rotated features.

Percentage correct scores:

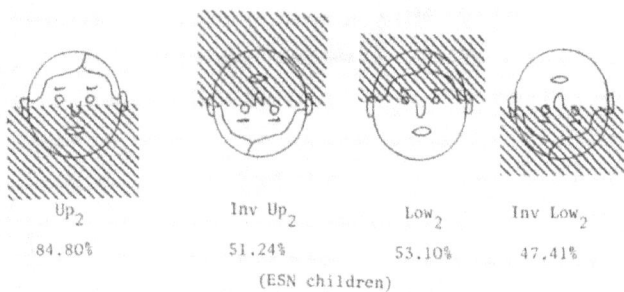

| Up$_2$ | Inv Up$_2$ | Low$_2$ | Inv Low$_2$ |
|--------|-----------|---------|-------------|
| 84.80% | 51.24% | 53.10% | 47.41% |

(ESN children)

3.   Inversion of the faces equally impaired the autistic children's ability to recognise them regardless of whether upper or lower halves or the whole face were seen.

Percentage correct scores

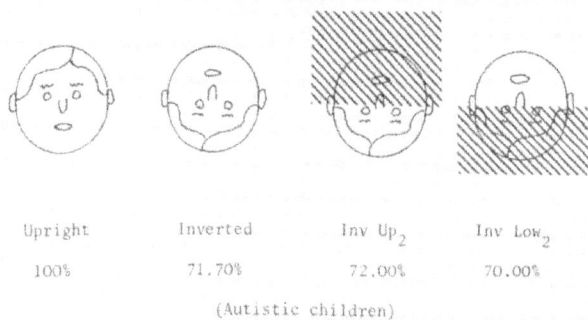

| Upright | Inverted | Inv Up$_2$ | Inv Low$_2$ |
|---------|----------|-----------|-------------|
| 100% | 71.70% | 72.00% | 70.00% |

(Autistic children)

Discussion

The results from the autistic children imply that they have a homogeneous knowledge of inverted faces as well as of upright faces. In the introduction it was suggested that the older autistic child's relatively good ability to recognise upside down faces might be due to his knowledge of the mouth area and the ease with which this area can be 'rotated mentally'. The results of the ESN children's performance support the contention that the mouth area is more easily mentally rotated (in that recognition of it is less affected by inversion) than the eye area is. However, the autistic children did not find the lower inverted halves to be easier to identify than the upper ones. Thus, it is unlikely that the ease of mentally rotating the mouth area alone can explain the autistic children's above average ability to recognise inverted faces. If knowledge of the mouth area led the autistic children to have a superior ability to recognise inverted faces, then why was their ability to recognise upper inverted halves so good?

A number of workers have pointed out the possibility that inversion of faces may more radically affect recognition of them than it does any other stimulus that is normally only seen in one orientation (Hochberg and Galper, 1967; Yin, 1969; Rock, 1974; and Ellis, 1975). gives a summary). Rock (ibid.) noted that when a face is inverted a complex of familiar spatial relationships is altered. Because one's scanning strategies may rely upon these relationships, inversion of the face might disrupt one's habitual face-scanning strategies. Noton and Stark (1971) found support for the idea that faces are scanned in a particular manner, and Smith and Nielson (1970) bolster this with their finding that people tend to scan faces from top to bottom.

One problem inherent in such work is the lack of a precise definition of what is meant by a stimulus which is usually only seen in one orientation (so called 'mono-oriented stimuli'). Written text for example is most often seen in the upright mode, and Rock (1974) draws attention to the fact that upside down hand writing can be very hard to read. On the other hand, although it is no indication that children are indifferent to orientation, they are nonetheless frequently observed to look at books and pictures which are held upside down. (Ghent, 1961; Phillips, 1977). If an explantion of why faces are peculiarly difficult to recognise upside down relies on defining them as mono-oriented, then this term must be defined more clearly. Additionally, if inverting faces disrupts one's natural scanning pattern for them, then it remains to be shown that one's scanning pattern for faces is unique to faces alone.

Yin (1970) notes that the face serves two functions. It provides information about the identity of the person, and it also reveals something about the person's inner state. It is the latter, more social, aspect which Yin feels is involved in the abnormal difficulty in recognising inverted faces. It is, as many others have said (see Phillips, 1977), very difficult to tell the expression of an upside down face. However, there is a possibility which Yin does not discuss, namely that recognition of expression in the eye area is more radically affected by inversion than that in the mouth area. There is no data in the literature which is directly relevant to this point, but it is of potential relevance to the present study. It seems that the normal person's recognition of a face is strongly bound up with his ability to identify expression in that face: he tends not only to identify faces according to specific facial features but also according to typical expression.

In a sense, recognition of features and recogniton of typical expressions are two sides of the same coin. For the manner in which a particular expression manifests itself on a person's face is a function of the physical characteristics of his face. His expression is a pattern of his facial features and the spatial relationships between them. Thus to talk of the disruption of one's ability to recognise features is ipso facto to be talking of the disruption of one's ability to identify expression, too.

The important point to be made here is that emotional expression might be difficult to discern in inverted faces because the discernment involves the integration of several features and their inter-relationships into a whole or 'gestalt'. Consequently, the eye area is possibly harder to recognise upside down not only because it contains more elements than the mouth area, but also because the relationships between the components must be 'mentally rotated' and not just the individual features themselves. If this is true, then the normal and ESN child's natural propensity to integrate the parts of his perceptions into a meaningful whole might on the one hand allow him to understand facial expression but on the other hand hamper his ability to recognise both identity and expression in upside down faces. By reverse logic the autistic child's abnormally good ability to identify inverted faces might be due to him lacking the normal propensity to integrate his perceptions. If this is true then one can make two predictions: the older autistic child's good ability to recognise inverted stimuli should not be restricted to faces and his ability to identify facial expressions should be deficient (especially where correct identification involves the integration of several components and the relationships between them).

It would thus be of interest to test the ESN and autistic children's abilities to identify other stimuli which are usually seen one way up and which usually involve the integration of their parts into a whole. One example of such stimuli is the written word, which as soon as a child can read will be viewed as a whole rather than as a series of letters and their sounds.

## Summary and conclusions

It was hypothesised that the older autistic child's superior ability to recognise inverted faces is due to his possessing a more detailed knowledge of the mouth area, which, it was suggested, might be easier to 'rotate mentally'. To test this hypothesis the children were shown inverted halves of peers' faces in photographic form, and their performance was compared with that of matched ESN children. If the mouth is a more easily mentally rotated feature, then it would be expected that recognition of lower halves of faces is less affected by inversion than that of upper halves. This was found to be true for the ESN children but not for the autistic children. The autistic children found both of the inverted halves equally easy to identify. The results were discussed in the light of other workers' suggestions as to why inverted faces are so hard to recognise. It was concluded that one's ability to identify emotional expression in another's face may be important in recognising his identity, and that such recogniton might be drastically affected by inversion. It was finally suggested that the normal and ESN child's difficulties with recognising inverted faces might be due to their natural propensity to integrate their within-modality perceptions into wholes or 'gestalten'; thus, the autistic children may not integrate their perceptions so readily, and consequently they might possess knowledge of individual components which are easier to recognise when inverted.

207

Figure 3.12  <u>Words in the test of inverted and</u>
<u>upright word perception</u> (after the
'Burt Word Reading Test', Hodder
& Stoughton, 1976).


to      is      up      he      at

for     my      sun     one     of

big     some    his     or      an

went    boys    that    girl    water

just    day     wet     pot     things

no      told    love    now     sad

nurse   carry  quickly village   scrambled

journey terror  return  twisted  shelves

beware  explorer known  projecting tongue

serious domineer obtain belief  luncheon

emergency events steadiness nourishment fringe

formulate scarcely universal commenced overwhelmed

circumstances destiny urge labourers exhausted

trudging refrigerator melodrama encyclopaedia apprehend

motionless ultimate atmosphere reputation binolcular

economy theory humanity philosopher contemptuous

autobiography excessively champagne terminology perambulating

efficiency unique perpetual mercenary glycerine

influential atrocious fatigue exorbitant  physician

microscopical contagion renown hypocritical fallacious

phlegmatic melancholy palpable eccentricity constitutionally

alienate phthisis poignancy ingratiating subtlety

It was proposed that the next step should be to find out whether the autistic children's abnormally good ability to identify inverted stimuli is specific to faces. Hence a study was made of their ability to read inverted words, and the results of this study are presented in the following section.

### 3.4.2    Recognition of Inverted Words

The purpose of this investigation is to determine whether or not the older autistic children's superior ability to recognise inverted stimuli is specific to faces. To this end the children were required to read words which were presented upside-down and then to read them the right way up. If the older autistic children's ability is not specific to faces, then one would expect that, like the ESN children, their ability to read upright words would be better than their ability to read inverted ones but that inversion would affect them less than it would affect the ESN children.

### Materials

The intention of this experiment was to administer the Burt Word Test to the children with the words first being presented upside-down and then the right way-up. However, in its original form the word test has the test material printed in various print sizes. It was felt that this was potentially a confusing factor, and thus the words were re-typed using an IBM typewriter with "pica" typeface (see figure 3.12).

### Methodology and Procedure

Each child was shown the words on the test sheet, one at a time and upside-down. The procedure of the Burt Word Test was followed with the child seeing progressively more difficult words until he failed two complete rows of words. Having administered the test in this inverted mode, the child was immediately given the test again in the normal upright manner. In the first presentation of the words the child was given no feedback as it was felt that learning of the test material might occur before the retest.

## Results

An analysis of variance on the data revealed a main effect of conditions ($F = 3.01$, $p < 0.05$) and an interaction of groups-by-conditions ($F = 3.82$, $p < 0.01$). This reflected the fact that in accord with prediction both groups found the words easier to read when they were seen upright ($t = 4.78$, $p < 0.01$ for the autistic children; $t = 5.19$, $p < 0.001$ for the ESN children). The difference between the number of correct upright and the number of correct inverted words for each child was calculated for the two groups and these were compared using an unrelated t-test; the source of the above interaction was thus discovered to be that inversion of the words affected the ESN children's scores much more than it did the autistic children's ($t = 3.93$, $p < 0.005$). The lack of a 'groups' effect was due to the lack of difference in their ability to read the words when they were presented in the normal upright mode ($t = 0.29$, $p > 0.1$), and one may therefore conclude that the reading ability of the groups was statistically equal.

A note was made of the types of error that the members of each group made, and there were significant group differences. Errors of reversal of letters (eg. b for d) were more frequent in the ESN group than in the autistic group (12 in the ESN group compared to only 3 in the autistic group). Similarly, the ESN children were found to make more errors of inversion of letters (eg. t for f) than did the autistic children (again, 12 errors by the ESNs but only 1 by the autistics). However, errors of displacement of letters (reading "on" for "no" for eg.) did not differentiate the groups (the ESN children made 6 such errors and the autistic children only made 5).

Discussion

Whilst both the autistic and the ESN children found inverted
words harder to identify than upright ones, the autistic children's
ability was less affected by inversion of the stimuli.  Because the two
groups had statistically equal reading ages in the upright mode, one
may conclude that the difference in abilities on the inverted mode was
not due to a mismatch of their reading abilities.  Thus the older
autistic children's superior ability to identify inverted stimuli is
not specific to faces and extends at least to the identification of
written words.

It was notable that the autistic children made fewer errors of
inversion and reversal of the letters.  The presence of reversal errors
in young children's reading is common (see Gibson and Levine, 1976),
and these alongside inversion errors tend to imply that the ESN children
were trying to read the words as 'gestalten'.  That is, they were tending
to read in terms of the relationship between the various individual
components of the printed words.  Thus reversal and particularly inversion
errors are a natural consequence of attempting to 'mentally rotate' each
word in its entirety.  If by contrast a child were to read in a more
piecemeal fashion, noting how each component looks iconically, then he
may also approach the reading of inverted words in a similar manner.
Hence he would invert each letter individually rather than attempting
to invert the word as a whole.  This would give rise to fewer errors of
inversion and reversal, and describes very well the performance of the
autistic children.  Whilst this is not firm evidence (other factors
might explain the results), it may be that the autistic children tended
not to integrate the letters into whole words when they read as much
as the ESN children.  Support for this comes from the responses of one

autistic child who frequently half-spelt and half-pronounced each word (eg. 'g-l-ycerine' for 'glycerine'). The contention is also in line with the findings of the previous experiment, in which it was also suggested that the autistic children tended not to integrate their perceptions into meanginful wholes as readily as the ESN children.

### 3.4.3 General discussion of the inverted mode studies

In the original experiment on face perception, it was found that the older autistic children were exceptionally good at recognising upside-down faces. The older autistic children were also found to be equally good at recognising both upper and lower inverted halves of a face. This finding thus eliminated the possibility that it was solely their knowledge of the mouth which led to their abnormally good ability to identify upside-down faces.

It was noted that the literature favours a link between one's ability to identify emotional expression in a face and one's problems with identification of faces seen upside-down. It was also noted that the identification of expression is inextricably bound up with the ability to process one's perception of a face in terms of both its featural components and the relationships between them. Integration of one's perceptions is thus vital to accurate perception of facial expressions. By reverse logic it was suggested that the autistic children had less of a tendency to process their perception of faces in such an integrative manner. The advantage to expect of a less holistic knowledge of a stimulus is that one can recognise it more readily when it is upside-down. The price paid, though, was hypothesised to be a lesser ability to discern facial expression. The latter point will be investigated later in this thesis, but the former point would seem to fit the previous results of the autistic children.

If the autistic children's good ability to recognise inverted
faces is based on a lesser tendency (or ability) to integrate parts
of their perception into wholes or 'gestalten', then there is no reason
to suppose that it is specific to faces.  This was found to be true,
and they displayed a better ability to identify inverted words than
matched ESN children.  Further, the lack of errors of reversal or
inversion of the letters by the autistic group was noted to be possible
evidence for their not reading words in as holistic a manner as the
ESN children.

To integrate the 'parts' which make up one's perceptual world into
'wholes' is a necessary aspect of normal human cognition.  But if this
integration simply takes the form of 'chunking' or 'clustering' then
the processes of categorisation and symbol  formation will be greatly
impeded.  One must be able to go beyond that which is immediately
given or temporally adjacent and be able to bring together disparate
elements to form a single thematic unity.  Clearly, although it may be
going beyond the data of the above experiments, one may nonetheless hold
in mind that the older autistic children's superior ability to recognise
inverted stimuli may reflect a deficiency in their ability to perceive
gestalten through the integration of component parts into meaningful
wholes.

This theoretical proposition will be returned to later, though
for the moment one may note that the fact that the face serves several
functions may be an important aspect of the present enquiry.  Up to this
point the studies have dealt with the autistic child's ability to
recognise faces and have investigated the hypotheses that arose in
consequence.  However, as was mentioned above, recognition of a face's

identity may be linked to one's ability to discern the expression on that face. It remains a possibility therefore that ESN children find it difficult to recognise inverted faces because they find the expressions on them hard to discern.

But if feature- and expression-identification are probably linked for the ESN child, it is not clear from the above study that this is also true for the older autistic child; and one is in no position to propose that it is true for the younger autistic child either. In fact, clinical observation suggests that both younger and older autistic children are poor at understanding other people's non-verbal behaviour of which facial expression forms a part (Wing, 1976a). Consequently, one may hypothesise that in a study of their ability to identify expression, autistic children would be shown to be less able than ESN children. Further, while the ESN children's ability to identify expressions would be greatly affected by inversion, it is possible that the autistic children's ability to identify facial expression would be generally much poorer, but what ability they have would be less affected by inverting the faces.

For the above reasons, the following two chapters will be concerned with the identification of expression by ESN, normal and autistic children. The first of these chapters deals with an overview of the literature on normal children's ability to identify facial expressions and the ontogeny of their ability. The second chapter deals with an experimental study of the autistic and ESN children's skills in this area.

Before moving on to these topics, though, it is worth noting that the literature on the identification of facial expression also concerns itself with the production of expressions. The ability to understand another's expression is intertwined with one's ability to experience that expression. Similarly, the ability to correctly label a facial expression is bound up with one's ability to produce it (although it will be noted that for acquired expressions comprehension seems to precede performance). Hence, the following chapter will discuss details of those expressions which may be innate and those which are more probably acquired. Suffice to say at this juncture that in early life spontaneous production of expressions precedes recognition of them; and this in turn precedes the ability to produce them to order. Thus it would be of interest to study the autistic children's abilities to produce facial expressions, both spontaneously and to order. Therefore, Chapter 5 will deal with this topic too.

3.5 Summary of and Conclusions to the Studies so far

In the first study the autistic children's ability to recognise peers' faces from isolated facial features and from inverted portrayals was compared with that of matched comparison groups of normal and ESN children. The results of the normal and ESN children were similar across age levels and showed them to be more able to recognise faces from upper features than from lower ones. In contrast, both younger and older autistic children were more able than their comparison groups to recognize lower facial features.

However, whereas the younger autistic children found the lower features easier to recognize than the upper ones, the older autistic children found the faces to be almost equally easy to recognise from any facial area. Neither autistic group were found to be less able than the comparison children to recognize the faces from the eye area. Whilst the comparison groups and younger autistic children found inverted faces harder to recognize than upright ones, the older autistic children were found to have an ability to recognize inverted faces superior to that of all the other groups. This ability was nearly as good as their ability to recognize upright faces.

As a result of these findings, it was suggested that the autistic children might have a tendency to scan the lower halves of all objects. To test this they were required to sort schematic houses into two piles according to their similarity to two basic house designs. The houses to be sorted were made up of elements of the basic houses. By noting onto which pile the child placed any, one could infer whether the child was tending to sort according to upper or lower features. The autistic children's performance on this test was compared with that of matched

ESN children. There was no evidence to indicate that the autistic children tended to scan lower areas since they showed no evidence for abnormal sorting by lower features.

A second possibility was that the autistic children's better than normal knowledge of lower facial features might be due to them tending to lip-read. The validity of such an assertion was first tested by investigating the ability of hard-of-hearing subjects to recognise peers' faces from upper and lower halves. It was found that, in accord with prediction, they were more able to recognise faces from the lower area than were subjects with normal hearing. However, it was noted that they were still somewhat less able in this regard than the autistic children.

Some of the autistic children were compared with matched ESN children for their ability to lip-read peers' names. The two groups were equally able to do this task. A more elaborate task was devised in order to investigate whether the two groups differed in their reliance upon the mouth area for cues about the content of spoken communications. The autistic children were once again found to be as able as the ESN children at lip-reading. However, the other findings were more confusing. First, the autistic children were less affected by the presence of white noise when they had to report words heard via headphones. Second, the ESN children did not perform in the expected manner when they were presented with conflicting auditory and visual information and were asked to repeat the word they had perceived. Normal children have been shown (Dodd, 1977) to rely more on visual input than auditory input when either modality presented alone would dictate that the children would

give the same percent correct. In contrast, the ESN children reported
heard words and seen ones with equal frequency. When the noise level
was reduced they quickly switched to reporting the words that they heard.
The autistic children's performance differed from this in that at the
balance position they tended to report what they heard, and as the noise
level was reduced they changed more slowly than the ESN children to
reporting the heard words with greater frequency. The meaning of these
findings was not clear, but the autistic children did not seem to exhibit
an abnormal reliance upon lip-read information. Instead, it seemed that
a poor ability to integrate the seen and heard sources of information from
spoken messages was implicated.

The older autistic children's superior ability to recognise inverted
faces was further investigated. It was suggested that they might possess
a superior knowledge of the mouth area which is easier to identify when
upside down. However, whilst the ESN children's ability to recognise
lower halves of faces was less affected by inversion than their ability
to recognise upper halves the older autistic children's ability was equally,
and only slightly, affected by inversion. Thus, a superior knowledge of
the mouth area could not explain the autistics' results. The ability
of the children to identify inverted words was also investigated to find
out if the older autistic children's superior ability to recognise inverted
stimuli was restricted to faces. This was not found to be so, for
their ability to identify upside-down words was also better than that
of matched ESN children. Furthermore, the autistic children made fewer
errors of inversion of letters (mistaking 't's for 'f's and so on) and
fewer reversal errors, too (such as saying 'on' when they'd read 'no'
upside down). It was concluded that the older autistic child's superior
ability to recognise inverted stimuli is not restricted to faces but

probably remains constant for all so called 'mono-oriented' stimuli.
The most probable interpretation of the results was that the autistic
children were not tending to view words or faces as 'gestalten' and
thus retained a more fragmented knowledge of the stimuli. Such a
fragmented knowledge might have enabled the autistics to identify
inverted stimuli, since recognition of individual inverted features
is easier than that of a whole which must be mentally rotated in its
entirety before identification can take place.

The general conclusion is thus that the autistic children have
showed several instances where their abnormal performance might be
accounted for by a failure to integrate their perceptions and form
meaningful gestalten. The failure to do this could explain why they
were so good at identification of inverted stimuli and would also account
for their abnormally homogeneous knowledge of the-face. However, it is
the ability of other children to form such meaningful gestalten that
allows them to have a full concept of 'facial expression'. That is,
only by integrating the information gathered from the various parts of
the face over a course of time can ... one to determine how another
feels. It was thus decided that it would prove fruitful to know more
about the autistic child's ability to discern facial expressions. It
was further noted that the ability to identify expressions has been
discussed along with the ability to produce expressions in the literature
on normal children, and thus it was decided to investigate this topic, too.

Chapter 4

THE IDENTIFICATION AND PRODUCTION OF FACIAL EXPRESSIONS: THE NORMAL CHILD

"The human face is a masterpiece..The eyes reveal the soul, the mouth the flesh, the chin stands for purpose, the nose means will; but over and behind all is that fleeting something we call 'expression'.

(Elbert Hubbard, 1895 - 1915)

## 4.1  Introduction

In the context of this thesis there are several questions regarding the face's role in revealing the inner state of a person.  To what extent are facial expressions innate?  To what extent are they learnt?  Does recognition of an expression go hand-in-hand with the ability to produce it, or does recognition only follow much later?  Finally, to what extent do the production and recognition of expressions play a part in a child's communication with others?

It is difficult to answer any of these above questions with total confidence.  However, it is possible to go some way toward answering them: while there is strong evidence for an innate element in early expressional behaviour, many specific expressions seem to be learnt from within the context of social interaction.

Facial expression is an important aspect of the newly-born's pre-linguistic non-verbal communication.  As was previously noted, autism is mainly described in terms of an impaired ability to communicate and a lack of affective contact.  It is thus of particular interest to compare the development of expression in autism with that in normal children; especially bearing in mind that by definition autism has its onset in the early (pre-linguistic stage of life)  Thus the beginnings of what may be called a "communication deficit" must be present in the stages of life which are precursory to speech production.

The questions raised above will be examined through reviewing our present knowledge of the development of expressional behaviour in normal children and then comparing this knowledge with that of the expressional behaviour of autistic children. The review of normal development in this chapter will draw heavily on the excellent summary by Charlesworth and Kreutzer (1973).

4.2 Emotional expression in the normal infant and young child

Darwin wrote one of the earliest accounts of emotional expression of the human infant (1877). In this he charted the development of his own son's expressions during his first year of life. He felt strongly about the innateness of many facial expressions and their place in the phylogenesis of the species. He saw the vast majority of expressions as having evolved from more primitive inborn forms, and he noted that almost all of the complex expressions which an adult can display are to be seen in infancy in a simpler form. This, he felt, was particularly true of such basic emotions as pleasure, displeasure, anger, joy, sorrow and disgust. On the subject of much more complex emotions, he was willing to concede that they were largely affected by learning and cross-cultural variation. However, as Charlesworth and Kreutzer (1973) rightly pointed out, many psychologists today are unwilling to come to such absolute conclusions regarding the innateness of expressions.

It is worth noting, however, that some of Darwin's (1872) observations do at least have a common sense validity. For instance, he noted that some emotional expressions seem to have a specific

function other than communication with others. For instance, when
surprised, our eye-brows rise and our eyes open. It is a state of
hyper-alertness in which the senses are 'cleared' in readiness for
action. In contrast, one screws up one's eyes momentarily<sub>∧</sub>. The
                                                    when startled.
behaviour protects the eyes from the unexpected, but may also serve
to reduce visual input. Laughter and crying, on the other hand, may
be examples of the release of internal tensions. This leads to an
important point: there is quite a difference between the somewhat
'reflex' expressions which may communicate feelings to others but
are not primarily intended to do so, and those whose primary aim is
to inform others of personal feelings. Perhaps the former reflex
expressions are largely innately determined and consistent cross-
culturally, whereas the latter are learnt and are as culturally
specific as any verbal language.

Blatz and Millichamp (1935) found that emotional episodes in
infancy are very frequent, but they are often not easy to trace to
specific environmental stimuli. Again, Herzka (1965), in his
study of the range of facial expressions displayed by infants,
confirmed that the range was very large - from an "angelic smile"
to complicated and adult-like displays of disgust, anger, and even
what looked like "wisdom". However, the specific onset of most
emotional expressions is not easy to define with precision.

Probably the first expression that a Western baby displays
is crying/distress, for this has been frequently induced at birth
by obstetricians (see Le Boyer, 1975 ). But the best documented
and most studied expression is the smile. Data from the study of
it provides some of the strongest evidence available for the

innateness of emotional expression. It would seem that the onset
of the full social smile comes quite consistently at around 46 weeks
after conception (Bower, 1977). This is true of any child, apparently,
regardless of when he is actually born. Thus premature babies,
although they may be argued to have had longer to learn the expression,
do not smile any earlier ("conceptually") than do full-term neonates.

Further support for the innateness of the smiling response
comes from the work of Dennis (1938). Dennis studied a pair of twin
girls who were reared from one month of age with very little social
contact. They were never given the opportunity to see a human face,
and they were cared for in such a way that they could not come to
associate any pleasurable release with the human face or voice.
Nonetheless, they too each began to smile on schedule at 46 weeks
after conception. Although it will be discussed more fully later
in this chapter, the study of blind babies is also relevant. They,
too, begin to smile at the same time after conception: however, at
first their smiles are not generally found to be as intense or
sustained as those of a normal sighted baby (Charlesowrth & Kreutzer,
1973).

Having presented a fairly strong case for the innateness of
the smiling response, can anything be said about the factors that
elicit it? The human voice and face have both been described as
powerful elicitors of smiles especially when the face is seen en face
(e.g. Spitz & Wolff, 1946). However, Bower (1977) discusses the
reasons why some believe that the face per se is not a prime stimulus
for bringing forth the neonates' first smiles. For instance, the
evidence presented above by Dennis and also that from studies of the

blind seems to indicate that it is not necessary for the infant to see a face in order for him to smile. In the early chapter of this thesis it was mentioned that it is not necessarily the 'human' aspects of a face that cause an infant to smile vigorously - a pair of black dots on a white card will suffice (Ahrens, 1954). Somewhat more enigmatic is the consistent findings that more than one pair of dots will produce more smiling than will a single pair (Ahrens, 1954).

It should be made clear at this point what is meant by the 'social smile'. This label is generally given to the full smiling response that occurs around six weeks of age and is most readily elicited by a human face. It follows a period in which full smiles have just emerged in the infant's repertoire (at about three weeks) but only in response to the human voice; the response being far greater to the female voice than to sounds such as bells ringing. The response is not enhanced by the presence of any visual stimulus, the human face included (Bower, 1977). Thus, the label 'social smile' may say more about the adult's interpretation of the infant's behaviour than about the infant's view of the world. It is rather ironic that research should indicate that, for the baby, smiling at a face at this stage of life is not 'social' at all in the sense of being directed specifically to a human being.

Bower (1977) introduced the idea of the infant's perception of contingency between two events in his experience. Bower notes that there is a substantial body of evidence to support the connexion between the infant's appreciation of contingency and the onset and vigour of his smiling (e.g. Watson, 1973). This result was also obtained by Papousek (1969) who clearly demonstrated that the goal of the action (such as the illumination of a light) was not the cause of the infant's

smiling. Rather it was specific to his discovery of a connexion
between an action on his part and an event in his environment.

Bower (1977) cites a retarded infant who, whilst she had had
ample exposure to human faces, had not smiled by eight months of age.
Her first full smiles came only after she had been exposed to a situation
in which she could discover contingency. Similarly, a blind baby who
could not be argued to have his smiles elicited by visual stimulation,
first smiled in response to a situation in which he had contingent
control over an auditory mobile (see Bower, p.45). Bower further notes
that the vast majority of games which adults play with infants can be
seen to be "contingency games" (such as 'peek-a-boo'). In fact, Watson
(1973) goes so far as to say:

> ....the contingency detection game is not important
> to the infant because people play it; rather people
> become important to the infant because they play the
> game.

Bower goes on to point out that this view may offer an explanation
for previous findings by Watson (1966) in which he found that infants
smile most at faces which are in the same orientation as their own. This
is so in spite of the fact that during feeding, washing and changing a
baby, an adult's face is most frequently not en face, but rather rotated
at some angle. Bower makes the connexion that it is only in the context
of contingency games that the baby sees an adult's face full on and
upright. In consequence, this orientation may come to be associated
with a smile producing situation, and thus itself evoke smiling.

However, it is clear that this cannot be the entire answer. Why,
for instance, should a pair of black dots on white card be such an
effective early evoker of smiles in most infants? Moreover, why should

a similar card with three pairs of dots on it elicit an even stronger smiling response? Bower has made the point that the two dots are, of course, associated with the eyes, and yet whilst they are present in all facial orientations the infant smiles most at upright faces. How can this be so if the child is smiling in response to dots? From the review in chapter 2 of the ontogenesis of face perception, it is clear that the response to this question is that at this stage the infant is no longer smiling at dot pairs. Watson's (1966) study involved fourteen-week-old infants, and the data which relates dot pairs to the smiling response is referring to six-week-olds. As was noted in the early section of this thesis, Caron et al (1973) found that at about fourteen- to sixteen-weeks-old the infant becomes sensitive to the position of the eyes vis a vis the facial outline. That is, he has located them in the upper region of the face and has come to expect them to be side by side and symmetrical in their placement. It is more likely that the confirmation of this discovery causes the fourteen-week-old infant to smile particularly strongly at upright faces. Nonetheless, it would be of interest to know whether such an orientation specific response still occurs in babies who are brought up by adults who purposely avoid playing contingency games in the normal orientation.

It is of interest to note that in the above paragraph the idea that contingency discovery is an important releaser of smiles has not been disgarded; rather it may have indicated how our conception of this might be enriched and expanded. For instance, it might be possible to talk of "discovery" alone, rather than "contingency discovery" and thus of the more basic idea of an "ah-ha!" response (see Koestler, 1971). That is, whenever the child makes a discovery, or has a previous discovery or hypothesis confirmed, he reflects this by smiling. Consequently, an infant may be expected to smile not only when he perceives a correspondence between two events or between an action on this part and an external event, but also when a perception confirms (or conforms to) a newly formulated schema.

To conclude this discussion of the smiling response, it can be said that whilst it appears that the discovery of contingency can elicit smiling from an infant, it remains to be shown either that this is the earliest releaser of smiles (predating the response to dot-pairs, for instance) or that it is the major factor involved. It may well be found that the readiness to smile under certain conditions is 'gentically programmed' but that a wide variety of factors may be able to contribute towards these necessary conditions. It seems certain, though, that whilst there may be uncertainty as to what these factors are and why they produce smiling, the specificity of the onset of smiling does suggest the innateness of this emotional expression.

In comparison to the amount of work that has been devoted to smiling in babies, there is a lamentable lack of information regarding other expressions of emotion in early life. Laughter, for instance, seems to be a difficult expression to define. Its onset has been set at anywhere between four and sixteen weeks of age (Washburn, 1929; Stroufe, 1971). This disparity would seem to be totally due to the different workers' definition of the label (see Dennis and Dennis, 1937; Charlesworth & Kreutzer, 1973).

J.B. Watson (1919) considered anger to be one of the triumvirate of emotions which appear at birth (along with smiling/laughter and crying). However, it would seem that an unequivocal facial expression of anger is

absent until several months after birth. The earliest signs of
"affection" seem to come at about four months (Banham, 1950). However,
the scoring of such an emotion is extremely subjective. How, for
instance, can one be certain that the child's expression is not simply
one of pleasure?

Charlesworth and Kreutzer report that the first appearance of "fear"
totally depends (again) upon the criteria used. Stirnimann (1940), for
example, would claim that the expression of it is present from birth,
but at the other extreme Peiper (1963) is adamant that "no expressive
movement of fear or horror exists during infancy". However, such a
statement has its origins in the concept that by definition fear requires
a fairly high level of cognitive ability; a level which a child does
not reach within the first six months of life. There may well be two
types of fear in fact. On the one hand a 'reflexive' or 'primitive'
response to intense or aversive stimuli; and on the other hand a more
advanced form which results from incongruity between the expected
properties of a stimulus and those which are actually experienced
(Jones, 1930; Schaffer, 1969); the former making its appearance
substantially before the latter.

The element of expectancy is an important one in the discussion
of emotional expression for it also differentiates two confusable
expressions - surprise and startle. These have been referred to as
'epistemic' in that they involve a person's expectations regarding an
event in contrast to what is actually experienced. The difference
between the two expressions is subtle, yet very real: surprise is
the result of a misexpected event, whereas a startle reaction follows

an unexpected happening. Charlesworth (1966) tells us that a "surprise face" is rare within the first seven months, but the basic expression would appear to be established within the first half of the second year. The basic startle reflex, however, seems to be present from very soon after birth (cf. Bower, 1977).

It is rather difficult to distinguish "shyness" from "fear" in the neonate, but shyness would seem to be unquestionably present from around the end of the first eighteen months. Shame and embarrassment make their debut in the child's repertoire at a relatively late stage, being dependent upon fairly advanced cognitive abilities and an awareness of one's own appearance.

In general, then, it can be seen that a very great number of emotional expressions appear within the first years of life. Also, it would seem to be safe to postulate the innateness of at least a few of these expressions (e.g. the 'laugh' and cry/fret behaviour). It would appear that younger children generally express themselves in more extreme form than older children - flailing their limbs and rolling on the floor in rage (Darwin, 1872; Bridges, 1931). However, undoubtedly social factors play a large part here (consider such a commonplace phrase as "big boys don't cry", for example.) Infants not only show greater extremes of emotion, but are frequently noted to shift suddenly from one expression to another. Gradually the changes become more subtle (Charlesworth & Kreutzer, 1973) as the infant matures.

## 4.3 The recognition of emotion

Are infants and children equally able to recognize expressions as they are to produce them? It seems clear that by about six months infants can discriminate at least the two basic expressions of smiling (positive) and anger (negative) (Buhler and Hetzer, 1928). Spitz and Wolff (1946) noted that prior to about six months of age the infant will smile at any widely drawn mouth - even at a rictus which would produce a response of fear in an older child. One point of interest is that infants of around six months will also respond to the presentation of a 'positive affect' or 'negative affect' face by producing a similar expression (Charlesworth and Kreutzer, 1973). According to them, an element of internalization has occurred that allows the child to copy expressions.

One of the earliest developmental studies of the child's ability to recognize emotional expression was that of Gates (1923). He assessed 458 children in an age range from three to fourteen years on their ability to identify the expression of a so-called "Ruckmick" photograph. It is of interest that Gates not only required the subjects to label expression but also to adequately communicate them to him as well. Adults had also been tested on such a task and found to be extremely accurate (84% to 100% correct) on the identification of six basic expressions: laughter, anger, surprise, fear, scorn and pain.

A developmental trend was in evidence for the children. The subjects of three years of age or less could recognize laughter with greater than 50% accuracy, but it was not until around five or six years of age that more than 50% of the subjects could recognize pain. Anger was not recognized until seven years, and fear was identified correctly

after nine years.  Surprise became generally recognizable by around

ten and a half years, but the ability to recognize scorn was still

not established in more than half of the fourteen-year-olds.  However,

this study is open to criticism (Jenness, 1932) because only one

photograph was used to represent each of the six emotions.  In

consequence ,it may well have been the case that a poor photographic

representation of an expression could only be correctly labelled by

the older and more intellectually agile children.

Ekman and Friesen (1971) explored the ability of 130 children

from the Fore of New Guinea to recognize expressions.  Each child was

asked to choose one of six emotions that fitted each of several stories.

The stories contained a description of a character who clearly felt one

of the following: happy, angry, sad, surprised, fearful or disgusted

(two examples).  The children ranged from around six- to fifteen-years.

When the six- to seven-year-olds were compared with the fourteen- to

fifteen-year-olds there was no statistically significant difference

in their abilities to recognize the above emotions.  Their findings

were thus at variance with Gates on the ability of the younger children

to identify "fear" and "surprise", for Ekman and Friesen found them

to be fairly good at these expressions.

Honkavaara's (1961) study produced the interesting finding that

young children tend to be misled by irrelevant cues as to a person's

emotional state.  For instance, he found that more than half of the

three- to -four-year-olds that he studied mistakenly identified a

sad girl in a red dress as happy.  However, this may be partly due to the younger child not quite clearly understanding what is being

asked of him. Certainly, if the child has latched on to an erroneous

correspondence between "redness" and "happy" then this must have some

basis in the child's development. Possibly, for instance, the label

"pretty" has been given to pictures of children dressed in brightly

coloured clothing and, almost inevitably, shown to be smiling. Thus a

confusion of the categories might be expected at an early stage before the

child has clearly defined to himself the meaning of the adult's utterance.

Honkavaara also noted that the correct labelling of actions precedes

that of passive displays. Thus laughing and crying are seemingly

recognized earlier than happiness and sadness. Charlesworth and Kreutzer

(1973) draw attention to the fact that this finding is consonant with our

knowledge of early verb acquisition: the young child will often describe

an object by what it does rather than what it is.

However, a reservation to the above is added that the young child's

ability is "seemingly" biased towards recognition of action at first. Once

again the situation arises in which the child must learn to delineate what

an adult means by a word such as "sad" or "miserable". The attachment of

a label such as "crying" to another who is exhibiting a well defined

pattern of behaviour is relatively easy when compared to the cognitive

and empathic/sympathetic processes involved in the correct use of more

abstract labels. Hence the child's awareness of the fact that another is

"miserable" may well precede by some considerable time his ability to

utilize this label correctly in his everyday speech.

The main point here is that a child's competence may be greater than

his performance implies it to be, which is essentially the point Odom and

Lemond revealed in their 1972 study. They required 32 kindergarten and
32 fifth grade children to identify eight facial expressions and then to
produce the same expressions. The older children were not only more accurate
in their ability to recognize the expressions but also produced them more
accurately. Both groups, however, showed a significant lag in their ability
to produce the expression compared to their ability to identify it.

Charlesworth and Kreutzer (1973) suggest that this finding may contradict
observations that spontaneous expression precedes identification. However,
it is perhaps unnecessary to suggest, as they do, that such a contradiction
may be resolved by consideration of the scoring difficulties and specific
photographs employed. In fact it is not at all clear that a contradiction
even exists. Why should a lag between requested production and recognition
be argued to be antagonistic to findings regarding spontaneous production?
Intuitively one might expect (as is found) that spontaneous production
precedes the recognition of production in others, which in turn precedes
the ability to imitate that production. Nonetheless, an uncontrolled
factor in Odom and Lemond's study was that of the age of the people who
posed for the photographs. The photographs used were of adults (Izard,
1971) and the expressions were "idealized" in form. Because of the
idealization of the expression they may well have been easier to recognise
than produce, the latter involving relatively unnatural facial movements
for the young child who is unaccustomed to acting.

Thus far it has been noted that the infant and the young child both
have a quite wide repertoire of facial expressions and an almost equivalent,
if lagging, ability to identify these expressions. However, to what extent
does learning play a part in the expression of emotion?

## 4.4 Lack of opportunity to learn expressions

Davis (1940, 1947) described a child who was kept confined to her room for the first six years of life. During this period the mother engaged in an absolute minimum of social interaction with her. When discovered, the girl produced virtually no facial expressions at all, but after only a day or so in a more "normal" environment she would smile when coaxed to do so. Later still she smiled more willingly, and in about six weeks even actively sought to be tickled. The mother was severely retarded and thus this factor may have had other effects upon the child apart from simply "social deprivation". It is important also to be wary of interpreting the absence of expression in a child found after several years of deprivation in terms of a lack of innateness of the production of expressions. Clearly we cannot be certain whether such a child once showed any expression and only later failed to show it due to the lack of positive reinforcement for its presence.

So called "feral" children also fit into this category of children who have been deprived of normal social stimulation in early childhood. Zingh (1940) in his review of such children, since about 1857, concluded that they generally did not laugh or cry when first discovered. However, many such children have been described as "wild" in their behaviour and somewhat aggressive in their manner. Itard's (1932) "Wild Boy of Aveyron" (Victor) is a prime example of such a child. Itard described how Victor showed no signs of affection at first. His facial expression would suddenly shift for no apparent reason from seeming melancholy to peals of laughter. In fact, this form of behaviour has been noted in autistic children, too, and along with the presence of such characteristics as "want for sameness" has led some workers to propose that Victor may well have been autistic (this is reviewed by John Wing in Wing, 1976).

It is possible that such cases provide some information about emotional expression in children deprived of the opportunity to learn about it from others. However, a problem still exists in that although it may be possible to conclude that such children often have a scant expressional repertoire when discovered, it is not possible to say whether they never learnt them or whether they possessed them as part of an innate endowment but lost them due to the absence of social reward for their presence. Certainly, at least the propensity to rapidly acquire expressional behaviour is present in many of these children (see Davis' study above).

Charlesworth and Kreutzer (1973) indicate that the behaviour of 'feral' children is not harmonious with Darwin's (1872) hypothesis that laughing and crying exist to reduce tensions. In fact, no such definitive statement can be made in this regard from the above evidence. For instance, one might propose that such a releasing effect might only be subserved by expressional behaviour early on in life. Thus, by the time that most of the deprived children were discovered the function (or functions) which any particular expressive behaviour might serve may have changed. In the normal child such changes might take the form of a more 'primitive' reflexive expression later becoming transformed into a considerably more complex social behaviour which is embued with communicative intent (see Bruner, 1975a, b).

There are, of course, other forms of childhood deprivation, the study of which can give us some insight into the nature of expressional behaviour: notable amongst these is congenital blindness. The study of such children (e.g. Freedman, 1964, 1965) has led workers to the conclusion that the smile response is innate. However, strictly speaking, this statement should be limited to the conclusion that the visual modality is not the only one via which stimulation may arrive to precipitate a smile. However, it is of interest to note that the early social smile which blind babies produce is much more fleeting than that of a normal infant. It is rather like the 'smile' which a normal infant produces with his eyes closed within the first month of life. Nonetheless, the blind child's social smile does start at the same time of life as the normal infant, and by around six months the blind baby will be smiling for a more normal duration within a social situation.

An earlier study by Thompson (1941) gives us a more thorough picture of the development of facial expression in blind infants. She studied a wide range of blind children from seven weeks to 13½ years old, half of whom had been blind since birth and half had become blind in the period up to about three years of age. These children, along with a comparison group of sighted children, were filmed in both natural and contrived situations which were likely to elicit emotional responses.

Crying, smiling and laughter were found in all the children, with no detectable differences in the manner of production between the blind and the sighted. She also noted that displays of anger, annoyance and sulkiness were very similar in the two groups, and appeared only in appropriate situations.

Thompson also noted that the congenitally blind children smiled less as they became older. Strangely, she attributed this decrease in facial activity to maturation in the blind child, which is masked

in the normal child by the effects of social mimicry. However, it
does seem more likely, as Charlesworth and Kreutzer (ibid) point out,
that the blind child's facial activity becomes less due to the lack
of feedback from the facial expressions of others.

She also noted that there was far less variation in the expressions
displayed by the sighted children than by the blind children. This,
she argued, was due to the conformatory effects of social mimicry,
which serve to stylize expressions.

Goodenough (1932), Charlesworth (1970) and Eibl-Eibesfeldt (1970)
have each noted that expressions of emotion seem to be fairly normal
in older blind children. Goodenough reported that a congenitally
blind and deaf girl had fairly normal expression of such emotions as
laughing, resentment, anger, and astonishment. In fact, with the
exception of a few abnormal expressions, her 'normal' facial behaviour
seems to provide good evidence for the contention that such expressions
do not require visual learning.

Charlesworth (1970) produced further parallels between the
expressional behaviour of sighted and blind individuals. He studied
the responses of fourteen congenitally blind and eleven normal children
in situations where their expectancies were not fulfilled. No
significant group differences were found. However, quite contrary
to expectation the children did not produce a stereo-typed surprise
reaction or startle response.

A clinical study of eight blind infants was undertaken by Fraiberg (1968). She found that the rage reactions of these children were abnormal in so far as they mainly consisted solely of yelling and were not accompanied by such behaviours as kicking, banging the floor, or facial expressions. This is not in line with the fairly normal facial behaviours of blind children mentioned above. Charlesworth and Kreutzer (1973) note that this may in part be due to the fact that Fraiberg's subjects tended to be younger than those in other studies. However, if this is accepted then it must stand as evidence for later onset of expressional behaviour in blind infants, for it is clear that visual learning cannot account for the later presence of such behaviour. It may also be noted that her infants were not younger than those of Thompson (1941) who reported a great similarity between the facial expressions of blind and sighted infants.

## 4.5  Acting expressions

Dumas (1932) asked 33 congenitally blind persons (most were twelve-
to twenty- years old) to act afraid, sad, angry and happy.  The blind
subjects were normal in their spontaneous expressional behaviour, but
were totally unable to act out these expressions.  Charlesworth (1970)
also asked blind and sighted children to produce expressions and again
found that the blind children were either unable or far worse than
normal at doing so.

Fulcher (1942) compared the abilities of 50 blind and 118 sighted
children to produce facial expressions upon request.  In brief, his
findings were that the blind children produced less facial activity
than the sighted subjects, although there was a great similarity
between expressive behaviours that the two groups exhibited.  He also
claimed that his data showed evidence of an increase in facial activity
with age in the sighted subjects, but a decrease of such activity in
the blind children.  However, Fulcher did not subject his data to
statistical analysis.  Charlesworth and Kreutzer (1973) feel that the
intergroup differences may not in fact be significant - neither for the
amounts of facial activity or the differential amounts of it as a
function of age.

However, these findings simply show that a lack of opportunity to
learn the visual/motor correspondances of facial expression tend to
lead to a deficiency in the production of expression to order.  They
cannot tell us anything directly about the innateness of such expressions.

The results of such studies would seem to support Darwin's basic
hypothesis that visual learning is not a necessary requirement for the
possession of a seemingly normal repertoire of facial expressions.

Nonetheless, it cannot be concluded from this that facial expression is innate - it can only be said that the visual modality is unnecessary for its acquisition.

4.6  The presence of opportunity

Most infants have the opportunity to learn facial expressions;
from within a few hours of life they have visual contact with other
people's faces.  It has also been found that neonates can imitate
tongue protrusion (Zazzo, 1957;  Gardner and Gardner, 1970) as well
as other simple actions such as the opening and closing of the mouth.
Guernsey (1928)studied imitation in 200 infants from two-to twenty-one-
months of age.  She found that at two months the infant engages in
reflexlike or passive imitation;  at around four months imitation
becomes more conscious and active;  at eight months delayed or memory-
based imitation begins.  Buhler and Hetzer (1928) also reported that
infants in their fifth to sixth month imitate facial expressions.

However, Spitz (1946) in his monograph on the smiling response
argues quite conclusively that the early imitations that an infant
engages in require far more simple facial movements than are involved
in smiling.  Thus he argues that the response is innate and not due
to any form of imitative learning.  It was also noted in an earlier
chapter of this thesis (which had a section devoted to the ontogenesis
of face perception) that the neonate has a limited perceptual ability:
evidence exists that suggests that he does not perceive the face as
a whole until fairly late in the first year of life - an ability which
is surely necessary for him to successfully imitate a fully smiling
face, even given that his imitiative abilities are greater than his
mimicry of simple motor movements would imply.

THE IDENTIFICATION AND PRODUCTION OF FACIAL EXPRESSIONS:

THE AUTISTIC CHILD

## 5.1 The Identification of Expressions

### 5.1.1 The abilities of autistic children

There is no literature which deals directly with the ability of autistic children to identify facial expressions. There is, however, frequent mention of them being poor at non-verbal communication (e.g. Tubbs, 1966; Rutter, 1974; Ricks & Wing, 1976). The poor ability both to use and identify others' gestures would seem to be connected to their relative inability to display a normal range of facial expressions or understand those of others (Wing, 1976). Thus while the available anecdotal evidence would seem to indicate that autistic children are poor at identifying others' expressions, there is as yet no experimental evidence to support these observations.

In Chapter Three it was shown that the autistic children knew the lower facial areas better than did normal or ESN children who were matched for age and intelligence. The autistic children's knowledge of the lower halves of faces was also not accompanied by a weaker performance in recognition of the upper halves of faces. One was drawn to the conclusion that the older autistic child's relatively homogenous knowledge of upright faces was extant in the inverted mode of presentation. The possibility was suggested that the normal and ESN child's ability to recognise a face may be related to their ability to identify that face's expression, and that it is this factor in particular which makes inverted faces so hard for them to identify. Because the autistic child's knowledge of the face would appear to be more homogeneous than that of the normal or ESN child, it was suggested that he may not view faces as socially meaningful. This factor may also account for the older autistic child's superior ability to

243

recognize inverted faces, although his ability does not seem to be restricted to faces.

The intention of the following experiment was thus to investigate the autistic children's ability to identify facial expressions. It was decided that it would be profitable to investigate their ability not only in the upright mode but also in the inverted one, too. If the suggestions made above are correct, then one would expect that the normal and ESN children would be less able to identify expression in an upright face than in an inverted one. However, one would expect that the autistic children's ability to identify expression would be relatively poor, but their ability in the inverted mode would depend to a great extent upon the strategy which they adopt to label expressions. If, as seemed to be the case with their ability to recognize faces, they are able to identify some expressions by seeing only a small area, then it may be that they are able to identify the expression of an inverted face almost as well as when the face is upright. If, on the other hand, their appreciation of a person's feelings is arrived at after viewing his face in a more holistic manner (as may be the case for the normal child), then one would also expect that inversion of a face would greatly affect their ability to identify its expression.

The literature contains very few examples of attempts to test the abnormal child's ability to understand facial expressions. Odom et al (1973) examined the deaf child's ability to identify facial expressions by testing how well he could correctly match an expression to an emotion-arousing situation. Deaf children, like autistic children, have been noted to have a lack of empathy (Altschuler, 1963, 1964, 1967; Baroff, 1963; Levine, 1956, 1960). Odom et al therefore decided to test their

Drawing representing surprise.

Drawing representing fear.

Figure 5.1.  Contextual clues given 'for a facial expression test
          by Odom et al (1973).

ability to choose which expression would be appropriate for several situations and compare it with that of hearing children. They chose nine affect categories after those used by Izard (1971). These were: interest, joy, surprise, distress, disgust, anger, shame, fear and contempt. They found the deaf children to be generally less able to match the correct expressions to each of thirty-six situations (four of each affect; see figure 5.1, for examples of their pictorial situations). However, they found that this was not due to the deaf children being less able than the hearing children to sort the photographs of the expressions into piles according to similar affect. They thus concluded that the deaf child's lack of empathy is connected to his inability to relate a particular expression to a situation and not to his inability to identify expressions in general. However, one may note that Odom et al. required their subjects to put photographs of faces with similar expressions into separate piles and rightly concluded that the deaf children did not seem to have a perceptual problem in identifying which expressions went together. Nonetheless, it is possible that the deaf children may be less able to label the expressions or describe how a person with a certain expression is feeling. Thus one may take issue with their final conclusion that the deaf child has difficulty in analyzing and interpreting emotion-producing situations: he may well do, but he may also have problems with the understanding and labelling of facial expressions, too.

This experimenter's initial intention was to repeat Odom et al's task with the autistic children; however, it was found that none of the children tested so far in this thesis could understand the requirements of the task. In fact, after discussion with the children's teachers

TABLE 5.1    Subjects in the study of identification of facial
expression

| Group | N | Mean C.A. (sd) | Mean Full IQ (sd) |
|---|---|---|---|
| Younger autistic | 9 | 10.66 yrs (1.37) | 64.67 (12.10) |
| Older autistic | 9 | 14.93 yrs (0.98) | 60.11 (14.02) |
| ESN | 10 | 12.27 yrs (2.21) | 61.20 (8.17) |

and the care-staff it seemed unlikely that the autistic children would
be able to identify any more complex expressions than happiness or
sadness. A pilot study tended to support this. Then autistic children
were shown pictures of facial expressions and asked to identify them
(these were the same as Odom et al had used, together with a 'sad'
face, also from Izard, 1971). It was found that on the basis of verbal
labelling they were unable to identify all but the happy and sad faces
(and some of the children tested in this pilot could not do this even).
However, a further pilot study revealed that all of the children to be
tested in the following experiment (see later for details) were able to
correctly identify simplistic schematic representations as: (☺)
and (☹). It was thus decided to test these children's ability to
sort photographs of happy and sad faces into two piles, and in accordance
with the discussion at the beginning of this section, to test their
ability in both upright and inverted modes. The ability of the autistic
children was compared with that of ESN children.

5.1.2    The identification of expression in upright and inverted faces

Subjects

Initially two groups of ten autistic and ten ESN children were chosen
and matched for age and general intelligence. However, after testing
these children in the following experiment, it was found that there were
some distinct age trends among the autistic children, but none among the
ESN children. A further eight autistic children were tested, increasing
the group to eighteen and nine of them were designated the "older" group
and the other nine designated the "younger" group. There being no age
effect in the ESN group, it was decided to retain just the original ten
subjects and to compare the performance of the two autistic groups with
this single ESN group. Details of the subjects are given in table 5.1.

Figure 5.2. Actor making sad and happy faces (top); the parted and complete composites are shown below.

## Materials

The stimuli for this experiment were photographs of actors' faces. The actors were asked to produce happy and sad faces in such a way that it was clear from both the upper and lower areas of their face what the expression was (i.e. they were required to "smile with their eyes" as well as their mouth, and to couple a sad mouth with a frown). The upper and lower halves of twenty faces thus produced (ten of each type) were shown to twenty undergraduate students, each of whom correctly identified the intended expression. The photographs were black-and-white and measured approximately 14cm by 10 cm. Figure 5.2 gives examples of the photographs.

## Method and Procedure

The subjects were initially required to sort the inverted upper and lower halves of the faces into two piles according to whether they thought the face was happy or sad. Each child was first shown the upper halves of the faces upside-down. The instruction given in each case was put the "happy" faces on one side of a line and the "sad" faces on the other side. If the child had any trouble in understanding what was required of him, then he was shown the schematic representations of happy and sad faces to exemplify the sorting.

Having sorted the upper inverted halves, the child was asked to sort a pile of lower inverted halves into the same two piles. This completed, the child was required to sort the whole, uncovered upside-down faces into the two piles. Once the child had sorted all the faces in the inverted mode, then he was asked to repeat the procedure with the halves and whole faces now seen in the upright mode. Again he was first asked to sort the upper halves, followed by the lower halves, and and finally the uncovered faces.

TABLE 5.2     Mean percent correct for each group when sorting
upright and inverted full and half expressional
faces. (Note 50% is a chance sorting)

| Group | Upright | | | Inverted | | |
|---|---|---|---|---|---|---|
| | Full | Low | Up | Full | Low | Up |
| Younger autistic | 76.40 | 77.10 | 50.70 | 77.80 | 76.60 | 50.00 |
| Older autistic | 93.10 | 92.60 | 63.70 | 90.56 | 88.20 | 53.70 |
| ESN | 98.80 | 98.20 | 72.20 | 96.00 | 98.30 | 48.20 |

Results

(i) Between groups comparisons.

(a) The Upright Faces

The results are shown in table 5.2. A multivariate analysis of variance was computed for the present study. The two conditions described in the next experiment were also included in this analysis, because the same children and stimuli were involved. A significant result was obtained when the equality of all mean vectors was tested ($F_{16,36}$=2.488; $p < 0.012$); and a test for individual effects of groups and conditions was also significant ($F_{8,18}$=5.004; $p < 0.002$). The younger autistic children were found to be significantly inferior to the ESN children in their ability to correctly sort either the half or whole upright faces (whole: $t$=2.96; df=17, $p < 0.01$; lower half: $t$=2.58, df=17, $p < 0.002$; upper half: $t$=5.06, df=17, $p < 0.001$). They were also less able than the older autistic children to sort the lower halves of the upright faces ($t$=1.87, df=16, $p < 0.05$), or the whole upright faces ($t$=1.95, df=16, $p < 0.05$). A trend existed for them to be less able at the upper halves, too ($t$=1.66, df=16, $p < 0.07$). The reason for the non-significance of this last difference was that all the younger autistic children were performing at chance on the upper halves, whereas some of the older autistic children were able to do the task above a chance level.

The older autistic children were slightly less able to sort according to the whole faces and the upper halves than were the ESN children (whole: $t$=1.89, df=17, $p < 0.05$; upper halves: $t$=1.75, df=17, $p < 0.05$). However, one should note that both groups were performing at around 100% correct. The older autistic children were as able as the ESN children to sort according to the lower halves ($t$=1.62, df=17, $p < 0.01$). It is thus possible that it was the older autistic children's poorer ability to ascertain expression in the upper halves of the faces which led them to be slightly less able to recognize the uncovered faces.

252

(b)  The Inverted faces

The ESN children were as able to sort inverted lower halves and whole faces as they were to sort upright ones. This was also true for the younger autistic children, and thus they were once again less able on these two conditions than the ESN children. However, in the inverted mode the ESN children's ability to sort according to the upper halves dropped to chance, and they therefore became no more able to sort these than were the younger autistic children.

The older autistic children were as able as the ESN children to sort by the whole inverted faces and by the inverted upper halves (both groups performing at chance on the latter). However, the ESN children were slightly more able to sort according to the inverted lower halves than were the older autistic children (t = 1.80, df = 17, p $\langle$ 0.05).

(ii) Within group comparisons

For the upright faces the ESN children were as able to sort according to the lower halves as by the whole faces. However, they were significantly less able to sort by the upper halves (upper versus lower halves: t·= 7.57, df = 9, p $\langle$ 0.005). The picture was similar in the inverted mode: but their ability to sort by upper halves dropped to chance, whereas they were no less able to sort by the lower halves or whole faces (lower versus upper inverted halves: t = 22.51, df = 9, p $\langle$ 0.001). The picture for the older autistic children was almost identical to that for the ESN children (lower versus upper upright halves: t = 4.37, df = 8, p $\langle$ 0.01; lower versus upper inverted halves: t = 5.17, df = 8, p $\langle$ 0.005). Whilst the younger autistic children were also as good at lower halves as at whole faces, and also better on these than on the upper halves (upper versus lower halves: $t = 2.83$, $df = 8$, $p < 0.025$), their ability was not altered by inversion of the faces. Thus the older autistic and ESN children showed a better than chance average ability to sort according to upper halves in the upright mode, and this fell to chance in the inverted mode. In contrast, the younger autistic children's performance was not significantly above chance in either mode.

## Summary of results

1. The ESN and the older autistic children showed fairly similar performances in this experiment. Both groups were very able to sort the faces according to the lower halves and the whole faces, but were somewhat less able to sort by the upper halves. However, the older autistic children were not quite as good as the ESN children at sorting by the whole faces or by the upper halves.

2. The younger autistic children were less able than either of the other groups to sort by either the upright halves of the face or the upright whole faces. Their ability on the upper halves of the upright faces was no better than chance.

3. The abilities of the older autistic and the ESN children to sort by the lower halves and whole faces were not affected by inversion. However, when the faces were seen upside-down their abilities to sort according to the upper halves dropped to a chance level.

4. The younger autistic children's abilities to sort by the lower halves and whole faces was also not affected by inversion. Because they had performed at chance on the upright upper halves, there was no change in their ability to sort by these halves after the faces had been inverted.

The results may thus be seen to offer some support to the contention that one's ability to identify a person's facial expression from the lower half of their face is less affected by inversion than is one's ability to judge expression from the upper halves.

Discussion

The pilot study mentioned in the introduction to the above experiment found that all the autistic children were able to label schematic representations of happy and sad faces correctly. It is thus not surprising that they all showed themselves to be able to sort the real photographs of happy and sad faces into two piles at above chance level. However, while it was found that the older autistic children were only a little less proficient at sorting the expressions than were the ESN children, the younger autistic children were considerably less able. The differences were particularly noteworthy in their ability to sort the upper halves of the faces.

The pattern of performance by the ESN children indicated that they found it easier to tell if someone was happy or sad when they saw the person's mouth than when they saw the person's eye area. Clearly, a happy mouth is characterised by up-turned edges and a sad one by down-turned edges. The identification of happiness or sadness in the mouth area is thus not complicated by the need to obtain an overall view of the disposition of several features. However, in order to tell the expression displayed in the eye area it is necessary to take into account the relationship between various aspects (such as positions of the eye-brows, how wide the eyes are open, presence of wrinkles as when one smiles, etc.). Thus the task of telling someone's feelings from the eye area alone is relatively difficult when it is seen out of the context of the rest of the face.

The fact that the ESN children's ability to identify expression in the upper halves of the faces dropped to a chance level when the faces were seen upside-down supports this reading of the data. It was

proposed in the final section of Chapter Three that a difficulty
that one has in recognising inverted faces is that one may have to rotate
several aspects of the faces at once mentally. That is, because a face
is usually viewed as a gestalt, one has not only to imagine what the
individual features look like upside-down, but also what the disposition
of them one-to-another would be like. Given that the identification of
expression in the mouth area involves very little integration of
component features, one's ability to recognise expression in this half
will be relatively unaffected by inversion. However, identification of
expression in the eye area might be greatly affected.

Turning to the results of the autistic children, one notes that the
older autistic children were almost as good at identifying the expressions
as the ESN children. The younger autistic children, in contrast, were
significantly worse than either of the other groups at this task. They
were particularly poor at sorting the expressions according to the upright
upper halves, where they performed at a chance level. It would seem to
be harder to tell expression in the eye area than in the mouth area
because the former requires that one be able to integrate the various
components and arrive at an overall view which implies "happiness" or
"sadness". One may therefore suggest that the younger autistic children's
performance reflects their relatively poor ability to integrate aspects
of their perception in order to obtain meaningful wholes. Because the
older autistic children were able to sort the expressions by the upper
halves at a level which was on average about 10% above chance, one may
presume that they possess at least the rudimentary ability to perceive
the relationships between features which is necessary in order to arrive
at the conclusion that the person is happy or sad.

In the recognition of identity (see Chapter Three) the ESN
children were far more able to recognise upper halves of the face than
the lower halves. However, it has been found above that they were more
able to sort expressions according to the lower halves than the upper
ones. Thus it would appear that the ESN child tends to use the upper
half of the face to determine someone's identity, but the lower half
to determine how the person is feeling (although it is uncertain how
far the above findings would be generalisable to other facial expressions).
The younger autistic children, in contrast, were found to have an abnormally
good ability to recognise faces from the lower halves, and were unable to
sort the expressions according to the upper halves. The older autistic
children differed again, in that they had a fairly homogeneously good
knowledge of the face as far as identity was concerned and had a similar
pattern of ability to determine expression as that of the ESN children
(if a little lower in their ability). The fact that the older autistic
children were relatively good at recognising people from upper halves
of inverted faces and yet poor at identifying expression in the inverted
upper halves may be seen as support for the idea that identification of
expression is not connected to the recognition of features in a simple
way.

It was predicted in the introduction that the autistic children
might show evidence of viewing faces less as socially meaningful stimuli
than do the ESN children. What may now be said in this regard? The
results of the younger autistic children support this in so far as they
were generally less able to sort the expressions, and were particularly
poor at sorting the upper halves of the faces. However, this effect
was not so clear for the older autistic children, and yet it was they who

took part in the study of recognition of faces from inverted halves which gave rise to the predic tion. Nonetheless, the older autistic children were not as able as the ESN children to sort the expressions and, like the younger autistic children, the difference was most marked for the sorting of upper halves. Indeed, whilst the means do not reflect it, five of the nine older autistic children were unable to sort the upright upper halves at a level above chance.

Thus there would seem to be some support for the hypothesis that autistic children tend to view faces less as social meaningful stimuli than do ESN children of similar age and intelligence. This is certainly backed by the pilot studies undertaken before the above experiment and by anecdotal reports. The above-mentioned pilot studies found that the autistic children were able only to name happy and sad faces, whereas a small sample of the ESN children had relatively little difficulty in doing so. Teachers' and caretakers' reports bear out the autistics' poor knowledge of expression.

It was mentioned above that identifying the expression displayed in the mouth area involves less ability to integrate features than does the appreciation of expression in the eye area. It may thus be more accurate not to talk of the autistic children as being less social in their looking at faces (although this may well be so) but to refer to the fact that identifying someone's facial expression requires the ability to integrate facial features into a meaningful whole. And integration is far less necessary for the identification of happiness and sadness (where one can rely upon the appearance of the mouth) than for other more complex expressions.

It is thus of interest to compare the ESN and autistic children's abilities to sort faces into two piles according to whether they appear as happy or sad when they contain elements of both expressions. If the upper half of a face were to contain one emotion and the lower half the other emotion, then one could infer by the way that the children sort the faces which half of the face their perception is dominated by. It may also be possible to obtain an idea of the extent to which the child is integrating the features into a unity - that is, whether he perceives a single complex emotion or is aware that the face contains two conflicting ones. The following experiment was designed to investigate this.

### 5.1.3: The identification of expression in faces containing two conflicting expressions

The aim of this study was to investigate the autistic and ESN children's abilities to determine expressions in faces which display more than one emotion. It has been discussed above that one tends to view a face as a whole, a gestalt, and not as a collection of unrelated components. Thus, it would seem that one perceives a face's expression by gaining a holistic impression of its entirety, and one does not usually judge whether someone is surprised, frightened, etc., on the basis of looking at a single feature. If there is conflict between the expression that a person tries to communicate and what she/he really feels (eg. "putting on a brave face"), then one usually knows this is so. But one does not perceive two distinct expressions in the face of such a person; instead one sees a single complex expression which reflects the emotions that are pretended and felt. It is usually said to be the eyes which reveal the "true" emotion which a person is feeling (Ekman, 1973). Thus if one views a face with the upper and lower halves displaying contrasting emotions, then one's perception of the face's expression will be biased towards the emotion conveyed by the eye area.

If a child is tending to view facial expressions in this manner,
then one would expect him to tend to sort a face with a smiling mouth
and a frowning eye area as a "sad" face. And one would expect this trend
to exist despite the fact that he is more able to sort expressions
according to the lower halves than according to the upper halves. In
addition, one would rarely expect a child who is perceiving faces as
"wholes" to comment that there are two distinct expressions present in a
face. On the other hand, one might expect him to say something like "That
person looks happy, but he's really sad" when there is a smiling mouth
and sad eyes.

In contrast, a child who does not tend to view faces in a holistic
manner may not find the emotion which the eyes convey to have such a
compelling influence on his perception of facial expression. Thus, if
such a child is presented with a face in which the upper half is sad and
the lower half is happy, then he may label such a face as "sad" as
frequently as he does "happy". Or, to be more precise, he may sort by
the mouth's expression more frequently simply because he finds it easier
to discern emotion in the lower half. Equally, one would not expect
such a child to make such a searching comment (about "apparent" and "real"
emotions) as was cited above. But one might expect him to mention that
"the mouth is happy, but the eyes are sad".

If one is correct about the normal tendency to view faces as wholes,
and consequently see only a single expression, then it may be possible
to break-up the holism of a face by presenting it in photographic form
with the lower half separated by a gap from the upper half. If this does
have the effect of breaking up a holism, then one would expect it to
change the way that the normal child would sort composite happy/sad faces

but to have no effect upon the sorting of a child who did not perceive it as a whole to begin with.

It may be proposed that the autistic children will perform as if they do not perceive wholes. The ESN children, on the other hand, might be expected to perform as if they perceive faces in a holistic manner.

## Subjects

The same children who took part in the previous experiment also acted as subjects for the present one.

## Materials

The same photographs of faces used in the last experiment were used to prepare the composite photographs for this study. Each actor who posed for a happy face also posed for a sad one. It was thus possible to make composite pictures using the lower half of one of the expressions posed by an actor and the upper half of the other expression. This was done by cutting carefully prepared photographs in half and sticking them onto pieces of card. Care was taken to make the head size of each of the photographs the same, and to print the faces such that there was a minimum of difference between the tonal qualities. The two halves, one sad and one happy, were stuck next to each other and the resulting montage was reproduced on a high quality photocopying machine. With this done it was difficult to tell that the two halves of the resulting face were a montage of two different photographs (see figure 5.2). The composite faces to be used in the second half of the study where there is an attempt to break-up the holism were prepared in a similar manner, except that the two halves were glued onto the card with about one inch separation.

TABLE 5.3   Mean percent correct by each group, scored by the
mouth's expression, for the parted and complete
composite expressional faces

| Group | Split composite | Combined composite |
|---|---|---|
| Younger Autistic | 76.40 | 74.00 |
| Older autistic | 82.00 | 80.80 |
| ESN | 81.70 | 90.30 |

The two types will be referred to as 'combined-half' and 'split-half'. Their sizes were about the same as those in the last experiment (14 cm by 10 cm).

## Method and Procedure

This experiment was either run on the same day as the previous one or as soon afterwards as possible; in all cases this was within a week. Once again, the children were told to sort the photographs of faces into two groups depending upon whether they thought the person looked happy or sad. The children were not introduced to these faces as being in any way special compared to the foregoing ones, as it was felt that this might draw attention to the composite nature of the stimuli. Each child was shown all possible composites, in both the combined-half and split-half conditions, in a random order. He was encouraged to decide one way or the other, although hesitations and reasons given for hesitations were noted down. Once a face had been sorted it was turned over to avoid the child comparing it with faces he might sort onto the same pile later.

## Results

The results are shown in table 5.3.

(a) The ESN children

Scoring the performance of the ESN children in terms of percent correct for the mouth's expression, revealed that they were tending to sort by this and not by the expression conveyed in the eyes. Still, this does not go against the predictions mentioned above. One must test the difference between their ability to sort the combined halves with that they showed for the upright lower halves in the previous experiment. If there is no significant difference between the scores, then one can infer that the ESN children sorted the combined halves purely according to the mouths. If there is a significant difference, though, then one may infer that the contrasting emotion conveyed by the eyes affected their choice. In fact, the latter was found to be true: treated in terms of sorting by the mouth's expression, they were significantly better at the upright lower halves than at the combined halves (t = 4.56, df = 9, p < 0.001. One is also interested in whether the splitting of the face had an effect upon their sorting choices. In fact, it was found that it did (t = 2.43, df = 9, p < 0.05). That is, in terms of sorting the faces correctly according to the mouth's expression the sorting showed them to be more often correct in the combined-half condition than in the split-half one. The ESN children were also found to report that there were two separate expressions (or two faces) more frequently when the faces were parted by an inch gap (an average of 6.1 occurrences for the split-half condition compared to an average of only 1.2 for the combined-half). All the above results are concordant with the hypothesis that ESN children perceive facial expressions holistically: this is supported by the fact that four of the ESN children mentioned that a person in the combined-half condition "looked happy but is really sad", whereas none made such remarks in the split-half condition.

(b) The Autistic Children

The younger autistic children performed these tasks as if they were sorting according to the expression revealed by the mouths. Comparing their performance on the combined-halves with that on the upright lower halves from before revealed no significant difference (t = 1.24, df = 8, p > 0.1). And there was no significant difference between their performance on the combined-halves and the split-halves (t = 1.05, df = 8, p > 0.1). This of course was only as expected since it was discovered previously that their ability to sort according to expression in the eye area was no better than chance. Thus, as expected, they showed no evidence of perceiving faces as gestalten.

The older autistic children were found to be better when sorting the upright lower halves than when sorting the combined-halves in terms of percent correct by the mouth (t = 3.17, df = 8, p<0.01). They were, however, no better on the combined-halves than on the split-halves by this criterion (t = 0.23, df = 8, p>0.1). Thus, like the ESN children the older autistic children showed evidence that they took some account of the contrasting expression of the eyes in the combined-half condition. But unlike the ESN children, the parting of the faces made no difference to their performance. The older autistic children reported about as many times in both composite conditions that there were two expressions (average of 3.3 in the split-half, and 2.7 in the combined-half; no significant difference). The last two points taken together would seem to imply that the older autistic children, like the younger ones, were not tending to perceive facial expression holistically. Finally, none of the autistic children ever remarked that any person "looked happy/sad) but is really sad/happy").

### Discussion

The initial predictions were confirmed. By performing differently when sorting incongruous combined-half and split-half faces than when sorting upright lower halves, the ESN children revealed that their perception of combined halves was affected by the conflicting expressions which the eyes conveyed. Support for the interpretation that this was due to their perceiving facial expression holistically came from three sources. First, their performance was different when they sorted the split-halves than when they sorted the combined-halves; and it was conjectured that this could only be true if the gap in the face had broken the holism. Second, they tended to report that there were two expressions in the combined-half condition much less frequently than in the split-half condition. Third, whilst a few ESN children remarked that a face in the combined-half condition looked happy but that the person was really sad, none of them made such a comment about a split-half face.

In contrast, the autistic children did not show this evidence for viewing facial expression holistically. The lack of ability for the younger autistic children to sort by the upper halves of faces was once again evident. They sorted both types of composite face as if they were simply sorting by the mouth's expression. The older autistic children however, were more like the ESN children in that they also did not sort the combined-half faces by the mouth's expression alone. Thus the older autistic children also seemed able to take account of the expression conveyed by the eye area. Nonetheless, it seems wrong to attribute the same type of performance to the ESN and autistic children. The older autistic children, unlike the ESN ones, performed no differently on the two composite face conditions. That is, the gap present in the split-half condition's faces did not seem to break the holism for the older autistic children. At least, one can infer that a lack of difference between their performance on the two conditions indicates that the unity of the face is less crucial to the autistics' perception of faces than to the ESNs'.

The older autistic children did not tend to report that there were two expressions in the face more frequently in the split-half condition than in the combined-half one. As was noted above, if a child tends to perceive faces as gestalten, then he would most probably note that there are two expressions in a face which has been split in two than one which is whole and complete. Lastly, the conclusion that the autistic children tended not to view the faces holistically was supported by the fact that none of the autistic children made a comment like, "He looks happy, but he's really sad". Such a comment implies that a child is perceiving a face in its entirity and is able not only to report his global impression of the facial expression but also to perceive that a conflict can exist between the global expression conveyed by a face and what the person is really feeling.

Once again, then, the ESN children's perception of expression was dominated by that which the mouth displayed (cf. section 5.1.2). They were able to take into account the emotion revealed by the eyes, but this seemed to mainly affect their appreciation of what a person was 'really' feeling and did not dominate their overall view of the face's expression. Furthermore, they showed evidence of having an overview of the face's expression. In terms of happy and sad faces, then, it seems that ESN children's perception of facial expression is dominated by the lower half of the face, whereas their perception of faces for identity is dominated by the upper facial features. Perception for identity did not indicate that the autistic children (younger or older) tended to view any one facial area, but when perceiving expressions they were dominated by what was conveyed in the mouth area. The reason for the abnormal performances of the autistic children can be explained in terms of their not tending to integrate their perceptions into meaningful gestalten. These points will be discussed later in this thesis in Chapter Seven.

5.1.4  Discussion of studies on identification of expressions

Section 4.3 of the previous chapter outlined the normal child's ability to recognise emotion in people's faces.  It would seem that by around six months of age the normal child will respond differently to a "negative affect" face than to a "postive affect" one (Buhler and Hetzer, 1928; Charlesworth and Kreutzer, 1973).  Gates' study (1923) showed that normal children can correctly label happy faces before three years of age, and this would seem to be confirmed by Ekman and Friesen's (1971) study of the Fore of New Guinea.  Ekman and Friesen's study also seems to have shown that by about six years old a child can recognise facial displays of sadness, surprise, fear, anger and disgust.  One can thus surmise that the child's ability to recognise happy and sad faces develops very early in life.  One should certainly be surprised not to find it in a child of about eight years, even if his mental faculties were mildly retarded.

The ESN children performed up to expectation in the above experiments. The suggestion from the pilot studies that they were able to correctly identify such expressions as joy, surprise, distress, anger, fear etc. also conforms to one's expectations of children with mild mental retardation in the eight to eleven year age range.  The autistic children, in contrast, clearly have a much poorer ability to identify expression than one would expect from their general mental abilities.  Indeed, the fact that the younger autistic children were so poor at identifying happiness and sadness implies that they have less ability in this regard than the normal child has attained by the third year of life.  This ability is obviously below that expected at their average mental age level of about five and a half years.

One can thus conclude with confidence that the autistic children's abilities to identify facial expressions are out of keeping with their mental ages. Wing and others (see Wing, 1976) have mentioned that the autistic child fails to understand other's feelings, and such arguments infer that any inability these children have in identifying facial expressions stems from a basic absence of empathy. However, the present studies have drawn attention to the fact that the autistic child may lack the ability to integrate aspects of his perceptual world into meaningful wholes. It has been argued that this inability causes him to be particularly poor at the identification of expression, except where identification can take place in the absence of such integration - e.g. when identifying happiness and sadness from a single feature, such as the mouth.

Whilst the process by which normal children come to be able to identify facial expressions remains unknown, it would seem safe to hypothesise that certain factors must be involved. The child must be able to recognise that a person (or several different people) disply a certain facial configuration in certain situations or following events of a particular nature. For example, they must be at least able to recognise the fact that a face with a widely drawn mouth with up-turned eges, raised eyebrows, etc. (i.e. the attributes of a happy face) tends to go with or follow soon after a "happy" event. There must, presumably, be an element of empathy in that the child is aware that the other may feel "happiness" in certain circumstances, just as he would. Thus, to obtain a full understanding and ability to recognise when another is pulling a happy face the child must be able to combine his past and present knowledge about his feelings in certain situations, the facial display of others that goes with those situations, and be able to put these items of information together.

Of course, to be able to simply put a "correct" label to a facial display or sort it consistantly may not involve such a degree of empathy as has been implied above. But the child must at least be able to extract those aspects from faces to which he consistently applies the label. Given the complexity of facial expressions and the fact that one must be able to see what is common about a display of emotion, regardless of the particular physical attributes of the face which is displaying it, then it seems highly likely that an inability on the part of the autistic child to integrate his perceptions into meaningful wholes would necessarily mean that he would be poor at identifying people's facial expressions.

These points will be returned to later in the thesis, but suffice it to note at this juncture that those aspects of recognising expression at which the autistic child is fairly able, are those which are not greatly affected by temporal changes. That is to say, the physical characteristics of happy and sad mouths are reasonably consistent regardless of who exhibited them and when. In contrast, emotion displayed in the eye area, being more complex, is more variable between faces and, to a lesser extent, within each individual face over time. Additionally, it would seem reasonable to suggest that the recognition of a gestalt from a complex of components must involve the integration of several characteristics and relationships in a finite period of time. This process is qualitatively different from the identification of a single characteristic feature such as a smiling mouth, which has little need for temporal processing.

## 5.2 The Production of Facial Expressions

### 5.2.1: The autistic children's abilities

It was hypothesised above that one aspect of a child's ability to identify facial expressions might be his degree of empathic understanding. Given, too, that a correspondance was noted between a normal child's abilities to identify expressions and to produce them, it would be pertinent to investigate the autistic child's ability to produce expressions.

Ricks and Wing (1976) seem to be in little doubt about the fact that autistic children are usually able to smile, laugh, weep and show signs of fear and anger. But they tend only to show extremes of such emotions. However, virtually no non-verbal communication (as defined by Argyle and Cook, 1972, for example) appears to be universally present in the autistic child's repertoire. Insofar as facial expressions are part of one's non-verbal communicative abilities, it may be suggested that the autistic child's expressional behaviour reflects their innate "reflex" emotional response to their environment rather than an intent to communicate their feelings.

It was decided that the most valuable first step was to undertake a survey of the expressional ability of the autistic children studied. Two approaches were taken. First, the teachers and houseparents were given a list of basic expressions and asked to comment upon the children's ability to execute them. To supplement this the author visited the schools for an average of two days per week for two months in an attempt to observe the range of expressions which the children displayed, and to make a photographic record where possible.

Because of the informal nature of this survey, the results will
be presented informally. The findings of Ricks and Wing were broadly
confirmed in that most of the children were said to be capable of
smiling, laughing, weeping, and showing signs of fear and anger.
However, the teachers pointed out that expression of even these emotions
were not common, and most of the children were characterised by an
apparent flatness of affect. When emotion was displayed by facial
expression it tended to be fairly extreme, with shades of emotion
being almost totally absent. It was also of interest to note that
most people who worked with the children felt that many     expressed
emotions which were not seemingly contingent upon what had happened
or was happening to them. Other workers have also noted the existence
of inappropriate affect in the autistic child (Wing, 1965). Many of
the adults who knew the children felt that the children had at sometime
shown a reflex startle reaction; but none of them had ever displayed
an obvious expression of overt surprise. That is, whilst the children
had been known to react to an event as "unexpected", they had not shown
that they had "misexpected" an event (see Charlesworth, 1972, for a
discussion of the distinction between these two expressions).

All these points were supported by the author's own observations
of the children. The only expression which was noted that was not
brought to light by the houseparents or the teachers was that described
as "puzzlement". Kanner (1943) drew attention to the fact that most
autistic children do not look subnormal, whereas many other children
who score well below average on IQ tests do. Kanner went so far as
to claim that autistic children have intelligent physiognomies.
The present survey could only attribute this observation to the general

TABLE 5.4    Details of the subjects in the study of elicited
             expressions

| Group | N | Mean C.A. (sd) | Mean Full IQ (sd) |
|-------|---|----------------|-------------------|
| Autistic | 10 | 13.78 yrs (1.32) | 61.20 (14.17) |
| ESN | 9 | 13.91 yrs (1.02) | 60.09 (7.82) |

lack of expression the children displayed coupled with the aforementioned puzzled look, which might be said to give a child the
appearance of someone who is rapt in thought or intelligently reflecting
upon some matter.

Such factors as these may well have led some autistic children to
be thought of as enigmatic, or to be wrongly diagnosed as a normally
intelligent child who is going through a phase of withdrawal. Indeed,
such factors as their apparently normal and intelligent appearance
have been the primary motivation of many psychogenetic theories who
would have the "blame" for the child's condition fall on the parents
and their methods of child rearing.

This initial survey has thus set the scene in which one may view
the autistic child as being relatively affectless and generally
incapable of using facial expressions intentionally to communicate
their feelings to others. But if their ability to
produce facial expressions spontaneously is poor, are they equally
unable to produce expressions to order? A study was devised to
investigate the autistic children's ability to pull happy and sad
faces, compared with that of a group of ESN children.

## 5.2.2: Elicited Expressions

### Subjects

Ten autistic children were chosen from those who had taken part
in the previous studies of this thesis. These children's ages spanned
those of the children who had previously taken part. Nine ESN children
matched to the autistic children for chronological age and general
mental ability were also chosen. Details of these children can be
found in table 5.4.

Method and Procedure

Each child was taken on his own to a well-illuminated quiet room. He was told that he would be asked to make a couple of faces, and some pictures would be taken of him as he did so. The child was first asked to make a happy face, and a photograph was taken when the experimenter and an independent observer agreed that the child was doing his best. This necessarily introduced an element of subjective evaluation, and hence potential error, yet it was nonetheless felt to be a justified and reliably realistic measure of the children's abilities. Once this was done, the child was asked to make a sad face, and again the child's best effort was photographed. It should be noted that the child's teacher was also present to enable all possible methods of communicating requirements to the child to be made. Thus if the child seemed not to understand either the phrase "pull a face" or "make a face", then such phrases as "try to look happy/sad" would be used.

For five of the ESN children, pictures of their "happy" faces were not taken. Instead three independent observers from the children's school were asked to be present and to judge each child's performance on a seven point scale from "good" to "poor".[*] For the poor expressions of these children and for both expressions of the rest of the ESN children and of the autistic children, the photographs were given to ten independent raters who were naive as to which of the two expressions had been demanded of the children, or which type of child any particular photograph was of. These raters were asked first to classify each photograph as happy or sad, and then to judge how good an example of that expression each was on a seven point scale from "good" to "poor".

---

* Footnote: This was not the best methodology, and it is suggested that all children's expressions be recorded if this study is replicated.

TABLE 5.5    Mean scores given by raters to each groups' attempts
to pull happy and sad faces.  The raters scored on a
seven-point scale, with the correct expression giving
a positive rating, and an incorrect expression giving
a negative rating (hence the high sd of the autistic
children on happy faces).  Note a high score represents
a good example of the expression.

| Group | Happy (sd) | Sad (sd) |
|---|---|---|
| Autistic | 2.88 (3.38) | 3.06 (1.36) |
| ESN | 6.02 (0.17) | 3.50 (0.78) |

Results

The results are shown in table 5.5. A 2-by-2 ANOVA was computed and revealed a main effect of groups ($F_{1,36}$ = 9.45; $p < 0.01$), and a group-by-conditions interaction ($F_{1,36}$ = 5.91; $p < 0.025$). The results were indicative of the fact that the subnormal children were generally more able to pull accurate facial expressions than were the autistic children. The subnormal children were more able than them to pull happy faces (t = 2.87, df = 18; $p < 0.02$), but each was equally able at the sad faces (t = 0.36, df = 18, $p > 0.1$). And whilst the autistic children were equally good at both types of expression (t = 0.36, df = 9, $p > 0.1$), the ESN children were better at the happy ones than the sad (t = 8.47, df = 9, $p < 0.001$).

Thus whilst both groups were fairly poor at pulling sad faces, the ESN children alone were good at pulling happy faces. The similarity, though, between the two groups' responses when trying to pull sad faces belies the fact that the autistic children responded quite differently to the ESNs. Whereas the autistic children seemed genuinely unable (or barely able) to pull either face very well, the ESN children made much more thoughtful attempts to pull the sad faces. Their low scores may reflect the fact that they tended to report feeling self-conscious about pulling a sad face, and consequently tended to smile a little as the photographs were taken. There was also a tendency for them to report that "sadness" was something which one kept inside - and thus they simply rendered it by a passive "sad face" staring at the ground. This pose, however, was not one which the raters tended to score very highly, despite its possible realism.

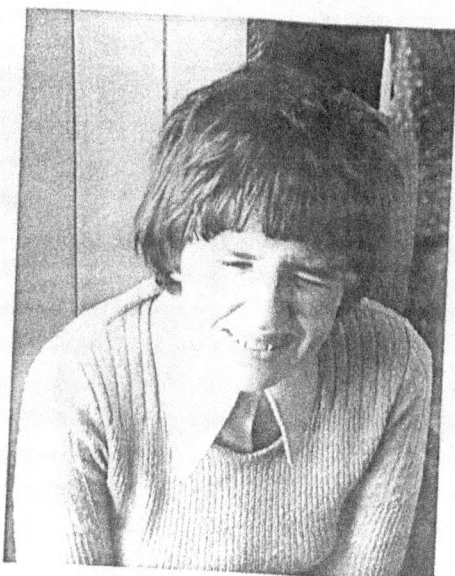

Figure 5.3a. Autistic girl's attempts at sad (top) and happy faces.

Figure 5.3b. A more able autistic boy's attempts (note expression almost totally in the mouth).

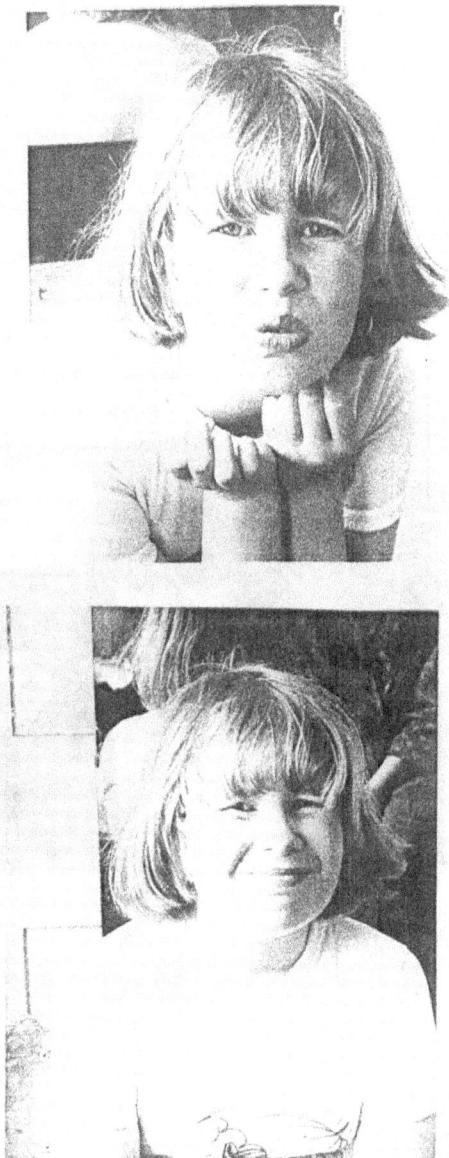

Figure 5.3c.  Another autistic girl's attempts.

Figure 5.3d. ESN girl's sad face which was typical of a type
not scored highly yet arguably "realistic".

A revealing finding was that two of the autistic children obtained an overall negative score for their attempt to pull a happy face. That is, one of them was judged on average to be pulling a poor sad face, and the other was generally judged to be pulling a good sad face! In all, six of the autistic children were given a negative score by at least one rater, whereas none of the ESN children were.

It should finally be noted that the five ESN children who were rated at the time of testing were all thought by the raters present to be pulling unequivocably good happy faces. Support for having done this is gained from the fact that the other ESN children also obtained a similar average ability for their attempts at the happy face.

In this experiment each child needed to understand what was required of him when he was asked to "pull a happy/sad face", for there were no models for him to copy. Thus it is possible that the superior performance by the ESN children noted above might have been partly due to their superior linguistic abilities. For this reason it was decided to undertake a study of the children's abilities to copy a facial expression which is demonstrated by a model. The following study reports the findings of such an investigation.

5.2.3: Copying Facial Expression

Subjects and Procedure

In this study autistic and ESN children matched to the autistic children for general ability were compared for their ability to copy a facial expression displayed by a model. It was also decided to add to the design of the experiment the factor of whether or not the child

TABLE 5.6    Details of the subjects in the study of copied
             expressions

| Group | N | Mean C.A. (sd) | Mean Full IQ (sd) |
|-------|---|----------------|-------------------|
| Autistic | 8 | 13.51 yrs (1.24) | 60.90 (13.92) |
| ESN | 8 | 13.44 yrs (0.98) | 61.24 (7.72) |

Figure 5.4. Autistic boy's attempts to copy an expression without feedback (top) and with feedback.

Figure 5.4b. ESN girl's attempts at copying with and without feedback.

had feedback of how well he was doing.  Eight of the children from each
of the groups who took part in the above experiment acted as subjects
in this study (see Table 5.6 for details).  Each child was taken alone
to a quiet well lit room in which was positioned a large mirror against
one wall.  At first the child was asked to stand with his back to the
mirror and to look at the face of a female model who was pulling "a
funny face" (figure 5.4 shows an example of it).  The child was asked
to "do as the lady is doing - pull a funny face like hers".  All
children seeemed to understand the requirements of the task and
immediately looked at her face and attempted to copy it.  A photograph
was taken of their best effort, and this was done such that it included
the model's face, too, reflected in the mirror behind the child's back.
The child was then asked to turn around and face the mirror so that he
or she could see both his or her own face and that of the model.  With
the visual feedback which this allowed each was asked to have a second
attempt at copying the model's facial expression.  Once again a
photograph was taken of the child's best attempt.  The photographs
were later given to each of a panel of ten raters who were asked to
score each photograph on a seven point scale for the accuracy of the
child's attempt to imitate the model (the scale ran from "very
inaccurate" to "very accurate").  The raters were not told what the
purpose of the experiment was, and they were given the photographs
in random order so that it was not possible to tell from which group
each child came.  All the photographs were in black and white, and each
was given the same attention to quality of the print.  Examples are
given in figure 5.4.

TABLE 5.7    Mean scores given by the raters on a seven point scale
             when the children were trying to copy a model's
             expression once without visual feedback, and again with
             feedback.    (Note a high score represents a judgement
             of good imitation).

| Group | Copy without feedback (sd) | Copy with feedback (sd) |
|-------|----------------------------|-------------------------|
| Autistic | 3.46 | 3.06 |
|  | (1.45) | (0.92) |
| ESN | 3.17 | 4.35 |
|  | (1.18) | (1.03) |

## Results

The results are shown in table 5.7. A two-by-two analysis of variance was computed on the results and revealed only a significant interaction of groups-by-condition ($F_{1,36}$=6.02; $p < 0.025$). This interaction reflected the fact that both groups tended to do equally well at copying the model (t = 1.83, df = 30, $p < 0.05$). Although there was, in fact, a trend for the ESN children to do a little better than the autistic children. However, the source of the interation resided in the fact that only the ESN children improved their performance when they were allowed access to visual feedback (t = 2.48, df = 7, $p < 0.01$, for the ESN children; and t = 0.88, df = 7, $p > 0.1$ for the autistic children). This finding is in concord with findings reported by Hermelin and O'Connor (1970) when (in conjunction with Frith) they gave autistic and subnormal children the task of following a 'maze' like track with a metal stylus. The children were required to do this with and without visual feedback of their efforts, and only the autistic children failed to gain from the availability of the visual information.

Given, then, that the autistic children showed a fairly good ability to copy facial expression, it may be noted that it is unlikely that their limited repertoire of expression is the result of their being unable to imitate the expressions of others.

Discussion

The ESN children were generally able to  pull happy and sad faces.

To the extent that they failed to pull sad faces convincingly it seemed

to either be due to their embarrassment or to their understanding of

the feeling which led them to pose in a fairly expressionless manner.

The autistic children, on the other hand, were less able to pull happy

and sad faces. Several of the autistic children pulled expressions

which were seen by some raters as being of the opposite kind of that

requested. Indeed, two autistic children attained overall averages

which implied that their happy faces were judged to be sad. This was

not true for any of the ESN children.

In Chapter Four a distinction was made between 'reflex' and 'non-

reflex' expressions of emotion. The former are spontaneous and may

communicate one's inner state to another but are not consciously

intended to do so. The primary intention behind the non-reflex

expressions is, by contrast, to communicate to another how one feels.

These expressions are thus part of the nonverbal complement to verbal

language. As with verbal language, these intended expressions must

be learnt by the child.

Babies are noted to show a very wide range of facial expressions,

and many of these are said to be surprisingly adult in their form

(Herka, 1965). However, there is evidence to suggest that the infant's

expressions do not always relate to the inner states they would be

expected to correspond to if they were an adult's. Bower (1974) notes

that there are several quite distinct facial displays which babies

show that are said to be a 'smile'. Moreover, all these different

displays tend to happen in quite different circumstances. It is thus

rather misleading to refer to all of the expressions by the same label.
An infant's earliest smiles may not only reflect happiness, but may
also indicate other internal states such as having wind. Similarly,
one cannot attribute an adult meaning to an infant's expression simply
because it looks like an adult's expression.

It may be that while certain facial displays are reflex expressions
of such inner states as 'happiness', 'anger', 'fear', or 'discomfort',
others may be relatively unrelated to any particular inner state. The
latter may be in some ways similar to infantile babble. Babble is a
necessary precursor to speech proper, and might be part of the child's
discovery that he can emit sounds. Although the theory is speculative,
it may be that early utterances which at first carry no specific
meaning (none which is socially defined anyway) come to acquire meaning
through the child's interaction with an adult. The adult marks the
child's utterances and shapes them towards more socially acceptable
usage. At first these utterances may be idiosyncratic to the infant,
but it is important that the adult impute meaning to the child's
behaviour and thus meet his needs. Through the adult's meeting of the
infant's needs, and thus showing the baby that there is a correspondence
between his utterances and things being done to him, the baby may come
to imbue his utterances with intent. In this way the baby can progress
from a stage of pure demanding to being able to request. There is
growing evidence that this is true (see Bruner, 1975a, b) and that
such early utterances develop into spoken language proper in order
to fulfil the need to regulate joint attention between mother and
child.

In a similar sense, early facial displays may be a necessary
precursor of later more socially acceptable communication of feeling.
Adults may   serve a similar purpose to that in the child's development
of speech by shaping the child's displays by marking them in a
consistent manner.  Thus, mothers may say such phrases as "Who's a
happy boy then?" in situations when the infant is thought to be
displaying happiness.  Consequently, if the infant starts life by
producing a 'smile' in several diverse situations, then this shaping
by his caretaker will lead him to emit it mainly in one type of
situation and not others;  therefore in this case he will learn to
smile when he is happy and not when he is not.

The strength of this theory is that it avoids having to explain
how a child is able to imitate the facial display he would need in
order to produce any given expression.  However, this is not to say
that imitation does not play a part in the child's acquisition of
facial expressions.  It does.  But the importance of imitation in
the first months of life may not only be in terms of the child's
acquiring the ability to produce facial displays;  in a similar way,
imitation does not simply lead to the child's acquisition of his
first words.  Rather, it may be that the adult imitates the infant's
expressions, and through this   the infant comes to associate certain
expressions in other's faces with certain types of feeling or
experience of his own.  Indeed, there is a growing body of evidence
that this is the case (eg. Pawlby, 1977).

The consequence of the infant coming to associate a certain
feeling in himself with the expression on another's face, is that
the perception of the expression may come to evoke the corresponding

feeling in him. That is, seeing a smiling face may-evoke the feeling
of pleasure that he felt whenever he previously viewed the display
and the adult was imitating him. Thus viewing a smiling face may cause
a baby to smile not because he is copying the facial expression, but
because it evoked a feeling within him that he associates with seeing
that expression. It then seems a natural step for the baby to
associate expression in others with feeling in himself and later to
understand that he too makes such expressions. This is surely a basis
for the acquisition of empathy. But one may note here that a baby
will only be able to follow this course of development if he is able
to put together the differing aspects of his perceptions - an empathy
with what he sees, and the contingency of other's behaviour upon his own.

Obviously there are other factors involved in the acquisition of
a full range of facial expressions. Many require complex social
learning, and it is thus not surprising that they develop much later
in life (see Gates, 1923). Imitation of others' expressions may play
an increasingly important role in the acquisition of facial expressions
with age. Insofar as this is the case, it would seem that the autistic
child is able to imitate others' expressions - thus his major problems
with producing facial expressions must lie elsewhere.

His major problems may lie in his behaviour in the first year of
life, and the consequences of his innate cognitive deficit. To
summarise what the normal infant might require in order to gain a
basic ability to produce and identify expressions:

1. The infant must produce a sufficient range of facial
   expressions for the mother to respond to. That is, if
   the mother's copying and marking of the child's behaviour
   is important, then clearly the infant must produce
   sufficient behaviour.

2. The mother must copy those examples of the baby's facial
   displays which she feels reflect the socially acceptable
   emotion or feeling for that display (e.g. reinforcing
   smiling when the child's inner state is pleasure and
   not at other times).

3. The infant must produce his displays with sufficient
   consistency such that the mother can gauge which facial
   displays go with which inner states (i.e. insofar as
   there may be several different types of smile, for instance,
   the baby must be consistent as to which type he produces
   when he's happy).

4. The baby must be able to detect and encode the fact that
   a facial display on the mother's part tends to go with
   a certain type of feeling in himself.

5. It may be that as time passes the baby should have the
   feeling evoked in him whenever he sees the expression
   if empathy is to develop and he is to appear to copy his
   mother. This may be rewarding for her.

It is not claimed that this list is complete, but nonetheless
let us consider that these factors may be essential to the development
of facial expression and an understanding of its use and meaning.

In the above experiments it was found that the ESN children's
abilities to recognise and produce expressions were equally good, and
they had no history of being poor at expressing emotion early in life.
On the other hand, the autistic children were both less able to
recognise and to produce facial expressions. Although the data was
not available for the present children, autistic babies are frequently
reported to have been generally affectless during their development.
Many autistic babies are said to be exceptionally passive or to fret
and cry and be very difficult to comfort. Thus it seems that whilst
some autistic babies may produce insufficient facial displays for the
mother to mark and copy, others may produce them for reasons which
are hard to discern. In addition, autistic infants have been described
as showing little willingness to interact with their caretakers (Wing,
1976a; Newson, 1980). And there is also evidence to show that autistic
babies fail to exhibit normal pre-verbal conversation patterns of turn
taking and so forth (Newson, op.cit.).

Bearing in mind the above mentioned five points it seems that the
autistic child may be ill-equipped on all fronts. He may produce too
few expressions or may produce them with insufficient consistency.
The studies so far reported also support the contention that the
autistic child may have difficulties in integrating his perceptions
both over time and over different aspects of ongoing experience.
Consequently he may be unable to perceive the links between his inner
states and the expressions displayed by the mother. A failure to
perceive such links may mean that the baby fails to smile back at his
mother and is thus considerably less responsive than a normal baby.
This inability to link inner states with other's facial expressions
may lead to a lack of understanding as to what facial expression of
emotion is about, what its purpose is.

The literature also suggests that autistic children may have had abnormal or deficient babble (Wing, 1976; Bartak et al, 1975) and idiosyncratic pre-verbal utterances (Ricks, 1972, 1975). Thus it seems that the autistic child has abnormalities in both the verbal and non-verbal precursors of communicative ability. Consequently, a failure to integrate perceptions into wholes or thematic classes may be coupled with a lack of production of necessary precursury behaviours in the autistic child, and it may lead to his poor and abnormal communicative abilities. This point will be returned to in Chapter Seven.

In summary, the autistic child seems to have a fairly normal range of spontaneous or reflex expressions, which are not primarily intended to communicate something to others, but he may fail to grasp what conscious expression of emotion is _for_ due to an inability to integrate the various aspects of his perception. However, he may show fairly good ability where he need not interpret the meaning of his perception, for example, when he is required to reproduce a facial expression exactly as seen. He is thus at least able to act as if he comprehends the connexion between facial expression by others and his own facial displays. Hence any theory which contends that he has a defect in sensory processing that affects the integration of perceptions must take this possible comprehension into account.

CHAPTER 6

EYE MOVEMENTS WHEN PERCEIVING FACES

6.1: Introduction

This chapter will deal with a computerised study of the eye movements of autistic and ESN children whilst looking at faces. Because the study was undertaken after the main body of work on this thesis was complete, different children were used (Dutch ones, in fact). The study also made use of a piece of apparatus which the author had on loan for a short while. Hence the experiment stands only as a pilot project in this area of study.

To date very little is known about the details of autistic children's gaze behaviour. On an anecdotal level, they have been reported to look out of the corners of their eyes and to use peripheral vision to inspect objects. But this has so far been a clinical impression - without specialised equipment it is not possible to say for certain that a child tends to use peripheral vision when inspecting his environment. On a less anecdotal level, Hermelin and O'Connor (1970) have reported that autistic children are characterised by relatively brief fixation times. They also noted that the autistic children made fewer comparative gaze movements between objects. That is, they were unlike the subnormal children tested insofar as they tended not to compare and contrast the pairs of stimuli they were presented with. Rather they would tend to shift their gaze from figure to ground and back to figure again.

Apart from the above, our knowledge about their gaze behaviour must be drawn from inference. For instance, it is said that autistic children actively avoid eye contact (Hutt et al., 1965), although others

Figure 6.1.  Eye movements when viewing a face (Yarbus 1967)
Compare this to Figure 3.1 and note the greater
scanning of the mouth of the smiling face.

have disputed this (Hermelin and O'Connor, 1978; see Chapter Two). If this is so, then one can conclude that their gaze behaviour shows a certain amount of selectivity and is by no means random. However, as to the precise nature of their gaze when looking at faces, for example, one is unaware whether they have well defined scanning strategies relatively longer fixations on some parts more than others, and so forth.

Turning for a moment to the literature on normal peoples eye movements when looking at faces, one notes that there is a host of evidence to suggest that scanning patterns are unique and selective (see Argyle and Cook, 1976). Yarbus (1967) found that subjects fixate areas of maximum interest for periods of about one third of a second. These fixations on such points of interest are linked by saccades and are repeated in cycles. In the case of faces people look mainly at the eyes and the mouth (see figure 6.1). Walker-Smith and her colleagues (1977) also studied eye movements of adults when looking at faces. In one task subjects were required to match a test face with a previously presented target face, and in a second task they had to compare two simultaneously presented faces. Walker-Smith et al. found that each subject tended to have a preferred feature which they would fixate when trying to tell whether they had seen a face before or whether two faces were the same. Moreover, the preferred features were mainly the eyes and the mouth, with some subjects choosing the nose as well.

Studies of the eye movements of abnormal subjects seem almost entirely restricted to an interest in schizophrenic patients. There have been many studies on this (Holzman et al, 1973, 1974, 1975; Shagass et al, 1974; Lindsey et al, 1978) and they have generally claimed that schizophrenics have impaired smooth-pursuit eye movements (SPEMs).

Apparently between 65% and 80% of schizophrenic patients and about 45%

of the first degree relatives have shown disordered SPEMs, in contrast

to about a 6% prevalence in the normal population. The reasons for this

remain obscure, and as yet the measurement of eye movements seems more

concerned with a method of diagnosing schizoprenia.

It is noted that none of the above studies of the eye movements of

normal or abnormal subjects have involved children. Thus in many ways a

study of the eye movements of autistic children will be breaking new

ground. For this reason few predictions can be offered. In the following

section various aspects of the gaze behaviour of autistics will be discussed,

and expectations regarding their gaze behaviour whilst viewing faces

will be outlined.

6.2 Computer Based Study of Autstic Children's Eye Movements

After the body of work which makes up this thesis was complete, the author was given the use of a G & W Applied Science Laboratories "Eye View Monitor System" (sold under the trade name of Wittiker, model 1998). This apparatus is one of the more advanced of its kind and has particular advantages over other systems when working with abnormal children. It requires the subject to sit in a fairly relaxed manner, but has a computerised system which tracks head movements and thus can allow the child to move a little during measurements. It relies upon a corneal reflection measurement of the position of the eye. Information about where the subject is looking is obtained by means of an infra-red light which is bounced off the subject's eye and back into an infra-read camera. Hence there is no need for the subject to have anything on or near his person, and he will be unaware that his eye movements are being measured.

It has been noted several times in this thesis that it would be of great interest to have details of autistic children's eye movements when they look at other's faces. Although it was not possible to use the computerised eye-movement recorder with the children who acted as subjects in the previous experiments, it was nonetheless felt to be of value to investigate the eye movements of another sample of autistic children.

One aspect of autism which the study of face perception in section 3.1 tried to deal with was whether or not the autistic child avoids eye-contact. Whilst the study of face perception indicated that it was unlikely that he does, it is noted that the indication was based upon the assumption that if normal people know the eye area of faces well because they look at eyes, then autistic children should not know the eye area well since

they avoid eye-contact. This point could be investigated directly by
the use of an eye-movement recorder which allows one to quantify the
autistic child's eye movements when he's looking at faces.

## Gaze Avoidance in Autism

In section 2.3, a survey was presented on the various views of an
empirical evidence relating to the topic of gaze-avoidance in autism.
It was noted that very few studies of the topic have been undertaken.
One of the most often quoted studies is that of Hutt and Ounsted (1966),
in which they proposed that the autistic child is over-aroused and that
he avoids mutual gaze to prevent his level of arousal becoming any higher.
Whilst there have been a few studies which have provided support for such
a claim (eg. Richer and Coss, 1972), these have been highly criticised.
The work of Hermelin and O'Connor (1967) on this subject has received less
criticism, although its experimental approach has been termed "unnatural"
(see, Mittler, 1971). Their studies led them to posit that the autistic
child's "gaze avoidance" might only be apparent and due to their having
a very low fixation time on all things. As Beate Hememlin has put it:
"If you were a table, you too would complain that the autistic child
avoids your gaze".

Section 2.3 concluded that while the experimental work left an unresolved
picture, it nonetheless seemed from the clinical evidence that the autistic
child may not avoid gaze contact, but may rather be indifferent to it or
use it abnormally.

Because the measurement of a person's eye movements in a totally
natural setting is beyond the technology available at the present time,
it was felt that a laboratory based approach that attempted to be as

natural as possible was justified. It was thus decided to adapt and extend Hermelin and O'Connor's (1967) study of gaze aversion by the utilization of the computerised eye movement recorder. In their study Hermelin and O'Connor asked the child to look into a box which had a black interior. At the far end of its interior the child could see an illuminated live face. This face was seen by each subject once with its eyes open and once with them closed. Through another apperture in the box a second researcher was able to note the length of time each child spent looking at each of the faces. They used this experimental set-up to compare the gaze behaviour of autistic children with that of a matched group of normal controls. They found that the autistic children looked less long at each face than did the normal children. However, both groups looked at the face with its eyes open and the one with them closed for equal lengths of time. Thus Hermelin and O'Connor concluded that the autistic children did not evidence gaze aversion to the face with its eyes open.

In the same paper (1967), Hermelin and O'Connor also studied the eye movements of autistic, ESN and normal children when looking at other stimuli. They found that the tendency for the autistic children to have very brief visual fixations was general to all the stimuli they required then to look at, but that they did spend longer looking at the human faces than at other stimuli. Because the interior of the box in which the stimuli were seen was blackened, it may be noted that the autistic children can be said to have engaged in more non-directed gaze than the other children. They also spent far less time looking from one stimulus to the other (when a pair were presented) and instead tended to look from stimulus to background and back to stimulus again.

The present study thus had four main goals:

1. To investigate the gaze behaviour of autistic children whilst
   looking at faces in a situation allowing them to exhibit a
   natural pattern of gaze activity.

2. To compare the gaze behaviour of autistic children with that
   of ESN children matched for mental and chronological age.

3. To extend the study by investigating the autistic child's
   gaze when viewing other types of face (smiling, talking, etc.)
   and other stimuli.

4. To repeat Hermelin and O'Connor's study of the autistic child's
   eye movements when looking at faces with open and closed eyes.

## Methodology and Predictions

It was stated above that present technology does not allow one to
measure a child's eye movements whilst he is going about his normal daily
activities. Thus one must necessarily put the child into an 'unnatural'
situation in the sense that he will not be used to it. Because eye
movement recorders which do not require the subject to wear a piece of
apparatus generally need fairly low light levels (to obtain a large pupil
diameter), and a reasonably motionless subject, there are certain
constraints which one must immediately put upon the testing situation.
A full description of the testing procedure and the conditions of testing
will be given later, however, it will be noted that given the requirements
of the eye movement recorder the present study was made as natural as
possible.

It was decided that not only should the subjects see faces with open
and closed eyes, but they should also see smiling faces, sad faces, talking
faces, and ones that look away. These additional stimuli were chosen to

test the aforementioned hypotheses of gaze avoidance and also provide
further information about the gaze activity of autistic children whilst
viewing faces displaying emotional expression. Several predictions may
be made regarding the gaze of autistic children whilst viewing these
faces:

1. Hutt et al. have proposed that autistic children avoid eye contact,
or indeed looking at faces in general because they find them too arousing.
However, arousal is a complex topic, and it is somewhat reductionist to
talk simply in terms of faces arousing autistic children above an already
abnormally high baseline. Nonetheless, Hutt et al.'s predictions may be
tested in the present study. It is possible that some faces are more
'arousing' than others. Certainly one would expect them to look less at
a face which was looking at them than at one with its eyes closed or
which is looking away. But there is also the implication in Hutt et al's
work that emotional expression and social contact is arousing to the
autistic child, and thus one would expect them to avoid this, too. That
is, one might tentatively predict that Hutt et al.'s theory suggests that
an autistic child would look less at a smiling face than at a passive one,
and perhaps he would also look less at a person who was trying to talk
to him than at either of the other two faces. Similarly, if the autistic
child understands what a 'sad' face is then perhaps he will also look
less at this than at a passive face. In the present study the sad face
was also averting gaze. Thus, because the elements which make up the
passive face with averted gaze and the sad face are the same, if the
child shows different gaze behaviour to the two kinds of face this implies
that he viewed them as different, and possibly he has understood that
one was expressing emotion and the other was not. Likewise, if the smiling
face looking at the child is inspected in a different manner than the
passive staring face, then once again one can conclude that he saw the
two faces as different.

2.  As indicated above, if the autistic child appreciates facial expressions then he should respond differently to the sad averted face than to the passive averted one. He should also respond differently to the smiling face than to the one which is passively staring at him.

3.  It was suggested in section 3.1 that the autistic children's above average knowledge of the mouth area of faces might be due to their tending to use lip-read cues. If this is true, then one would expect it to be evidenced in their gaze behaviour by their tending to look at the lower half of the face. Whilst this might not be so for all faces, it should certainly be true in response to the talking face.

4.  Support for the findings of Hermelin and O'Connor would be found if the autistic child looks less long at faces than does the ESN child. Further support would be gained if both types of children tended to look as often at the face with its eyes open as the one with its eyes closed. One would also expect from their work that the autisitcs' fixations would be briefer than those of the ESN children, and that they would engage in fewer comparative shifts of gaze from one part of the face to another.

Finally, if the autistic child views faces as qualitatively different from other visual stimuli, then his eye movements should reflect this. Thus if the autistic child is presented with a schematic house to look at, then he should exhibit gaze activity different from that he exhibited when looking at faces. Moreover, by showing the children such pictures of houses one would be able to test the results of the sorting experiment in section 3.2, which found no evidence that autistic children tend to look at the lower half of all things. Naturally,

TABLE 6.1    Details of the three subjects tested in the computerized
study of eye movements while looking at faces.
(M.A. calculated using "De Snijders-Oomen Niet-Verball
Intelligentieschaal", by Snijders, J.T.H. and Snijders-
Oomen, N. (1975); Groningen).

| Child | Onset of symptoms | C.A. | M.A. |
|-------|-------------------|------|------|
| Autistic boy | < 30 months | 11.42 yrs | 4.90 yrs |
| Autistic girl | < 30 months | 10.58 yrs | 5.08 yrs |
| ESN girl | (from birth?) | 10.67 yrs | 5.21 yrs |

all the results obtained with the autistic children could also be compared with those of an ESN child so that any abnormalities in the autistic children's gaze behaviour may be more certainly attributed to their 'autism'.

It will be noted that this study has pertinence to nearly all of the foregoing experiments reported in this thesis, and thus may give rise to some potentially unifying conclusions.

Subjects

This study took place in Holland, and thus the subjects who had taken part in the other studies reported in this thesis were not available. There was also a time limit on the availability of the eye movement recorder. Consequently it was decided to run only a small selection of children. The main criterion for selection of the autistic children (beyond the assessment of their condition, which had to be in line with Rutter's 1978 description) was that they had to be able to sit reasonably still during the time of testing and not be distressed by the testing situation. Two autistic children met these requirements, one boy and one girl both of whom were particularly "classic" in their autistic symptoms. Both children had an air of aloofness and showed very little contact with people. The boy had no spoken language and had never been seen to use gesture to indicate his needs. The girl had a few words, no gesture, and was a little more sociable than the boy (in that she seemed more aware of the presence of other people). Details of these subjects are given in table 6.1. As can be seen from the table, both autistic children had an onset of symptoms within the first thirty months of life. To compare the performance of these two autistic children, an ESN girl of similar general ability but exhibiting no signs of autism, was chosen.

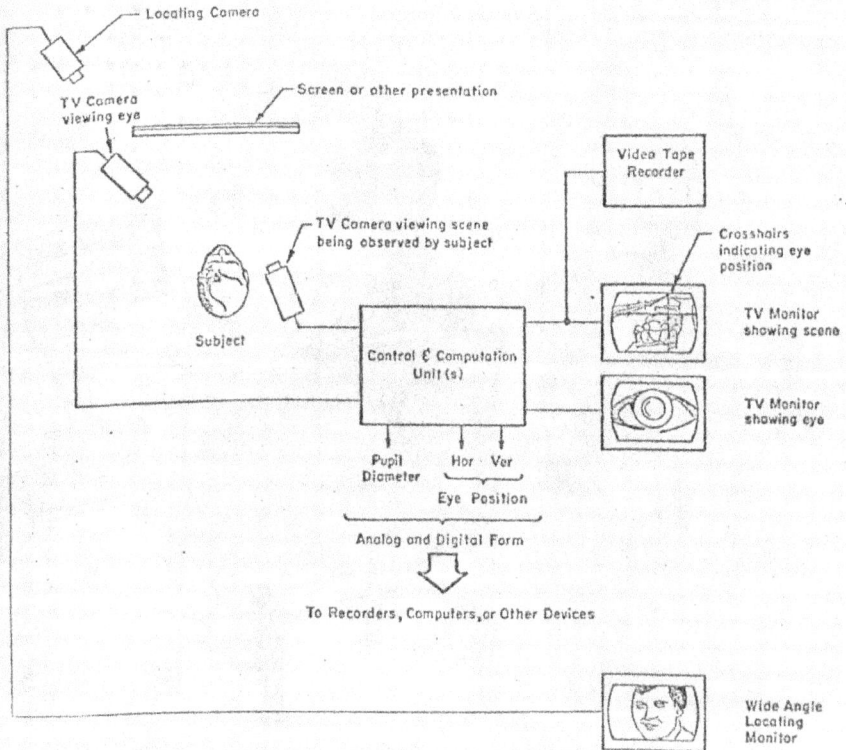

Figure 6.2  Eye View Monitor System Configuration.

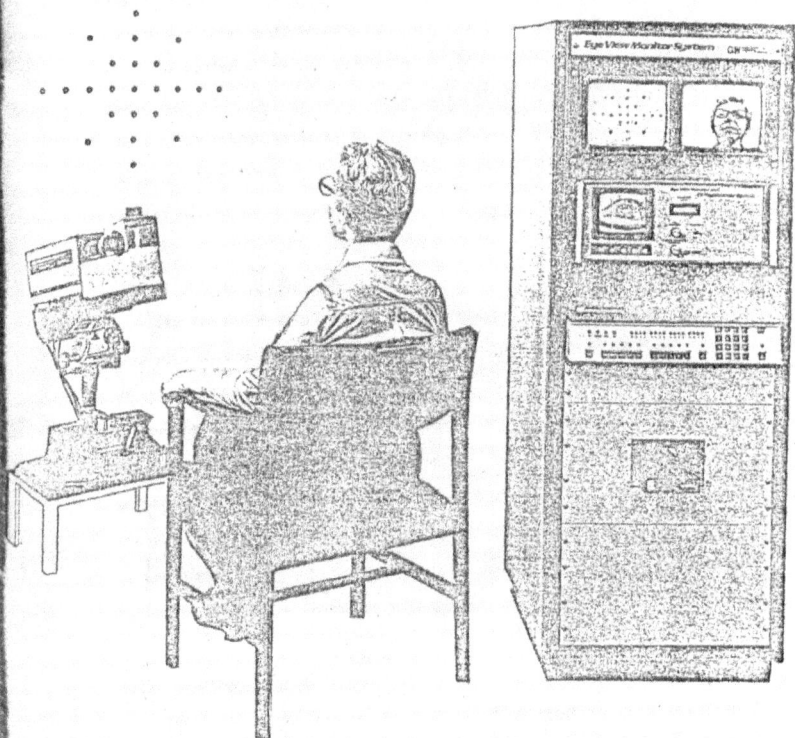

Figure 6.3. **Subject seated at F**... (from equipment manual).

Equipment and Materials

The main piece of equipment used in this study was the G & W model 1998 "computer based head tracking eye view monitor system". A schematic representation of the components of the system is shown in figure 6.2. Figure 6.3 shows a photograph of a subject's eye-movements being measured with the equipment whilst looking at an idealised display. It will be noted that this picture omits the camera which would be positions behind the subject's head in order to have a record of what they are seeing (although the output from such a camera is shown in the upper left monitor of the control panel).

(i) Principles of operation

The subject's eye rotation (as opposed to translation resulting from head motion) and his point of fixation are determined by the measurement of the centre of the pupil with respect to the centre of the corneal reflection. The two features of the eye move together with head motion but move differentially with eye rotation, hence the difference in their positions is indicative of the eye's point of fixation. In this way the eye position is independent of head position as long as the pupil image is contained within the field ov view of the camera. This allows the system to tolerate a degree of head motion, talking, etc.

(ii) Components of the system

The heart of the system was an all-purpose computer which was linked to three television cameras. In front of the child, and below the display he was to watch, were placed two cameras (see figure 6.3) and an infra-red projector. One of the cameras was used to record the infra-red beam after it had been bounced off the subject's eye, and thus provided the computer with the above mentioned information regarding pupil and corneal reflection positions. The second camera had a wide-angle lens on it for

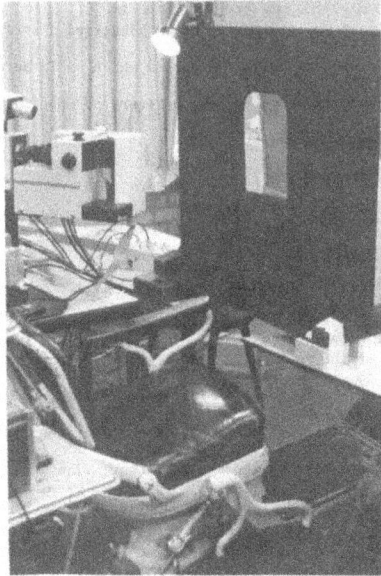

Figure 6.4. Early version of this study's set-up.

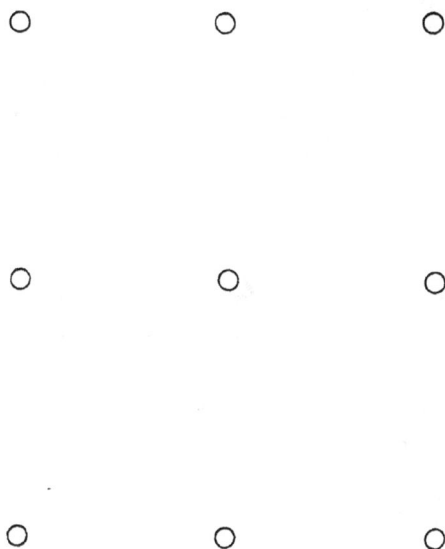

Figure 6.5 Calibration grid shown approximately half
full size. The cirles were drawn on a red transparent sheet of plastic and a light shone from
behind for the child track visually.

monitoring the general position of the child's head. This was necessary in order to line up the infra-red beam on the child's eye and to keep it there. A simulated output from these two cameras is shown in the upper right and lower left monitors of the control panel in figure 6.3. The position and focus of the two cameras in front of the child could be altered from the control panel. The apparatus in front of the child also contained an automatic head-movement monitoring system. This kept the child's pupil in the camera's view by using a second infra-red beam system to give feedback to a mirror, the position of which was altered in accordance with the head position. A third camera was placed behind the child in order to obtain a record of what he was seeing. The output of this camera was also displayed on the main control panel (see figure 6.3).

The child sat in a highbacked chair of the kind which dentists use. This allowed one to adjust the position of each child such that his face could be set at one metre away from the stimulus. Such a chair also minimized forward and backward movements for which the recorder cannot compensate. In front of the child was a table around which was draped a black cloth which hid the rear of the table from the child's view. On top of the table a screen was placed which was painted matt black, and measured approximately one metre by one metre (see figure 6.4, for a photograph of this in an early pilot of this study - the black cloth is absent and the measuring cameras are placed higher). In the centre of the screen was a rectangular window a little bigger than a person's head. There were two doors attached to the back of this window so that either could be shut across it. One of these was a black wooden door which prevented the subject from seeing what was happening behind the screen. The other "door" was used for calibration purposes. This was made from a wooden frame across which was stretched some transparent red plastic. On this plastic were drawn nine black circles of about 4mm diameter. These circles mapped out a rectangular grid of about 17 cm by 25 cm (see figure 6.5).

The subject was to see a face appear at the screen's window, and thus a spot light which threw a sharp circle of light onto the window was set up behind the child's chair. With this light shining upon the presenter's face it was impossible for her to see the child, thus a dim (15 watt) light was set up above the child so that the presenter of the faces could see him, which was important if the situation was to be as natural as possible.

The child's fixation point was displayed by cross-wires which were superimposed upon the output of the camera filming what the child was seeing. A Phillips video-recorder was used to make a video record of the resulting picture.

(iii)Calibration procedure

Once the infra-red beam had been set-up in the correct position on one of the child's eyes, then calibration could begin. Essentially the child was required to look at each of the nine circles in turn that were drawn on the red plastic covering the window in the screen (the circles were numbered 1 to 3 on the top row, 4 to 6 on the middle row, and 7 to 9 on the bottom row). However, it was not possible to use speech to ask the autistic children to do this. Hence it was decided to use a 4 mm spot of light held up to the back of the red plastic at the point where the circles were. This spot of light could be made to "dance around" in order to attract the child's attention but once attracted the spot was held still for the calibration of that point. With the computer in the "DAT" mode one simply had to get a child to look at circle number 1 and then press button 1 on the computer facia. One then would press button 2 when the child looked at circle number 2 and so forth. In this fashion the calibration procedure could be completed very quickly, and such a procedure considerably increased the likelihood that the child could be calibrated before he tired of the situation (as might have been the case with the autistic children). The computer instantly calculated the position of the eye with respect to each of the 9 points in space, and thus a second run through the circles found that the cross-wires would cross exactly over the circle being fixated. Because all that the child would see was to be within the area defined by the 9 point grid one could be certain of the child's fixations on the stimuli to within 1 degree of visual angle (according to the maker's claims this corresponds to an area of about 1 cm diameter at the screen). Considerable movement could be tolerated by the child before recalibration would be needed, and this was not found to be necessary for any of the children tested.

Method and Procedure

Each child was tested individually. The eye-movement recorder demanded a fairly low level of lighting. But in order to allow him to acclimate himself to the room the child was introduced to it with the lights fully on. Only when the child had had ample opportunity to see the room and become accustomed to it were the lights lowered. The child sat in a high-backed chair which supported his head at a position of about one metre from the screen. The calibration procedure was carried out first in the manner described above. The child then saw a person's face appear at the screen's window. This face was that of a female undergraduate. She displayed the following in random order: a happy face which looked at the child's eyes, a sad face which looked away from the child, a talking face which spoke to the child in a social manner (saying "Hello N", and such like, in a conversational way), an expressionless face which looked at the child

# Figure 6.6

Included here are examples
of the houses shown.

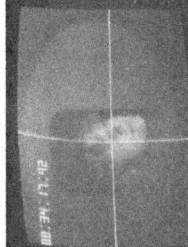

(a) Passive averted

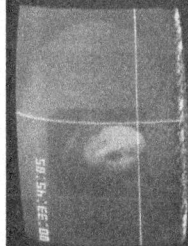

(b) Sad averted

(a) Eyes closed

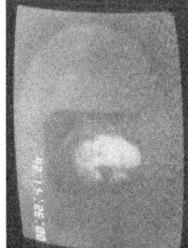

(d) Talking face

(e) A house

(f) A house

(g) Passive stare

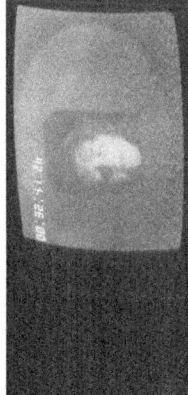

(h) Three frames of autistic girl viewing face with its eyes closed.

and tried to gain eye contact, an expressionless face which looked
away from the child to a point behind and to one side of him and finally
an expressionless face turned in the direction of the child but with
eyes closed.

The child saw each of these conditions twice and for about fifteen
seconds each time. During the presentation of a condition the spotlight
was switched on, and between them it was switched off so that the child
could only see the unilluminated homogeneously black screen. The period
between presentations lasted about five seconds. In practice it was found
that this speed and duration of presentation of the conditions provided
a rapid pace and ample eye movement data while minimising distraction on
the part of the child. However, the presentation was not thought to be
so fast as to 'overload' the child with too much information in too
little time. The only restriction placed on the order of presentation
was that two of the same condition should not follow consecutively.

When the different displays of faces had been seen, the child was
shown two more stimuli; these were both schematic representations of
houses and were both shown for about fifteen seconds with a gap of about
five seconds intervening (see figure 6.6).

When all these conditions had been shown to the child, the calibration
screen was put back in place and the child's attention was drawn to a
few of the circles by the use of the spot of light. It was thus possible
to ascertain whether the child's eye movements had remained calibrated
throughout the session.

Figure 6.7a Examples of the recordings (see also Fig 6.6)

(a) Three frames of the autistic boy looking at the smiling face – note fixations of the order of a few hundredths of a second are typical for him.

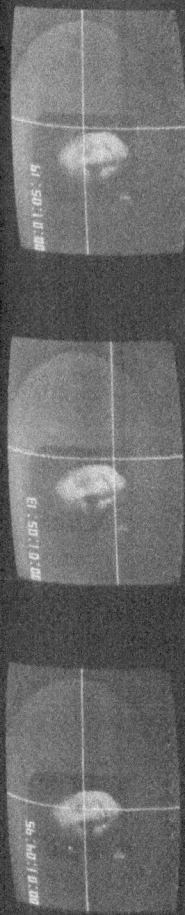

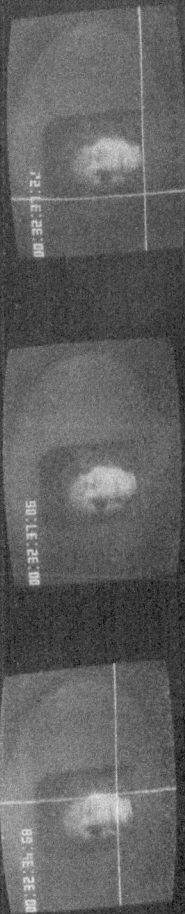

(b) Six frames from the autistic girl viewing the face with its eyes closed. Note the tendency to shift from face to off-screen to face again.

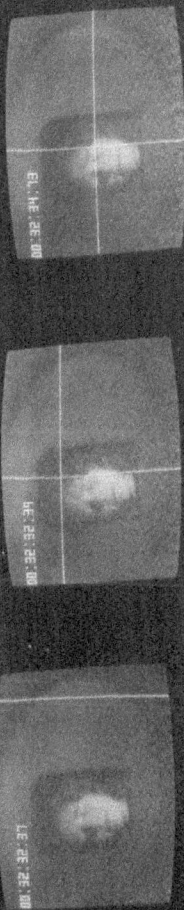

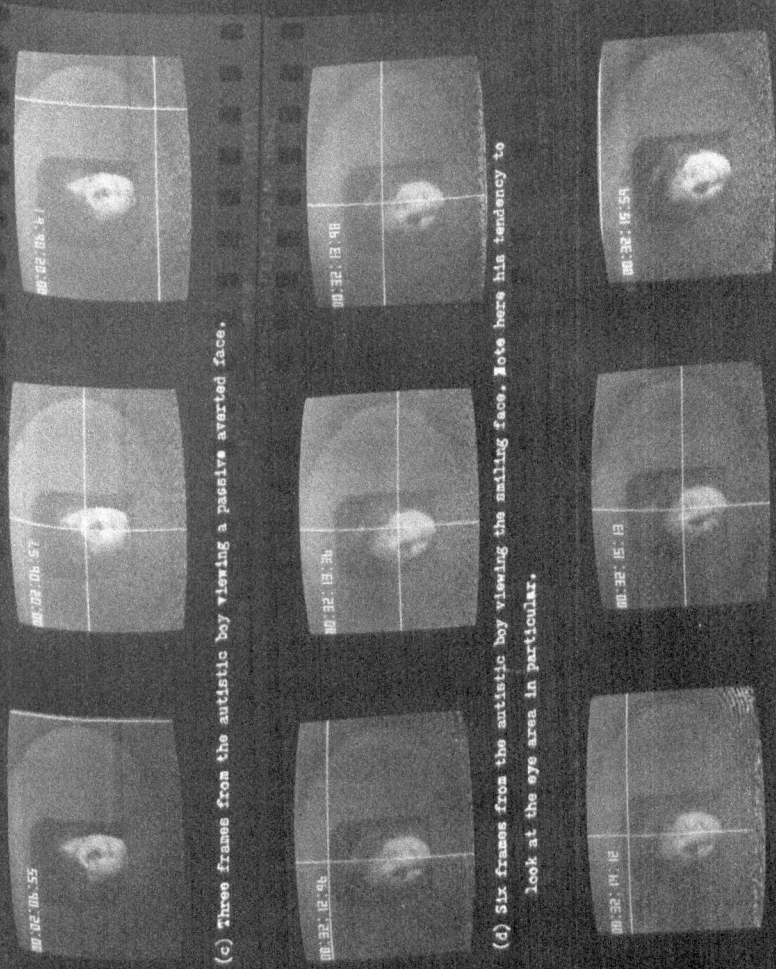

Figure 6.7b Examples of recordings.

(c) Three frames from the autistic boy viewing a passive averted face.

(d) Six frames from the autistic boy viewing the smiling face. Note here his tendency to look at the eye area in particular.

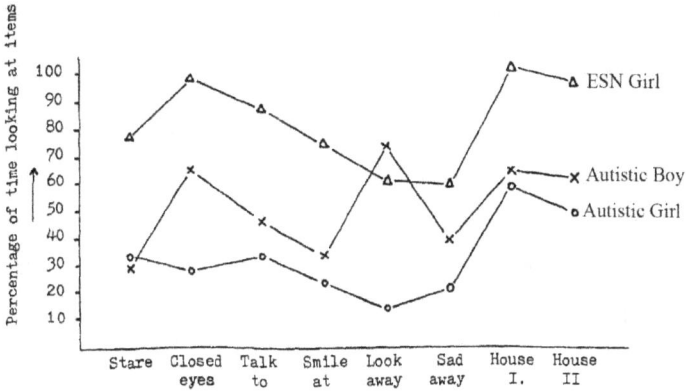

Figure 6.8  Average percentage of time spent by each child
looking at each of the items.

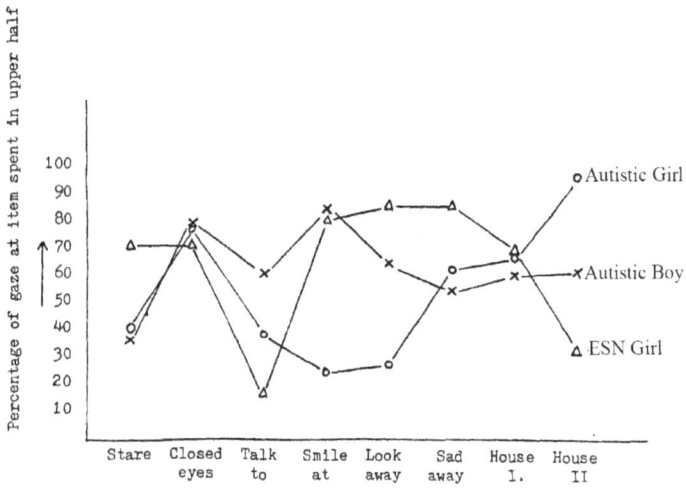

Figure 6.9 Each child's percentage of gaze at the upper
half of each item.

TABLE 6.2  Average fixation times when looking on the stimuli; and when looking at them, the average fixation times in the upper and lower halves.

| | Passive Stare | | | Eyes closed | | | Talk to | | | Smile at | | | Look away | | | Sad away | | | Houses | | |
|---|---|---|---|---|---|---|---|---|---|---|---|---|---|---|---|---|---|---|---|---|---|
| | On | Up | Low | On | Up | Low | On | Up | Low | On | Up | Low | On | Up | Low | On | Up | Low | On | Up | Low |
| Autistic Girl | 0.64 | 0.55 | 0.72 | 0.58 | 0.91 | 0.25 | 0.89 | 0.70 | 1.04 | 0.88 | 0.57 | 1.06 | 0.61 | 1.38 | 0.45 | 0.42 | 0.49 | 0.35 | 0.91 | 1.29 | 0.42 |
| Autistic Boy | 0.70 | 0.64 | 0.74 | 1.29 | 1.33 | 1.19 | 0.89 | 1.08 | 0.71 | 1.01 | 1.2 | 0.56 | 0.94 | 1.06 | 0.76 | 0.89 | 1.05 | 0.76 | 0.86 | 0.95 | 0.75 |
| ESN girl | 1.75 | 2.47 | 1.02 | 1.33 | 1.87 | 0.79 | 2.25 | 1.19 | 2.78 | 0.99 | 1.68 | 0.35 | 1.05 | 1.52 | 0.38 | 1.69 | 2.73 | 0.45 | 1.94 | 2.48 | 1.56 |

The child's eye movements were recorded onto video and were superimposed on the picture of what he was seeing at the time.  A digital
timing record was superimposed on the recording of what the child was
seeing and allowed one to study the timing of the children's eye movements
to within one hundreth of a second.  Examples of these recordings are
shown in figure 6.7.  It should be noted that if the child did not look
at the face (or house) when the spotlight was on, then he could only look
at the surrounding black board of the screen - no other objects were
visible.

## Results and discussion

All three children's eye movements were found to have remained calibrated
during the testing periods.

The data was analysed in three main ways:  first, in terms of the time
spent looking at each stimulus;  second, in terms of the children's average
fixation times when looking at the stimuli, and third, in terms of the
number of fixations on each stimulus.  All three measures were also
analysed separately for the upper and lower halves of the stimuli.
Graphs displaying the first and third measures are shown in figures 6.8
and 6.9.  Table 6.2 shows the results of the calculation of the average
fixations times.  For the purpose of this analysis a 'fixation' was
taken to be an arrest of gaze motion on an area for a period exceeding
one tenth of a second.  As can be seen from table 6.2 the fixations were
typically somewhat longer than this, though.

Because there were only three subjects in this experiment and they
only saw each condition twice, the results could not be subjected to
statistical analysis.  However, the data will be inspected and the results
discussed with reference to the predictions made in the introduction.

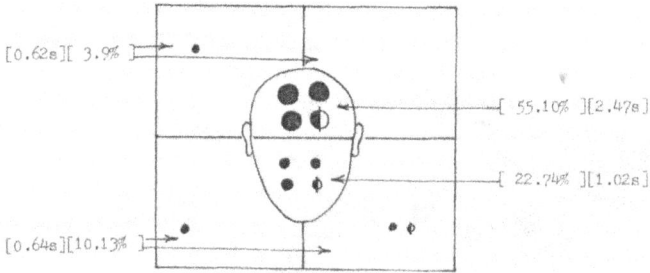

Passive staring

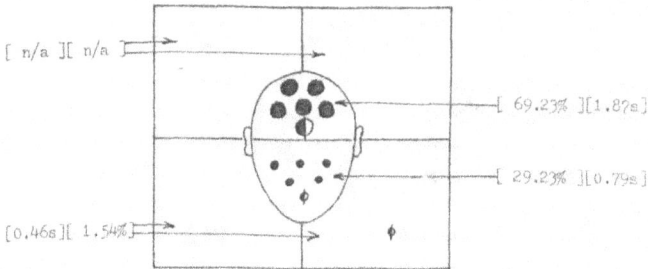

Eyes closed

Figure 6.10  The ESN girls results.

(Note that here and on the ensuing figures the percentage time
looking at a face and the average fixation time are given. The
number and size of the dots and positions relate to fixation time
and area of fixation)

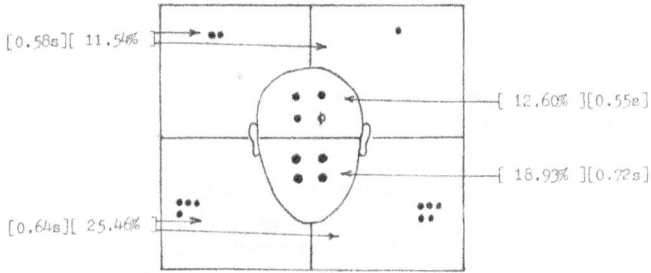

[0.58s][ 11.54%]

[ 12.60% ][0.55s]

[ 18.93% ][0.72s]

[0.64s][ 25.46%]

Passive staring

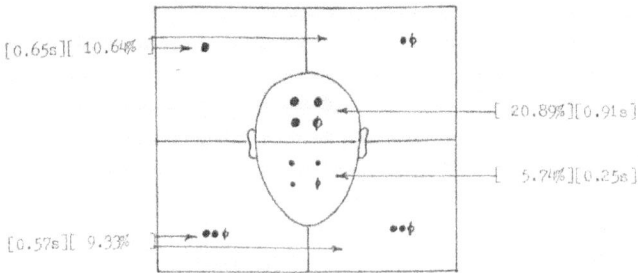

[0.65s][ 10.64%]

[ 20.89%][0.91s]

[ 5.74%][0.25s]

[0.57s][ 9.33%]

Eyes closed.

Figure 6.11 Autistic girl's results.

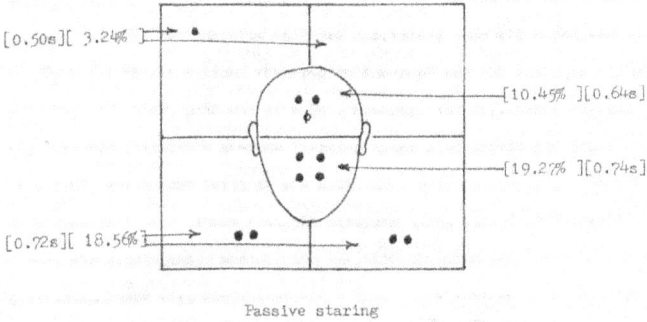

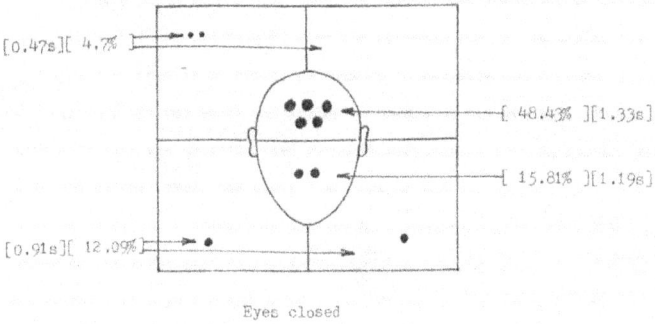

Figure 6.12  The autistic boy's results.

1.   Overall fixation times

One prediction mentioned in the introduction related to the findings
of Hermelin and O'Connor (1967). They found that the autistic children they
tested tended to have very brief fixation times, and it was posited that
this might lead to an appearance of gaze avoidance. Looking at the overall
average fixation times, regardless of condition, in the present study,
reveals that the two autistic children did indeed show a tendency to have
a very brief fixation times compared to those of the ESN child (t = 4.00,
$p < 0.01$; t = 2.67, $p < 0.05$; df = 5). However, the difference between the
two autistic children's average fixation times also approached significance
(t = 2.55, which just fails at p = 0.05; df = 5). An inspection of the
data (see table 6.2) shows that the fixation times varied considerably
across the conditions. Whereas the autistic children generally had shorter
fixations, there were conditions where their fixations were not shorter
than those of the ESN child. This point will be returned to in the
individual evaluations of the various conditions.


2.   Passive staring face and the one with closed eyes

Figures 6.10, 6.11 and 6.12 show the results for these two conditions.
A comparison between the results when the children saw the face with its
eyes closed or open is of direct pertinence to Hermelin and O'Connor's study.
When the face was one which was trying to establish eye contact, the autistic
children's gaze was characterised by relatively little looking at the face
(only 30% of the time), and short fixations when they did look at it.
There was a slight tendency for them both to look more frequently and
longer at the lower half of the face. For the autistic girl this effect
was minimal, athough she did spend a further 25% of the time looking at
the area of board around the lower half of the face. For the autistic boy
the effect was stronger, but still only slight.

The ESN girl, on the other hand, looked at the face most of the time. Her observation of it was characterised by long fixations on or near the eye area, and an equal number of shorter fixations near the mouth. Because all three children had about as many fixations on the face and about as many in each half of the face, one may note that it was primarily the fact that the autistic children displayed relatively brief fixations times which differentiated their performance from that of the ESN girl. Whilst the autistic children's fixations were only a little more than half as long as the ESN child's in the lower half of the face, they were between four and five times shorter in the upper half. Thus, whereas the ESN child showed a very strong tendency to prefer the upper half of the face, the autistic children showed a slight tendency to prefer the lower half. The difference between the types of child was thus mostly in terms of the length of their fixations upon the upper half of the face.

When the face's eyes were closed the autistic girl spent virtually no more time looking at it, nor made significantly more fixations on it. However, the pattern of her gaze when looking at this face was quite different. This time she spent considerably more time inspecting the upper half than the lower one. Because she had about as many fixations on each half of the face as she had before (thus her fixations were evenly spread), the difference was primarily in the length of her fixations on the lower half. Those on the upper half were about twice as long as before, whereas those on the lower half were extremely brief.

The autistic boy's gaze behaviour was in even starker contrast to that which he exhibited to the previous facial display. Like the autistic girl, he now showed a tendency to inspect the upper half of the face; but all of his fixations were longer than before and especially those

TABLE 6.3    Details of the average number of fixations on, and
average time spent looking at, the passive face and
the one with its eyes closed for the two girls.
(Note that the number of fixations on-from-off the
face are given, and thus differ from those shown in
figure 6.12 especially).

|  | Passive Staring face | Eyes Closed |
|---|---|---|
| **Autistic girl** | | |
| (i)  % time spent on the face | 31.53 | 26.63 |
| (ii) no. fixations on the face | 7.5 | 7.0 |
| **ESN girl** | | |
| (i)  % time spent on the face | 77.84 | 98.46 |
| (ii) no. fixations on the face | 2.5 | 1.5 |

on the upper half. He spent approximately half of the available time
looking at the upper half of the face. However, his fixations on the
upper half were still not as long as those displayed by the ESN girl.
She again spent a lot of the available time looking at the upper half
of the face and made as many, but much shorter, fixations on the lower
half. Her fixations were both more frequent and shorter than they were
when she looked at the face with its eyes open. Thus the effect that the
closing of the eyes had on her gaze was to increase the number of her
fixations on the face and to reduce their duration;    consequently
she spent only a little longer looking at the face than she had done before.

How do these results compare with those of Hermelin and O'Connor?
First, it should be noted that the two autistic children responded similarly
but      the change in gaze activity between the two faces was more
dramatic in the boy. It is uncertain to what extent this change might
be attributed to the difference in their sex, verbal ability, or social
responsiveness. However, considering just the two girls and reducing the
data to the two measures used by Hermelin and O'Connor reveals an
interesting finding. Table 6.3 shows the result of doing this. As can
be seen, both children were fairly constant in the number of fixations
they had to the faces and how long they spent looking at each one. This
is in agreement with the findings of Hermelin and O'Connor. However, as
was discussed above, the analysis of the pattern of fixations when the
children were looking at the face differentiated.the two types of child.
Whereas the ESN girl tended to look at the upper half in both case, the
autistic girl tended only to do so when the eyes were closed.

Consequently, although it would be dangerous to draw conclusions
based upon so little data, it seems possible that evidence has been obtained

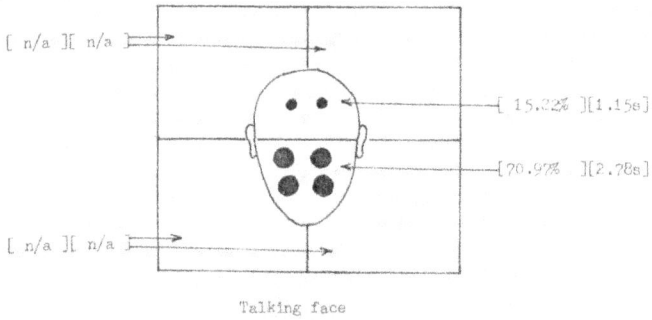

Talking face

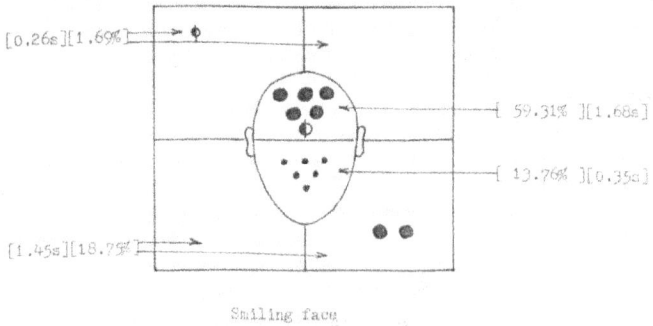

Smiling face

Figure 6.13 The ESN girl's results.

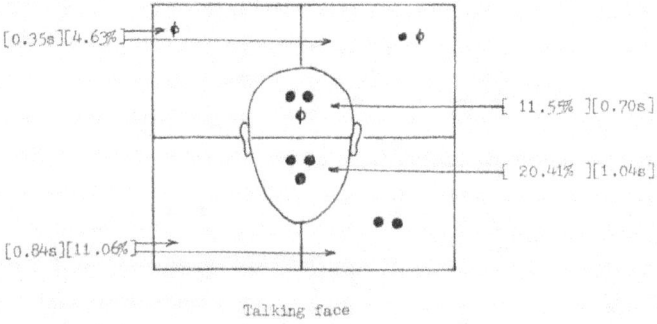

[0.35s][4.63%]

11.55% ][0.70s]

20.41% ][1.04s]

[0.84s][11.06%]

Talking face

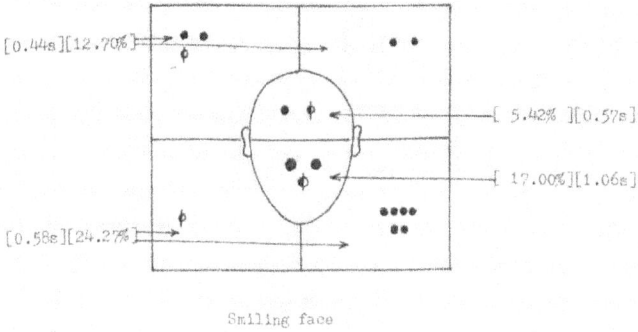

[0.44s][12.70%]

5.42% ][0.57s]

17.00%][1.06s]

[0.58s][24.2%]

Smiling face

Figure 6.14  The autistic girl's results.

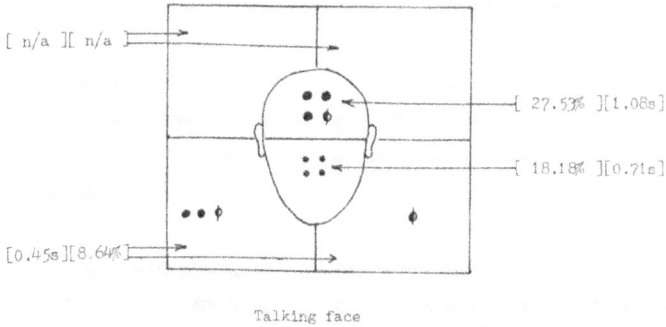

Talking face

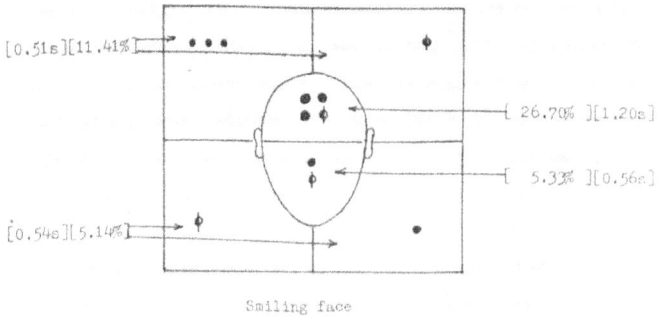

Smiling face

Figure 6.15  The autistic boy's results

which both supports the findings of Hermelin and O'Connor and leads to
an alternative interpretation of their findings. Clearly, the autistic
children responded differently to the face when its eyes were open than
when its eyes were closed, and the change in their gaze activity indicated
that they were not tending to make gaze contact. In contrast, the ESN
girl showed clear evidence for mutual gaze contact and a tendency to
fixate the upper facial areas even when the eyes were closed.

One may note that the fact that the autistic girl did not look at
one of these faces more than the other implies that no simple theory of
gaze 'avoidance' due to over-arousal can adequately account for the
findings.

3.  The passive staring face and the smiling face

Having found above that the autistic children tended not to look at
the upper half of faces with open eyes, one would also expect them to
show similar gaze behaviour when looking at a smiling face which was
also looking at them. In fact, it might be argued that a smiling face
is even more arousing than a passively staring one (this was reasoned
above, and the problems of reducing arousal to a simple factor were
noted). Moreover, if Hutt et al. were correct in their hypothesis that
autistic children avoid looking at faces because it arouses them too
much, then greater avoidance should occur when they view a smiling face.
Figures 6.13, 6.14 and 6.15 show the results of the eye movement
recordings for the smiling face.

The gaze behaviour of the autistic girl reinforced the above
conclusion that she tended not to make gaze contact. She spent even
less time looking at the face. However, the reduction in the amount of
time she spent looking at the face was almost entirely restricted to

the upper area. She looked as long at the lower area as before, but her
fixations were fewer and longer. Her fixations on the upper half, in
contrast, were as long as before, but very few. Leaving the results of
the autistic boy for the moment, one may note that the ESN girl's gaze
when looking at a smiling face was fairly similar to that when she looked
at the face with its eyes closed. That is, she looked as long at the
face as when the eyes were open and the face expressionless, but her
fixations were shorter and more frequent. It is possible that the ESN
girl was more excited by the smiling face and hence her gaze was more
erratic. But it is also possible that frequent eye movements are more
appropriate when looking at a face expressing feeling (this will be returned
to later).

The results of the autistic boy confuse the picture so far constructed.
Although he had about as many fixations on the smiling and passive faces,
he spent considerably longer looking at the smiling face, hence, his
fixations were longer. Such a finding was quite contrary to the predictions,
as was also the fact that when he looked at the smiling face he tended to
almost exclusively fixate the upper area. These results do not conform to
an interpretation that he was tending to avoid gaze contact, and thus doubt
must be shed upon the interpretation of his results in the above comparison
between the face with its eyes open and the one with them closed.

The picture is thus unclear as to which predictions (if any) the
experiment so far supports with certainty. Once again, the results of the
autistic girl conformed to the prediction that autistic children tend not
to make gaze contact. Her results might also be taken as evidence that
the lack of gaze contact is due to 'over arousal' because she looked at
the eyes even less when viewing a smiling face. However, it has been noted

above that a simple theory of arousal cannot explain the autistic
child's gaze behaviour. This was illustrated by the results of the
autistic boy, who actually increased his fixations on or near the eyes
when the face was smiling. It was of particular interest that the present
results are not at variance with those of Hermelin and O'Connor (1967)
when one reduces the measures taken to those which they used. Finally,
it is noted that the difference between the two autistic children's
results cannot be explained in terms of accuracy of diagnosis, for both
of them were equally 'classic' in their symptoms and history.

4.  The talking face

The results of the eye movement recordings when the children looked
at a face which was talking to them are shown in figures 6.13, 6.14 and
6.15. It was expected that the talking face would be more arousing in
ethological terms than the other faces, and thus would give rise to
greater gaze avoidance if the theory of Hutt et al could be upheld. It
was also suggested that autistic children might tend to look at the lower
half of a talking face in an attempt to compensate for an inability to
process auditory information.

The autistic girl's gaze behaviour when looking at this face was
similar to that when she was looking at the smiling and staring faces.
The major difference was that she tended to have fewer fixations offthe
face and on the board just below the chin. It is thus difficult to
attribute her tendency to fixate the lower area to the fact that the face
was talking. There was an increase in the number of her fixations which
were off the video screen, which may be due to the more arousing or
demanding nature of the stimulus.

The autistic boy, in sharp contrast, responded to the talking face
by tending to look at the upper facial features more frequently and longer
than he had when presented with the passive staring face. In fact, his gaze
behaviour when viewing the talking face was most like that when he viewed
the smiling face. This finding is not in line with prediction. As with
the passive staring face, though, more than half of his fixations were non-
directed and off the video screen. The literature does not contain any data
on children's eye movements when looking at people when they talk, however,
there is some data on infant perception of talking mothers. Haith et al
(1977) found, contrary to their predictions, that infants of two to three
months looked at their mother's eyes even more intensely when she started
to speak than they had when she was passively staring at them. Haith et al
were unable to come to any conclusions as to why this might have been so.
However, they offered the possible interpretation that the eyes have
acquired signal value in social interaction, and possibly the infant in
increasing his mutual gaze encourages his mother to continue talking by
showing that he is attending to her. The factor of intention implied
here is questionable, yet nonetheless it is possible that a similar process
leads to the heightened mutual gaze noted in these infants. Can such an
interpretation be applied to the present data of the autistic boy? If it
can, then one might expect that the ESN girl would also show such heightened
fixation on the eyes of a talking face.

The results of the ESN girl, however, were quite different. She tended
to look nearly all of the time at the mouth area of the talking face, with
few but extended fixations. Thus her results support the view proposed
in section 3.1, that movements of the mouth attract one to look at it in
order to obtain information about the visual component of speech; thus
the performance of the ESN child offers no support for the explanation
given above for the results of the autistic boy.

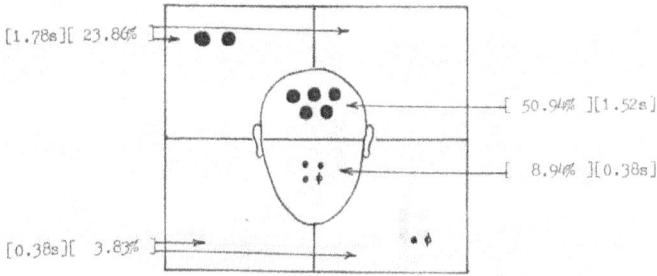

[1.78s][ 23.86%]

[ 50.94% ][1.52s]

[ 8.94% ][0.38s]

[0.38s][ 3.83%]

Passive averted

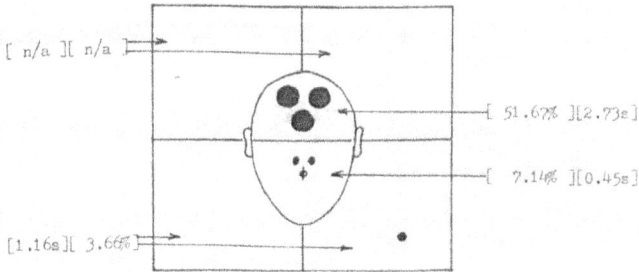

[ n/a ][ n/a ]

[ 51.67% ][2.73s]

[ 7.14% ][0.45s]

[1.16s][ 3.66%]

Sad averted

Figure 6.16  The ESN girl's results.

[0.75s][ 9.73% ]

[ 4.48% ][1.38s]

[ 7.33% ][0.45s]

[1.66s][ 43.15% ]

Passive averted

[0.58s][ 5.64% ]

[ 12.64% ][0.49s]

[ 7.91% ][0.35s]

[0.68s][17.50%]

Sad   averted

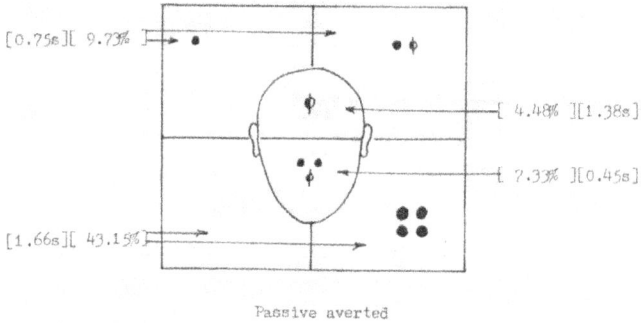

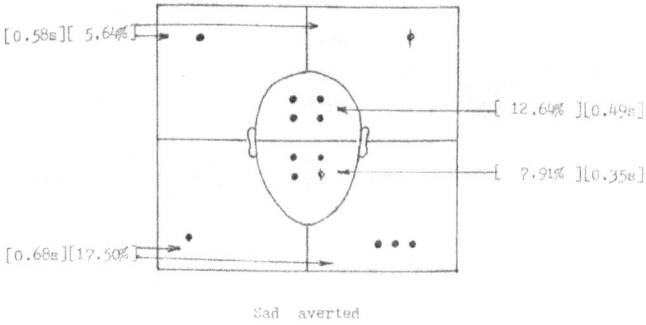

Figure 6.17  The autistic girl's results.

[0.73s][ 9.49%]

[ 48.30% ][1.06s]

[ 22.23% ][0.76s]

[0.77s][ 5.01%]

Passive averted

[ n/a ][ n/a ]

[ 20.52%][1.05s]

[ 17.26%][0.76s]

[0.89s][22.06%]

Sad averted

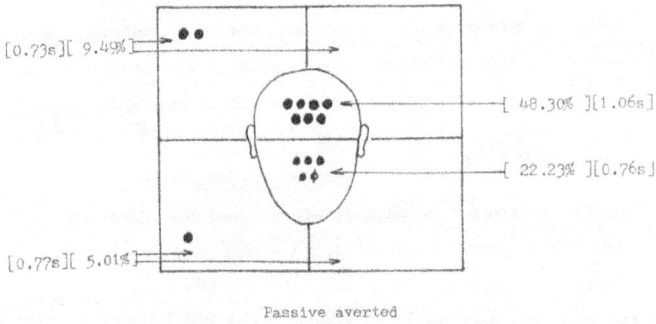

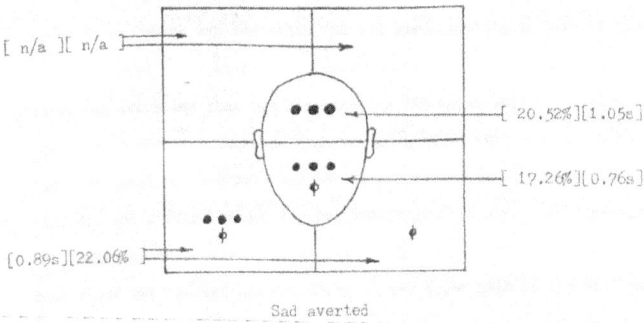

Figure 6.18  The autistic boy's results.

Apart from the possibility that the autistic boy was very immature in his gaze behaviour, it may be the case that when he looked at faces he tended to fixate those areas that were least arousing. Consequently when looking at a passive staring face he fixated the lower half most often, and when looking at faces which involve mouth movements - smiling and talking - he tended to fixate the upper areas. Whilst feasible for these conditions, it is not clear how such an explanation can account for his tendency to look at the upper areas of the face with closed eyes or his pattern of gaze at the two averted faces (see below).

5.  The passive and sad averted faces

The results obtained when the children saw the averted faces are shown in figures 6.16, 6.17 and 6.18. It was hypothesised that the children's gaze should not differ when looking at these faces unless they have some appreciation of the meaning of the sad face. The fact that all of the children showed different gaze behaviour when looking at the sad than when looking at the passive averted face is thus of significance.

The ESN girl only spent about 58% of the time looking at each of these faces, which was less than she had spent looking at each of the previous faces. The major difference in the way in which she looked at these two faces was that her fixations in the upper half were more frequent and briefer when the face was passive and averted than when it was sad. The time spent on each half and the length of the fixations in the lower half did not differ between the two conditions. However, in contrast to her fixations on previous faces, the brevity of her fixations on the lower half stood out against all but those on the lower half of the smiling face. It is also worthy of note that in response to the sad averted face she spent some 40% of the time gazing out of the screen area, quite far from the face, while she spent less than 15%, and typically 10%, of the time doing this with the other faces. This constitutes the longest period of non-directed gaze recorded for the ESN child. A possible explanation is that she was troubled by the unhappy face, while the other faces were either unthreatening or actively friendly and sociable. All of these differences in the way in which she looked at the passive and sad averted faces may be taken as evidence that she appreciated that the sad face conveyed something about the inner state of the person.

The autistic boy also spent about half of the total time looking at the upper half of the passive averted face. He displayed fairly long fixations compared to those he generally exhibited. However, his fixations in the mouth area were neither as infrequent nor as brief as those displayed by the ESN girl. This pattern of gaze most resembled that of his looking at the face with its eyes closed: these findings are once again difficult to marry with the idea that he was avoiding the most arousing facial areas.

Contrary to his gaze-pattern when looking at the passive averted face, when looking at the sad face he made as many fixations on the upper half as on the lower half. Those on the upper half were generally longer; thus he spent a little more time looking at this half. However, the difference between the time spent on each half was by no means as large as that for the other averted face. Like the ESN girl, the number of fixations which went off the screen area when he was presented with the sad face was greater than when he was looking at any other face.

When she was shown the passive averted face, the gaze behaviour of the autistic girl was quite different from that of the other two children. She spent very little time looking at the face at all (a total of about 12% of the time). When she did look at the face she tended to fixate on the lower area. The outstanding feature of her gaze pattern was that she spent a lot of time looking at the area below and to the right of the face (about 43% of the time), and her fixations in this area were the longest that she displayed during the experiment. Although the face was averted in this direction, it will be noted that she displayed a tendency to look at this area whenever a face with eyes open was presented to her (cf. her results for the smiling face, for example).

When she looked at the sad averted face she spent very little more time looking at the upper half of the face than the lower and although she spent more time looking at this face than the last, she nonetheless only looked at it for about 20% of the time. She spent about 60% of the time engaged in non-directed gaze which was outside the camera's view. Still, note that she also responded in this way to the talking face and the one with its closed eyes. For this reason it would not seem possible to connect the amount of time she spent in such non-directed gaze with the different arousing properties of the faces. In consequence, one cannot necessarily conclude that she possessed any appreciation of the meaning of the sad face from this face alone. However, her gaze was certainly different when looking at this face than at the passive averted one, and this might indicate that she possessed the rudiments of understanding emotional expression in faces.

6.  The schematic houses

Two hypotheses were formulated with relevance to the perception of the houses: first, if a child views faces as qualitatively different from other stimuli, then this should show in the change in his gaze patterns when looking at the houses; second, as was suggested in section 3.1,

[ n/a ][ n/a ]

[49.83%][2.48s]

[47.46%][1.58s]

[ n/a ][ n/a ]

ESN girl

[ 0.85s][8.29%]

[42.18%][1.29s]

[11.03%][0.42s]

[ 0.66s][6.42%]

Autistic girl

[ 0.81s][7.88%]

[37.20%][0.95s]

[24.36%][0.75s]

[ n/a ][ n/a ]

Autistic boy

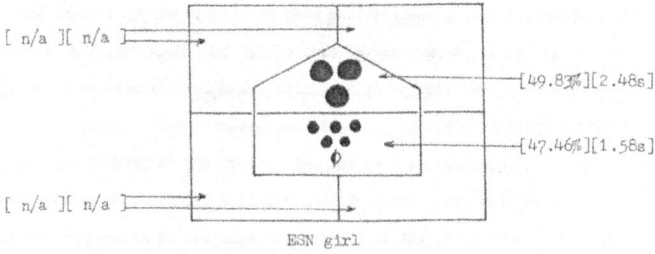

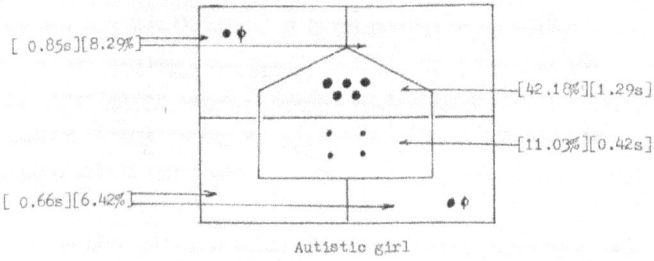

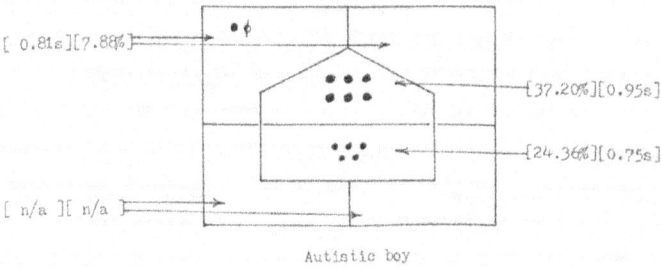

Figure 6.19 The results of the three children when viewing houses.

autistic children might tend to look at the lower half of all things, and thus they should tend to look at the lower half of the houses.

The results of the recordings when the children viewed the houses are shown in figure 6.19. As can be seen in the figure, there are differences between the responses which the three children gave, but still there exists a trend toward similarity. The ESN girl spent virtually all the time looking at the houses, and her gaze was characterized by long fixations on the upper half and more frequent but briefer fixations (amounting to the same total time) on the lower half. She thus distributed her gaze in a more even fashion across these stimuli than she had across the faces, i.e. in terms of time she had no tendency to look at one half more than the other. It is not possible to say whether the fact that her fixations were typically twice as long in the upper half is due to her habitual manner of scanning all stimuli, or whether it is an acquired scanning strategy which has its roots in the processing of meaningful stimuli like faces.

The autistic girl spent considerably longer looking at the upper half of the houses, and did so with fixations which were about three times longer than those of the lower half. Although she only engaged in non-directed gaze which went off the screen about 32% of the time, this does not represent a departure from her gaze patterns when viewing the faces. She also spent about the same amount of time in such non-directed gaze in response to the passive averted face and the passive staring face. However, in terms of the percentage of time she spent looking at the stimuli there were differences between her gaze when looking at the houses and at the faces. By spending some 42% of the time looking at the upper half of the houses she viewed this half of these stimuli at least twice as long, and

typically three to four times as long as of any of the faces, hence
it would seem that her tendency not to look at the upper halves was
restricted to faces. It certainly does not seem true that she had a
tendency to look at the lower half of all things, certainly not houses.

The autistic boy also looked for longer and with longer fixations
at the upper half of the houses than at the lower half. But the differences
in the amount of time he spent looking at each half and the average
fixation times in each half did not contrast so sharply as with the
autistic girl. Neither the time spent looking at either half of the
houses nor the time spent in non-directed gaze conclusively differentiates
the manner in which the autistic boy viewed the faces and the houses.
However, bearing in mind the varied responses he made to the various
faces, it would be wrong to interpret this lack of difference in his
gaze behaviour between faces and other stimuli in terms of  'asociability'.

It is noted that both autistic children once again displayed relatively
short visual fixations as compared with the ESN girl.

In conclusion, then, it appears that the two girls both viewed faces
in a different manner than they viewed schematic houses. The autistic
boy showed less variation in his gaze activity depending on whether he
viewed a face or a drawing of a house. But, the lack of a general
difference may only reflect the wide range of gaze behaviour that he showed
in response to the faces. All the children certainly shared the common
feature of having longer fixations when looking at the upper half of the
houses, which is contrary to the hypothesis that the autistic children
tend to look at the lower halves.

TABLE 6.4    Average number of the two types of gaze shift exhibited by the children for all the stimuli,
            for just the faces, and for just the schematic houses.   (Note the increase in feature-to-feature
            shifts by the autistic children when viewing houses rather than faces.  Note, too, their
            relatively greater number of shifts from stimulus to ground and back).

| Child | Overall | | Just faces | | Just houses | |
|---|---|---|---|---|---|---|
| | Stimulus to ground | Feature to feature | Stimulus to ground | Feature to feature | Stimulus to ground | Feature to feature |
| Autistic girl | 7.14 | 2.00 | 7.08 | 1.67 | 7.50 | 4.00 |
| Autistic boy | 7.93 | 3.50 | 7.92 | 3.00 | 8.00 | 6.50 |
| ESN girl | 3.36 | 5.71 | 3.67 | 5.58 | 1.50 | 6.50 |

7.  Gaze shifts and non-directed gaze

Hermelin and O'Connor (1967) found that autistic children tend
to engage in fewer figure-to-figure gaze shifts and more figure-to-
ground ones than do ESN or normal children.  They also found that the
autistic children differed from the others in that they tended to engage
in a lot of non-directed gaze.

The latter point has certainly been borne out by the present study.
Both of the autistic children tended to spend less than half of the time
looking at the stimuli, be they faces or houses, whereas the ESN girl
typically spent some 70% to 80% of the time looking at the stimuli, at
least.

It was also possible to calculate the number of times each child
shifted his or her gaze from stimulus to the background, or vice versa,
and the number of times their gaze shift tended to be from one half of
the stimulus to the other.  The results of such analysis are shown in
table 6.4.  As can be seen in this table, the autistic children engaged
in many more eye movements which went from stimulus-to-ground or ground-
to-stimulus than did the ESN child.  The ESN girl also showed between
two and three times as many shifts of gaze from one half of the stimulus
to the other.

Hermelin and O'Connor have pointed out that a tendency not to
'compare' stimuli and to only fixate on them for only brief periods means
that the autistic child's visual learning, visual identification, and
visual discrimination problems are even more acute than those of the
subnormal child.  If one considers that the perception of a face involves

scanning it to ascertain its identity, expression, and so forth, then
there is a need to 'compare' the various parts of the face in order to
come to a 'meaningful' appreciation of it. The lack of such feature-to-
feature gaze shifts in the autistic children could mean that they are
more handicapped in the perception of the social aspects of faces - and
this problem would only be exacerbated by their abnormally brief fixation
times.

Looking at the gaze shift measures for the individual conditions
reveals that the autistic boy engaged in feature-to-feature gaze shifts
most often when the face he was watching was either looking away or had
its eyes closed. This might be taken to indicate that the least threatening
faces which allowed him to scan them in a more normal fashion, although his
stimulus-to-ground scores for these two conditions were as high as ever.
It is also of interest that both autistic children tended to do more
feature-to-feature gaze shifts when looking at the houses than when
looking at most of the faces; however, here again they tended to shift
their gaze from figure-to-ground frequently too.

6.3 Summary and general conclusions

Two autistic children and one ESN child were required to view various facial displays and some drawings of houses. Whilst they viewed these stimuli their eye movements were recorded onto video and superimposed upon a record of what they were seeing. By also recording a timing device on top of the video recording, it was possible to make detailed analyses of the children's gaze behaviour. The children saw a face which stared at them, one with its eyes closed, one which was talking to them, an expressionless face with averted gaze, a sad face with an averted gaze, a smiling face looking at them and two drawings of houses for comparison purposes. The results for each of these conditions may be summarised as follows:

1. Fixation times

The autistic children both had much shorter average fixation times than the ESN girl.

2. Staring face and the one with closed eyes

A comparison of the children's gaze behaviour when looking at these two faces indicated that the autistic children tended not to look at the upper half when the eyes were open, but they looked more at this half when the eyes were closed. In contrast, the ESN child looked mainly at the upper half of the face in both cases.

3. The smiling face

The autistic girl once again tended to look at the lower half of a face which was looking at her. The ESN girl continued to prefer to look at the upper half of the face. On the other hand, the autistic boy's gaze went against prediction, and he looked more at the upper half than the lower half.

4.   The talking face

When looking at a face which was talking to her, the autistic girls'
fixations resembled those she evinced when the person smiled at her or
just stared.  That is, she tended to look more at the lower half of the
face.  In contrast, the autistic boy responded to the talking face looking
more at the upper half.  Thus he looked at it in the same way he did the
smiling face but differently from the staring face.  The ESN girl tended
to look at the mouth of the talking face.

5.   The passive and sad averted faces

All three children responded differently to these two faces, but they
all showed that they regarded an emotional face as distinct from an
expressionless one.  The ESN girl looked less at these faces than any of
the former ones.  Her fixations on each were similar and mainly on the
upper half, but those to the passive averted face were shorter and more
frequently.  The autistic boy's gaze behaviour was similar to the ESN girl's
insofar as he also spent more time looking at the upper half of the faces.
He also had more frequent fixations on the passive averted face.  However,
he spent more time overall looking at the passive face because he spent
longer looking at the upper half of that face.

The autistic girl's gaze behaviour differed from the other two
children.  She spent very little time looking at the faces.  When she
looked at the passive averted face she tended to fixate the lower area,
but when she looked at the sad face she fixated on both areas almost
equally.

6.   The schematic houses

The ESN girl spent as long looking at the upper and lower halves, but
her fixations on the upper half were much longer (and thus less frequent).

The autistic girl spent considerably longer looking at the upper half of the houses, and did so with fixations that were much longer than those to the lower half.  The autistic boy also looked more at the upper half of the houses than the lower half, but the difference in time spent on the two halves and the difference in length of fixation on the halves was much less marked.

7.  Gaze shifts and non-directed gaze

The autistic children spent much more time in non-directed gaze - that is gaze directed away from the stimuli.  The ESN girl, in contrast, spent most of the available time looking at the faces and houses.  The autistic children tended to shift their gaze from stimulus to background and back again, rather than from one part of the stimulus to another.  The reverse was true for the ESN girl.

8.  The results of Hermelin and O'Connor

Both Hermelin and O'Connor findings of shorter fixation times by autistics and of the autistics having more non-directed gaze with fewer comparative gaze shifts were supported by the present study.  Their results regarding the children's fixations on faces with open and closed eyes were also confirmed, but the interpretations were extended.  If the data was reduced to the number of fixations on the two faces, then both girls had an equal number to each face.  But analysis of the halves of the faces on which their fixations fell differentiated the two types of children.  The ENS child looked always more at the upper half of the face, whereas the autistic girl looked at the lower half more when the eyes were open and more at the upper half when they were closed.

6.4  General discussion

Do the results support the theory that autistic children avoid gaze contact?  Had one only compared the children's gaze when looking at the faces with open and closed eyes, then it might have been possible to conclude that autistic children do indeed avoid mutual gaze.  Both autistic children looked more at the lower half of the face when the eyes were open and more at the upper half when the eyes were closed. The ESN child, in contrast, always looked more at the upper half. However both types of children made about equal numbers of fixations on both of the faces. Moreover, the autistic children's relatively brief periods of viewing were held true not just for their perception of faces, as they made very brief fixations upon the drawings of houses too. More important, the autistic boy spent more time looking at the upper half of a face which was smiling at him and trying to gain gaze contact. Because this face might be seen as more 'arousing' or 'threatening' (in ethologists' terms, and hence in terms of Hutt et al.'s and Tinbergen and Tinbergen's theoretical framework), one would have expected more gaze avoidance to this face than to the passive staring one. Furthermore, the most sociable face might have been the one which was talking to the child and trying to make gaze contact, too. Still, the autistic boy also spent more time looking at the upper half of this face than at the lower half.

The autistic girl showed gaze behaviour which was more in line with a theory of gaze avoidance insofar as she spent more time looking at the lower facial features whenever the face was looking at her. When the face's eyes were closed she had a slight tendency to look more frequently and for longer at the upper facial area, but the tendency was not great. In addition, when the face was averted (with and without expression displayed on it), she looked at it far less than when it was smiling, talking, staring passively or had its eyes closed. In terms of Hutt et al.'s theory, one would have expected the averted faces along with the one with the eyes closed to offer the least threat and be the least 'arousing'. Indeed, Hutt and Ounsted (1966) claim that autistic children monitor people's faces when the other's face is averted, and avert their gaze as the other turns

toward them. The present study found no evidence to support this.
Thus, even though the gaze behaviour of the autistic girl offered more
support for the contention that she avoided mutual gaze, her results
nonetheless contained elements which are difficult to explain within a
simple 'gaze avoidance' theory framework.

It was not possible to explain the difference between the two
autistic children in terms of the girl being 'more autistic' than the
boy. In fact, although both children were chosen as fairly classic in
their symptoms and history, the boy was a little more distant and less
sociable than the girl. While the boy was mute, the girl had a few
words which she used in an obsessional manner. It may be noted that
neither of the autistic children were indifferent to the fact that a face
was looking at them or whether or not it was expressive or expressionless,
thus it may be that the explanation of the autistics' results lies in a
consideration of their ability to understand what gaze contact and facial
expression can be used for. This point will be returned to later.

Did the autistic children have an abnormal tendency to look at the
lower half of all stimuli? Clearly not. They were in fact found to fixate
the upper half of the drawings of houses, and their fixations on the
halves of the faces were not independent which face they looked at. Thus
the hypothesis proposed in section 3.1 to explain the autistics' good
ability to recognise the lower halves of faces is not supported.

Was there any evidence that the autistic children had an abnormal
tendency to look at the mouth area of talking faces? Once again, this
was clearly not so. The ESN child did look at the lower area of the

talking face. This she did not do in response to any of the other

faces. Thus some support is gained for the contention made in section 3.1

that a tendency to lip-read whilst another is talking may lead one to

fixate the mouth area. However, neither of the autistic children tended

to look more at the lower half of the face when it was speaking compared

to when it was not. Whilst the autistic girl did have a slightly greater

tendency to look at the lower half of the talking face than the upper

half, she also possessed a similar tendency when looking at the smiling

and passively staring faces. In contrast, the autistic boy differed

most from prediction in that he tended to fixate the upper half of the

talking face. In fact he responded to it in much the same way he had

to the smiling face. No firm explanation emerged to account for the

autistic boy's results. It was mentioned that Haith et al (1977)

found that babies tend to gaze even more intensely at their mother's

eyes when she starts to talk to them; but it seems unlikely that the

autistic boy's gaze activity reflects such extreme immaturity. It is

more likely that he views both the smiling and talking faces in a similar

a social way, not as stimuli which possess information relevant to

inerpersonal communication. He may have found the movement in the upper

facial areas more interesting when the face was smiling or talking than

when it was staring passively. Hence his differential response to the

passive, smiling and talking faces might reflect an inability on his

part to process faces for meaning but to tend to look at the most

attractive features regardless of their potential value as sources of

information about interpersonal communication. The lack of difference

between the way the autistic girl looked at the smiling, passive and

talking faces might also be explained by a similar argument; thus, she

too may lack the ability to understand what facial expression is used

for, but by possessing a rudimentary appreciation of it she may tend to

avoid facial features which are puzzling to her.

But was there any evidence that the autistic children perceived that some of the faces displayed emotional expression? The critical tests for this were thought to be whether the children viewed the passive and smiling faces differently and whether they viewed the passive and sad averted faces differently. Both autistic children responded differently to the two averted faces. The autistic boy responded differently to the smiling face than to the passive staring one, but the girl responded the same to both. Obviously there is some evidence for the supposition that the autistic children saw the expressive faces as being distinct from the expressionless ones, but the evidence was stronger in the case of the boy. However, the data is confounded by the fact that in both the above comparisons the expressionless face was motionless whereas the expressive face contained some movement. It is thus possible that the autistic children's differential responses were due to the factor of movement.

More circumstantial evidence may be gained from the results of the ESN child. When she viewed the smiling face she made many more comparative eyes movements between the upper and lower halves than when she saw the passive staring face. This might have been due to the fact that comparative eye movements are more appropriate when one is processing a face for meaning. Such comparative gaze shifts may gain a gestalt impression of the face. Neither of the autistic children increased the number of their fixations in this manner. They certainly did not increase their comparative gaze shifts which were uniformly very infrequent. However, the fact that the autistic girl spent less time looking at the smiling face than the passive one may be due to her having a rudimentary appreciation of facial expression but an inability to understand it may lead to her having more erratic gaze behaviour. That is she might be 'troubled' by the expressive face. The fact that she scanned the sad averted face more than the

expressionless averted one may be seen as support for this idea.
In summary then, it is uncertain whether the autistic boy's responses
were due to his attraction to the movement in the expressive faces or due
to his appreciation of their expressive character. The autistic girl,
on the other hand, may have had a rudimentary appreciation of facial
expression which affected her gaze behaviour. These conclusions are noted
to fit with the clinical observation that the girl was a little easier
to make contact with than the boy.

The finding that the autistic children had both shorter fixation
times and fewer comparative (feature-to-feature) gaze shifts may be of
great theoretical value. It has been suggested several times in this
thesis that autistic children have an inability to integrate their
perceptions into meaningful wholes or themes. Their low fixation times
and lack of comparative gaze shifts supports this contention. Hermelin
and O'Connor. (1970) have pointed out that a tendency not to compare
stimuli and to only fixate on them for brief periods, means that the
autistic child's visual learning, visual identification, and visual
discrimination problems will be even more acute than the subnormal child's.
Scanning faces and comparing the various features is essential if one is
to ascertain what its expression is, thereby coming to a meaningful
appreciation of it. Determining who a person is does not require such
comparisons, for one need only detect a known feature.

There are, consequently, two aspects of integrative ability that
should be reflected in one's gaze activity. First, to gain a meaningful
appreciation of the stimuli presented one needs to compare and contrast
the various features, taking into account their relative positions and
relations. However, it is also critical that one compare the data in

one's present perceptions with that gained from previous ones. To
do this surely requires that one fixate features for a reasonable length
of time. In addition, given that one must compare past and present
relative dispositions of features to determine expression, for example,
then fairly lengthy comparative scans would be appropriate. There are
other factors, too, of course: the comparison of past and present
internal states with the perception of expression in others (as discussed
in previous sections), calls for fairly sustained comparative gaze
fixations.

The results of this study have thus been pertinent to almost all
the foregoing experiments reported in this thesis. They have broadly
confirmed the results of the previous studies, and have allowed one to
expand upon some of the theories previously proposed. In brief, it
seems that the most parsimonious explanation of the autistic children's
results throughout this thesis is in terms of their possessing an
inability or poor ability to integrate their perceptions into meaningful
wholes and themes. It further seems that this inability prevents the
autistic child being able to understand the uses to which facial display
can be put in interpersonal communication. Chapter Seven will deal
with the theoretical aspects of these contentions in greater detail.
It will also deal with various issues which relate to the findings
of this thesis and which are of theoretical interest to the study of
autism. Finally, Chapter Seven will present suggestions for further
research on autism.

PRESENT FINDINGS, THEORETICAL
IMPLICATIONS AND SUGGESTIONS
FOR FURTHER RESEARCH

CHAPTER 7

PRESENT FINDINGS, THEORETICAL IMPLICATIONS AND SUGGESTIONS
TO FURTHER RESEARCH

*Science is always wrong. It*
*never solves a problem without*
*creating ten more".*

\- George Bernard Shaw

7.1: Introduction

Inevitably, this thesis has thrown up more questions about the nature
of autism than it has answered. The purpose of this chapter is thus to
summarise the results of the twelve studies, and to outline the questions
which should now be asked. As was concluded in Chapter One, autism is most
likely due to some form of brain damage or dysfunction which gives rise to a
cognitive deficit having specific characteristics. It is thus pertinent
to ask whether the results of the present studies point to any particular
neurological impairments in the autistic child, and to discuss what the
findings imply with regard to the delineation of the features and boundaries
of a cognitive deficit.

Thus, the following section will present an overview of the present
findings, and secondly outline the questions which these findings raise
The third section will then consider the theoretical implications of the
findings in the light of present knowledge about neurophysiology and
cognitive functioning. Finally, a fourth section will deal with suggestions
for further research.

7.2: A summary of the present findings

The first study investigated normal, subnormal and autistic
children's abilities to identify upright faces from isolated features
and from inverted presentations. The autistic children had a more complete
knowledge of the faces, and in this sense they were better than the non-
autistic children at face recognition. In particular, both the younger
and older autistic children were better than the other children at
recognising the lower facial areas. The younger autistic children
found the lowermost features easier than the uppermost ones (which they
identified less well than their control subjects), whereas the older
autistics had a homogeneously good ability to identify all the facial
areas. The older autistics' complete knowledge of faces extended to
the inverted mode, too, because they were also better at recognising
upside-down photographs than were any of the other children. It was
noted that neither the younger nor the older autistic children were
abnormally poor at recognising the eye area of the faces. Thus, it
seems unlikely that the autistic children avoided gaze contact, for
this would have led them to know the eye area less well.

The results can be viewed in one of two ways: either the autistic
child has something akin to the normal child's tendency to view the
upper halves of faces and has an additional reason for looking at, and
hence knowing well, the lower facial areas; or the autistic child
lacks the normal child's tendency to focus upon the eye area of faces,
but instead views faces as a collection of unrelated features rather
than as a whole. These two possibilities thus led to several predictions.
In terms of the first of the two alternatives, it was suggested that

autistic children might either tend to look at the lower half of all
stimuli or that they might have an abnormal tendency to use lip-read
information in face-to-face interactions.

With regard to the suggestion that the autistics might tend to look
at the lower half of all things, it was noted that the older autistics
did know the uppermost areas of faces very well. This observation,
coupled with the finding that the autistic children did not sort schematic
houses according to their lower features, led to the conclusion that
it is extremely unlikely that the autistics' abnormal knowledge of
faces is due to them focussing on the lower half of all stimuli.

A study of hard-of-hearing subject's abilities to identify faces
from the upper and lower halves found that they too knew the lower
facial features better than normal hearing subjects. Thus evidence
was gained to support the idea that lip-reading might lead to an
enhanced knowledge of the mouth area. However, the hard-of-hearing
subjects' ability to identify lower features was not as outstanding
as that of the autistic subjects, and hence it was concluded that a
tendency to lip-read probably could not totally account for the
autistic children's face recognition performance.

A test of the autistic children's ability to lip-read supported
the above conclusion, and found them to be as (but not more) able as
ESN children who were matched for age and general intelligence. The
lip-reading test also allowed one to gauge each child's reliance upon
either the visual or auditory modalities whilst lip-reading. While the
ESN children tended to have a fairly equal reliance upon both modalities
when the modalities were presenting conflicting information, the autistic

children tended to report what they heard more than what they saw. In addition, the autistic children needed more noise in order to lower their ability to report the heard-only words to a level which was equal to that of their seen-only ability (and also equal to that of the ESNs). The meaning of these findings was not clear, but the most parsimonious explanation was that the autistic children were poor at integrating the seen and heard aspects of spoken communication.

The older autistics superior ability to identify inverted faces was further investigated in comparison to the ability of matched ESN subjects. It was noted that two explanations were possible as to why the older autistics were so good at this task. First, the autistic children had already been shown to know the lower facial features better than the ESN children. It was thus possible that because the mouth may be an easier feature to 'rotate mentally', the autistics' greater knowledge of this area might suffice to enable them to be superior at identifying inverted faces. Second, the literature on face perception strongly suggests that normal subjects view faces as perceptual gestalten, and it is because this holistic impression of the face is difficult to rotate mentally, that normal subjects find inverted faces exceptionally difficult to identify. Thus the normal subject perceives faces not only in terms of their individual features, but also in terms of the inter-relationships between them - he is integrating his perceptions into a unified gestalt. When the normal subject is asked to view an inverted face he is confronted with the task of not only trying to imagine what the features look like upside-down, but also what their disposition would appear like. The normal subject is thus not especially adept at identifying individual features. In contrast, there was evidence from the first experiment that autistics have a much more evenly distributed knowledge of facial features. If this is true, then a tendency for the autistic child to view faces as a collection of parts rather than integrating them into gestalten might paradoxically lead him to be better able to recognise inverted faces.

To test these two ideas the children were required to identify inverted upper and lower halves of faces. If it is the autistics' knowledge of the mouth which enables him to be better at recognising inverted faces then one should find that he is considerably better at recognising inverted lower halves than inverted upper halves. If, on the other hand, it is because the autistic child has a more piecemeal knowledge of faces which enables him to identify inverted faces, then there should be little difference between the effect which inversion has on his ability to identify upper halves and the effect it has on his recognition ability to lower halves. Further, if the above proposal about the relationship between the tendency to view faces as gestalten and finding them difficult to identify when inverted is true, then one may hypothesise that this would be reflected in the results of this study. That is, it seems reasonable to suggest that for the normal subject the mouth area might be easier to identify when upside-down because there are fewer elements involved for one to rotate in one's mind than when viewing the eye area. The eye area, then, presents a more complex collection of parts which the normal subject integrates into a whole. In consequence, the non-autistic child can expect his recognition ability of upper halves to be more radically affected by inversion of the face than his ability to identify lower halves. In contrast, the second hypothesis above indicated that once again the autistics' ability to recognise each facial half should be equally affected by inverting the faces.

The results revealed that inverting the faces had much more affect upon the ESN children's ability to recognise upper halves than lower ones. In contrast the autistic children were equally handicapped in their ability to identify both halves. Moreover, their ability to identify inverted halves was not greatly different from their ability to identify inverted whole faces. The results of the ESN children thus supported the proposition that they tend to view faces as gestalten, and that the eyes form a more complex perceptual gestalt which is difficult to rotate mentally. The results of the autistic children, by contrast, support the contention that they view faces in a more piecemeal manner and not as meaningful wholes. The superior ability of the autistics was thus not simply due to their better knowledge of the mouth area.

If the autistic children's superior ability to identify inverted faces is due to their being poor at integrating the various features of a stimulus into a gestalt, then this effect should be observable from their ability to identify other stimuli upside-down which are also usually integrated into meaningful wholes by normal subjects. An example of such stimuli are words. When a child has learnt to read he no longer views words as a collection of individual graphemes, instead he perceives a perceptual gestalt which he 'reads' as a single sound entity. Inverted text can be difficult to read because one has a natural tendency to view words as wholes and it can pose great problems when one tries to rotate mentally a line of letters and their relationship to each other. Inverted script can be exceptionally difficult to read for this reason. If, on the other hand, one was to have a propensity to read words in a more piecemeal manner then inversion of them should have far less affect upon one's ability to read them. It was thus decided to test the autistic and ESN children's abilities to read inverted text.

On testing the children's reading ability in the normal fashion (with
upright words) it was found that the two groups of children had almost
identical average reading ages. However, the autistic children were
much more able to read the inverted words. Moreover, whereas the ESN
children made mistakes which reflected that they were trying to rotate
mentally a perceptual gestalt (such as mistaking a 'n' for a 'u', or
a 'd' for a 'b'), the autistic children showed very few such errors.
It seems, then, that autistic children view faces and words in a
similar way - as collections of unrelated features rather than as
unified meaningful wholes.

As a consequence of the above findings, it was decided that the
autistic child's ability to identify facial expression should also be
investigated. There is strong indication in the literature that the
normal subject's tendency to view faces as conveying meaningful
expression is bound up with his proclivity to view faces as gestalten.
That is, in order to discern the expression of a face one must be able
to integrate the disposition of the various facial features into a
meaningful whole - indeed this is what one is referring to by the phrase
'meaningful whole'. If the autistic child has difficulty in integrating
his perceptions into meaningful wholes then one can predict that he
will be poor at identifying facial expressions. However, it is possible
that the autistic's ability to discern facial expression may not be so
poor when the expression may be gauged fairly accurately by the shape
or disposition of a single feature such as a smiling mouth.

In a test of their ability to sort photographs of happy and sad
faces into two piles, younger autistic children were found to be worse
than either older ones or a comparison group of ESN children. However,

the older autistic children were as good as the ESN children at sorting whole faces. Both the older autistic and the ESN children found it harder to sort the faces by the upper halves than the lower halves, but the older autistic children had notably more trouble sorting the upper halves than did the ESN children. Similarly, the younger autistic children found it easier to sort the lower facial areas, and in fact performed at a chance level when sorting the upper halves.

The ability of the children to sort inverted happy and sad faces and halves of faces was also studied. Both the older autistic and the ESN children could sort the lower halves equally well when they were seen upside-down. But when they had to sort inverted upper halves the performance of both groups dropped to chance. The younger autistic children's sorting ability was not affected by inversion of the faces; they too could sort the inverted lower halves as well as they did the upright halves, and their ability to sort upper halves remained predictably at chance.

The results thus did offer support for the contention that it is easier to tell facial expression from inverted lower halves of faces than from inverted upper halves. What was noteworthy, though, was that the older and more sociable autistics were better at identifying facial expressions and thus, presumably, better at integrating facial features. However, there does remain the possibility that the older autistics are still poor at integrating features into wholes, but that they have developed strategies to cope with the identification of expression in the eye area which do not involve the ability to integrate their perceptions. What militates against this, though, is the finding

that like the ESN children the older autistics ability to identify
facial expression in upper halves of faces falls to chance level when
the area is viewed in the inverted mode.

To test the contention that autistics have problems with perceptual
integration in more depth, the children were required to sort photographs
of faces which contained two emotions into two piles according to whether
they appeared sad or happy. These composite faces were made up of the
upper half of either the happy or sad face used in the last experiment
together with the lower half of the opposite expression posed by the
same person. In this way it was possible to compose faces which had
genuinely 'sad eyes' with 'happy mouths' and vice versa. Two versions
of the composite faces were made. In one there was no gap between
the upper and lower halves and every attempt was made to make each
face not look like a composite of two others. In the second kind a
gap of about one inch was left between the upper and lower halves.
It was argued that this gap had the effect of disrupting the holism
of the face.

The ESN children's responses showed that although they mainly
sorted by the mouths they took into account the expression conveyed
by the eyes when sorting both types of composite face. Further, they
performed differently when sorting the composite faces which were made
to look complete than when sorting the ones with a gap in them. When
sorting the former type they sorted less according to the eyes'
expression than when sorting the latter type. The ESN children were
also more likely to point out that they thought that there were two
expressions present when the faces were split apart than when they were
joined together. All these results indicated that the ESN children were

able to take into account the expression of both halves of the face when
the halves presented conflicting information, and that they tended to
view the faces in a gestalt manner.

The autistic children's results were quite different. The younger
autistic children's responses agreed with those in the previous experiment
insofar as they appeared to be unable to sort according to the upper
halves. Hence for both composite faces they sorted as if they were just
judging by the mouth's expression alone. The older autistic children,
in contrast, once again showed that they had a rudimentary ability to
tell the expression in the eye area. They sorted both types of composite
faces with some reference to the expression conveyed by the eyes. However,
the older autistics differed from the ESN children in that they did not
sort the two types of composite face differently. Thus there was some
evidence that the older autistic children were not perceiving the faces
as gestalten which could be disrupted by a gap between the upper and
lower halves. Further evidence that this was true came from the fact
that the autistic children did not tend to report that there were two
expressions present any more frequently when the faces were split apart
than when they were joined together. Finally, whilst the ESN children
tended to report that, for instance, a person looked happy but was
really sad (when there was a smiling mouth and sad eyes), no autistic
child reported anything like this. This was taken as additional evidence
that the ESN children alone were perceiving the faces as gestalten.

Although it was only a trend, it seemed significant that the autistic
children were more likely to report that two emotions or faces were
present when the halves of the face were made to appear complete than

did the ESN children. This may also reflect the autistic's lack of ability to integrate his perceptions, and may indicate that autistic children have a better than normal ability to distinguish a figure from its ground.

It was noted that in normal development the ability to identify expressions is concurrent with the ability to express them. Hence the autistic children's abilities to display emotions were also tested. The children had to pull happy and sad faces and their ability to do so was compared with that of matched ESN children. The autistic children were poorer than the ESN ones at pulling happy faces. Both groups were equally poor at pulling sad faces though; but the ESN children's poor ability on sad faces was partly due to them conceptualising sadness as an emotion to be kept within (and hence not scored highly as sadness by the raters who saw the photographs), whereas the autistic children seemed to have genuine difficulties with pulling this expression. A surprising finding was that a few of the autistic children had their attempts at one of the expressions rated as the opposite by a panel of scorers. In fact, one autistic child had her attempt at a happy face rated as a good attempt at a sad one. None of the ESN children's attempts were confused in this manner.

It was noted that the above study required that the children understand what was asked of them. Consequently it may have been that the autistic children were handicapped by the verbal nature of the task's instructions. Hence the childrens' abilities to copy a facial expression was studied. This was done under two conditions: in one situation the child faced the model, and in the other the model was by the child's side and both looked into a mirror. In the first case the child had no visual feedback

as to how well he did, whereas in the second case such feedback was
available. Both groups copied the model equally well when no visual
feedback was available. However, when the children could see how well
they were doing only the ESN children benefited from this knowledge
and improved their performance. Thus, the autistic children's limited
repertoire of facial expression is unlikely to be mainly due to their
being unable to imitate other's expressions. Also, their inability to
take advantage of the visual feedback may be seen as further evidence
that they tend not to integrate their perceptions.

It was noted that a survey of the clinical and anecdotal evidence
suggests that autistic children are generally able to display 'reflex'
emotions, but are very poor at acquired facial expressions which are
intended to communicate their inner feelings to others. Hence their
limited repertoire of facial expressions may be seen as part of their
more general inability or poor ability to communicate with others. It
was noted that normal babies may learn how to express their inner state
to others through early interaction with adults. Part of this early
interaction involves the baby being able to perceive contingencies
between his behaviour and that of the adult, and between ongoing events
and those he has experienced in the past. Thus, once again the possible
importance of the child's ability to integrate his perceptions into
meaningful wholes and themes was highlighted. Not only may the autistic
baby be poor at recognising the relationships between his perceptions,
but he may also produce far fewer consistent expressions of emotion for
the mother to react to. In consequence the autistic child may be
abnormally unresponsive to interact with, and thus abnormally unrewarding
for the mother too.

371

Finally, a computerised study of children's eye movements whilst looking at faces was reported. Although this study could only take an exploratory form, the results were nonetheless of pertinence to most of the above findings. Two autistic children and one ESN child had to look at various faces, some of which expressed emotion whereas some did not, and some tried to make eye contact whilst others did not. They were also required to look at some schematic representations of houses. The results were fairly complex, but seemed to offer no clear evidence for gaze avoidance in autistic children. One of the clearest results was that both autistic children had far briefer fixations times than the ESN child.

The autistic boy spent a greater proportion of his time looking at the upper halves of faces which were talking to him or smiling at him than the autistic girl . However, this could not be explained by the girl being more 'autistic' than the boy, for the boy was if anything less sociable.

The ESN child tended to look more at the mouth of talking faces than of other faces, and thus provided support for the idea that people tend to switch their attention to other's lip movements when they talk. However, neither of the autistic children showed any unusually strong tendency to fixate the lower facial area of talking faces. In fact the autistic boy looked mostly at the eye area of talking faces.

The responses of the children when viewing the expressive faces indicated that the ESN child had an understanding of their expressive nature. However, it was suggested that whereas the autistic girl had a rudimentary comprehension of facial expression (which occasionally led to more erratic gaze), the autistic boy's gaze behaviour was determined by less socially guided stimulus properties.

None of the children showed any tendency to look at the lower halves of the houses. Thus there was no support for the above mentioned idea that autistic children tend to fixate the lower half of all things. The brievity of the autistic children's gaze fixations was also true for looking at houses, too. Thus one cannot conclude that they tended to only look at faces for a very brief time. It was noted that these findings concur with those of O'Connor and Hermelin (1967). It was also noted that the autistic children generally made fewer feature-to-feature gaze shifts than the ESN child. Instead, they tended to look from a feature to the background and back to a feature again. This manner of looking at things is inappropriate for the extraction of information which might help a child's visual learning, visual identification, and visual discrimination problems. In particular it is inappropriate if the child wishes to compare the various aspects of his perceptions and gain an overall gestalt view of an object. Such gestalt perception of stimuli is undoubtably important in the identification and appreciation of facial expressions.

7.3: Theoretical implications

The two major findings of this thesis are that autistic children are particularly good at recognising faces but they are rather poor at identifying facial expressions. The purpose of this section is to consider these findings in the light of what is known about the way the brain functions and the psychological implications of its functioning. For instance, is there any particular area of the brain which has been connected with the ability to recognise faces, or which is known to deal with the identification of expression? First, then, the evidence which has been provided to suggest that face perception is an innate ability will be discussed.

7.3.1    Is face perception innate?

In Chapter Two the possibility was mentioned that babies may possess an innate tendency to seek out 'dot patterns' which resemble eyes. It was concluded that the evidence for such an innate tendency specifically geared to the development of gaze contact is weak. Although the area of study is as yet still confused, it seems that the infant is born with certain tendencies to seek out stimulation such as brightness, contrast, critical levels of complexity, movement, and contingency on his own behaviour. Human beings are almost unique amongst the stimuli that the newborn encounters in possessing these qualities - and in particular people's eyes. As a consequence of tending to fixate other's eyes it seems possible that the baby comes to appreciate the significance of faces and gradually learns to extract more and more information from them. Hence, such evidence suggests that there is nothing innate about perceiving faces per se. Thus early face perception may help one understand why the autistic child fails to understand expressions (this will be returned to later), but does not relate to the matter of why they are so good at recognising faces.

7.3.2    Is face perception unique?

Other workers have searched elsewhere for evidence of the uniqueness of faces as perceptual stimuli. For instance, some have claimed that transformations of faces (such as viewing them upside down or in photographic negative) make them harder to identify than any comparable stimuli. Galper (1970) has tested people's ability to identify faces which are seen in photographic negative, and reported that her subjects found negative faces very hard to recognise. She argued that the same pattern information is available in both positive and negative photographs of faces, thus the difficulty in identifying the negative ones must be due to factors other than the ability to identify pure pattern. However, her conclusion that it is solely the difficulty in recognising the expression of negative faces which causes the difficulties is not defendable. As Phillips (1972) has pointed out, transforming a photograph into a negative changes the whole range of brightness relationships. He argued that it might be the changes in these brightness relationships which causes one to find negative faces harder to identify (although he agreed with Galper that the expression of photographic negatives of faces is difficult to discern). His attempt to reconcile the question involved requiring subjects to view lithographic positive and negative photographs of faces. The lithographic process turns all the darker greys into black and all the lighter ones into white, thus producing an entirely black and white picture with no half tones. His argument was that if the brightness relationships led Galper's subjects to find negative faces hard to identify, then negative 'lith' pictures should not be harder to identify than positive ones because the brightness relations remain the same. However, he found that subjects made more errors when trying to identify famous people's faces from 'lith' negatives than from 'lith' positives. Nonetheless, this should not be seen as evidence against the validity of Phillips' initial criticism, for it is still possible that brightness relations play a part in the exceptional difficulty one has in identifying negatives faces. Phillips was not justified in inferring that the problem his subjects would encounter when viewing 'lith' negatives was merely that they were reversals of 'lith' positives already seen. Considered in terms of information processing, there is undoubtably a certain amount of redundant information present in a face; this means that it may still be reasonably easy to identify if it has been partly degraded in some fashion as it is in the lithographic process. However, whilst this process might be equivalent to seeing "THS CRT SAT ON THD MAT" (a degradation of THE CAT SAT ON THE MAT), the negative of this process would be more like "TAM DHT NO TAS TRC SHT" (the reverse of the degraded version), than white print on black as Phillips implies. One has only to consider that a simple schematic face drawn in black ink upon white paper would be equally easy to identify in the negative.

To date no one has undertaken a thorough study of people's ability to identify other equally complex stimuli in photographic negative, thus it is unlikely that this can be seen as evidence that faces are exceptional.

It has also been noted that the same pattern information is present when a face is seen upside down, and yet recognition of upside down faces appears to be exceptionally difficult. The face has been referred to as a 'mono-oriented' stimulus because it is usually seen only in one orientation. Such mono-oriented stimuli are reknown for being difficult to recognise when seen upside down compared to right way up (Ellis, 1975). However, it seems that faces are particularly difficult to recognise in the inverted mode (Hochberg and Galper, 1967; Yin, 1969). Yin (1969) reported that his subjects found recognition of faces was more affected

REALITY/FANTASY, upside-down design, by Henry M. Swope,
Braden, Tenn.

Figure 7.1.   Examples of the difficulty one experiences
in perceiving identity and meaning in complex
inverted stimuli.

by inverting them than was recognition of houses and matchstick-men designs. He also noted that his subjects reported viewing the upright and inverted faces in different ways, whereas they viewed the other stimuli in the same manner regardless of orientation. That is, they viewed all the stimuli but the faces by looking for individual features to recognise them by, whereas they viewed upright faces as gestalten and switched to trying to identify some individual feature when the faces were seen inverted. This point is important and will be returned to later.

Rock (1974) has pointed out that inversion of faces alters spatial relations which are very familiar, and this could result in a disruption of subject's scanning strategies. He goes on to note that other stimuli are also very difficult to identify upside down, such as written script, and this might be for similar reasons (see figure 7.1 for examples of the difficulties involved in identifying inverted stimuli). Circumstantial support for Rock's ideas comes from several sources; writing is usually read from left to right, and many workers have claimed that faces are scanned from top to bottom (Noton and Stark, 1971; Smith and Nielson, 1970; see Ellis, 1975 for a review). However, it has yet to be shown either that people scan other 'mono-oriented' stimuli in radically different ways, or how a scanning strategy specific to the viewing of faces might be peculiarly affected by transformations of the stimulus. One might also question whether the other mono-oriented stimuli that have been used in studies (such as planes, houses, matchstick-men; see Ellis, 1975) are solely seen only in one orientation. Children frequently view pictures in their books upside down and such pictures are often of the kind chosen by researchers. Although this does not mean that children can equally easily recognise the pictures in either modality (Ghent, 1961), it certainly throws doubt on the claim that such stimuli are purely mono-oriented.

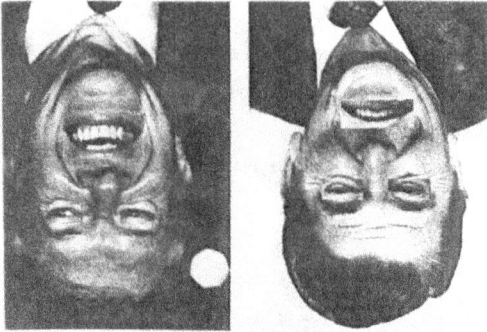

Figure 7.2.  Facial expression can look very different
depending on whether the face is upright
or inverted.

Bradshaw and Wallace (1971) argued that the difficulties in recognising inverted faces may just be because they are rarely seen that way up. They attempted to train their subjects to identify inverted faces, and found that they could eventually achieve almost as high a recognition of inverted faces as of upright ones. However, the method they employed suggests that the training of the subjects to recognize inverted faces involved an enhancement of their ability to identify faces from isolated features, rather than by identifying faces as gestalten both ways up (see Homa, et al., 1976).

It is thus not possible to conclude from the above evidence that faces are exceptional as visual stimuli. Stronger evidence for the 'specialness' of faces comes from a consideration of the fact that faces also carry expression, and the related consideration that the right cerebral hemisphere has been implicated in the processing of both spatial and emotional material.

### 7.3.3    Facial expression and its relation to identity

Yin (1970), Galper (1970) and Galper and Hochberg (1971) have argued that facial expression is important in one's recognition of faces. Yin (1970) suggested that the reason people have great difficulty recognising upside down faces is because they cannot discern facial expression in them (see figure 7.2). Galper and Hochberg (1971) supported their claim that facial expression plays a large role in facial recognition by testing subjects' retention of identity and expression of faces over a period of a few days. They found that the subjects could recall both the faces and the expressions with a high accuracy, but that their ability to recall the faces was better than recall of expressions. However, to conclude from this, as they did, that the difference between the recall scores is indicative of a role played by the faces' expressions is a non sequitur.

If the subjects had been unable to recall the expressions then one may
have made a case for the independence of recall of expression and
identity. But the fact that the expressions were recalled does not
provide evidence that they were used to aid recall of identity.

There is, in fact, a basic difficulty in arguing that one recognises
faces according to the expressions which they usually produce. By
definition the identity of a face must be relatively independent of
the expression it conveys or of paraphernalia (such as beards, glasses,
etc.), or else one would have to relearn who someone was each time
their facial features shifted position or were covered by something.
Put simply, Joe Smith looks like Joe Smith whether he's smiling or
scowling( even if one has only seen him once before when he was fairly
expressionless). Thus, to say that recognition of inverted faces is
difficult because identification of expression in inverted faces is
hard is also a non sequitur. Certainly though, recognition of identity
and expression are related, for expression is the spatial disposition
of the individual features which are also used in recognition of identity.

### 7.3.4    Hemispheric processing and face recognition

A host of studies have demonstrated a right hemisphere (left visual
field) advantage in the processing of photographs or schematic depictions
of faces (Geffen et al., 1971; Rizzolatti et al, 1971; Hilliard, 1973;
Ellis and Shepherd, 1975; Patterson and Bradshaw, 1975; Klein et al,
1976; Moscovitch et al., 1976; Young and Ellis, 1976). This is in
addition to other visio-spatial abilities possessed by the right
hemisphere (Corkin, 1965; Warrington and Kinsbourne, 1966; Levy et al.,
1972), and contrasts with the verbal and analytical abilities attributed
to the left hemisphere (Milner, 1971; Gefen et al., 1972; Kimura, 1963;

Marcel and Rajan, 1975). Gazzaniger (1970) and White (1969) both give
reviews of the literature on the cerebral hemispheres.

There is some doubt, however, whether the left hemisphere is devoid
of ability to identify faces. Marzi and Berlucchi (1977) provide evidence
for the left hemisphere being better than the right at identifying well
known faces. Other studies have reported similar results (for instance,
Marzi et al., 1974). Marzi and Berlucchi suggest that the reason for
this superior recognition by the left hemisphere is that when viewing
well known faces one may rely upon the detection of isolated features,
which the left hemisphere is found to be good at. They support their
ideal by referring to Patterson and Bradshaw's study (1975) in which
they found that schematic drawings of faces were discriminated better
by the right hemisphere except when the faces had to be discriminated
on the basis of a single facial feature. It therefore seems that the
left hemisphere too can identify faces, and it does so better (or quicker)
than the right one when detection of a single feature is critical.

There is also some doubt as to whether the right hemisphere's ability
to identify faces is just due to it possessing a good ability to deal
with spatial material in general, or whether it indicates the presence
of 'face-specific analysers' in the right hemisphere. The main evidence
for the possible existence of face-specific analysers being present in
the right hemisphere comes from studies of brain damaged patients. In
particular evidence has been drawn from studies of patients suffering
from 'prosopagnosia' which is the inability to recognise the faces of
even near relatives or friends.

People suffering from prosopagnosia may complain of an overall
blurring and a difficulty in interpreting fine shadow and soft forms
of the face. They may be able to identify individual features but
be quite unable to gain any idea of the expression being conveyed by
a face. Hence they may try to identify people by their voice, gait,
clothes, hair length, and so on (see: Bay, 1953; Pallis, 1955; Macrae
and Trolle, 1956; Beyn and Kayazeva, 1962; Cole and Perez-Cruet, 1964).
Although the syndrome is rare, several cases have been reported since
Charcot first described it (see Hecaen and Angelergues, 1962). Bodamer
(1947) labelled it prosopagnosia in order to underscore his belief that
a face-specific process is damaged in such patients. This apparent
specificity has led workers to postulate the existence of face-
specific analysers which are impaired in prosopagnosic patients
(Hecaen and Angelergues, 1962; Konorski, 1967; Yin, 1970). However,
as Ellis (1975) points out, there are a number of objections which can
be raised to the simplicity of this idea.

First, the patients usually also suffer from other 'agnosias'
such as: an inability to tell one chair from another (Bay, 1953; Critchley,
1953), or problems identifying food and animals (Pallis, 1955), or being
unable to tell a cow from a dog (Macrae and Trolle, 1956), or frequently
colour agnosia (Bay, 1953; Pallis, 1955; Beyn and Knyazeva, 1962;
Cole and Perez-Cruet, 1964; Gloning et al., 1970). Visual field defects
are not unknown in such patients (Bay, 1953), and some experience
distortions of patterns such as crosses and swastikas (so called
'metamorphosia'; Benton and Van Allen, 1968). As Ellis (1975) notes,
it is hardly surprising that clinicians and patients most frequently
mention the difficulty with faces (De Renzi et al., 1969), but the fact
that this aspect of the patient's problems gives most concern is not
an argument for the presence of a face-specific analyser system. In

the absence of a pure case of facial agnosia it remains a possibility
that the patient's visual processing problems are causing facial agnosia
as one among many symptoms.

Second, it is noted that there is no single area of the brain which
has been implicated in prosopagnosia.  Damage has been reported in the
parietal-temporo-occipital junction (Hecaen and Angelergues, 1962),
bilateral occipital lobes (Beyn and Knyazeva, 1962) and right temporal
lobe (Cole and Perez-Cruet, 1964), and in bilateral parieto-occipital
regions (Gloning et al., 1966).  Whilst is is true that most of the damage
implicated has been to the right hemisphere (Hecaen and Angelergues, 1962),
it seems unlikely that one specific area is involved.  Rather it seems
that there may be several sub-processes in the identification of faces,
governed by several areas of the brain, and that damage to any one part
of the process can lead to some form of facial agnosia.  The many different
reports of what patients have described their vision of faces to be like,
and the theories that have been built upon such descriptions, also implicate
several processes that may be involved in face perception (Faust, 1947;
Bay, 1953;  Pallis, 1955).

Experimental studies of patients suffering from unilateral brain
damage have shown that damage to the right-hemisphere more radically
affects a person's ability to identify faces than damage confined to the
left-himisphere (De Renzi and Spinnler, 1966;  Warrington and James, 1967;
Benton and Allen, 1968;  Milner, 1968;  De Renzi et al., 1969;  Jones,
1969;  Tzavaras et al., 1970;  Yin, 1970).  The important question, of
course, is whether such damage ever only affects a person's ability to
recognise faces.  Tzavaras et al. (1970) believe that the damage may be
restricted to problems with facial recognition.  They compared right-
hemisphere lesioned patients with left-hemisphere damage ones and normal

subjects for their abilities to recognise faces which had been disguised
in various ways (with beards, shadows etc.), and their abilities to
recognise particular stimuli from amongst an array of similar stimuli.
They found that the right-hemisphere lesioned patients were much poorer
than the control subjects at recognising the disguised faces. The right-
hemisphere damaged subjects were also worse at the other non face-like
patterns, but the effect was not so great. There was, however, no control
for the difficulty which each task provided for the subjects. For instance,
the controls had very few problems with any of the tasks except the one
involving faces. It is therefore possible that the task with faces was
simply harder than the rest, and showed up the right-hemisphere lesioned
patients' problems with spatial tasks in general. Tzavaras et al.'s
findings cannot thus be taken as evidence that there are face-specific
analysers in the right hemisphere.

Yin (1970) showed that patients with damage to the posterior sector
of the right hemisphere did significantly less well on a test of face
recognition than did either left posterior hemisphere damaged patients
or normal controls. However, the patients with right posterior hemisphere
damage were able to do as well as those with left side damage at
recognising pictures of houses. Yin took this to be further evidence
for his previous (1969) contention that the right-hemisphere is specialised
in perceiving faces. He supports his argument with the results of the
same subject's performance at recognising inverted faces and houses. In
this case the right posterior hemisphere damaged patients did better
than any of the subjects with other unilateral brain damage at recognising
inverted faces (in fact, the left posterior hemisphere damaged group
did worse than chance). But once again they were about as good as the

controls at recognising inverted houses. In consequence Yin argued
that there is a face-specific analyser in the right-hemisphere which
is also orientation specific. However, Yin omitted any discussion
of the interesting results of the left posterior hemisphere damaged
group. Whereas the right-hemisphere lesioned patients were about as good
as normal controls at recognising inverted faces, the left-hemisphere
lesioned patients were considerably worse. This may indicate that
there is an important element of verbal coding or analytic processing
involved in the identification of inverted faces. This may also relate
to Marzi and Berlucchi's (1977) finding, mentioned above, that the
left hemisphere is better at identifying well known faces. They argued
that this might be because the left-hemisphere is specialised at
analytical processing of information, and thus is more able to detect
critical features by which to recognise faces. The suggestion that
one may adopt different strategies for looking at upright and inverted
faces is also of relevance here (Yin, 1970; Ellis, 1975; see above).
If one tends to view upright faces as gestalten but inverted faces as
a collection of individual features, then it is possible that damage to
the right hemisphere would affect identification of upright faces more
than inverted ones, and damage to the left hemisphere would have the
opposite effect. This is in accord with the findings of Yin's work,
and does not implicate the presence of face-specific analysers in the
right hemisphere.

More recent studies have provided evidence which develops Yin's
findings. Leehey et al. (1978) noted that Yin's finding that damage
to the posterior sector of the right-hemisphere does not effect patient's
ability to identify inverted faces, does not mean that other areas of
the right-hemisphere are not crucial to the identification of inverted
faces. To test this possibility they used a tachistoscopic technique

to present upright and inverted faces to the left and right visual fields
(LVF and RVF). They argued that if the right-hemisphere is specialized
in the recognition of upright faces then faces presented in the LVF should
be recalled well when upright but poorly when inverted. In contrast, the
faces presented in the RVF should be reported equally poorly regardless
of their orientation. This was in fact what they found, and they thus
concluded, "This pattern of results supports the existence of a right-
hemisphere specialization for upright faces in addition to the right-
hemisphere specialization for visuo-spatial patterns." (Authors'
emphasis). They note that their results are at variance with Ellis and
Shepherd's (1975) work in which they found a LVF advantage for both
upright and inverted faces. Leehey et al. claim that the reason why
their results support Yin's (1970) - whereas Ellis and Shepherd's do
not, is that the latter used too brief fixation times. Ellis and Shepherd
only allowed their subjects to see that faces for 15ms and Leehey et al.
argue that this was insufficient time to allow enough depth of processing
(Craik and Lockhart, 1972) such that the stimuli were not viewed as faces.
Stated thus Leehey et al.'s criticism of Ellis and Shepherd's procedural
method is nonsensical for the subjects certainly reported that the stimuli
were faces. Nonetheless, the fact that the subjects recalled vastly more
faces in the LVF when allowed a longer fixation time is indicative of
the nature of the process which can give the right-hemisphere its advantage
over the left one.

Leehey et al.'s claim that the right-hemisphere has a specialization
for upright faces in addition to one for visuo-spatial patterns can also
be criticized. The basis for this claim in their conclusion is unclear
but would seem to rely upon the assumption that upright and inverted faces
represent equally complex figures, and thus perception of them by a
hemisphere specialized in visuo-spatial material should not be better for

one than the other. However, there is ample evidence in the literature, as noted above, that inverted and upright faces may not be equated in terms of their objective difficulty as patterns: clearly upright faces are much more familiar than inverted ones, any scanning patterns appropriate for an upright face will not be appropriate for an inverted one, and subjects have reported viewing upright faces as gestalten and inverted ones in a more piecemeal manner. In summary, then, neither of Leehey et al.'s conclusions can be agreed with. There is neither evidence provided by their study for the right hemisphere being specialized for upright faces in particular, nor for it being specialised for face perception above and beyond its specialized perception of other visuo-spatial patterns.

7.3.5     Hemispheric processing and the identification of facial expression.

Bradshaw and Wallace (1971) have pointed out that "....the human face can be viewed as a complex visual pattern subserving two purposes: communication and identification." The above studies have generally dealt with subject's abilities to identify faces, but is there any evidence for asymmetry in the brain's processing of communicative aspects such as facial expression? There is in face a wealth of evidence to suggest that the right-hemisphere is more involved than the left in the processing of emotional stimuli (for example: Goldstein, 1939; Hecaen et al. 1951; Denny-Brown et al., 1952; Perria et al., 1961; Gainotti, 1972). Early evidence was gained from brain damaged patients, and Goldstein was the first to note a common emotional response to left-hemisphere lesions, which has been attributed to a freeing of the 'emotional' right hemisphere. Goldstein termed this the 'catastrophic reaction'. Later, Hecaen et al. and Denny-Brown et al. described a complementary pattern of emotional response after right-hemisphere lesion which has been termed the 'indifference reaction'. Gainotti's work with unilaterally brain damaged patients has confirmed these earlier reports. The catastrophic reaction was found by Gainotti to include anxiety, crying, hostility and compensatory boasting, whereas the indifference reaction included jocularity, minimization, anosognosia, and a lassez faire attitude.

There has also been evidence for hemispheric asymmetry of affective memory processes. Wechsler (1973) found that unilaterally brain damaged subjects short-term memory for the affective aspects of stories was worse when they had right- and left-hemisphere lesions. Haggard and Parkinson (1971) also gained evidence for right-hemisphere processing and emotional stimuli. They found that judgements about emotional tone of sentences (anger, boredom, happiness, distress) heard in one headphone whilst 'babble' was heard in the other, were significantly more accurate on left-ear presentations (which are processed by the right-hemisphere). Carmon and Nachson (1973) also used a dichotic listening procedure to investigate hemispheric asymmetry when perceiving nonverbal sounds such as cries, shrieks and laughter. They also found a slight but nonetheless significant left ear advantage for these emotional sounds.

Safer and Leventhal (1977) required subjects to listen to taped passages of text which were of three emotional kinds: positive, negative, and neutral. These passages were then read in three tones of voice, with the positive passages being read in a happy manner, the negative ones read in a strong almost angry manner, and the neutral ones read in an objective way. Whilst the subjects were not told which cue to use to rate the passages, 29 of the 36 subjects who listened to the left ear used the tone of voice to rate the passages. Conversely, 21 of the 36

subjects who listened to the right ear rated the passages according
to their linguistic content. This provides further evidence that the
right-hemisphere is involved in processing stimuli which have emotional
content carried by intonation, pitch and rhythms.

Dimond and Farrington (1977) showed subjects films which were either
unpleasant or humorous, and measured their heart rate as they viewed
them. They were able to present the films to either one hemisphere
(visual field) or the other and    consequently gain evidence for
asymmetry of response by the two hemispheres. They found that the
subjects' heart rate was higher when the unpleasant film was presented
to the right-hemisphere than to the left one. In contrast, the heart
rate was higher when the humorous film was shown to the left-hemisphere.
Despite this left-hemisphere effect they interpreted their findings as
support for the right-hemisphere bearing "responsibility for 'emotion'
viewed in the broad sense" (p.259).

Suberi and McKeever (1977) presented subjects with faces in a
tachistoscope in such a way that the faces were off-set and fed to one
hemisphere or the other. The faces were either emotional or neutral
as judged by independent raters. Suberi and McKeever found that the
subjects' reaction times when identifying previous seen faces were
faster when faces were seen in the left visual field (LVF). Moreover,
the reaction times favoured the LVF more strongly for subjects who had
memorised emotional faces than those who had memorised neutral ones.
Whilst this does not show that a LVF superiority for processing emotional
stimuli, it nonetheless indicates that faces are generally better
identified by the LVF when affect is present in the stimuli.

Ley and Brydén (1979) also presented faces unilaterally to subjects by using a tachistoscope. Subjects saw cartoon drawings of men's faces. There were five different cartoon characters and each was shown displaying each of five different facial expressions. These expressions ranged from a very 'positive' one to a very 'negative' one (happy to angry) with the stages between being judged as distinguishable and valid steps by separate raters. After presentation subjects were later asked to compare a presented face with the ones seen before and to say whether they had seen the character before, or the expression. As with the above studies, Ley and Brydon found a significant LVF superiority for both character and emotion recognition. However, statistical analysis revealed that the two effects were independent. That is the LVF superiority for emotions was correlated with the degree of affective expression, whereas that for character recognition was not.

Ley and Brydén note that there are many characteristics for right-hemisphere functioning that may uniquely bias it for the processing of affective information. For instance, Semmes (1968) has proposed that elementary functions are focally represented in the left-hemisphere and more diffusely represented in the right-hemisphere. This diffuse organization is hypothesised to lead to a more proficient integration of dissimilar units and a specialization for multimodal coordination, such as visuo-spatial abilities (see Corkin, 1965). Ley and Brydon suggest that the recognition of emotion entails an integration of stimulus information from a variety of sources (both sensory and motor) and across space and time. Semmes' model would argue that such synthesis would take place in the right-hemisphere. This right-hemisphere superiority for synthesising diverse units of information is closely allied to its often described 'holistic' or gestalt processing capabilities (Bogen, 1969; Levy, 1972; Ornstein, 1972; Safer and Leventhall, 1977). Ley

and Bryden go on to note that a third characteristic of emotional
processing can also be associated with right-hemisphere functioning,
namely its involvement with processing and forming 'images' (Davidson
and Swartz, 1976). Safer and Leventhall (ibid.) made the point that
imagery is often associated with emotions. Hence, Ley and Bryson
conclude, "....synthetic and integrative characteristics, a holistic
and gestalten nature, the imagic associations are three features of
processing affective material that would differentially favour right-
hemispheric mediation of the task."

Thus one may understand the right-hemisphere's excellent performance
at processing emotions in terms of its more basic mode of functioning.
What is interesting here (and Lee and Bryson omit to mention it) is that
precisely these right-hemisphere abilities to integrate and synthesis
information have been referred to by other workers as possible reasons
why it is so good at recognising faces. Their experiments with brain
damaged patients led De Renzi and Spinnler (1966) to speculate that
individuals with right-hemisphere damage are deficient in the high-level
integration of visual data. In support of this view, Jones (1969)
reports that right-hemisphere damage can impair visual search efficiency.
Jones argued that because many tests of face recognition involve patients
having to decide which of an array of faces they have seen before, the
patients inability to extract meaning from complex arrays might cause
them to appear to be less able to recall faces than they in fact are.
Jones backed up his argument by showing that such patients were more
able to recall faces when they had to choose between two faces, one
of which they had seen earlier, than when they had to pick which the
face was from a large array of photographs.

Clearly, the deficiency suggested above is not face-specific, and might be expected to reveal itself in response to the perception of any complex stimulus which tends to be viewed in a global rather than analytic manner. Moreover, by reverse argument one may posit that the right hemisphere is normally superior at recognising faces simply because it possesses an integrative mode of functioning. Thus, not only does it seem that there is little or no evidence for 'face-specific analysers' in the right-hemisphere, but that the reasons why the right-hemisphere is so good at face perception and good at processing emotional information may be identical. That the right-hemisphere's ability to integrate and synthesise information may be central to both recognition of faces and emotional expression is borne out by Bodamer's (1941) description of one of his prosopagnosic patient's view of faces:

> "(He) could disciminate the various parts of the face but all faces appeared to him to be spiritless and lacking in expression, individuality and meaning. Mimicked expressions were clearly perceived but could not be interpreted".

>                                  (Quoted in Hecaen and Angelergues, 1962).

It is notable that the assumption that the right-hemisphere's ability to process information holistically and the left-himisphere's tendency to process data analytically can account for nearly all of the above mentioned findings about face recognition and identification of expression. If the ability to integrate sensory information is fundamental to both the perception of identity and expression, then it is predictable that both of these activities will be impaired by inversion of the stimuli. That is, when looking at inverted faces it is difficult to make use of a 'gestalt' mode of perception, because the gestalt as it is normally viewed has had all its relations inverted in an unfamiliar manner.

It thus becomes unnecessary to postulate that faces are difficult to recognise when upside down because one cannot discern their expressions. Equally, it becomes unnecessary to assign any special significance to the fact that the hemispheres are differentially affected by inversion of the stimuli. The left-hemisphere's analytical mode of processing information is as appropriate for upright faces as inverted ones, for the detection of an individual feature does not depend upon its disposition with respect to other features. Equally, it accounts for the left-hemisphere's inability to perceive emotion in faces (of the reference to Bodamer's patient above), for to do so requires a synthesing and integrating mode of processing. However, this view does not indicate that the left-hemisphere cannot identify faces, only that it will be better at doing so when an analytical mode of perception might be advantageous. Such a mode would be advantageous when viewing inverted faces, and seemingly when looking at highly familiar faces as Marzi and Berlucchi (1977) found.

In conclusion, one is drawn to propose that the manner in which one views faces is related to the fact that one usually wishes to extract meaning from them about the inner states of other people. Because this is a primary reason for fixating others' faces, the manner in which we look at them is bound to favour a holistic mode of processing. In consequence when one fixates others' faces one rarely focuses attention upon the individual features, and thus one's ability to recognise them when they are seen upside down will be impaired. This is not true for almost every other visual stimulus which human beings perceive in daily life, and hence it is little wonder that there might misleadingly seem to be 'face-specific analysers' in the brain. It is possible that written words come closest to faces as

complex stimuli which require holistic processing (although they are
neither so complex nor require the same degree of gestalt perception);
thus it is noteworthy that researchers are unable to agree as to whether
'dyslexia' represents a 'specific word blindness' or is only one aspect
of a more general problem that such people have with processing visual
stimuli (Griffiths, 1972). The above argument suggests that the latter
may be the case, but it is outside the domain of this thesis to speculate
further.

Thus, whilst there is no unequivocal evidence that face perception
is innate, it seems that the innate tendency of the right-hemisphere to
process information in a gestalt and integrative manner allows it to be
superior at the recognition of faces and their expressions.

### 7.3.6   Neurological aetiologies of autism suggested by other authors

Many theories about the neurological aetiology of autism have been
proposed, but this section will confine itself to those which have a
bearing upon person perception in relation to possible hemispheric
asymmetries.

First it should be noted that in at least one study about a third of
autistic children who were followed up from early childhood to adolescence
showed some signs of brain damage such as epileptic fits (Rutter, 1970)
and this has been supported by others (Lotter, 1966, 1967). There is
thus good evidence for detectable brain damage in a sizeable number of
autistic children. Even in the remaining two thirds of autistic children
it seems most likely that they were born with some form of brain dysfunction,
as psychogenic theories of causes of autism have received no empirical
support to date. The apparent specificity of the syndrome has led many

workers to suggest certain areas of the brain as locii of dysfunction.
For instance, Crawley (1971) has suggested damage to the association
areas, Hermelin (1966) and Ricks (1972) have suggested damage to the
dominant hemisphere and Wing (1969) has indicated the possibility of
damage to other areas concerned with language.

Gellner (1959) has suggested that autistic children suffer damage
to the corpora quadrigemina, the medial and lateral geniculate bodies,
and tracts carrying exteroceptive, proprioceptive and interoceptive
impulses to and from these ganglia. She hypothesised that such lesions
would lead to a failure of incoming stimuli to be integrated with
interoceptive impulses from the autonomic nervous system. Such a lack
of integration might lead to difficulties with comprehension and with
perception. Whilst Gellner's ideas are noteworthy for attempting to
explain many of the symptoms of autism, they are nonetheless highly
speculative and unproven. Indeed, many of the functions that she has
assigned to the above areas of the brain have more recently been
associated with other areas such as the posterior sector of the right
hemisphere, the frontal lobes, and so forth (see Luria, 1973).

Several theories have implicated the recticular formation as being
the locus of damage (MacCulloch and Sambrooks, 1972; DesLauriers and
Carlson, 1969; Hutt et al., 1964, 1965; Hutt and Hutt, 1970; Rimland,
1964). The major reason for this is that damage to this area can lead
to abnormalities of arousal and attention. However, it has frequently
been noted (Wing, 1976a; Hermelin and O'Connor, 1970) that a simple
theory of abnormal arousal cannot account for the diverse symptoms seen
in the autistic child. This is particularly true for those with near
normal intelligence. More specifically, it does not seem that an arousal
theory can account for the autistic child's manner of perceiving people.

Perhaps the most immediately attractive theory of autistic behaviour has been that there is damage to the left hemisphere (see Prior and Bradshaw, 1979). Autistic children invariably have poor language skills, but they may excell at spatial, mathematical, musical and rote memory tasks. Autistic children are also noted for their lack of symbolic thought. Viewing the dichotomies suggested for the two hemispheres reveal the reason for thinking that autistics possess mainly right hemisphere abilities.

| Left-hemisphere | Right-hemisphere |
|---|---|
| linguistic verbal | visual-spatial |
| symbolic | mathematical |
| discrete | diffuse |
| logical | musical |

(after Bogen, 1969)

But some doubt may be shed on any simple theory immediately, by considering a few more of the dichotomies.

| Left-himisphere | Right-hemisphere |
|---|---|
| rational | emotional |
| numerical | geometric |
| digital | analogic |
| sequential | imaginative |
| analytic | integrative * |

(again after Bogen, 1969)

---

* The right hemisphere is also said to deal with intonation, pitch and rhythms -- each of which autistic persons have trouble perceiving and producing in speech.

Thus if one considers the hemispheres to be specialized for language and symbolic functioning (left) and visuo-spatial, musical and mathematical abilities (right), then there seems to be some sense in proposing that autistic children possess almost entirely right-hemisphere abilities and virtually no left-hemisphere ones. However, this is not true. Autistic children are very conscious of order, as is revealed by their rote memory abilities, want for sameness and repetitive behaviours. In addition, they tend to learn language in a one-to-one fashion and not in the holistic-categorical manner characteristic of the right-hemisphere. Moreover, they are noted to lack imaginative and affective abilities both of which have been attributed to the right-hemisphere. Although the topic will be returned to later, it will also be noted here that the normal child tends to be good at face perception and identification of facial expression mainly because he perceives faces in a holistic fashion utilising his right hemisphere's advantages in these areas. The autistic child, by contrast, would seem to be poor at the identification of expression because he lacks the normal ability to integrate perceptions, and his relatively good performance at face recognition tasks seems, paradoxically, to be due to his tending to process faces as collections of disparate features rather than as gestalten. Hence, this data also argues against the autistic child performing as 'a right-hemisphere processor'.

More important to theories of damage to higher cortical functions is the face that theorists have been unable to account for the fact that autism typically begins in the first thirty months of life when the brain is still relatively 'plastic'. If the child were born with right-hemisphere damage the left-hemisphere should take over the functions of the right in addition to those of its own. The only reason why this might not happen would be if the corpus collosum is damaged too, and there is no evidence that autistic children have such damage.

Nonetheless, a few workers have attempted to search for asymmetrical functioning in autistic children (Kugler, 1975; Libbard, 1979; Prior and Bradshaw, 1979; Blackstock, 1978). Kugler presented her work as a pilot study, giving little detail. However, she claimed to have obtained preliminary evidence that autistic children do not possess a normal left-hemisphere superiority for verbal material as measured by ear advantage in a dichotic listening test.

Libbard (1979) did further work on autistic children's cerebral processing abilities. She too used dichotic listening tasks. She describes three experiments with a group of autistic children in which she compared the performance of these children with that of matched groups of subnormal and normal children. In her first study she presented pairs of words simultaneously, one to each of the child's ears. The words were carefully prepared to be in synchrony and all were single syllable nouns having a common middle vowel and a common final consonant (eg: pet, met, net). Both the normal and subnormal children showed a preference for reporting the word which they heard in their right ear (and which was presumably being processed by their left hemisphere). In contrast, the autistic children showed no ear preference. This finding thus supported the contention that autistic children have a left-hemisphere deficit. The autistic children also made more errors overall than did either of the other groups, which further supports the observation that they have problems with the processing of verbal input. However, Libbard did not discuss the possibility that other language impaired children might also fail to show a right-ear advantage in this type of paradigm. In the absence of any results from dysphasic children on a similar task it is difficult for one to conclude that Libbard's results show anything more than that language impaired children do not show a 'normal' response on a language related task.

In her second study, Libbard presented non-verbal sounds
dichotically to the children's ears, as the right hemisphere is purported
to be specialised in processing such non-linguistic sounds. Thus one
would expect a subject to report those sounds heard by his left ear
more frequently than those heard by his right and the experiment
therefore sought evidence for a possible right-hemisphere deficit.
However, no such evidence was obtained for any of the three groups.
In fact, all the children failed to show an ear preference for the non-
verbal sounds, including the normals. This absence of the expected
response pattern from the normal children makes this experiment difficult
to interpret, and it would be interesting to repeat this study with
stimuli which were first determined to elicit a left-ear advantage
in normal children. Only by doing this could one come to any meaningful
conclusions about the absence of such an ear advantage in autistic
children.

Libbard's third study involved the children of matching by touch
alone various grades of sandpaper according to which was roughest. She
had the child feel the two pieces of paper whilst they were out of sight,
and required him to feel the pieces once with just one hand and then
later with a different hand for each piece. Because the left hand feeds
information to the right-hemisphere and the right hand feeds information
to the left-hemisphere, it was thus possible to compare the children's
tactile discrimination abilities both unilaterally and cross-laterally.
She found that all the children were quite able to discriminate the
pieces of sandpaper regardless of whether they were compared with the
same hand or different ones. It thus does not seem that autistic
children have any callosal problems, at least for tactile information.

Blackstock (1978) claimed to provide evidence from two studies that autistic children are 'right-hemisphere processors'. Blackstock defines a right-hemisphere processor as one who has relatively intact visuo-spatial skills but poor language skills. His reason for inferring left-hemisphere damage in autistic children is thus solely because they tend to have poor linguistic skills and yet are good at visuo-spatial tasks. This simplistic view of hemispheric function was discussed and rejected above as being inadequate. His first study was based upon the clinical observation that autistic children seem to like listening to music. His hypothesis was that given the choice between listening to music and listening to a spoken story autistic children would choose the former and normal children would choose the latter. Autistic and normal children were selected and matched for chronological age. The result of this matching, though, was that the language skills of the normal children were considerably higher than those of the autistics. The child was shown an apparatus which had two levers on it, the pulling of one allowed the child to hear a burst of music and the pulling of the other caused a burst of spoken text to be heard. The child could not pull both levers at the same time.

Blackstock claimed that the results of this study clearly revealed that the autistic children preferred to hear music whereas the normal children preferred to hear spoken words. However, his analysis of the data is open to many criticisms as is his choice of control subjects. He reported that the mean frequency of pulling each lever differed between the groups and went on to test the differences between the mean frequencies using a Chi squared test. But it is not adequate to test mean frequencies in this manner. Further, he gave no idea of the

total number of pulls each type of child produced in the session.
If the normal children gave many more such responses than the autistics
(as seems quite possible from clinical knowledge of these children)
then this would further complicate Blackstock's analysis of his results.
More important, his choice of normal children as 'controls' who were
linguistically far more able than the autistic children tends to
invalidate any comparisons between the groups. How can one be certain
that any child with as little linguistic competence as the autistic
children would not also choose the music in preference to the speech?
Perhaps better controls would have been subnormal children matched on
verbal IQ, or better still, dysphasic children matched in a similar way.

Blackstock's second experiment also investigated the possibility
that autistic children prefer to listen to music rather than speech.
However, the added dimension of ear preference was introduced by
playing the music and speech as a very low level and thus requiring
the child to put his ear to a loudspeaker to hear anything. Two tables
were placed in the middle of a room, and there was a loudspeaker on
each of the sides of both tables (eight in all). One table had three
speakers producing musical sounds with a fourth speaker remaining silent,
and the other table had three speakers emitting spoken words, and a
fourth which remained silent. The silent speakers were included for
control purposes only. There were three types of music (rhythmic,
melodic and harmonic) and three types of speech (a Russian lesson, a
story, and some poetry). The children were allowed to wander in the
room for a period of time, first having been shown that by putting
their ears up to the speakers they could hear the various sounds. As
they wandered a note was made of which speaker they listened to, for
how long and which ear they put up to the speaker.

Both Blackstock's predictions and his results are puzzling. He predicted that it would be normal for a child to put his left ear to a speaker playing music and his right ear to one playing speech. However, Blackstock offers no reason as to why this should be expected, nor does the literature contain any evidence for supporting such a notion. Unless there is competition between the inputs to the two ears, sound entering one ear will go equally to both hemispheres and not to the contralateral one. Moreover, Blackstock seems to presume that information fed to one ear is processed by the contralateral hemisphere even in the absence of any competing information to the other ear. Blackstock's predictions, then, that normal children would tend to spend more time listening to the words than the music and do so mostly with their right ears, whereas the autistic children would spend most time at the music table and show no ear preferences is rather difficult to justify.

His results are also puzzling. In this study the normal children failed to show any preference for listening to music or speech. The autistic children, in contrast, were found to prefer to listen to the music. However, what is puzzling is that Blackstock did report ear preferences when there is no reason to expect them. He found the normal children preferred to listen to the story and the poetry with their right ear, but failed to show any preference when listening to the other four sound sources. The autistic children tended to use their left ears to listen to the three music sources and to the Russian, but showed no clear preference when listening to the other two spoken sources. However, the picture is less clear when, instead of analysing the mean number of times each type of child put his ear to any speaker he analysed according to the difference score for each subject when listening to each speaker by subtracting the percentage of listening time with the right ear from that with the left ear. The means for the groups were then treated by an analysis of variance. When this was done the only group differences were on the musical melody source and the story telling. While normal children tended to listen to the story with their right ears, the autistic children tended to listen to both sources with their left ears. Blackstock offers no suggestions as to why this should be so, or why there were no group differences for the other four sound sources. The results are thus very unclear, and certainly do not, as Blackstock maintains, allow one to conclude that autistic children tend to listen to sounds primarily with their left ears whereas normals tend to listen with their right ears.

In conclusion to Blackstock's experiments, it is very difficult to agree with his contention that he has provided evidence that autistic children are 'right hemisphere processors'. His evidence at best suggests that differences exist between autistic and normal children of similar age in their use of one ear or the other to listen to certain sound sources. However, the data does not even allow one to say that a normal child listens to speech with his right ear and music with his left, let alone to conclude that autistic children lack such a tendency. It remains quite possible that many of the group differences which Blackstock found were due to the normal children being far more linguistically competent than the autistic children.

The only other experimental work on hemispherical processing by autistic children was undertaken by Prior and Bradshaw (1979). Like Libbard (1979) they too gave a group of autistic children a dichotic listening test, and they also gave several tests for handedness to the children. They used five measures of handedness, cleaning teeth,

writing on paper, throwing ball, kicking a ball, and striking or
pretending to strike a match. Their performance on both the handedness
measures and the dichotic listening task were compared with that of a
group of normal right-handed children matched for mental age. They
found that of twenty-three autistic subjects seventeen were clearly
right-handed, none were left-handed and six showed a mixture of hand
preferences (the criterion being taken as at least four of the five
tests indicating the same handedness).

On the dichotic listening task the children were presented with
competing words to each ear and had to repeat what they heard. As
predicted, the normal children tended to repeat what they heard in
their right ears. However, there was considerable variance in the
autistic group. Five autistic children showed a clear right ear
advantage (out of nineteen who took part), seven showed a left ear
advantage, and the remaining seven showed no ear preference. There
seemed to be some indication that ear preference (and hence laterality)
was more common for the higher IQ children who also tended to be those
who gained speech before five years of age.

Prior and Bradshaw's results on the dichotic listening test were
thus similar to those obtained by Libbard and lend support to the
conclusion that as a group autistic children tend not to show strong
ear advantages for verbal material. However, Prior and Bradshaw also
found that about a third of the autistic children that they tested
nonetheless evidenced a right-ear advantage for verbal material, thus
one cannot simply conclude that such an advantage is absent in autistics.
The question of accuracy in matching controls also arises in Prior and
Bradshaw's work. While they matched for mental age and thus controlled

to some extent for verbal ability, it is still possible that dysphasic
or subnormal children might resemble autistics in showing a lack of ear
preference for dichotically presented verbal material.

The results that Prior and Bradshaw obtained from meausres of
handedness reflected those obtained by other workers (Hauser et al.,
1975; Boucher, 1977; Colby and Parkinson, 1977). In general, while
some researchers have noted that autistic children may be left-handed,
there is little evidence that the incidence of left-handedness in
autism is greater than would be expected in the general population.

In summary, there seems very little evidence to suggest that autistic
children's problems are primarily due to their having sustained damage
to their left cerebral hemispheres, although there is some indication
that speech does not become as strongly or as early lateralised in
their left hemispheres as it does with normal children of similar
mental ability.

As was mentioned above, there still remains the problem that autism
begins in the first year of life at a time when the brain is still
relatively 'plastic'. It is thus difficult to explain why a lesion of
the left-hemisphere would not lead to the right-hemisphere taking over
the damaged area's functions. One possible explanation lies in the
consideration of the subcortical areas as the site of the damage or
dysfunction (Hauser et al., 1975; De Long, 1978). Hauser et al. proposed
that autism might be due to damage to the hippocampal/limbic system
areas of the brain, and noted that damage to these areas on one side of
the brain may not be compensated for by equivalent areas on the other
side.

Hauser et al. and DeLong draw parallels between the behaviour of animals which have suffered temporal lobe damage and the behaviour of autistic children. They note that both the animals and the autistics tend to show repetitive and stereotyped behaviour. A problem here, though, is that such activities alone are not unique to autism and thus the parallel is perhaps rather tenuous. They also note that there are similarities between adults with the Kluver-Bucy syndrome and Korsikov's syndrome and autism. Both of these adult syndromes are due to damage to the temporal lobe area. More important, Hauser et al. were able to report that fifteen of their seventeen language impaired autistic subjects had abnormal pneumographic recordings which indicated enlargement of the left ventricular horn. These findings have yet to be replicated, but as yet stand as the strongest evidence available that at least some autistic children have sustained damage to the left temporal area. Lastly, it is worthy of note that the function of the limbic system has been linked to memory processes and that Boucher and Warrington (1976) have provided at least some suggestions which link autism with amnesia in childhood. This topic will be returned to later.

### 7.3.7: Some Theoretical Considerations

*I can't believe that! said Alice. "Can't you? said the Queen in a pitying tone. "Try again: draw a long breath and shut your eyes." Alice laughed. "There's no use trying", she said: "One can't believe impossible things". "I daresay you haven't had much practice," said the Queen. "When I was your age, I always did it for half an hour a day. Why sometimes I've believed as many as six impossible things before breakfast".*

(Lewis Carrol: Alice Through The Looking Glass)

This section will attempt to draw together the findings presented
in this thesis.  There are five main areas it will address itself to:
the possibility and consequences of autistic children possessing a
perceptual integration deficit;  the implications of possible cognitive
and perceptual deficits to the acquisition of language;  the subject of
the possession and understanding of abilities in contrast to the use of
them;  the implications that the results have for theories of possible
sites and mechanisms of brain dysfunction;  and finally, a discussion
of the extent to which autistic children may be born without certain
normally 'innate' factors which lead a child to be empathic,
inquisitive and gain communicative competence.

Given that the areas of perceptual processing, language acquisition
and brain functioning are still relative 'grey areas' in psychological
theory, this section will be necessarily somewhat speculative.  Moreover,
it should be borne in mind that many of the considerations presented
here are not to be understood simply as logical extensions of the
experimental findings presented in this thesis.  Although implications
of the findings will be discussed, the discussions will also range
somewhat beyond the results obtained in order to indicate ways in
which future research might profitably develop.

a)   Perceptual integration deficits in autism

Section 7.2 summarised the findings of this thesis and concluded
that the most parsimonious explanation of the results obtained from the
autistic children was that they were not tending to integrate their
perceptions into meaningful wholes.  That is, whilst the normal child
is capable of both holistic and analytic processing of sensory input,
it seems that autistic children tend to only operate in a limited

analytic mode. Their main problem then, seems to lie in the formation of perceptual 'gestalten', either of inputs from two or more modalities (hence intermodal integrations; see the lip-reading study and studies reported by Hermelin, O'Connor and Frith), or various perceptions arriving at the same time through the same modality (hence intramodal integration; see the other studies in this thesis).

The normal child seems to begin life by having a relatively global and holistic view of his world, and only later is he able to break up his perceptions into meaningful inter-related parts. These perceptions by virtue of their relations are later perceptually integrated once more, but now imbued with meaning which stems from his knowledge of his world. For instance, young children have great difficulty identifying 'figures' from complex 'grounds' in standard gestalt perception tests (Ghent, 1956). But later they are able both to discriminate the parts and integrate them back into a whole again. Bower (1979) has also suggested that a normal baby is born having a high degree of perceptual synthesis such that he will turn his head and eyes and reach towards a noise which he hears. Bower suggests that the baby may only be coding at first that 'something happened to my right', and not whether it was felt, seen, smelt or heard. Moreover, the normal baby seems to possess an innate tendency to seek out relations and associations between perceptual inputs - he is born trying to simultaneously differentiate and integrate his perceptual world and attach semantic cue value to what he perceives.

Autistic children, by contrast, seem to be born tending to view the world as a collection of disparate parts rather than as being comprised of integrated wholes. Thus for them perceptual 'events' both within a

modality and between two or more, may begin and remain relatively
separate. Yet it is only by the realisation of possible interrelationships
of such 'events' that a meaningful perception of the world can emerge.
Clinical and anecdotal evidence supports this view. For instance,
autistic children may be seen to put jigsaw puzzles together with
the pieces upside-down or face-downwards, and they may do so with
great ease. There is frequently a notable lack of trial and error
in the way that they place each piece as if being able to see precisely
which space any given piece fits into.

Autistic children also exhibit so called 'want for sameness' and
they may throw a tantrum if, upon returning to a room, one small object
is not quite in the same position it was in when they were last there.
Such unerring ability to notice one detail of a complex whole again
tends to support the suggestion that autistic children perceive the
world as a collection of parts.

Concomitant to this ability, to identify isolated parts of complex
wholes is the tendency to store perceptions without interpreting them,
i.e. to store them exactly as they were experienced. Thus some autistic
children have been known to have phenomenal rote memory abilities,
such as being able to recall the birthdays of a long list of unfamiliar
people, or the names on a randomly chosen page of a telephone directory.
This last example is typical of their tendency to recall (and to become
obsessed with recalling) lists of items for no practical reason. Even
less able autistic children may show some ability to recall what they
have perceived very accurately, throwing a tantrum if something or some
routine in their life is changed. Islets of special ability in autistic
children are frequently rote memory feats or mathematical abilities which

entail a good memory (c.f. the accounts of idiosavants). One child, for example, was claimed to be able to multiply and divide large decimal numbers in his head very quickly. The boy was very bright and seemed to have gained his ability since acquiring a calculator for Christmas. However, when the present author asked him a few problems it was noted that of a range of equally difficult ones he could do some extremely quickly and others he laboured over extensively. Discussing his ability with him was possible and very revealing. It appeared that he spent a great deal of his time running through many calculations on his calculator and memorising the answers. This ability to memorise his calculator display together with his not mediocre mathematical abilities meant he could frequently surprise people with quick answers to lengthy problems - but the answers were only very quick when he had run the particular calculation before and memorised the answer.

But if this boy had a fairly good comprehension of the number system together with his memory ability, often autistic children will at first seem to have a grasp of a concept when they actually do not. For instance, it is quite possible that an autistic child of low intelligence could not only lay a table for six people with all the correct cutlery, etc., but also lay one place setting in green plastic ware, another in red and so forth, exactly as had been demonstrated to him. Although there may be better examples, abilities like this can lead an inexperienced person to assume that the autistic child in question understands the quantity 'six', the colours involved, and so on. In fact, it is very likely that this is not so beyond his basic ability to discriminate and reproduce what he has seen. Indeed, had one demanded that he lay a similar table with similar coloured cutlery then one may have found that he would have been totally at a loss.

This ability to recall things exactly as they were experienced (even down to surprisingly accurate copies of others vocal pitch and characteristics) has also been noted in the experimental literature. Hermelin and O'Connor (1970) noted that the autistic children they tested exhibited an 'echo-box' type memory. This type of memory system is characterised by a recall of only the last items heard and a failure to make use of structure present in the input to aid recall beyond one's digit span. Echolalia occurs frequently in autism and is often the cause of much frustration when trying to interact with the autistic child:

| Teacher: | "...and now what?" |
| David: | "All the things." |
| Teacher: | "All the things?" |
| David: | "The dreams." (mishears) |
| Teacher: | "The dreams! Did you mention a brick?" |
| David: | "A brick." |
| Teacher: | "Okay, a brick. Should I move the brick?" |
| David: | "Move the brick" |
| Teacher: | "Okay, is that better?" |
| David: | "Better". |

(From a study reported elsewhere: Langdell 1980a,b, 1981).

It is of interest in the above example that both teacher and child are echoing each other, but whereas the child's echoing is devoid of communicative intent, the teacher is using her echoing in an attempt to confirm that she had understood the child correctly. This topic of the use of ones abilities will be returned to later.

b) Possible connections between an integration deficit and language
and thought

Accompanying such memory characteristics in autistic children is the
rigid and concrete nature of their thought processes. Autistic children
usually acquire language in an inflexible manner, taking words to be
labels or 'signs' for specific objects which they saw at the time when
they heard the word, rather than as generic (categorical) nouns for
many objects with similar qualities. Hence an autistic child may not
understand that a tall blue cup with straight sides and a white handle
is called a 'cup' as well as one which is smaller, red, has sloping
sides and has no handle. Even variations in colour alone can lead some
autistics to refuse to use the same label. This is reminiscent of
incidents in which some autistic children fail to recognise even their
own mother simply because she has had a new hairstyle. Autistic children
may also become distressed if told that the same object can have two
different labels (a pail and a bucket for example). Such lack of
flexibility can cause great difficulties where, for instance, one
person can have several different 'names' such as 'sister', 'Sally',
'daughter', 'cousin', 'neice', and if she's married, 'wife'. The
normal child quickly grasps that his sister, named Sally, is older
than him and married and is called by other terms according to how
the person who is speaking is related to her. Such systems of naming
may evade even brighter autistic children who are otherwise very able
in terms of their performance on standard IQ tests and so forth.

Some autistic children have been noted for the extremely literal
way in which they interpret what is said to them. Many mothers have
cursed the day that they unintentionally said phrases like "Don't cry
your eyes out". Two autistic boys at school one day showed how they

both interpreted what the teacher said literally when she left the room absent-mindedly saying that they should "brush the paper off the table onto the floor" (meaning for them to knock it off with their hands). When she returned some while later the boys were wandering around aimlessly. She enquired what was the matter and why the paper was still on the table. "Oh," replied one of the boys, "We're looking for a brush to brush it off with." Even more amusing perhaps was the anecdote about another autistic boy who, upon being shown around a house, was asked if he needed the toilet as they were near it. His reply was "No thank you, we already have one at home". What is interesting is that all of these linguistic errors are primarily in the pragmatic realm rather than the syntactic, semantic or phonological realms (although overlaps between pragmatic and semantic aspects are inevitable). That is, autistic children seem to mainly have problems understanding what language is used for, and what is likely to be communicated in a given context. In linguistic terms it means that they may have a basic grasp of the production of signs/symbols* (phonology), of the relationships between signs (syntax), and of the relationships between signs and their referents (semantics), but lack the ability to comprehend the use of signs in human social context (pragmatics). However, there is some reason to believe that autistic children may also have difficulties in the semantic and syntactic realms, too (see Hermelin and O'Connor, 1970; Simmons and Baltaxe, 1975).

Another way in which one can refer to the mode of thought which autistics exhibit is as 'all-or-none' rather than as relativistic. Names of things are learnt in a one-to-one fashion with little

---

\* Footnote: Morris (1938) who defined these divisions between the realms, referred to linguistic 'signs' but perhaps 'symbols' is the more correct term because of the arbitary nature of the relationship between words and their referents.

generalisation, and rules once acquired or generated tend to be applied by the autistic child with excessive rigidity. This is in marked contrast to the young normal child who seems to 'play' with language, and who gives many different things or events the same vocal label as if by way of experimentation. Whereas for the autistic child perceptions are stored as separate entities, for the normal child they seem to be processed and stored in a relativistic manner - relative to what the child already knows and to what else is happening or can be perceived at the same time.

However, the normal child's relativistic manner of perception cannot simply involve attempts on the child's part to compare incoming information with past perceptions or other ongoing perceptions. Such a view is too mechanistic and does not account for the active seeking of specific stimuli and the spontaneous labelling which young normal children engage in. It is thus important to emphasise the forward looking anticipatory element of cognitive perceptual processing. The normal baby, it is suggested, may be better regarded as a 'hypothesis tester' rather than as a passive integrator of past and present experience. It is further suggested that some autistic children may lack this mode of processing whilst others are deficient in their development of it. The hypotheses which infants form may be seen as precursors to later 'concepts' and thus early perceptual processing can be regarded as 'protoconceptual'.

One also cannot regard the normal child as simply attempting to integrate specific stimuli, or comparing those in ongoing experience with those specific ones already perceived. No two stimuli are ever exactly the same (or rarely sees even the same cup from precisely the same viewpoint twice), and moreover the context of the perception will always be different, both in terms of what else can be perceived at the time, and in terms of the knowledge (the internal context, if you will) that the child brings to the moment of perception. It is thus in the nature of the normal child's perceptual processing that he is predisposed to encode his perceptions in a relativistic manner; and the perceptions are encoded as relative to other ongoing perceptions, other internally stored past perceptions, and the relationships between such stored items.

Thus it may be proposed that the question a young child is asking is not "Have I experienced this before?" but, "What is the probability that I have experienced this before?". That is, because the child is processing his perceptions in a relativistic manner, his hypotheses about what he is perceiving will be probabilistic rather than absolute. An example of the normal process would be if one were to walk down a country lane at twilight and see out of the corner of one's eye a movement in the hedgerow. The context is that of the countryside where one is likely to see small animals or birds and so on. If one has noted that the air is fairly still with no breezes then one might interpret the movement as being due, say, to a small bird in the undergrowth. Moreover, for a fraction of a second one might actually 'see' a small bird. But perhaps then a faint breeze is detected, and one glimpses fallen leaves in the vicinity. Very suddenly one interprets the situation quite differently (the context has changed because one has attended to different internal and external cues), and one sees that it was merely a leaf shifting in the wind.

The consequence of this mode of processing, then, is that the child begins life as a categoriser who is effectively making covert propositions about the world he experiences. Such covert propositions may become overt when the child begins to indicate aspects of his perceptual world to his caregiver by pointing and otherwise drawing his partner's attention to a common point of reference. Such behaviour on the child's part has been referred to as 'protodeclarative' (Bruner 1975a, b; Bates, 1976, for example). But the suggestion being made here is that the nature of the child's mode of perceiving the world means that such gestures to another also possess a 'protopropositional' quality. The infant is not merely 'declaring' that he has seen something he is also seeking confirmation that what he has indicated is actually an entity worth indicating. This is not to say that the child is aware that the adult can provide feedback as to the appropriateness of his gesture (and later his utterances). Nonetheless the adult thus has the role of marking the child's experience and helping him to make sense of what he perceives, and by doing so the adult is effectively giving the child clues as to what the socially and culturally 'correct' hypotheses are to make. The caretaker will thus respond to an infant's proto-declarative acts with such phrases as "Yes, that's a doggy isn't it?". Later the caretaker's feedback can help the child improve upon his hypotheses, such as when a child points to a cat and says "Doggy!", whereupon the adult remarks something like, "No, it looks like a doggy doesn't it? But we call it a cat".

This has as its consequence that one will tend to encode perceptions as being integrated with each other rather than disparate. For the normal child it becomes as important to be able to differentiate the parts from wholes as it does to be able to integrate the various parts back into wholes again. In this manner the child is able to simultaneously hold in his mind both the 'ground' or 'context' and the 'feature' or focus of his attention. For example, he becomes able to focus upon one feature of a person's face and yet still maintain a global impression of the entire face, and consequently of its expression.

Language is also very much connected with the ability to consider both parts and wholes or contexts. For instance, it is vital that a child is able to know what is likely to be said to him in a given situation in order to interpret what is actually being said. Many errors which autistic children make with language were noted above to be pragmatic in nature, and they result from their inability to know what language is used for and what another is likely to be saying in a given context. This topic has been discussed more fully elsewhere (Langdell, 1980a, b, 1981) and will be returned to in the next subsection. It seems likely though from the above discussion that the autistic child's problems with language reflect a more basic problem he has with processing his perceptions.

To gain further insight into how the autistic child's problems might have begun, one needs to turn to a consideration of his development in the first year of life. It is known that autism starts within the first thirty months of life, and it was argued earlier that there is every reason to believe that in most cases the child is born with the syndrome. Autism thus begins at a preverbal stage in development.

Bruner (1975a, b) has outlined several stages which he feels a
normal child must progress through before being able to acquire language
or, at first, primitive speech acts. The first stage Bruner calls a
'demand mode' and it refers to the baby's earliest communicative routines
such as crying when hungry. Bruner notes that in practice the needs of
the child are usually responded to with the effect of establishing
expectancies in the child. When such expectancy is established changes
occur (see Bruner, 1975a) which mark the start of the 'request mode'.
In this mode the primitive egocentric demanding of the infant is
transcended and routines begin whereby the baby can request attention,
feeding, and so on. In this mode, where the baby's acts may be said
to be 'protoimperatives', it is notable that the baby now shows signs
of expecting a response to his behaviour. There is thus indication
that, although Bruner does not emphasise the point, the baby has made
the important transition from communication without intent to
communication with intent. This intent may also be interpreted as
reflecting the beginnings of hypothesis-testing (i.e. "when I cry in
a certain way I'm more likely to get fed). Although Bruner does not
discuss it, there are other ways in which the baby now starts to show
that he is expecting certain things to happen and certain patterns to
ensue. For instance, babies start raising their arms in anticipation
of being lifted up. Elsewhere (Ratner and Bruner, 1977) though, Bruner
does refer to the making and breaking of expectancies as forming an
essential aspect of early mother/infant play (peek-a-boo, for example).

After the 'request mode' Bruner suggests that the child enters an
'exchange mode' in which the beginnings of turn-taking emerge, and then
a 'reciprocal mode' which is characterised by turn-taking. The
reciprocal mode may be said to form the basis for human communication
proper.

Several aspects of autism are relevant here: first, there is a wealth of anecdotal and clinical evidence suggesting that autistic babies differ from normal ones in important ways. Autistic babies are noted to be either particularly 'good' babies who rarely cry or seem to need attention, or they are extremely difficult babies who cry and scream unconsolably (Wing, 1976b). Their babble has also been noted to be diminished and/or abnormal (Bartak et al., 1975; Ricks and Wing, 1976), and their preverbal utterances are frequently very idiosyncratic (Ricks, 1972). They have also been noted to fail to form an anticipatory position prior to being picked up, or to accommodate their position to the shape of the mother when lifted.

It will be recalled that in order to enter Bruner's 'request mode' the infant must first begin to expect certain behaviours on his part to have predictable outcomes. If the autistic child has a poor ability or deviant ability to predict events, as was suggested above, then it is unlikely that his progression to even this early stage of development will occur without abnormality. The autistic child will thus tend to be very rigid about his ordering of the world, or he will fail to order it in a coherent manner, this being the consequence of his making too rigid hypotheses or failing to make them at all. Consequently, the autistic child may be exceptionally unpredictable to his mother or paradoxically quite predictable but in idiosyncratic ways (this was reflected in Rick's work, 1972 ) If the child is unpredictable then her responses to him, no matter how constant, cannot establish shared exchanges and predictable sequences of demand-satisfaction-reward (smiles, passivity, etc.). Such a baby would be very unrewarding to interact with, and this in turn could not help but impair further the quality of the mother/baby relationship.

It was mentioned above that the normal baby may be thought of as a hypothesis tester who is constantly processing his input in a relativistic manner, both in terms of whatever else he is experiencing and what he has experienced before. It is inherent in this mode of processing that the normal child selectively attends to the familiar and the unfamiliar. Moreover, one may posit that perceptual events which challenge his hypotheses will receive most attention. Consequently the baby can be expected to selectively attend to those stimuli which are progressively less and less similar to his prior encoded perceptions. Language may arise partly as a tool for the management of this process. One may see a connection here with the contention that the child's earliest one-word utterances are chosen according to the 'principle of informativeness' whereby the child selects for encoding (and production) that element he perceives to be needed to resolve uncertainty (Greenfield and Smith, 1976). The one word stage may thus be seen as an extension of an earlier stage in which the child is forming and testing hypotheses. Most important, such a mode of thought presupposes the importance of distinguishing the old from the new, and thus may be linked to the ordering of early two-word utterances (which occur in a new/old order) and the precursors of backgrounding and foregrounding of information, deixis, anaphonic reference, etc.

It is noted that from early in life the normal child may be regarded as an active user of language and an active processor not only of his perceptions but of the hypotheses which underlie his perceptual realisations. Such processing of the hypotheses underlying perceptions is akin to the later activity of treating language as a 'problem space' (Karmiloff Smith, 1979) and to the presence of reflective thought, or 'inner language' (Vygotsky, 1962).

The child, then, who has a defect in such a mode of functioning will beimpaired on many fronts. He may, for example, not encode perceptions according to similarities but rather as isolated from each other. This in turn may lead to a failure to take context into account or paradoxically to take it too much into account. That is, he may be willing to call a cup a 'cup' only if it is seen in the particular situation it was in when first seen, or he may fail to account for the change in usage of terms depending on context (the use of 'I' and 'you' when the speaker changes, the fact that certain phrases are appropriate to say to one's mother but not to a stranger etc.). In consequence the child may produce inappropriate or irrelevant speech, or may be exceptionally rigid about his labelling of objects and events. This rigidity of thought patterns, and a tendency to learn words in a one-to-one fashion were mentioned above as uniquely characteristic of the autistic child. A too rigid manner of processing may also lead him to fail to break up some utterances which he hears (even though he may have shown himself able to break up utterances at other times) and thus incorrectly use long word strings where a simple label would suffice. Equally, the words may become linked to events in a stimulus/ response manner without gaining semantic cue value.

A failure to integrate experience and consequently to form inadequate hypotheses about his world, may lead the autistic child to wish to experience the same input over and over again. That is, the cognitive mechanism which effectively says "I've experienced this before and need not attend to it again" may be malfunctioning. Want-for-sameness as well as strerotyped and repetitive behaviours may also be seen as examples of the result of this malfunction. Most important, it is very unlikely

that a child with such deficit would be able to comprehend what
language (and linguistic coding) may be used for. Communication is
largely context-dependent and relies heavily upon one's ability to
take former knowledge into account and form efficient hypotheses about
possible shared understandings and others' points of view. Indeed,
it may be difficult for a child with such a deficit to appreciate that
others do have a separate point of view. This in turn may lead to
problems of use of personal pronouns and other deictic terms of reference.
That is, personal pronouns are relative insofar as who is 'I' and who
is 'you' are dependent upon who is speaking and who is
listening. An inability to process inputs in a relativistic manner
would cause great difficulties in the understanding of the relativity
of frames of reference in interpersonal situations. In addition, the
child's cognitive mode will lack a dynamic forward-looking aspect
which characterises the inquisitive nature of the normal child.

To recapitulate the main points, the normal child is conjectured
to process his perceptions in a relativistic manner, making probablistic
hypotheses about the nature of what he perceives. Thus it is suggested
that the mind does not process absolute items of perceptual data, but
rather concerns itself with the relationships between stored perceptions
and also between these and ongoing experience. The natural consequence
of such a manner of processing is that perceptions are necessarily
integrated to some extent from the beginning, for they are stored and
processed relative to each other rather than as isolated perceptual
events. In contrast, it is proposed that autistic children have problems
with integrating perceptions and that this is connected with a deficit
of forming efficient hypotheses about the nature of their perceptions.
It also seems to lead them to store perceptions as discrete entities
rather than as parts of a related system of percepts.

c)  Speculations as to the nature of brain dysfunction in autism

It will be noted at the outset of this subsection that the present author claims no expertise in neurology, and thus any speculation will be very tentative. In fact, no attempt will be made to claim a specific area of the brain as the site of dysfunction, but sites which may be involved will be suggested.

Perhaps the most important thing an experimental/clinical psychologist can do is to define the limits of observed consequences of the brain disorder. From the above it would seem that autistic children have problems with the formation of hypotheses about their perceptions and with the integration of their experience. It also appears that they have in consequence some problems with determining whether perceptions are novel or familiar. It has been argued above that such a deficit may account for the autistic child's problems with language and thought, but one is left unable to account for their problems in relating to others and expressing emotion. Although it seems possible that such a deficit may also go some way towards explaining the autistic's lack of sociability and empathy, but to state this categorically would be to go beyond the data obtained.

In considering possible sites of brain damage the above deficits must therefore be accounted for. It was noted in section 7.3.6 that a simple hemispherical-damage theory cannot suffice to explain the autistic child's problems. Whilst language deficits and problems with symbolic thought might implicate damage to the left-hemisphere, problems with perceptual integration, holistic processing, and emotional expression all (if anything) implicate damage to the right-

hemisphere. Indeed, it seems that the right-hemisphere is reputably
good at recognising faces and determining facial expressions for the
sole reason that it specialises in the synthesis and integration of
perceptions. It is good at both of these types of task because of its
proclivity to view objects as meaningful 'gestalten'. This is precisely
the area of functioning that the autistic child seems to have trouble
with, and his good ability to identify faces appears to be due to him
adopting the strategy of identifying individual parts rather than
looking at the whole. It was noted in section 7.3.4 that the left
hemisphere does in fact have some ability to identify faces, but that
it only exhibits an advantage in doing so when the identification of
a single feature is called for. There are thus some grounds for
viewing the autistic child's manner of perceiving faces in terms of
a left-hemisphere mode of processing.

Other reasons for discounting a simple hemispheric-lesion theory
include the fact that autism begins in the first year of life when the
brain is still relatively 'plastic', and any damage to one hemisphere
should be compensated for by the other. It has been noted that one
area of the brain which might prove to be damaged in autistic children
is the old cortex, and in particular the temporal lobes. Evidence has
already been presented to support the choice of this area as a location
of dysfunction by Hauser et al. (1975). A prime reason for the choice
of this area is that unlike damage to one hemisphere, unilateral
temporal lobe damage need not lead to the undamaged side taking over
the functions of the damaged area.

Credence for considering the temporal lobe as a site of damage
or dysfunction is gained by consideration of the work of such Russian
scientists as Luria (1973) and Vinogradova (1969, 1970) and that of the American
Pribram (1971). Vinogradova (ibid) has suggested that the hippocampus
serves to compare incoming stimuli with those already perceived in
order to differentiate those which are novel from those which are
familiar. Luria also ascribes this kind of function to the frontal
lobes, so caution should be exercised before taking this as clear
evidence for a temporal lobe deficit. Nonetheless, Luria is in
agreement with Vinogradova's ideas on the temporal lobes and points
out that this process is essential for selective attention and that it
is non-modality specific. Moreover, the temporal lobes (and particularly
the hippocampus) have been associated with one's ability to extinguish
tendencies to orient toward and attend to previously perceived inputs.
It is thus involved in the process of habituation. Once again, though,
it should be noted that the frontal lobes may also serve as a similar
function.

Given that some area of the brain does seem to be concerned with
the detection of novel and familiar stimuli, it is important to note
the point made above that no two perceptions are ever exactly the
same. Consequently it seems unlikely that any part of the brain is
asking "have I seen this before?", but rather "what is the probability
that I've seen this before?". Logically, then, the aforementioned
literature on the function of the limbic system gives some support to
the possible existence of a mechanism for hypothesis testing. Given
that such areas are also noted to be related to the ability to
extinguish old behaviours, one may postulate that damage to them may
explain why the autistic child frequently repeats certain behaviours

in a stereotyped fashion. It may also go some way toward explaining why many autistic children become so 'stuck' on the first example of anything they perceive (as when an autistic child accepts the label 'cup' for the first such object he is shown, but refused to use the term for any other cups he sees, no matter how physically similar).

Further reasons for considering the regions of the temporal and frontal lobes are drawn from Pribram's work (1971). It is of particular interest to the study of autistic children to note that Pribram has said,

> "There is a special affinity between symbols and other context dependent behaviours, such as those which guide interpersonal interactions because parts of the brain involved in symbolic behaviour (fronto-limbic forebrain, which includes the frontal cortex and the ...amygdala and hippocampus) are those which are involved in monitoring feelings - appetitive and affective interests ..."

(Pribram, 1971; p.308).

The characteristic symptoms of autism include an inability to form symbols and a lack of affective behaviour, and thus the possibility of a relationship between these deficits and damage to the fronto-limbic system is most compelling. However, one must bear in mind that not all neurologists are in agreement with Pribram's formulations.Nonetheless, it may be of importance to note that some areas of the brain are concerned with 'context dependent' processing and that such processing is indeed essential to symbol formation and much that is involved in interpersonal communication. This point has already been dealt with above, so suffice it to note at this juncture that autistic children seem particularly poor both at taking the context of events into account and being able to ignore the context when it is appropriate to do so.

d)   The possession of abilities versus the use of them

At several points in this thesis it has been noted that autistic
children possess certain abilities but seem to fail to use them. For
instance, it was concluded from the studies of face perception that
autistic children do not necessarily avoid eye contact with others so
much as fail to understand what mutual gaze may be used for. Again, it
was found that they are able to imitate facial expressions and their
repertoire of spontaneous expressions seems unusually limited. They
are particularly poor at using facial expression to communicate feelings
to others. Anecdotal evidence also indicates that they are able to
produce gestures to order, but they fail to use them spontaneously
(Langdell, 1980a, b, 1981). Bartak and Rutter (1976) reported that
this was the case; and recent studies by Attwood (unpublished) have
provided evidence that autistic children may be able to produce on
demand and understand many simple gestures, and yet they fail to know
how to use their knowledge and ability. Autism thus seems to be a form
of "apragmatism".

Several findings presented in this thesis suggest that the autistics'
difficulties in the use of their abilities may be related to their
cognitive/perceptual deficit. In Chapter Two it was suggested that the
most parsimoneous explanation for the infant's attraction to another's
eyes was in terms of the contingency of the eyes' movements to the baby's
behaviour. That is, along with the human voice (which also elicits
attention early on in the infant) the caretaker's eyes are unique
insofar as they change in accordance with the baby's movements and
vocalisations, and thus presumably bear some relationship to the baby's
inner state. A failure to integrate perceptions would lead to an

inability or poor ability to perceive that the eyes' movements possessed

contingency on one's behaviour, and in turn lead to a failure to

comprehend the meaning which the eye area can convey about another's

inner state, their direction of attention, etc.

Similarly, the autistic child's failure to integrate facial features

into a meaningful gestalten which reveals expression may also lead the

child to fail to perceive what facial expression might be used for.

That is, in order to see the potential use of facial expression a child

would need to comprehend that an expression on another's face 'goes

with' a certain feeling which one has experienced. It was tentatively

suggested earlier in this thesis that the caretaker's tendency to

imitate the infant may lead to a pairing of the infant's inner state

with an appropriate expression displayed on the adult's face. Hence

if the child is processing his perceptions in a relativistic manner he

might well form the hypothesis that 'that expression goes with this

inner feeling', and this was suggested to be a possible basis for the

emergence of empathy.

The picture of the autistic child's abilities and disabilities is

thus one of a child who is able to store discrete bits of information

and accurately recall them, and even accurately link various bits of

perceptual data in a one-to-one fashion, but is less able to integrate

his perceptions and perceive the relationship between them. In consequence,

he may be able to recognise faces very well, but because he fails to

form them into a perceptual gestalt which he notes to have some connection

with his inner states, he is unable to understand how one might use

facial expression communicatively. However, this does not leave him
totally unable to know what certain expressions mean, for he can link
certain discrete details (the shape of the mouth for instance) to
certain labels (up-curved mouth means happy). A similar process of
linking small details with certain labels may also enable the autistic
child to have a limited understanding of others bodily gestures (as
Attwood has noted) and as noted above this may explain the rigid one-to-
one fashion in which autistic children acquire, use and seem to understand
spoken language.

e)    Do autistic children lack any normally 'innate' behaviours?

In the chapter on facial expression a distinction was made between
those expressions which may be innate and those which are most probably
learnt. Many emotional expressions make their debut in the child's
first year of life, but it is difficult from the observations made to
date to say conclusively that any but the expressions of crying and
smiling/laughter are unequivocally innate. Nontheless, many facial
expressions are extremely similar from culture to culture (Ekman,
1973) and whilst people from quite different cultures are not able
to speak each other's verbal language on first meeting, they may
usually be able to communicate to a large degree by gesture alone.
Such observations are suggestive that many facial expressions and
bodily gestures may be innate and pan-cultural.

If the above is true, then autistic children certainly seem to
lack certain usually 'innate' patterns of behaviour. They display a
deficient repertoire of spontaneous facial expression and bodily
gestures from early in life. These deficiencies stand in marked
contrast to those of other children with 'language handicaps' (those

with receptive dysphasia, for example) insofar as these children usually possess a fairly normal range of facial expression (see Bartak and Rutter, 1976). It is noteworthy, too, that although blind children resemble autistic children in many ways (Fraiberg, 1977) in that they also exhibit stereotyped behaviours and abnormal social responses, they nonetheless seem to be born with a fairly normal range of spontaneous facial expression (see Chapter Four). It may be, though, that the similarities between the social incompetence of some blind children and that of autistic children reflects the fact that the source of many of the autistic's problems may not lie in damage to part of the brain usually concerned with affective behaviour, such as the amygdala, but rather in their problems with perceptual processing.

It thus seems possible that autistic children lack certain normally innate affective behaviours and expressions, but it also remains a possibility that their problems in these areas may be due to their inborn cognitive and perceptual deficits.

7.4: Suggestions for further research

Several hypotheses have been generated by the experiments reported
in this thesis, and each might be profitably explored using experimental
methods. For instance, it was suggested that there is ontogenetic
(and possibly phylogenetic) advantage in looking at another's eyes. It
was suggested that in order to gain all the information one requires
about another's inner state from the eye region one needs to fixate
the eyes foveally. By contrast, it was proposed that in order to
extract meaning from the mouth area one need only scan and monitor
the lower facial features with non-foveal vision. It was further
argued that this is because the determination of expression in the
eye area requires one to integrate one's perceptions to a much greater
degree than does the determination of the mouth's expression, and that
the perceptual analysis required for integration demands foveal vision.
This could be investigated by showing normal subjects expressive faces
in a tachistoscope. By setting the point of focus either in the lower
half of the face or nearer the eyes and having a brief presentation
time, one would be able to compare the subjects' abilities to tell
expression of such faces when forced to fixate on one half or the
other. A similar method to that used in Chapter Four might be employed
whereby the faces would contain two expressions, one in the upper half
and another in the lower half. One would thus be able to gain some
idea of the extent to which the expression in the area of the face
not in foveal vision affected his description.

It was suggested that autistic children possess a deficit in
perceptual integration, and first experimental evidence has been
provided to suggest that this extends to intramodal perceptual
integration, too. Further tests of this might be made by using

Figure 7.3 Example of the type of stimulus one might
present to children to test their figure/ground
perception. (Gregory,1971)

standard tests of gestalt perception. For instance, one might use methods similar to those employed by Ghent (1956) in which children had to detect simple shapes amidst complex 'grounds'. It should be hypothesised that autistic children would be unusually capable at detecting the shapes because unlike non-autistic children they would not have their performance marred by a natural proclivity to integrate their perceptions into wholes.[*]

One might also compare autistic and non-autistic children's abilities to recognise stimuli which require a degree of perceptual integration to be clearly discerned. For instance, photographs of stimuli may be 'degraded' by processing them as lithographs (in which all the greys are made either pure white or black). In this way it may be difficult to discern what the picture is of unless one is able to integrate the various patches of pattern into a complete whole (see figure 7.3). Another method would involve the use of blurred pictures. This method has the advantage that one can vary the degree to which the pictures are blurred and hence test degrees of integrative ability. The autistic children would be hypothesised to perform less well when required to recognise familiar objects which are either presented in degraded photographic form or seen out of focus.

Inter-modality integration might also be examined. For instance, McGurk (1977) has reported that one can create an auditory/visual illusion by presenting subjects with disparate visual and auditory information. This technique resembles that used by Dodd (1977) and used in this thesis too. Subjects are required to watch a television screen and are shown a film of someone speaking, but whereas they see one phoneme being mouthed they hear at the same moment a different

*Footnote: Since writing this the author's attention has been drawn to the work of Shah (1980), who has independently followed up this line of research. Shah, A. "Integration and Perception in Autistic Children" Masters' thesis, University of Surrey.

phoneme. It is found that rather than report either the phoneme that they heard (say 'ka') or the one they saw mouthed (say 'pa') they report a synthesis of the two which is different from either ('ta' for instance). The hypothesis, were such an experiment to be run with autistic and non-autistic children, would be that this effect would be demonstrated by the non-autistics, but the autistic children would show little or no synthesis of the two inputs. It would probably be important, however, to use real words carefully matched for phase and synchrony rather than nonsense phonemes with such children in order to ensure cooperation.

The possibility was raised in the last section that autistic children may be poor at using their knowledge of the world to anticipate events. Work has been carried out on this topic (Hammes and Langdell, 1981) and has supported the contention. However, further tests need to be done. For instance, it might be possible to study the autistic child's 'contingent negative variation' (CNV) when put in a situation in which it would be usual to expect certain events to follow one another. The CNV is a slow potential brain wave which is recorded from the frontal lobes (a possible site of dysfunction in autism , it will be recalled). In tests where a subject is required to press a button a set time after a light has been lit, the CNV increases during the period between the light coming on and the button needing to be pressed (Small et al. 1971). Small has already carried out some tests of autistics CNVs and found that they can produce them in the type of situation described above. However, her experiments were not designed to investigate thoroughly the autistic child's ability to use his perceptions to predict his world. Such experiments may well provide revealing data.

It was also suggested in the above section that autistic children may be poor at taking contextual cues into account. One way that this might be tested would be to first show autistics the same picture of something, say a dog, over and over again. If they habituate (that is, if 'proactive inhibition' is set up), then this should be measured by psycho-physiological techniques. If one is then able to train them to habituate to many presentations of different dogs then it may be inferred that they have some concept of 'dogginess' (obviously this would need to be undertaken with relatively high level autistics). One would then be in a position to present a blurred picture of a dog and see whether the autistic child is able to use the context, in which he has just seen and habituated to many different dogs, to facilitate his identification of the picture. As a cross-check on the child's ability one would need to also show similar blurred photographs out of context too. The hypothesis would be that perceptual integration is enhanced for the non-autistic child by the presence of strong contextual clues, whereas the ability of the autistic child is equally poor in both situations.

It would also be of interest to gain further information about the autistic child's ability to use the knowledge that he gains. To this end, it might be plausible to set up a situation wherein a child would need to utilise a tool or an apparatus to achieve a goal and receive a desired reward. One may then train the same child to achieve the same goal and reward using different means. Finally, one would create a situation in which the goal could only be obtained by a combination of the prior two means or methods. It would be hypothesised that whilst the non-autistics would be able to make such use of their prior

knowledge, the autistics would not. However, it might be rather
difficult to control for the intelligence of the two types of children.
To the extent that 'problem solving' is a measure of intelligence,
it might be somewhat circular and unproductive to match the children
for general intelligence.

Perhaps a more informative and more natural version of the above
study could be undertaken with an adult being present to act as a
possible provider of a means. In fact, an interactional version of
the study of context effects could be performed where an adult could
provide the contextual clues which a child could utilise to improve
his performance.

Finally, although there seems little reason to suspect that
autistic children possess a hemispherical deficit, it is noted that a
fairly simple test might be carried out to investigate this. It has
been found (Campbell, 1978) that people express emotion more extremely
with the left halves of their faces (camera-right) than with their
right halves. This is due to the fact that the normal person's left
half of his face is governed by his right hemisphere and this hemisphere
deals with emotional expression. It is possible to make left-left
photographic composites and right-right ones too, and one finds that
the faces made up of left-left (posers sides) are rated as having
more extreme expressions than the right-right composite faces.
One would therefore need to take photographs of autistic children
expressing emotion and prepare such composites. One would also need
to prepare such photographs of non-autistic subjects. Getting the
photographs of autistic children expressing emotion could present
problems, but as was discovered when the present author undertook
experiments in this realm, the difficulties are not as great as one
first expects.

The foregoing is a selection of further experimental studies which this thesis's results suggest should be carried out. However, there would no doubt also be great value in attempting to investigate further the nature of the autistic child's 'apragmatism' and the possible connections of such disabilities with problems in the cognitive and perceptual realms. Perhaps the most rewarding method of investigating such possible interconnections would be by the study of autistic infants and very young autistic children. It would be of interest to see if like normal children -autistic children are born with highly organised behaviours (Condon, 1974), having many features in common with the behaviours of the caretaker. It would also be of interest to investigate possible problems with the timing and phasing of behaviours in the autistic infant and the possible maldevelopment of such prelinguistic features as 'protoimperitives' and 'protodeclaratives'. Undoubtedly, it would be difficult to find a sample of autistic infants simply because there is no known easily identifiable characteristic which would allow their detection. In addition, the very low incidence of autism (about 4 in 10,000 live births) may also mean that on purely statistical grounds they would be difficult to find early in life. Nonetheless, it might be possible to set certain 'best guess' limits on the features an autistic infant might possess. For instance, one might screen a large population of babies who are all either extremely passive or virtually unconsolable (these being features which many mothers of autistic children reported retrospectively that they possessed). One might also hypothesise that autistic children have problems with timing behaviours and thus may not show normal patterns of forming routines or 'burst/pause' patterns in their feeding behaviour. Such screening restrictions might possibly increase one's chances of detecting an autistic child to one in a thousand or perhaps even considerably better.

To end on an optimistic note, if it is indeed the case that autistic children are born exhibiting behaviour which betrays their handicap, then by refining the presently available behavioural observation techniques, through such means as the computer analysis of slowed-down video taped recordings, one may be able to detect autism in infancy and develop methods for more adequate intervention.

APPENDIX 1

| Seen | Heard | Related Distractor | Unrelated Distractor |
|------|-------|--------------------|-----------------------|
| Chair | House | Hat | Book |
| Ball | Hat | Cat | Tree |
| Cup | Plane | Cat | Shoe |
| Car | Book | Boy | House |
| Clock | Shoe | Cake | Dog |
| Dog | Hen | Frog | Tree |
| Bed | Girl | Boy | Hen |
| Boy | Cat | Hat | Train |
| Train | Fish | Tree | Boy |
| Frog | Horse | Dog | Cat |
| Bird | Cake | Cat | House |
| Ship | Tree | Shoe | Clock |
| House | Chair | Hat | Ball |
| Hat | Ball | Girl | Shoe |
| Plane | Cup | Ship | Dog |
| Tree | Ship | Shoe | Cat |
| Book | Car | Cat | House |
| Shoe | Clock | Cake | Ball |
| Hen | Dog | Hat | Cup |
| Girl | Bed | Boy | Train |
| Cat | Boy | Hat | Frog |
| Fish | Train | Plane | Bird |
| Horse | Frog | House | Bird |
| Cake | Bird | Clock | Hat |

Appendix 1: The words which were presented orally and
visually in the test of the contribution of lip -
reading to speech perception. See Chapter Three.

References

Ahrens, R. (1954). Beitrag zur entwicklung des physiognomie und
mimikerkennens. Z. exp. angew. Psychol., 2, 412-454.

Alpern, G.D. (1967). Measurement of "untestable" autistic children.
J. Abnorm. Psychol., 72, 478.

Altshuler, K.Z. (1963). Sexual patterns and family relationships. In
J. Rainer, K. Altshuler and F. Kallmann (Es.) Family and Mental Health
Problems in a Deaf Population. Columbia Uni. Press; N.Y.

Altshuler, K.Z. (1964). Personality traits and depressive symptoms in
the deaf. In J. Wortis (Ed.), Recent Advances in Biological
Psychiatry. Plenum Press: New York.

Altshuler, K.Z. (1967). Theoretical considerations in development and
psychopathology of the deaf. In J. Rainer and K. Altshuler (Eds.)
Psychiatry and the Deaf. (U.S. Department of Health Education and
Welfare), Washington D.C.: U.S. Government Printing Office.

Ambrose, J.A. (1961). The development of the smiling response in early
infancy. In Foss, B.M. (Ed.) Determinants of Infant Behaviour.
Vol. II; Wiley, New York.

Ames, E.W. and Siffen, C.K. (1965). Methodological issues in the study
of age difference in infants' attention to stimuli varying in movement
and complexity. Paper presented at the meeting of the Society for
Research in Child Development, Minneapolis, March, 1965.

Anthony, E.J. (1958). An experimental approach to the diagnosis of psychosis in childhood. Z. Kinderpsychiat., 25, 89-96.

Argyle, M. and Cook, M. (1976). Gaze and Mutual Gaze . Cambridge University Press, Cambridge.

Asperger, H. (1944). Die Autistischen Psychopathen im Kindesalter. Arch. Psychiatr. Nerventer, 117, 76.

Atteneave, F. and Benson, B. (1969). Spatial coding of tactual stimulation. J. Exp. Psychol., 81, 216.

Baltaxe, A.M. (1977). Pragmatic deficits in the language of autistic adolescents. J. Pediatr. Psychol., 2(4), 176-180.

Baltaxe, C.A.M. (1979). Acoustic characteristics of prosody in autism. Proc. Internat.Cong. Ment. Def., Univ. Park Press.

Baltaxe, C.A.M. (1980). Prosodic abnormalities in autism. J. Speech Hearing Dis., in press.

Baltaxe, C.A.M. and Simmons, J.Q. (1975). Language in childhood psychosis: A Review. J. Speech Hearing Dis., 40, 439-458.

Baltaxe, C.A.M. and Simmons, J.Q. (1977). Bedtime soliloquies and linguistic competence in autism. J. Speech Hearing Dis., 42, 376-393.

Baltaxe, C.A.M. and Simmons, J.Q. (1977). Language patterns in adolescent
autistics: A comparison between English and German. Proc. Fourth
Congr. Internat.Assoc. Sci. Study of Ment. Def., Baltimore: Univ.
Park Press.

Banham, K.M. (1950). The development of affectionate behaviour in infancy.
J. Genet. Psychol., 76, 283-289.

Baroff, G.S. (1963). Rorschach data and clinical observations. In
J. Rainer, K. Altshuler and F. Kallmann (Eds.) Family and Mental Health
Problems in a Deaf Population. Columbia Univ. Press; New York.

Bartak, L. and Rutter, M. (1976). Differences between mentally retarded
and normally intelligent autistic children. J. Aut. Child Schizo, 6,
109-120.

Bartak, L., Rutter, M. and Cox, A. (1975). A comparative study of infantile
autism and specific developmental receptive language disorder. I.
The Children. Br. J. Psychiat., 126, 127-148.

Bates, E. (1976). Language and Context: The Acquisition of Pragmatics.
Acad. Press: N.Y.

Bay, E. (1953). Disturbances of visual perception and their examination.
Brain, 76, 515.

Bender, L. (1947). Childhood schizophrenia: A clinical study of 100
schizophrenic children. Amer. J. Orthopsychiat., 17, 40-56.

Benjamin, J.D. (1963). Further comments on some developmental aspects of anxiety. In H. Gaskill (Ed.) Counterpoint, Int. Univ. Press., New York.

Benton, A. and Van Allen, M.W. (1968). Impairment in facial recognition in patients with cerebral disease. Cortex, 4, 344-358.

Bettelheim, B. (1967) The Empty Fortress; Collier-Macmillan: London.

Beyn, E.S. and Kuyazeva, G.R. (1962). The problem of prosopagnosia. J. Neurol. Neurosurg. Psychiat., 25, 154-158.

Blackstock, E.G. (1978). Cerebral asymmetry and the development of early infantile autism. J. Aut. Ch. Schizo, 8, 339-353.

Blank, H.R. (1959). Psychiatric problems associated with congenital blindness due to retrolental fibroplasia. New Outlook for the Blind, 53, 237-244.

Blank, M. and Bridger, W.M. (1964). Cross modal transfer in nursery school. children. J. Comp. Physiol. Psychol., 58, 272-282.

Blatz, W.E. and Millichamp, D.A. (1935). The development of emotion in the infant. University of Toronto Studies, Child Development Series, No. 4.

Bleuler, E. (1919). Das Autitisch-Undisziplinierte Denken in der Mediziin und seine Uberwindung. Springer; Berlin.

Bodamer, J. (1947). Die Prosop-Agnosie. Arch. Psychiat. Nervenkr.,
179(6).

Bogen, J.E. (1969). The other side of the brain: An oppositional mind.
Bull. Los Angeles Neuro. Socs., 3, 135-162.

Boucher, J. (1977). Hand preference in autistic children and their
parents. J. Aut. Ch. Schiz., 7, 177-187.

Boucher, J. (1978). Echoic memory capacity in autistic children.
J. Ch. Psychol. Psychiat., 19, 161-166.

Boucher, J. and Warrington, E. (1976). Memory deficits in early
infantile autism: some similarities to the amnesic syndrome.
Br. J. Psychol., 67(1), 73-87.

Bower, T.G.R. (1974). Development in Infancy. Freeman: San Francisco.

Bower, T.G.R. (1977). A Primer of Infant Development. W.H. Freeman:
San Francisco.

Bower, T.G.R. (1977). The Perceptual World of the Child. Fontana/Open
Books.

Bower, T.G.R. (1979). Paper on the development of sensory perception in infancy given at the Institute of Education, London, March 1979.

Bradshaw, J.L. and Wallace, G. (1971). Models for the processing and identification of faces. Percept. Psychophys., 9, 443-448.

Bridges, K.M.B. (1931). Emotional development in early infancy. Ch. Dev. 3, 324-341.

Brooks, R.M. and Goldstein, A.G. (1963). Recognition by children of inverted faces. Child Dev., 34, 1033-1040.

Brown, R. and McNeill, D. (1966). The "tip of the tongue" phenomenon. J. Verb. Learn. Verb. Behav., 5(4), 325-337.

Bruner, J. (1975a). The ontogenesis of speech acts. J. Ch. Lang., 2, 2-19.

Bruner, J. (1975b). From communication to language - A psychological perspective. Cognition, 3, 255-289.

Buhler, C. and Hetzer, H. (1938). Das erste Verstandnis fur Ansdruck un ersten Lebensjahr. Zeitschrift fur Psych., 107, 50-61.

Campbell, R. (1978). Asymmetries in interpreting and expressing a posed facial expression. Cortex, 14, 327-342.

Carmon, A. and Nachson, I. (1973). Ear asymmetry in perception of emotional non-verbal stimuli. Acta Psychologica, 37, 351-357.

Caron, A.J., Caron, R.F., Caldwell, R.C. and Weiss, S.J. (1973). Infant perception of the structural properties of the face. Dev. Psychol., 9(3), 385-399.

Chance, J.E., Goldstein, A.G. and Schicht, W. (1966). Effects of acquaintance and friendship on children's recognition of classmates' faces. Paper presented at the Meetings of the Midwestern Psychol., Assoc., 1966.

Charlesworth, W.R. (1966). Persistance of orienting and attending behaviour in infants as a function of stimulus - locus uncertainty. Ch. Dev., 37, 473-491.

Charlesworth, W.R. (1970). Surprise reactions in congenitally blind and sighted children. National Institute for Mental Health Progress Report.

Charlesworth, W.R. and Krentzer, M.A. (1973). Facial expressions of infants and children. See Ekman, P. (1973).

Chess, S. (1971). Autism in children with congenital rubella. J. Aut. Ch. Schizo, 1, 33.

Churchill, D.W., Alpern, G.D. and DeMyer, M.K. (Eds.) (1971) ∧ Infantile
Autism: Proceedings of Indiana University, Colloquium. C. Thomas:
Springfield, Ill.

Churchill, D.W. and Bryson, C.Q. (1972). Looking and approach behaviour
of psychotic and normal children as a function of adult attention
and preoccupation. Comp. Psychiat., 13, 171-177.

Clancy, H., Dugdale, A. and Rendle-Short, J. (1969). The diagnosis
of infantile autism. Dev. Med. Child Neurol., 11, 432.

Colby, K.M. and Parkinson, C. (1977). Handedness in autistic children.
J. Aut. Ch. Schizo, 7, 3-9.

Cole, M. and Perez-Cruet, J. (1964). Prosopagnosia. Neuropsychol., 2,
237-245.

Collis, G. and Schaffer, H.R. (1975). Synchronization of visual attention
in mother-infant pairs. J. Ch. Psychol., Psychiat., 16, 315-320.

Condon, W.S. (1975). Speech makes babies move. In R. Lewin (Ed.)
Child Alive, Temple Smith: London.

Conrad, R. (1964). Acoustic confusions in immediate memory.
Br. J. Psychol., 55, 75-84.

Corkin, S. (1965).   Tactually-guided maze learning in man:   Effects of
unilateral cortical excisions and bilateral hippocampal lesions.
Neuropsychologia, 3, 339-351.

Cornell, E.H. (1974).   Infants' discrimination of photographs of faces
following redundant presentations.   J. Exp. Ch. Psychol., 18,
98-106.

Coss, R.G. (1972).   Eye-like Schemata:   Their Effect on Behaviour.
Ph.D. Thesis, University of Reading.

Craik, F.I.M. (1966).   Short-term memory: echo box plus search process.
London Conference of the British Psychological Society.

Craik, F.I.M. and Lockhart, R.S. (1972).   Levels of processing:   a
framework for memory research.   J. Verb. Learn. Behav., 11, 671-684.

Crawley, C.A. (1971).   Infantile autism - an hypothesis.   J. Ir. Med.
Assoc., 64, 335.

Creak, E.M. (Chairman) (1961).   Schizophrenic syndrome in childhood:
progress report of a working party.   Cerebral Palsy Bull., 3, 501.

Creak, M. and Ini, S. (1960).   Families of psychotic children.   J. Ch.
Psychol., Psychiat., 1, 156.

Crichley, M. (1953).   The Parietal Lobes, Arnold: London.

448

Cross, J.F., Cross, J. and Daly, J. (1971). Sex, race, age and beauty as factors in recognition of faces. Percept. Psychophys., 10, 393-396.

Curico, F. and Piserchia, E.A. (1978). Pantomimic representation in psychotic children. J. Aut. Ch. Schizo, 8(2), 181-189.

Darwin, C. (1872). The Expression of the Emotions in Man and Animals. Murray: London.

Darwin, C. (1877). A biographical sketch of an infant. Mind, 2, 285-294.

Davidson, R. and Swartz, G. (1976). Patterns of cerebral lateralisation during cardiac biofeedback versus the self-regulation of emotion: Sex differences. Psychophys., 13, 62-74.

Davis, K. (1940). Extreme social isolation of a child. Am. J. Soc., 45, 554-565.

Davis, K. (1947). Final note on a case of extreme isolation. Am. J. Soc., 52, 432-437.

De Long, R. (1978). A neuropsychologic interpretation of infantile autism. In M. Rutter and E. Schopler (Eds.) Autism: diagnosis current research and management. Spectrum: N.Y.

DeMyer, M.K. (1971). Perceptual limitations in autistic children and
their relation to social and intellectual deficits. In M. Rutter (Ed.)
Infantile Autism: Concepts Characteristics and Treatment. Churchill:
London.

DeMyer, M.K., Alpern, G.D., Barton, S., De Myer, W., Churchill, D.W.,
Hingtgen, J.M., Bryson, C.Q., Pontins, W. and Kimblerlin, C. (1972).
Imitation in autistic, early schizophrenic and non-psychotic subnormal
children. J. Aut. Ch. Schizo, 2, 264-287.

Dennis, W. (1938). Infant development under conditions of restricted
practice and of minimum social stimulation. J. Genet. Psychol., 53,
149-159.

Denny-Brown, D., Meyer, J.S. and Horenstein, S. (1952). The significance
of perceptual rivalry resulting from parietal lesions. Brain, 75,
433-471.

DeRenzi, E., Faglioni, P. and Spinnler, H. (1968). Performance of patients
with unilateral brain damage on face recognition tasks. Cortex, 4,
17-34.

DeRenzi, E. and Spinnler, H. (1966). Facial recognition in brain-damaged
patients. Neurology, 16, 145-152.

DesLauriers, A.M. and Carlson, C.F. (1969). Your Child is Asleep.
Dorsey: Illinois.

Despert, J.L. (1951). Some considerations relating to the genesis of autistic behaviour in children. Am. J. Orthopsychiat., 21, 335.

Dimond, S.J. and Farrington, L. (1977). Emotional response to films shown to the right or left hemisphere of the brain measured by heart rate. Acta Psychologica, 41, 255-260.

Dodd, B. (1977). The role of vision in perception of speech. Perception, 1977, 1.

Dumas, G. (1932). La mimique des aveugles. Bull. de L'Academie de Medicine, 107, 607-610.

Eibl-Eibesfeldt, I. (1970). Ethology: The Biology of Behaviour. Holt:N.Y.

Eisenberg, L. (1957). The course of childhood schizophrenia. Arch. Neurol. Psychiat., 78, 69.

Ekman, P. (1973). Darwin and Facial Expression - A Century of Research in Review. Acad. Press: N.Y.

Ekman, P. and Friesen, W.V. (1971). Constants across cultures in the face and emotion. J. Person. Soc. Psychol., 17, 124-129.

Ekman, P., Friesen, W.V. and Ellsworth, P. (1972). Emotion in the Human Face, Pergamon: Oxford.

Ellis, H.D. (1975). Recognising faces. Br. J. Psychol., 66(4), 409-426.

Ellis, H.D., Shepherd, J. and Bruce, A. (1973). The effects of age and sex upon adolescents' recognition of faces. J. Genet. Psychol., 123, 173-174.

Ellis, H.D. and Shepherd, J. (1975). Recognition of upright and inverted faces presented in the left and right visual fields. Cortex, 11, 3-7.

Fagan, J.F. (1976). Infants' recognition of invariant features of faces. Ch. Dev., 47, 627-638.

Fantz, R.L. (1963). Pattern vision in newborn infants. Science, 140, 296-297.

Fantz, R.L. (1965). Pattern discrimination and selective attention as determinants of perceptual development from birth. In A.H. Kidd and J.L. Rivoire (Eds.), Perceptual Development of Children, Int. Univ. Press: N.Y.

Fanst, C. (1947). Partielle Seelenblindheit nach Occipitalverletzung mit besonderer Beeintrachtigung des Physiognomieerkennens, Nervenarzt, 18, 294-297.

Ferster, C.B. (1961). Positive reinforcement and behavioural deficits of autistic children. Ch. Dev., 32, 437.

Folstein, S. and Rutter, M. (1977). Infantile autism: A genetic study of 21 twin pairs. J. Ch. Psychol., Psychiat., 18(4), 297-321.

Fraiberg, S. (1968). Parallel and divergent patterns in blind and sighted infants. Psycho. Stud. Child, 23, 264-300.

Frai berg, S. (1977). Insights from the Blind. Souvenir Press: London.

Frith, U. (1968). Pattern detection in normal and autistic children. Ph.D. Thesis, University of London.

Frith, U. (1969). Emphasis and meaning in recall in normal and autistic children. Lang. Speech, 12, 29-38.

Frith, U. (1970a). Studies in pattern detection in normal and autistic children: reproduction and production of colour sequences. J. Exp. Ch. Psych., 10, 120.

Frith, U. (1970b). Studies in pattern perception in normal and autistic children: immediate recall of auditory sequences. J. Abnorm. Psychol., 76, 413.

Frith, U. (1980). Psychological abnormalities in childhood psychoses. Draft of a chapter to appear in a handbook of psychiatry edited by J. Wing.

Frith, U. and Hermelin, B. (1969). The role of visual and motor cues for normal, subnormal and autistic children. J. Ch. Psychol., 10, 153.

Frith, U. and Hermelin, B. (1971). Psychological studies of childhood autisms: can autistic children make sense of what they see and hear? J. Sp. Ed., 5(2), 107-117.

Frye, I.B.M. (1968). Fremde Unter Uns. Meppel: Boom Pers.

Fulcher, J.S. (1942). "Voluntary" facial expressions in blind and
seeing children. Arch. Psychol., 38(272), 1-49.

Gainotti, G. (1972). Emotional behaviour and hemispheric side of the
lesion. Cortex, 8, 41-55.

Galper, R.E. (1970). Recogniton of faces in photographic negative.
Psychon. Sci., 19, 207-208.

Galper, R.E. and Hochberg, H. (1971). Recognition memory for photographs
of faces. Am. J. Psychol., 84, 351-354.

Gardner, J. (1976). Three investigations into the nature of infantile
autism. Ph.D. Thesis, University of Leicester.

Gardner, J. and Gardner, H. (1970). A note on selective imitation by
a six-week-old infant. Ch. Dev., 41, 1209-1213.

Gates, G.S. (1923). An experimental study of the growth of social
perception. J. Ed. Psychol., 14, 449-461.

Gazzaniger, M. (1970). The Bisected Brain. Appleton-Century-Crofts:
New York.

Geffen, G., Bradshaw, J.L. and Wallace, G. (1971). Interhemispheric
effects on reaction times to verbal and non-verbal stimuli.
J. Exp. Psychol., 87, 415-422.

Geffen, G., Bradshaw, J.L. and Nettleton, N. (1972). Hemispheric
asymmetry: Verbal and spatial encoding of visual stimuli.
J. Exp. Psychol., 95, 25-31.

Gellner, L. (1959). A Neurophysiological Concept of Mental Retardation
and its Educational Implications. J.D. Levinson Research Foundation,
Chicago.

Geschwind, N. (1965). Disconnexion syndromes in animals and man. Part
II, Brain, 88, 585.

Ghent, L. (1956). Perception of overlapping and embedded figures by
children of different ages. Am. J. Psychol., 69, 575-587.

Ghent, L. (1961). Form and its orientation: A child's eye view.
Am. J. Psychol., 74, 177-190.

Gibson, E.J. (1969). Principles of perceptual learning and development.
New York: Appleton-Century-Crofts.

Gibson, E.J. and Levin, H. (1976). The Psychology of Reading. MIT Press:
Camb. Mass.

Glanzer, M. and Cunitz, A.R. (1966). Two storage mechanisms in free
recall. J. Verb. Learn. Verb. Behav., 5, 351-360.

Gloning, I., Gloning, K., Jellinger, K. and Quatember, R. (1970). A case
for 'prosopagnosia' with necropsy findings. Neuropsychol., 8, 199-204.

Goldfarb, W. (1961). Childhood Schizoprehnia. Cambridge, Mass: Harvard University Press.

Goldstein, K. (1939). The Organism: A Holistic Approach to Biology Derived from Pathological Data in Man. American Book: N.Y.

Goldstein, A.G. (1965). Learning of inverted and normally oriented faces in children and adults. Psychon. Sci., 3, 447-448.

Goldstein, A.G. (1975). Recognition of inverted photographs of faces by children and adults. J. Genetic. Psych., 127, 109-123.

Goldstein, A.G. and Chance, J. (1964). Recognition of children's faces. Child Dev., 35, 129-136.

Goldstein, A.G. and Mackenberg, E.G. (1966). Recognition of human faces from isolated facial features: a developmental study. Psychon. Sci., 6, 149-150.

Goodenough, F.L. (1932). Expression of the emotions in a blind-deaf child. J. Ab. Soc. Psychol., 27, 328-333.

Greenfield, P.M. and Smith, J.H. (1976). The Structure of Communication in Early Language Development. Acad. Press: N.Y.

Greenman, G.W. (1963). Visual behaviour of newborn infants. In A. Solnit and S. Provence (Eds.) Modern Perspectives in Child Development. Int. Uni. Press: N.Y.

Gregory, R.L. (1971). The Intelligent Eye. Weidenfeld and Nicholson: London.

Griffiths, P. (1972). Developmental Aphasia: An Introduction. Invalid Children's Aid Assoc: London.

Guernsey, M. (1928). Eine genetische studie uber Nachahmung Zeitschrift fur Psychol., 107, 105-178.

Haaf, R.A. (1974). Complexity and facial resemblance as determinants of response to facelike stimuli by 5- and 10-week-old infants. J. Exp. Ch. Psychol., 18, 480-487.

Haggard, M.P. and Parkinson, A.M. (1971). Stimulus task factors as determinants of ear advantages. Qu. J. Exp. Psychol., 23, 168-177.

Haith, M.M., Bergman, T. and Moore, M.J. (1977). Eye contact and face scanning in early infancy. Science, 198, 853-855.

Hammes, J.G.W. and Langdell, T. (1981). Precursors to symbol formation and childhood autism. Accepted by J. Aut. Devel. Dis., 1981.

Haslam, J. (1809). Observations on Madness and Melancholy. Hayden: London.

Hauser, S.L., De Long, G.R.and Rosman, N.P. (1975). Pneumographic findings in the infantile autism syndrome: A correlation with temporal lobe disease. Brain, 98, 667-688.

Haynes, H., White, B.L. and Held, R. (1965). Visual accommodation in human infants. Science, 148, 528-530.

Hecean, H., Ajuriaguerra, J. and Massonet, J. (1951). Les troubles visvo-constructifs par lesion parieto - occipitale dvoite. Roles des perturbations vestibulaires. Encephale, 1, 122-179.

Hecaen, H. and Angelergues, R. (1962). Agnosia for faces (prosopagnosia) Archs. Neurol., 7, 92-100.

Heller, T. (1930). About dementia infantalis. Reprinted in J.G. Howells (Ed.) Modern Perspectives in International Child Psychiatry. Oliver and Boyd: Edinburgh.

Hermelin, B. (1966). Psychological research, in Wing, J.K. (Ed.) Early Childhood Autism First Edition. Pergamon: Oxford.

Hermelin, B. (1978). Images and Language. In, M. Rutter and E. Schopler (Eds.), Autism: diagnosis, current research and management. Spectrum: N.Y.

Hermelin, B. and O'Connor, N. (1963). The response and self-generated behaviour of severely disturbed children and severely subnormal controls. Br. J. Soc. Clin. Psychol., 2, 37-43.

Hermelin, B. and O'Connor, N. (1964). Effects of sensory input and sensory dominance on severely disturbed children and an subnormal controls. Br. J. Psychol., 55, 201-206.

Hermelin, B. and O'Connor, N. (1967). Perceptual and motor discrimination in psychotic and normal children. J. genet. Psychol., 110, 117-125.

Hermelin, B. and O'Connor, N. (1968). Measures of the occipital alpha rhythm in normal, subnormal and autistic children. Br. J. Psychiat., 114, 603-610.

Hermelin, B. and O'Connor, N. (1970). Psychological Experiments with Autistic Children. Pergamon: Oxford.

Hermelin, B. and O'Connor, N. (1971). Spatial coding in normal, autistic and blind children. Percept. Mot. Skills, 33, 127.

Hermelin, B. and O'Connor, N. (1975). Location and distance estimates by blind and sighted children. Qu. J. Ex. Psychol., 27, 295-301.

Herschenson, M. (1964). Visual discrimination in the human newborn. J. Comp. Physiol. Psychol., 58, 270-276.

Herschenson, M. (1965). Visual discrimination in the human newborn. Dissertation Abstracts, 26, 1793 (Abstract).

Hershenson, M. (1967). Development of the perception of form. Psychol. Bull., 67(5), 326-336.

Hershenson, M., Kessen, W. and Munsinger, H. (1967). Pattern perception in the human newborn. In J.C. Mott-Smith, W. Wathen-Dunn, H. Blum and P. Lieberman (Eds.), Symposium on Models for the perception of speech and visual form. MIT Press: Camb. Mass.

Herzka, H.S. (1965). Das Gesicht des Saugtings: Ausdruck und Reifung. Schwabe: Basel/Stuttgart.

Hilliard, R.D. (1973). Hemispheric laterality effects on a facial recogniton task in normal subjects. Cortex, 9, 246-258.

Hochberg, J. and Galper, R.E. (1967). Recognition of faces. I. An exploratory study. Psychon., Sci., 9, 619-620.

Holzman, P.S., Levy, D.L., Uhlenhutt, E.H., Proctor, L.R. and Freedman, D.X. (1975). Smooth-pursuit eye movements and diazepan, CPZ and secobarbital. Psychopharmaco., 44, 111-115.

Holzman, P.S., Proctor, L.R. and Hughes, D.W. (1973). Eye tracking patterns in schizophrenia. Science, 181, 179-181.

Holzmann, P.S., Proctor, L.R., Levy, D.L., Yasillo, N.J., Meltzer, H.Y. and Hurt, S.W. (1974). Eye-tracking dysfunctions in schizophrenic patients and their relations. Arch. Gen. Psychiat., 31, 143-151.

Homa, D., Haver, B. and Schwartz, T. (1976). Perceptibility of schematic face stimuli: evidence for a perceptual gestalt. Mem. Cogn., 4, 176-185.

Honkavaara, S. (1961). The psychology of expression. Br. J. Psychol. Monog. Supplements, 32, 1-96.

Hudson, L. (1966). Contrary Imaginations. London: Methuen.

Hutt, C. and Ounsted, C. (1966). The biological significance of gaze aversion with particular reference to the syndrome of infantile autism. Behav. Sci., 11, 346-356.

Hutt, S.J., Hutt, C., Lee, D. and Ounsted, C. (1964). Arousal and childhood autism. Nature, 204, 908.

Hutt, S.J., Hutt, C., Lee, D. and Ounsted, C. (1965). A behavioural and electroencephalographic study of autistic children. J. Psychiat. Res., 3, 181.

Hutt, S.J. and Hutt, C. (Eds.) (1970). Behaviour Studies in Psychiatry. Pergamon: Oxford.

Itard, J.M.G. (1801). The Wild Boy of Aveyron. Eng. trans of two reports by G. and M. Humphrey, 1932; Appleton-Century-Crofts: N.Y., 1962.

Izard, C.F. (1971). The Face of Emotion. Appleton-Century-Crofts: New York.

Jaffe, J., Stern, D.N. and Peery, J.C. (1973). "Conversational" coupling of gaze behaviour in prelinguistic human development. J. Psycho-ling. Res., 2, 321-330.

Jones, A.C. (1969). Influence of mode of stimulus presentation on performance in facial recognition tasks. Cortex, 5, 290-301.

Jones, M.C. (1930). The development of basic emotions: The child's emotions. Proceedings of the Midwest Conference on Character Development. Univ. Chicago Press: Chicago.

Kagan, J. (1970). Attention and psychological change in the young child. Science, 170, 826-832.

Kagan, J., Henker, B., Hen-Tov, A., Levine, J. and Lewis, M. (1966). Infant's differential reactions to familiar and distorted faces. Child Dev., 37, 519-532.

Kaila, E. (1932). Die reaktionen die sanglings auf das menschliche Gesicht. Ann. Universitatis Aboensis, 17, 1-114.

Kanner, L. (1943). Autistic disturbances of affective contact. Nerv. Child, 2, 217-250.

Kanner, L. (1949). Early infantile autism. Am. J. Orthopsychiat., 19, 416.

Kanner, L. (1954). To what extent is early childhood autism determined by constitutional inadequacies? Proc. Assoc. Res. Nerv. Ment. Dis., 33, 378.

Karmiloff-Smith, A. (1979). A Functional Approach to Child Language. Cambridge Studies in Linguistics 24: Camb. Univ. Press.

Keeler, W.R. (1958). Autistic patterns and defective communication in blind children with retrolental fibroplasia. In P. Hoch and J. Zubin (Eds.) Psycho-pathology of Communication; Grune and Stratton: New York.

Kessen, W., Haith, M.M. and Salapetek, P.H. (1970). Human infancy: A bibliography and guide. In P. Mussen (Ed.) Carmichael's Manual of Child Psychology. (3rd ed.). Vol. 1. Wiley: N.Y. pp. 287-445.

Kessen, W., Salapatek, P. and Haith, M. (1972). The visual response of the human newborn to linear contour. J. Exp. Ch. Psychol., 13, 9-20.

Kimura, D. (1973). The asymmetry of the human brain. Sci. Am., 228, 70-78.

Klaus, M.H. et. al. (1971). Evidence for a sensitive period in human mothers of full-term infants. Paper to American Pediatric Society, Atlantic City. Quoted in M. Argyle and M. Cook (1976).

463

Klein, D., Moscovitch, M. and Vigna, C. (1976). Perceptual assymetries and attentional mechanisms in tachistocopic recognition of words and faces. Neuropsychologia, 14, 44-66.

Knoblock, H. and Pasamanick, B. (1962). Etiologic factors in "early infantile autism" and "childhood schizoprehnia". Paper given at 10th International Congress of Pediatrics, Lisbon, Portugal.

Koegal, R.L. and Lovaas, O.I. (1978). Comments on autism and overselectivity. J. Ab. Psychol., 87(5), 563-565.

Koegal, R. and Screibmann, L. (1974). The role of stimulus variables in teaching autistic children. In O.I. Lovaas and B. Bucher (Eds.) Readings in Behaviour Modification with Deviant Children.

Koestler, A. (1971). The Roots of Coincidence, Pan Books: London.

Kolvin, I., Ounsted, C., Humphrey, M. and McNay, A. (1971). The phenomenology of childhood psychoses. Br. J. Psychiat., 118, 385.

Konorski, J. (1967). Integrative Activity of the Brain. Uni. of Chicago Press: Chicago.

Koopman, P. and Ames, E. (1968). Infants' preferences for facial arrangements: A failure to replicate. Ch. Dev., 39, 481-487.

Kugler, B. (1975). Autism and Subliminal Perception. Ph.D. Thesis, University College, London.

Langdell, T. (1977) Cognitive Dysfunction and Social Incompetence in Autism. Paper presented to the 11th Postgraduate and Postdoctoral Conference; Hull University, April.

Langdell, T. (1978). Recognition of faces: An approach to the study of autism. J. Ch. Psychol. Psychiat., 19, 255-268.

Langdell, T. (1980a). Pragmatic aspects of autism: Or why is 'I' a normal word? Paper presented to the Conference of the Developmental section of the British Psychological Society, Edinburgh, September, 1980.

Langdell,T. (1980b). Pragmatic aspects of autistic children's verbal instructions to adults. Master's Thesis. Nottingham University.

Langdell, T. (1981). Pragmatic aspects of autism. Communication (NSAC), March, 1981.

Laufer, M.W. and Gair, D.S. (1969). Childhood schizophrenia. In L. Bellak and L. Loeb (Eds.) The Schizophrenic Syndrome: Grune and Stratton, N.Y.

Laughery, K.R., Alexander, J.F. and Lane, A.B. (1971). Recognition of human faces: effects of target exposure time, target position, pose position and type of photograph. J. Appl. Psychol., 55, 477-483.

Leboyer, F. (1975). Birth Without Violence. Wildwood: London.

Leehey, S., Carey, S., Diamond, R. and Cahn, A. (1978). Upright and inverted faces: the right hemisphere knows the difference. Cortex, 14, 411-419.

Levine, E.S. (1956). Youth in a Soundless World. New York: Uni. Press: New York.

Levine, E.S. (1960). The Psychology of Deafness. Columbia Uni. Press; New York.

Levy, J. (1972). Lateral specialisation of the human brain: behaviour manifestations and possible evolutionary basis. In J.A. Kiger (Ed.) The Biology of Behaviour. Corvallis: Oregon State Uni. Press.

Levy, J., Trevarthen, C. and Sperry, R. (1972). Perception of bilateral chimeric figures following hemispheric deconnexion. Brain, 95, 61-68.

Lewis, M. (1965). Exploratory studies in the development of a face schema. Paper presented at the symposium on The Origins of Social Behaviour. Am. Psychol. Assoc. Meeting, Chicago.

Lewis, M. (1969). Infants' responses to facial stimuli during the first year of life. Dev. Psychol., 1, 75-86.

Ley, R.G. and Bryden, M.P. (1979). Hemispheric differences in processing emotions in faces. Brain and Lang., 7, 127-138.

Libbard, S. (1979). An investigation into hemispheric functioning in autistic adolescents. Unpublished; Psychology Department, University College, London.

Lindsey, D.T., Holzman, P.S., Haberman, S. and Yasillo, N.J. (1978).
Smooth-pursuit eye movements: A comparison of two measurement
techniques for studying schizophrenia. J. Ab. Psychol., 87(5),
491-496.


Litrownik, A.J., McInnis, E.T., Wetzel-Pritchard, A.M. and Filipelli, D.L.
(1978). Restricted stimulus control and inferred attentional
deficits in autistic and retarded children. J. Ab. Psychol., 87,
554-562.


Lock, A. (1978). Action, Gesture and Symbol: the emergence of language.
Acad. Press: London.


Lotter, V. (1966). Epidemiology of autistic conditions in young children:
I prevalence. Soc. Psychia., 1, 124.


Lotter, V. (1967). Epidemiology of autistic conditions in young children:
II some characteristics of the parents and children. Soc. Psychia.,
1, 163.


Lovaas, I. and Koegal, R.L. (1973). Behaviour therapy with autistic
children. In Behaviour Modification, 72nd Year Book of the National
Society for the Study of Education; Uni. of Chicago Press: Chicago.


Luria, A.R. (1973). The Working Brain. Penguin Books: London.


MacCulloch , M.J. and Sambrooks, J.E. (1972). Concepts of autism: a
review. Paper presented at Burton Manor Symposium, "Recent
Developments in Psychiatry".

McGuigan, F.J. (1968). Experimental Psychology, Second Edition.

Prentice/Hall; Englewood Cliffs: N.J.

McGurk, H. (1977). Hearing lips and seeing voices. Paper read at

the Psychology Department, Birkbeck College, London.

Macrae, D. and Trolle, E. (1956). The defect of function in visual

agnosia. Brain, 79, 94-110.

Mahler, M.S. and Gosliner, B.J. (1955). On symbiotic child psychosis:

genetic, dynamic and restitutive aspects. Psychoanal. Stud. Ch.,

10, 195-214.

Marcel, T. and Rajan, P. (1975). Lateral specialisation for recognition

of words and faces in good and poor readers. Neuropsychogia, 13,

489-497.

Marzi, C.A. and Berlucchi, G. (1977). Right visual field superiority

for accuracy of recognition of famous faces in normals.

Neuropsychologia, 15, 751-756.

Marzi, C.A., Brizzolava, D., Rizzolatti, G., Umita, C. and Berlucchi, G.

(1974). Left hemisphere superiority for the recognition of well

known faces. Brain Res., 66, 358-359.

Maudsley, H. (1867). The Physiology and Pathology of the Mind.

Macmillan: London.

Maurer, D.M. and Maurer, C.E. (1976). Newborn babies see better than you think. Psychol. Today, October, 85-88.

Maurer, D. and Salapatek, P. (1976). Developmental changes in the scanning of faces by young infants. Ch. Dev., 47, 523-527.

Meili, R. (1957). Anfange der Charakterentwicklung. Huber; Stuttgart.

Mein, R. (1961). A list of words used in conversation of severely subnormal patients. Cell Barnes and Harperbury Group Hospital Management Committee.

Mein, R. and O'Connor, N. (1960). A study of the oral vocabularies of severely subnormal patients. J. Ment. Defic. Res., pp. 130-143.

Miller, R.T. (1974). Childhood schizophrenia: a review of selected literature. Int. J. Ment. Health, 3, 3-46.

Miller, G.A. and Selfridge, J.A. (1950). Verbal context and the recall of meaningful material. Am. J. Psychol., 63, 176-185.

Milner, B. (1968). Visual recognition and recall after right temporal-lobe excision in man. Neuropsychol., 6, 191-209.

Milner, B. (1971). Interhemispheric differences in the localization of psychological processes in man. Br. Med. Bull., 27(3), 272-277.

Morgan, G.A. and Ricciuti, H.N. (1965). Infants' responses to strangers during the first year. Unpublished paper, Cornell University. Quoted in Lewis (1969).

Morris, C. (1946). Signs, Language and Behaviour. Prentice-Hall: N.Y.

Moscovitch, M., Scullion, D. and Christie, D. (1976). Early vs late stages of processing and their relation to functional hemispheric asymmetries in face recognition. J. Exp. Psychol., 2, 401-416.

Nelson, K. and Kessen, W. (1969). Visual scanning by human newborns: responses to a complete triangle, to sides only, and to corners only. Proc. 77th Ann. Conven. Am. Psy. Assoc., 4, 273-274.

Newson, E. (1977). Diagnosis and early problems of autistic children. Communication (NSAC), XI (iii), 43-48.

Newson, E. (1980). Making sense of autism. Unpublished paper of the Child Development Research Unit, University of Nottingham.

Newson, J. (1974). Towards a theory of infant understanding. Bull. Br. Psychol. Soc., 27, 251-257.

Norman, E. (1955). Affect and withdrawal in schizophrenic children. Br. J. Med. Psychol., 28, 1-18.

Noton, D. and Stark, L. (1971). Eye movements and visual perception. Scient. Am., 224, 35-43.

O'Connor, N. (1971). Visual perception in autistic childhood. In M. Rutter (Ed.), Infantile Autism: Concepts, Characteristics and Treatment. Churchill-Livingstone: London.

O'Connor, N. and Hermelin, B. (1963). Measures of distance and motility in psychotic children and severely subnormal controls. Br. J. Soc. Clin. Psychol., 3, 29-33.

O'Connor, N. and Hermelin, B. (1965a). Visual analogies of verbal operations. Lang. Speech, 8, 197-207.

O'Connor, N. and Hermelin, B. (1965b). Sensory dominance in autistic imbecile children and controls. Archiv. Gen. Psychiat., 12, 99-103.

O'Connor, N. and Hermelin, B. (1967a). The selective visual attention of psychotic children. J. Ch. Psychol. Psychiat., 8, 167-179.

O'Connor, N. and Hermelin, B. (1967b). Auditory and visual memory in autistic and normal children. J. Ment. Def. Res., 11, 126-131.

Odom, P.B., Blanton, R.L. and Laukhuf, C. (1973). Facial expressions and interpretation of emotion-arousing situations in deaf and hearing children. J. Ab. Ch. Psy., 1(2), 139-151.

Ornitz, E.M. (1969). The disorders of perception common to early infantile autism and schizophrenia. Comp. Psychiat., 10, 259-275.

Ornitz, E.M. (1970). Vestibular dysfunction in schizophrenia and childhood autism. Comp. Psychiat., 11, 159-173.

Ornitz, E.M. (1973). Childhood autism: a review of the clinical and experimental literature. Calif. Med., 118, 29.

Ornitz, E.M. (1974). The modulation of sensory input and motor output in autistic children. J. Aut. Ch. Schizo., 4, 197-216.

Ornitz, E.M. and Ritvo, E.R. (1968). Perceptual inconstancy in early infantile autism. Arch. Gen. Psychiat., 18, 76.

Ornstein, R.E. (1972). The Psychology of Consciousness. W.H. Freeman:. San Fransisco.

Pallis, C.A. (1955). Impaired identification of faces and places with agnosia for colours. J. Neurol. Neurosurg. Psychiat., 18, 218-224.

Patterson, K. and Bradshaw, J. (1975). Differential hemispheric mediation of nonverbal visual stimuli. J. Exp. Psychol., Hu. Percept. Perform., 1, 246-252.

Pawlby, S.J. (1977). Imitative interaction. See H.R. Schaffer (Ed.) 1977,

Peery, J.C. and Stern, D.N. (1974). Gaze frequency distributions during mother-infant interaction. (Unpublished paper, College of Family and Child Development, Utah State University). Quoted in M. Argyle and M. Cook (1976).

Perria, L., Rosadina, G. and Rossi, G.F. (1961). Determination of side of cerebral dominance with amobarbital. Archs. Neurol., 4, 173-181.

Phillips, E.E. (1957). Contributions to a learning theory account of childhood autism. J. Psychol., 43, 117.

Phillips, R.J. (1972). Why are faces hard to recognise in photographic negative? Percept. Psychophys., 12, 425-426.

Phillips, R.J. (1977) Adult's Recognition of Faces and Other Stimuli. Ph.D. Thesis, London University

Piaget, J. (1929). The Child's Conception of the World. Paladin: Herts (reprinted 1973).

Piaget, J. and Inhelder, B. (1969). The Psychology of the Child. Routeledge and Kegan-Paul: London.

Pitfield, M. and Oppenheim, A.N. (1964). Child rearing attitudes of
mothers of psychotic children. J. Ch. Psychol. Psychiat., 5, 51.

Polak, R.H., Emde, R.N. and Spitz, R.A. (1964). The smiling response to
the human face: II visual discrimination and the onset of depth
perception. J. Nerv. Ment. Dis., 139, 407-415.

Potter, H.W. (1933). Schizophrenia in children. Am. J. Psychiat., 12,
1253.

Pribram, K.H. (1971). Languages of the Brain: Experimental Paradoxes
and Principles in Neuropsychology. Prentice-Hall. Englewood
Cliffs, N.J.

Prior, M.K. and Bradshaw, J.C. (1979). Hemisphere functioning in autistic
children. Cortex, 15, 73-81.

Prior, M. and Chen, C.S. (1976). Short-term and serial memory in
autistic, retarded and normal children. J. Aut. Ch. Schizo., 6(2),
121-131.

Rank, B. (1955). Intensive study and treatment of preschool children who
show marked personality deviations, or "a typical development" and
their parents. In G. Caplan (Ed.) Emotional Problems of Early
Childhood. Basic Books: N.Y.

Rank, B. (1959). Adaptation of the psychoanalytic technique for the
treatment of young children with a typical development. Am. J.
Orthpsychiat., 19, 130.

Ratner, N. and Bruner, J. (1977). Games, social exchange and the acquisition of language. J. Ch. Lang., 5, 391-401.

Rendle-Short, J. (1971). A paediatrician's approach to autism. In M. Rutter (Ed.), 1971.

Rheingold, H.L. (1961). The effect of environmental stimulation upon social and exploratory behaviour in the human infant. In B.M. Foss (Ed.) Determinants of Infant Behaviour, Vol. I. Wiley: New York.

Richards, M.P.M. (1971). Social interaction in the first weeks of human life. Psychiat. Neurol. Neurochir., 14, 35-42.

Richer, J. (1976). The social-avoidance behaviour of autistic children. Anim. Behav., 24, 898-906.

Richer, J. and Coss, R.G. (1972). Social looking in autistic and normal children. Unpublished, cited in Coss, R.G. (1972).

Ricks, D.M. (1972). The Beginnings of Verbal Communication in Normal and Autistic Children. M.D. Thesis: University of London.

Ricks, D.M. (1975). Vocal communication in pre-verbal normal and autistic children. In O'Connor, N. (Ed.), Language, Cognitive Deficits and Retardation. Butterworths: London.

Ricks, D.M. and Wing, L. (1976). Language, communication and the use of symbols. In L. Wing (Ed.) Early Childhood Autism, Second Edition; Pergamon: Oxford.

Rimland, B. (1964). Infantile Autism. Appleton-Century-Crofts: New York.

Ritvo, E.R. (Ed.) (1976). Autism-diagnosis, current research and management. Spectrum: N.Y.

Rizzolatti, G., Umilta, C. and Berlucchi, G. (1971). Opposite superiorities of the right and left cerebral hemispheres in discriminative reaction time to physiognomic and alphabetical material. Brain, 94, 431-442.

Robson, K.S. (1967). The role of eye-contact in attachment. J. Ch. Psychol. Psychiat., 8, 13-25.

Rock, I. (1974). The perception of distorted figures. Scient. Am., 230, 78-85.

Rutter, M. (1966). Behavioural and cognitive characteristics. In J.K. Wing (Ed.) Early Childhood Autism, First Edition; Pergamon: Oxford.

Rutter, M. (1968). Concepts of autism: A review of research. J. Ch. Psychol. Psychiat., 9, 1.

Rutter, M. (1970). Autistic children: Infancy to adulthood. Semin. Psychiat., 2, 435.

Rutter, M. (1971). The description and classification of infantile autism. In D.W. Churchill, G.D. Alpern and M.K. DeMyer (Eds.) Infantile Autism. Springfield, Illinois: Charles C. Thomas.

Rutter, M. (1972). Clinical assessment of language disorders in the young child. In, M. Rutter and J.A.M. Martin (Eds.) The Child with Delayed Speech. Clinics in Developmental Medicine, No. 43, Heinemann: London.

Rutter, M. (1974). The development of infantile autism. Psychol. Med., 4, 147-163.

Rutter, M. (1976). Infantile autism and other child psychoses. In M. Rutter and L.A. Hersov (Eds.) Child Psychiatry: Modern Approaches. Blackwell: Oxford.

Rutter, M. (1978). Diagnosis and definition. In M. Rutter and E. Schopler (Eds.) Autism: A Reappraisal of Concepts and Treatment. Plenum: N.Y.

Rutter, M. and Lockyer, L. (1967). A five to fifteen year follow-up study of infantile psychosis: I Description of the sample. Br. J. Psychiat., 113, 1169.

Rutter, M., Lebovici, L., Eisenberg, L., Sneznevsky, A.V., Sadoun, R., Brooke, E. and Lin, T.Y. (1969). A tri-axial classification of mental disorder in childhood. J. Ch. Psychol. Psychiat., 10, 41-61.

Rutter, M., Bartak, C. and Newman, S. (1971). Autism - a central
disorder of cognition and language? In, M. Rutter (Ed.) Infantile
Autism: Concepts, Characteristics and Treatment. Churchill: London.

Safrer, M. and Leventhal, H. (1977). Ear differences in evaluating
emotional tones of voice and verbal content. J. Exp. Psychol., 3(1),
75-82.

Salzen, E.A. (1963). Visual stimuli eliciting the smiling response in
the human infant. J. Genet. Psychol., 102, 51-54.

Schaffer, H.R. (1969). Cognitive structure and early social behaviour.
Paper presented at a study group on "The origins of human social
relations", London, July 1969.

Schaffer, H.R. (1971). The Growth of Sociability. Penguin Books:
Harmondsworth.

Schaffer, H.R. (1977) (Ed.). Studies in Mother-Infant Interaction.
Acad. Press: London.

Schaffer, H.R. and Emerson, P.E. (1964). The development of social
attachments in infancy. Monog. No. 94, Vol. 29, Society for Research
in Child. Dev.

Schopler, E. (1965). Early infantile autism and receptor processes.
Arch. Gen. Psychiat., 13, 327.

Schopler, E. (1966). Visual versus tactile receptor preferences in normal and schizophrenic children. J. Abn. Psychol., 71, 108-114.

Selfe, L. (1977). Nadia - a case of extraordinary drawing ability in an autistic child. Acad. Press: London.

Semmes, J. (1968). Hemispheric specialization a possible clue to mechanism. Neuropsych., 6, 11-26.

Shagass, C., Amadeo, M. and Overton, D.A. (1974). Eye tracking performance in psychiatric patients. Biol. Psychiat., 9, 245-260.

Simmons, J.Q. and Baltaxe, C. (1975). Language pattern of adolescent autistics. J. Aut. Ch. Schiz., 5,(4)

Small, J.G. (1971). Sensory evoked responses of autistic children. See Churchill et al. (Eds.) (1971)

Small, J.G., DeMyer, M.K. and Allen, J. (1971a). EEG dysrhymias in autistic, schizophrenic and emotionally disturbed children. J. Aut. Ch. Schizo.

Small, J.G., De Myer, M.K. and Milstein, V. (1971b). CNV responses of autistic and normal children. J. Aut. Ch. Schizo, 1, 215-231.

Smith, E.E. and Nielsen, G.D. (1970). Representations and retrieval processes in STM recognition and recall of faces. J. Exp. Psychol., 85, 397-405.

Spitz, R.A. (with Wolf, K.M.) (1946). The smiling response: a contribution to the ontogenesis of social relations. Gent. Psychol. Monogr., 34, 57-125.

Spitz, R.A. (1965). The First Year of Life. Int. Uni. Press: New York.

Sroufe, L.A. (1971). Research on infant's laughter. Quoted in W.R. Charlesworth and M.A. Kreutzer, 1973.

Stechler, G. (1964). Newborn attention as affected by medication during labor. Science, 144, 315-317.

Stechler, G. and Latz, E. (1966). Some observations on attention and arousal in the human infant. J. Am. Acad. Child Psychiat., 5, 517-525.

Stirnimann, F. (1940). Psychologie des neugeborenen Kindes. Munchen, Germany: Kindler Verlag.

Suberi, M. and McKeever, W.F. (1977). Differential right hemispheric memory storage of emotional and non-emotional faces. Neuropsychologia, 15, 757-768.

Taft, L.T. and Cohen, H.J. (1971). Hypsarrhythmia and childhood autism: a clinical report. J. Aut. Ch. Chizo., 1, 327.

Thomas, H. (1965). Visual fixation responses of infants to stimuli of varying complexity. Ch. Dev., 36, 629-638.

Thompson, J. (1941). Development of facial expression in blind and seeing children. Arch. Psychol. No. 264, 1-47.

Tinbergen, N. (1951). The Study of Instinct. Oxford Uni. Press: London.

Tinbergen, N. and Tinbergen, E.A. (1972). Early childhood autism - an ethological approach. Adus. Ethol., J. Comp. Ethol-Suppl. No. 10. Paul Parey: Berlin.

Trevarthan, C. (1974a). Conversations with a two-month-old. New Sci., 62, 230.

Trevarthan, C. (1974b). The psychobiology of speech development. In E.H. Lenneberg (Ed.) Language and Brain: Social and Pragmatic Factors in Language Acquisition. Wiley: London.

Trevarthan, C. and Hubley, P. (1978). Secondary intersubjectivity: confidence, confiding and acts of meaning in the first year. See Lock (Ed.) (1978)

Tubbs, V.K. (1966). Types of linguistic disability in psychotic children. J. Ment. Defic. Res., 10, 230.

Tzavaras, A., Hecaen, H. and Lebras, H. (1970). Le probleme de la specificite du deficit de la reconnaissance du visage humain lors des lesions hemispherique - unilaterals. Neuropsychol., 8, 403-416.

Urwin, C. (1978). Study of a blind child. See A. Lock (Ed.) (1978)

Vinogradora, O.S. (1969). Functional properties of cortical nuerons. In A.R. Luvion (Ed.) Higher Cortical Functions in Man, 2nd edn. Moscow University Press.

Vinogradora, O.S. (1970). The limbic system and registration of information. In, R. Hinde and G. Korn (Eds.), Short-term processes in Nervous Activity and Behaviour. Camb. Uni. Press.

Vygotsky, L. (1962). Thought and Language. M.I.T. Press: Cambridge, Mass.

Walker- Smith, G.J., Gale, A.G. and Findlay, J.M. (1977). Eye movement strategies involved in face perception. Perception, 6, 313-326.

Walters, R.H. and Parke, R.D. (1964). Social dependency and susceptibility
to social influence. In L. Berkowitz (Ed.) Advances in Experimental
Psychology, Acad. Press: N.Y.

Walters, R.H. and Parke, R.D. (1965). The role of the distance receptors
in the development of social responsiveness. In L. Lipsitt and
C. Spiker (Eds.) Advances in Child Development and Behaviour, Vol. 2.
Academic Press: N.Y.

Warrington, E.K. and James, M. (1967). An experimental investigation
of facial recognition in patients with unilateral cerebral lesions.
Cortex, 3, 317-326.

Warrington, E.K. and Kinsbourne, M. (1966). Drawing disability in
relation to laterality of lesion. Brain, 89, 53-82.

Washburn, R.W. (1929). A study of the smiling and laughing of infants
in the first year of life. Genet. Psychol. Monogr., 6, 399-537.

Watson, J.B. (1919). Psychology from the Standpoint of a Behaviorist.
Lippincott: Philadelphia.

Watson, J.S. (1966). Perception of object orientation in infants.
Mer. Pal. Qu., 12, 73-94.

Watson, J.S. (1973). Smiling, cooing and "the game". Mer-Pal. Qu., 18,
323-339.

Waugh, N.C. and Norman, D.A. (1965). Primary memory. Psychol. Rev.,
72, 89-104.

Wechsler, A.F. (1973). The effect of organic brain disease on recall
of emotionally charged vs neutral narrative texts. Neurology, 23,
130-135.

White, M.J. (1969). Laterality differences in perception. Psychol. Bull.,
72, 307-404.

White, B.L. and Held, R. (1964). Observations on the development of
visually directed reaching. Child Dev., 35, 349-364.

Winer, B.J. (1971). Statistical Principles in Experimental Design.
2nd Edn. McGraw-Hill: N.Y.

Wing, J. (1976). Kanner's syndrome: a historical introduction.
In, L. Wing (Ed.), Early Childhood Autism, Second Edition,
Pergamon: Oxford.

Wing, L. (1966). In J.K. Wing (Ed.) Early Childhood Autism, First
Edition, Pergamon: Oxford.

Wing, L. (1967). The handicap of autistic children - results of a
pilot study. In Proceedings of the Congress of the International
Association for the Scientific Study of Mental Deficiency.
B.W. Richards (Ed.), Mick and Jackson: England.

Wing, L. (1969). The handicaps of autistic children - a comparative study. J. Ch. Psychol. Psychiat., 10, 1.

Wing, L. (1975). A study of language impairments in severely retarded children. In N. O'Connor (Ed.), Language, Cognitive Deficits and Retardation. Butterworths: London.

Wing, L. (1976a). Diagnosis, clinical description and prognosis. In L. Wing (Ed.) Early Childhood Autism, 2nd Edn. Pergamon: Oxford.

Wing, L. (1976b). Epidemiology and theories of aetiology. In L. Wing (Ed.) Early Childhood Autism, 2nd Edn., Pergamon: Oxford.

Wing, L. (1978). In, M. Rutter and E. Schopler (Eds.) Autism: A Reappraisal of Concepts and Treatments. Plenum: N.Y.

Wing, L. (1980). Childhood autism and social class: a question of selection? Br. J. Psychiat., 137, 410-417.

Witkin, H.A., Dyk, R.B., Faterson, H.R., Goodenough, D.R. and Karp, S.A. (1962). Psychological Differentiation: Studies of Development. Wiley: New York.

Wolff, P.H. (1963). Observations on the early development of smiling. In B.M. Foss (Ed.), Determinants of Infant Behaviour, Vol. II, Wiley: N.Y. 113-138.

Wolff, S. and Chess, S. (1964). A behavioural study of schizophrenic children. Acta Psychiat. Scand., 40, 438-466.

Yarbus, A.L. (1967). Eye Movement and Vision. Translated by B. Hough Plenum Press: N.Y.

Yin, R.K. (1969). Looking at upside-down faces. J. Exp. Psychol., 81, 141-145.

Yin, R.K. (1970). Face recognition by brain-injured patients: a dissociable ability? Neuropsychol., 8, 395-402.

Young, A.W. and Ellis, H.D. (1976). An experimental investigation of developmental differences in ability to recognise faces presented to the left and right cerebral hemispheres. Neuropsychologia, 14, 495-498.

Zaslow, R.W. (1967). A psychogenic theory of the aetiology of infantile autism and implications for treatment. Paper given at meeting of Californian State Psychiatric Assoc., San Diego.

Zazzo, R. (1957). Le probleme de l'imitation chez le nouveau-ne Enfance, 10, 135-142.

Zingh, R.M. (1940). Feral man and extreme cases of isolation. Am. J. Psychol., 53, 487-517.

www.ingramcontent.com/pod-product-compliance
Lightning Source LLC
Chambersburg PA
CBHW070625270326
41926CB00011B/1820